play the king's Indian

a complete repertoire for black
in this most dynamic of openings

Joe Gallagher

EVERYMAN CHESS

www.everymanchess.com

First published in 2004 by Gloucester Publishers plc (formerly Everyman Publishers plc), Northburgh House, 10 Northburgh Street, London EC1V 0AT

British Library Cataloguing-in-Publication Data
A catalogue record for this book is available from the British Library.

ISBN 978 1 85744 324 0

Distributed in North America by The Globe Pequot Press, P.O Box 480, 246 Goose Lane, Guilford, CT 06437-0480.

All other sales enquiries should be directed to Everyman Chess, Northburgh House, 10 Northburgh Street, London EC1V 0AT
tel: 020 7253 7887 fax: 020 7490 3708
email: info@everymanchess.com; website: www.everymanchess.com

EVERYMAN CHESS SERIES (formerly Cadogan Chess)
Chief advisor: Byron Jacobs
Commissioning editor: John Emms
Assistant editor: Richard Palliser

Typeset and edited by First Rank Publishing, Brighton.
Cover design by Horatio Monteverde.
Printed and bound in the US.

CONTENTS

BIBLIOGRAPHY

Books

101 Attacking Ideas in Chess, Gallagher (Gambit 2000)
Beating the Anti King's Indians, Gallagher (Batsford 1996)
Beating the King's Indian and Benoni, Vaisser (Batsford 1997)
ECO Volume A and Volume E
King's Indian and Grünfeld: Fianchetto Lines, Janjgava (Gambit 2003)
King's Indian for the Attacking Player, Burgess (Batsford 1993)
NCO, Nunn, Burgess, Emms, Gallagher (Everyman/Gambit 1999)
Play the King's Indian Defence, Marovic (Pergamon 1984)
Sämisch King's Indian, Gallagher (Batsford 1995)
Starting Out: The King's Indian, Gallagher (Everyman 2002)
The Complete King's Indian, Keene and Jacobs (Batsford 1992)
The New Classical King's Indian, Nunn & Burgess (Batsford 1997)
Victor Korchnoi: My Best games Volume 1: Games with White, Korchnoi (Olms 2000)

Chess Software

MegaBase 2003
TWIC
Fritz

Internet Sources

ChessPublishing Website: King's Indian section by Martin, Gallagher and Mikhalevski

Magazines and Periodicals

Informators 1- 89
New in Chess: yearbooks and magazines
British Chess Magazine

INTRODUCTION

What? Another Gallagher book on the King's Indian, I hear you say. It seems like only yesterday when his last one was out. Yes, at times it feels a bit like that to me as well. But it is in fact well over two years since *Starting Out: The King's Indian* (Everyman 2002 and henceforth referred to as SOKID) was released and this book, which has been in the pipeline for sometime, was always intended as a sequel to that one. Let me quickly recap what SOKID was about and then highlight the similarities and differences to the current offering.

SOKID was a book primarily aimed at the inexperienced player or the more experienced player who was new to the King's Indian. It covered all the major variations in the King's Indian from an objective, middle of the road, viewpoint. It concentrated on explaining the first dozen or so moves of each line and it was heavy on verbal explanations and light on theoretical variations.

This book is aimed at all players who play the King's Indian, or who want to play it, and it assumes a slightly higher level of chess understanding than SOKID. Inexperienced players can still derive plenty of benefit from this book but I strongly recommend that they start with SOKID.

This book also deals with all the major variations of the King's Indian but strictly from a Black point of view. It is largely based on my own personal King's Indian repertoire and the variations that have served me well over the years. Some readers may be disappointed that their favourite variations are not included but in order to cover the chosen variations to the required depth I have had to be selective. Here is a brief overview of the repertoire this book provides against the main lines:

1) In the Classical both the main lines with 7...♘c6 and the modern 7...♘a6 are covered.

2) In the Sämisch I recommend that Black plays 6...c5.

3) In the Fianchetto Variation I recommend the classical 6...♘bd7, concentrating on the Gallagher variation and a closely related system based on 8...a6.

4) In the Four Pawns Black plays with 6...c5 and 9...♗g4.

5) In the Averbakh and early h3 systems Black plays, in general, for ...e7-e5.

Within the chosen repertoire, however, I do not restrict myself to one particular line of play and there is plenty of choice for the black player if one or two of the recommended lines run into trouble.

Whereas SOKID concentrated on the early stages of the opening this book devotes most of its firepower to the late opening/early middlegame stage of the game. There is a lot more analysis and theoretical variations than in SOKID but also plenty of verbal explanation. I have tried to reach a happy medium between the two. A myth I often hear spouted (in reviews, for example) is that books with plenty of prose are for the weak to average player whereas books that resemble the telephone directory are for the expert players. I strongly disagree and my personal opinion is that, especially in this database age, books that resemble the telephone directory are boring, irrelevant and for nobody.

I have used a complete games format to cover the material. On occasion this is merely window dressing but not here. In a book entitled *Play the King's Indian* I felt it was important to annotate the games fully throughout, although I have usually drawn the line at placing long endgames under the microscope.

One of the main dilemmas I have faced in writing this book is what to do about the overlap with SOKID. The fact is that in certain cases I have already said what I wanted to say about a position in SOKID. I have, on the whole, just decided to repeat what I said in SOKID here. The alternative was to refer the reader to SOKID for these parts, and whilst I have done this for the more basic explanations I didn't want to do this regularly as this is a stand-alone King's Indian book. The other option was to change things round a bit but this seemed like a waste of time (and a bit false) when I have already worked hard on a variation or on drafting a piece of text.

Apart from SOKID, I also wrote two other King's Indian books in the 1990's, *Beating the Anti King's Indians* (Batsford 1996) and *The Sämisch King's Indian* (Batsford 1995). Where appropriate, I have drawn on material from these works as well.

Another important source has been the ChessPublishing website. For some of 2002 and all of 2003 I produced a monthly article on the latest King's Indian games for this highly recommended openings site and the annotations to a number of games in this book have been adapted from what first appeared there.

It goes without stating, however, that everything from whatever source, has been updated and these are my King's Indian views of mid-2004.

This introduction has dealt mainly with technical issues but I would just like to finish on a more emotional note. During my chess career many openings have come and gone but only one has been ever present – the King's Indian. I started playing it at age 11 and have not stopped for nearly 30 years. It has brought many highs and some lows – it is not always easy playing Black no matter what opening you choose – but rest assured that if you master its secrets it will bring far more pleasure than misery.

Joe Gallagher,
Neuchattel,
September 2004

CHAPTER ONE

The Classical Variation: Modern Main Line

1 d4 ♘f6 2 c4 g6 3 ♘c3 ♗g7 4 e4 d6 5 ♗e2 0-0 6 ♘f3 e5 7 0-0 ♘c6 8 d5 ♘e7 9 ♘e1 ♘d7 10 ♗e3

The Classical is by far the most important variation in the King's Indian. You will probably have to face it as often as all the other variations put together. Consequently, it takes up about half the book. White's plan is simple and unassuming. He just develops his kingside sensibly and rapidly and awaits developments. Let us now consider the above sequence in detail.

1 d4 ♘f6 2 c4 g6 3 ♘c3 ♗g7 4 e4 d6 5 ♗e2 0-0 6 ♘f3 e5!

The best move and the only one we shall be looking at in the book. Alternatives such as 6...c5 and 6...♗g4 lead to completely different types of games where it is easier, in my opinion, for White to maintain an edge. In the past 6...♘bd7 was played sometimes as a means of preparing e5 but we can't do that unless we play the variation 6...e5 7 0-0 ♘bd7 (which we do not as Black is worse after 8 ♗e3!). The one plausible alternative to the text is 6...♘a6. This can be adopted by those of you who play the 7...♘a6 variation but wish to avoid, for example, the exchange variation in its purest form.

7 0-0

This is by far the most popular and flexible of White's 7th moves. The first five chapters are devoted to it whilst Chapter 6 deals with the alternatives, 7 d5, 7 ♗e3 and 7 dxe5.

7...♘c6

Now we are getting close to the territory which is simply described as the Main Line King's Indian. By playing 7...♘c6 Black invites White to close the centre with gain of tempo. He is even willing to have his knight driven to the inferior e7-square to achieve this central clarification. The reason Black wants the centre closed is that he wants to attack on the kingside and this is not possible with a fluid centre.

There are quite a few alternatives as the sharp theoretical battles that arise after 7...♘c6 are not too everyone's taste. 7...♘a6 is the most important alternative and it is covered extensively in Chapter 5.

8 d5

White usually accepts Black's invitation to close the centre as there are no promising alternatives. The one move that does occur from time to time is 8 ♗e3 (8 dxe5 dxe5 is completely harmless):

a) It would be played more often if it wasn't for the reply 8...♖e8! when the natural 9 d5 leads to complete equality after 9...♘d4! 10 ♘xd4 exd4 11 ♗xd4 ♘xe4 12 ♘xe4 ♖xe4 13 ♗xg7 ♔xg7. Therefore White's only try is the almost equally tedious 9 dxe5 dxe5 with the following possibilities:

a1) 10 ♕xd8 ♘xd8 (more reliable than 10...♖xd8) 11 ♘b5 ♘e6 12 ♘g5 ♖e7! (12...♘xg5?! 13 ♗xg5 ♖e7 14 ♖ad1 is unpleasant for Black) 13 ♖fd1 b6 14 a4 c6 15 ♘xe6 (15 ♘c3 ♘d4!) 15...♗xe6 16 ♘c3 ♖b8 (or 16...♖b7) 17 b4 ♖d7 18 f3 ♗f8 19 ♖xd7 ♘xd7 20 ♖b1 a5 with a level game, Hjartarson-Nunn, Szirak 1987.

a2) 10 c5 ♗g4 11 ♗b5 ♕c8 12 h3 ♗h5! is an idea of Smirin which diffused a White idea that was beginning to gain a supporter or two. The point is that it will now be difficult for White to break the pin (13 g4? ♘xg4). After 13 ♗xc6 bxc6, both 14 ♗g5 ♖b8 15 ♖b1 ♗xf3 16 ♕xf3 ♘d7 17 b4 a5, Oll-Smirin, Rostov 1993, and 14 ♕e2 h6 15 ♔h2 g5 16 ♕c4 ♖b8 17 b3 a5 18 ♘d2 g4 19 f3 gxh3 20 gxh3 ♖b4, Van der Sterren-Smirin, Tilburg 1992, were quite satisfactory for Black.

a3) 10 h3 ♗e6 11 c5 and now Black can choose between 11...♕e7, 11...a6 and 11...♘h5 all of which are thought to offer a roughly level game

b) Despite the fact that these lines offer Black easy equality most King's Indian players prefer to go fishing in murky water with 8...♘g4 9 ♗g5 f6 and now:

b1) 10 ♗h4 is not played so often when White has already castled as his options are severely reduced (in comparison to 7 ♗e3 ♘g4 8 ♗g5 f6 9 ♗h4, the Gligoric Variation, that is). The immediate 10...♘h6 is one possibility whilst 10...g5 11 ♗g3 ♘h6 12 dxe5 fxe5 is thought to be fine for Black, e.g. 13 c5 g4 14 ♘d2 dxc5 15 ♘b3 b6 16 ♕d5+ ♕xd5 17 ♘xd5 ♖f7 18 ♗c4 ♔h8 when White has compensation for the pawn but no more.

b2) 10 ♗c1 is more common and it transposes to the Gligoric System (see the introduction to that line in Chapter 6).

8...♘e7 9 ♘e1

For a lengthy explanation of this prophylactic retreat I refer you to SOKID.

We also have some pretty major alternatives here:

a) 9 b4 is the famous Bayonet Attack and that is the subject of Chapter 3.

b) 9 ♘d2 is not quite as popular as it used to be but is still an important line. That is covered in Chapter 4.

c) The interesting 9 ♗g5 is also covered in Chapter 4 along with other 9th move alternatives:

9...♘d7

Black gets ready to play ...f7-f5. As to why I prefer this move to 9...♘e8 I once again refer you to SOKID.

Now:

1) 10 ♗e3 is the subject of the remainder of this chapter. Our coverage starts after the additional and almost universal moves 10...f5 11 f3 f4 12 ♗f2 g5.

2) 10 ♘d3 and 10 f3 are seen in Chapter 2.

The Modern Main Line:
7...♘c6 8 d5 ♘e7 9 ♘e1 ♘d7 10 ♗e3

1 d4 ♘f6 2 c4 g6 3 ♘c3 ♗g7 4 e4 d6 5 ♘f3 0-0 6 ♗e2 e5 7 0-0 ♘c6 8 d5 ♘e7 9 ♘e1 ♘d7 10 ♗e3 f5 11 f3 f4 12 ♗f2 g5

This is one of the sharpest and most theoretical lines in the whole King's Indian. It also represents the King's Indian in its purest form. White will attempt to tear Black limb from limb on the queenside while Black will endeavour to hang, draw and quarter White on the kingside. Sometimes both players succeed in their aim and then Black wins. That is the advantage of attacking the king.

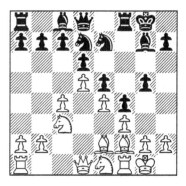

The great champion of this line with the white pieces is the legendary Grandmaster Victor Korchnoi. I have been fortunate enough to play in the same team as him on many occasions. We have had many lively discussions on the merits of the King's Indian. I am afraid he does not hold this opening in the same high esteem as I do. For example, when discussing Kasparov in his recent games collection Korchnoi lets slip, 'the World Champion habitually takes his life in his hands by depending on his miserable King's Indian'. Korchnoi is particularly scathing about 7...♘c6 in the Classical Variation and 10 ♗e3 is his weapon of choice.

I, on the other hand, used to be of the opinion that 10 ♗e3 just lost by force. Admittedly I was rather young when I held that view but I simply couldn't believe that anyone could be so generous as to let me play f5-f4 with gain of tempo. Of course, I now realise that things are not so simple. The bishop on f2 is perfectly placed to assist in the queenside attack while in other lines it becomes the white king's most valuable protector. However, it is also a target for a black pawn landing on g3. Black's main strategy in this line is based around playing g5-g4-g3. He doesn't care if it costs him a pawn as in return he will get open lines and outposts for his pieces. Perhaps the most important black piece in this line is the light-squared bishop. This is because if White meets ...g3 with h3 then Black may be able to sacrifice his bishop to rip open the white king position. You will find countless examples of ...♗xh3 sacrifices throughout this chapter. They are usually devas-

tating. The manoeuvre ...♖f6-h6, in order to gain a quick attack on the h-file, is also an important device. If White defends well then Black normally reverts to the strategy of playing for ...g4. Apart from in Game 1 where White's move order presented Black with an opportunity to block up the queenside, Black usually leaves this side of the board alone. Even if White attacks a rook in the corner, for example, then Black may ignore it in favour of continuing his kingside attack. In such a position every tempo is worth its weight in gold.

From the diagram position White has six reasonable moves and they are covered during the next five games. Game 1 deals with 13 a4 and 13 ♘b5, Game 2 with 13 b4, Games 3 and 4 with 13 ♖c1 and Game 5 with 13 ♘d3 and 13 g4. At the moment the most fashionable lines for White are 13 a4 and 13 ♖c1 but this can easily change as theory does not stand still in this sharp line.

The coverage of these lines is denser than in the rest of the book but this is unavoidable due to the tactical nature of the position. They are also very entertaining if you like sacrificial chess.

Game 1
Koutsin-Frolov
Kiev 1995

---

1 d4 ♘f6 2 c4 g6 3 ♘c3 ♗g7 4 e4 d6 5 ♘f3 0-0 6 ♗e2 e5 7 0-0 ♘c6 8 d5 ♘e7 9 ♘e1 ♘d7 10 ♗e3 f5 11 f3 f4 12 ♗f2 g5 13 a4

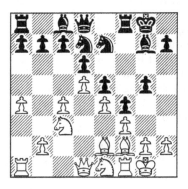

This move is an invention of Korchnoi. To understand why White wants to start his queenside attack with this particular move we must first look at another of Korchnoi's inventions, 13 ♘b5. This was introduced by Korchnoi back in 1987 when he was having a few problems with the more conventional lines. The basic idea is to play ♘a7 and ♘xc8 to remove the dangerous bishop on c8. Of course Black is not going to let this happen as then he will have nothing to sacrifice on h3. The most obvious try for Black is 13...a6 14 ♘a7 ♖xa7 15 ♗xa7 b6 as the bishop on a7 is in deep trouble. Korchnoi's idea is to play 16 b4 followed by c5 with every chance of extricating the bishop or, failing that, to at least ensure it is sold quite dearly. Black's results in this line were very poor but only, according to John Nunn, because he tried to win the bishop with moves such as ♗b7 and ♘c8. If instead he just got on with his kingside attack (16...♘f6, 17...g4) then the situation is not so clear.

Another line Black has tried is 13...♘f6, just sacrificing the a-pawn to give his bishop a square. The critical test is 14 ♘xa7 ♗d7 15 c5 and Black's results there do not inspire.

The third try is what put Korchnoi off 13 ♘b5: 13...b6 14 b4 a6 15 ♘c3. The position is the same as after 13 b4 (see next game) except that Black has two extra moves on the queenside. Korchnoi must have hoped that they would weaken his position but in practice they turned out to not be so damaging. Black can play 15...♘g6 or 15...♘f6 but there is another interesting idea, namely 15...♖f6. The rather crude idea is to play ...♖h6, ...♕e8, ...♕h5 and mate White down the h-file. This is possible in other lines as well (See Game 3) but it is particularly dangerous here as Black has been given the very useful move ...a6 for free. The point is that he doesn't have to worry about White playing ♘b5 (remember the queen is intending to leave d8). Kiltti-Maki, Tampere 1998 continued (after 15...♖f6) 16 ♘d3 ♖h6 (16...♖g6!?) 17 c5?! (17 ♗e1 in order to defend with ♘f2 and h3 is more to the point) 17...♕e8 18 ♔h1 bxc5 19 bxc5 ♘f6! 20 ♕d2 ♕h5 21 ♗g1 g4 22 ♘a4 g3 23 cxd6 (23 h3 ♗xh3) 23...♕g5! 24 dxe7 ♖xh2‡ 0-1.

So, discouraged with 13 ♘b5 Korchnoi went back to the drawing board and discovered that if only he could meet 13...b6 with a2-a5 Black would not be able to kick the knight with a6 as White just replies axb6. Unfortunately, pawns are not allowed to move this far so Korchnoi's idea was to start with 13 a2-a4, in order to 'threaten' 14 ♘b5' (not everyone agrees it is a threat) when 14...b6 can now be met by 15 a5.

Such is the way chess theory develops. It is often very hard to understand why a particular move is fashionable without understanding the history of a whole variation.

13...a5!?

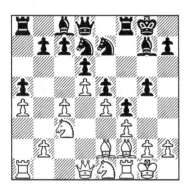

Black decides to try and punish White for his move order. By blocking the queenside with ...a5 and ...b6 he makes it impossible for White to achieve his most dangerous queenside advance c4-c5 (at least for a very long time). For a while 13...a5 was thought to be inaccurate because White is still able to develop his attack on the queenside by playing b4. The time that Black has spent on moves such as ...a5 and ...b6 could have been put to better use on the kingside, so the argument went. However, due to a lack of success with his other 13th moves Black started to examine 13...a5 again and this time found it much more to his liking.

The main line after 13 a4 was considered to be 13...♘g6 14 a5 ♖f7 but Black has been under pressure there on two fronts. The first nasty line is Kozul's pawn sacrifice 15 c5 (the main line runs 15...♘xc5 16 ♗xc5 dxc5 17 ♗c4 ♔h8 18 a6) while the second is Korchnoi's 15 b4 ♗f8 16 c5 ♘f6 17 c6!. Often it is possible to patch a line up against just one aggressor but when there are two it is usually time to move on. I also thought about recommending 13...♖f6 (I have played it myself) with similar ides to the previous note and Game 3. However, it is probably a slightly inferior version and I also want to look at a broader range of positions.

14 ♘d3 b6

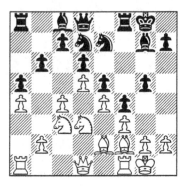

The consistent follow up. There is no point playing ...a5 if Black just allows White to play c5 afterwards.

15 b4

White must play b4 if he is going to open the queenside but he has several ways to implement this plan:

a) He can play 15 b4 and after 15...axb4 just recapture with the knight (see notes to move 16). The knight then has access to the hole on c6 but plays no part in the defence of the kingside.

b) He can play 15 b4 and meet 15...axb4 with 16 ♘b5 followed by ♗e1xb4. This was his choice in the main game.

c) There is a third way. White starts with 15 ♗e1 and follows up with ♘f2 and h3 in order to slow down Black's kingside attack. Only then does he play for b4. Certain sources have suggested that White can gain the advantage in this fashion but I don't really believe it. Let's have a look: 15 ♗e1 h5 16 ♘f2 ♘f6 17 h3 and now:

c1) 17...♖f7 (a typical manoeuvre which combines defence and attack) 18 b4 ♘g6 (on 18...axb4 19 ♘b5 White will play ♗xb4 followed by a5 so Black prefers to keep a pawn on a5 to prevent this; he understands that the pawn is likely to drop off but will hope to get

his attack underway while White is taking it) 19 bxa5 bxa5 20 ♘b5 ♗f8 21 ♗c3 ♖g7 22 ♖a2 ♘h8!? 23 ♕e1 ♘f7 24 ♗xa5 ♘h6 25 c5 g4 26 fxg4 hxg4 27 ♘xg4 ♗xg4 28 hxg4 ♘hxg4 29 ♗xg4 ♘xg4 30 ♖f3 dxc5 ½-½ Ikonnikov-Hassan, Egypt 2001.

White was much higher rated than his opponent so obviously wasn't too keen on his position.

c2) 17...♔h8 18 ♘b5 ♘eg8 (the ...♘e7-g8-h6 is another typical manoeuvre to try and force through ...g5-g4) 19 b4 ♖f7 20 bxa5 bxa5 21 c5 ♗f8 22 cxd6 cxd6 23 ♖c1 ♘h6 24 ♖c4, P.Nielsen–Kotronias, Hastings 2003/04, and now it is probably best for Black to play the immediate 24...g4 with unclear play.

15...axb4 16 ♘b5

After 16 ♘xb4 Black has a choice:

a) 16...♘c5!? 17 a5 bxa5 18 ♗xc5 dxc5 19 ♘d3 ♘c6! is a nice trick which has occurred a couple of times. The knight is heading for d4 and after 20 dxc6 ♕d4+ Black regains the piece with a good position. 17 a5 looks premature.

b) Black may prefer to bring his knight to the kingside. Yusupov-Kasparov, Yerevan Olympiad 1996 continued 16...♘f6 17 ♖a3 (17 ♘b5 transposes to the next note while on 17 ♘c6 Black should probably avoid 17...♕d7 on account of 18 a5 and play 17...♘xc6 18 dxc6 ♕e8 with unclear play) 17...♗d7 18 ♘b5 ♔h8 (18...g4 19 fxg4 ♘xe4 was a serious alternative) 19 ♗e1 ♖g8 20 g4! (otherwise White will come under a heavy attack) 20...fxg3 21 hxg3 g4 with equal chances according to theory. Given the choice I would take Black.

16...♘f6

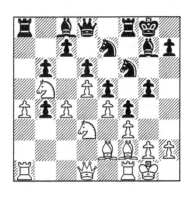

17 ♗e1?!

17 ♘xb4 g4 18 ♗h4 g3 19 h3 (as usual a line like 19 hxg3 fxg3 20 ♗xg3 ♗h6 would be fraught with danger for White; we will see many examples of similar positions) is given by Nunn as better for White. His assessment is based on the game P.Nielsen-Harestad, Gausdal 1996 which continued 19...♘g6 20 ♘c6 ♕d7 21 ♗xf6 ♖xf6 22 ♘ba7 but Black may be able to do better than this.

Firstly, the immediate sacrifice on h3 doesn't work. After 19...♗xh3 20 gxh3 ♕d7 21 ♔g2 ♘g6 22 ♗xf6 ♖xf6 23 ♖h1 ♘h4+ 24 ♔g1 Black can make no further progress on the kingside. The problem is that White's bishop has managed to get rid of an important knight, a knight that Black usually needs for the follow-up sacrifice on e4.

Instead of 19...♗xh3 Black should play the quiet 19...♗d7, covering c6 and threatening ♕c8 followed by ♗xh3. A possible continuation: 20 ♖e1 (so that he can defend with ♗f1) 20...♔h8 21 ♖a3 ♘g6 22 ♗xf6 ♖xf6 23 ♕a1 ♖a5!

There is also an argument for Black delaying g4 for a while. 17...♗d7 would lead to very similar play to the Yusupov-Kasparov game given above.

17...g4 18 ♗xb4

It was because the knight on b5 no longer protects e4 (as it did from c3) that Black was able to play g4 without further preparation. After 18 fxg4 ♘xe4 Black's central pawns are potentially deadly. After 19 ♗xb4 we have a couple of examples:

a) 19...♗d7 20 ♕c2 ♘g5 21 h4 ♘e4 22 ♗e1 ♘g6 23 h5 ♘g3 24 hxg6 ♕h4 25 ♘f2 ♗xb5 26 gxh7+ ♔h8 27 cxb5 e4 28 ♖d1 f3 29 gxf3 ♘xe2+ 30 ♕xe2 exf3 0-1 Chabanon-Degraeve, French Ch. 1999

b) 19...♘g6 20 a5 ♘c5 21 ♘xc5 bxc5 22 ♗c3 e4 23 ♗xg7 ♔xg7 (Fritz likes White here but I don't really care what it says; give me Black's centre any kingside attacking chances any day) 24 ♕c2 ♕e7 25 ♕c3+ (25 ♔h1 is Fritz's choice which is certainly a better move; Black should probably play 25...♗a6 and ♖ae8) 25...♘e5 26 ♖ae1 ♔g8 27 ♗d1 e3 28 g3 ♗xg4 29 ♗xg4 ♘xg4 30 ♖xf4 ♖xf4 31 gxf4 ♕e4 32 h3 ♕xf4! 33 hxg4 ♕g3+ 34 ♔h1 ♖e8 (the

knight on b5 is irrelevant) 35 ♖e2 ♕f3+ 36 ♔g2 ♕f1+ 37 ♔h2 e2 0-1 Nikitin-Solovjov, Alushta 2002.

18...g3 19 h3 ♗xh3!

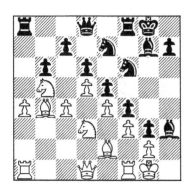

This bishop was born to lay down its life on h3. If Black delays then White will shore up his defences with ♖e1 and ♗f1. There is no reason to delay!

20 gxh3 ♕d7 21 ♕c2

The only variation that Black needed to calculate before sacrificing was 21 ♔g2? ♘g6 22 ♖h1 ♘h4+ 23 ♔g1 ♘xe4! 24 fxe4 f3 and White gets blown away. He didn't need to look at anything else because if White can't play ♔g2 then Black will pick up the crucial pawn on h3.

That's what I wrote in SOKID two years ago. Now we have an example that illustrates perfectly the danger of ignoring my King's Indian books. Pogorelov-Matamoros, Dos Hermanas 2003 actually reached the position after 24...f3 and the game concluded: 25 ♗d2 (25 ♗xf3 ♖xf3 is just hopeless for White) 25...f2+ 26 ♘xf2 (26 ♔f1 g2 mate would be a prettier way to go) 26...♖xf2 27 ♖h2 gxh2+ 28 ♔xf2 ♕xh3 29 ♕h1 ♖f8+ 30 ♔e1 ♕g2! 31 ♗f3 ♘xf3+ 0-1.

The game Krivoshey-Xie Jun, Linares 1997 deserves a mention. There White played 21 ♕d2 and now 21...♕xh3 22 ♗d1 ♘g6 23 ♕g2 would have transposed to the main game. However, Xie Jun preferred to manoeuvre her pieces into more threatening positions before capturing on h3. After 21...♘g6 22 ♗d1 ♗h6 23 ♘e1 ♔h8 24 ♖a2 ♖g8 25 ♕d3? (25 ♕g2 ♘h4 26 ♕h1 is not so clear) 25...♕xh3 26 ♖g2 ♘h4 27 ♕e2 ♖g5! my database says that a draw was agreed. I suspect this is a mistake and that White actually resigned. Black just plays ...♖h5 and delivers mate on the h-file.

21...♕xh3 22 ♗d1 ♘g6 23 ♕g2 ♕h6! 24 ♕h1

After 24 ♘xc7 ♘h4 25 ♕e2 ♘xe4! 26 ♕xe4 (both 26 fxe4 and 26 ♘xa8 are hopeless) the beautiful 26...♔g2! gives Black a winning attack. These tactics may look amazingly complicated but it is no surprise they work. The unifying theme is ...♘xe4 as this brings to life the other Black pieces (and pawns)

24...♘h4 25 ♘e1

If White can play just one more move, 26 ♘g2, then he should be able to beat off the attack. It's time for another sacrifice to keep up the momentum of the attack.

25...♘xe4!

For those of you who have been checking the variations in the notes this can come as no surprise.

26 ♘g2!

26 fxe4 f3 is completely hopeless for White

26...♖f5?!

Black had another fascinating possibility: 26...♘xf3+! 27 ♗xf3 ♕xh1+ 28 ♔xh1 ♘f2+ 29 ♖xf2 (29 ♔g1 e4! and despite the fact that queens have been exchanged and White has two extra pieces he is just lost) 29...gxf2 30 ♖f1 (there is nothing better, e.g. 30 ♗e4 ♖xa4!) 30...♖xa4 31 ♗a3 ♖xc4 32 ♖xf2 and the rook and five pawns should beat the three minor pieces. This looks more convincing than Black's choice in the game.

27 fxe4

White has to take one of the pieces; 27

♕xh4 loses immediately to 27...♖h5 and after 27 ♘xh4 ♖h5 28 fxe4 ♖xh4 29 ♕f3 ♖h2 Black also has a winning attack.

27...f3 28 ♗xf3

At first glance 28 ♕xh4 loses immediately to 28...fxg2 but White has the absolutely amazing move 29 ♖f4! Black still wins the rook but he doesn't get a new queen as well. After 29...♖xf4 30 ♕xh6 ♗xh6 Black is better but White can fight on.

28...♘xf3+ 29 ♖xf3 ♕xh1+ 30 ♔xh1 ♖xf3

The main wave of complications have ended and Black has emerged with the slight material advantage of rook and 2 pawns against two minor pieces (in an endgame anyway). Black's passed pawns on the kingside are potentially a decisive factor but for the moment it is the weakness of the respective queenside pawns that is the most relevant.

31 ♔g1!

Not falling for 31 ♘xc7 ♖xa4! 32 ♖xa4 ♖f1 mate.

31...♖b3?

Black needed to play one careful defensive move to keep the advantage. After 31...♗f8 32 ♘xc7 ♖c8 it is important that the d6 pawn is defended. White could try 32 a5 but the position after 32...bxa5 33 ♖xa5 ♖xa5 34 ♗xa5 ♖b1+ 35 ♘e1 ♖c1 is good for Black.

32 ♘xc7! ♗f8 33 ♗e1?!

White probably didn't like the look of 33 ♗xd6! ♖f2 but 34 ♖f1 holds the balance. Now Black is pressing again but the odds are still on White holding the draw. The remaining moves were:

33...♗f6! 34 ♘b5 ♗e7 35 ♖a3 ♖xa3 36

♘xa3 ♖f3 37 ♘c2 ♗g5 38 ♗b4 h5 39
♘ce1 ♖f6 40 a5 bxa5 41 ♗xa5 ♖f2 42
♗c7 ♗e7 43 ♘e3 ♖e2 44 ♘1g2 ♖a2 45 c5
♖a1+ 46 ♘f1 h4 47 ♘xh4 ♗xh4 48 ♗xd6
♖e1 49 c6 ♖xe4 50 c7 ♖c4 51 ♗xe5 ♔f7
52 ♘xg3 ♗xg3 ½-½

Game 2
Piket-Kasparov
Tilburg 1989

---

1 d4 ♘f6 2 ♘f3 g6 3 c4 ♗g7 4 ♘c3 0-0 5
e4 d6 6 ♗e2 e5 7 0-0 ♘c6 8 d5 ♘e7 9
♘e1 ♘d7 10 ♗e3 f5 11 f3 f4 12 ♗f2 g5
13 b4

In some ways this is White's most obvious
move. Now there is nothing Black can do to
stop White playing c5 but at least a tempo has
been spent to prepare it (there are many lines
where White gets to play c5 without b4). 13 b4
used to be considered as the main line but after
what happened to Piket in this game its popularity rapidly diminished.

13...♘f6

Sometimes the knight stays on d7 to prevent
c5 but after b4 this advance has become un-
stoppable. The knight may as well go and join
the kingside attack. From f6 it obviously has a
key role in supporting the advance g4.

14 c5 ♘g6 15 cxd6

When White plays the line with 13 b4 his
usual plan is to play c5, cxd6, ♖c1 and ♘b5. It
is also customary for him to play cxd6 before
Black can play ♗f8 as this gives Black the serious option of recapturing on d6 with the

bishop. For example 15 ♖c1 ♖f7 16 a4 ♗f8 17
cxd6 ♗xd6 18 ♘d3 b6, preventing ♘c5, is
supposed to be comfortable for Black.

I would like to look at another continuation
for White, 15 a4. If Black now continues as in
the main game with 15...♖f7 16 a5 ♗f8 we have
transposed into a position which is normally
reached via the 13 a4 move order. This position
is mentioned briefly in the 13th move notes to
the previous game. There it was pointed out
that Black has been suffering after the move 17
c6. The reason is that whilst 15...♖f7 is a good
reply to 15 ♖c1 (it defends c7 in anticipation of
White's planned invasion there) it is a little passive in reply to 15 a4. It is probably better for
Black to play 15...h5 with the following possibilities:

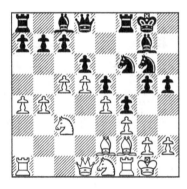

a) 16 a5?! (too slow) 16...g4 17 cxd6 cxd6 18
♘b5 g3! (this is the thematic breakthrough;
Black gives up a pawn to open lines on the
kingside) 19 hxg3 (White must accept as 19
♗xa7? loses by force in this position; Black
plays 19...♘h7!, threatening ...♕h4, and meeting 20 ♔h1 with 20...♖xa7! 21 ♘xa7 ♕h4 22
h3 ♗xh3) 19...fxg3 20 ♗xg3 a6 21 ♘a3 h4 22
♗f2 ♘h5 23 f4 (this is the only way for White
to try and defend the kingside) 23...♘hxf4 24
♘c4 ♕g5 with a clear advantage to Black,
Ftacnik-Smirin, Biel Interzonal 1993. Only one
side has an attack in this position.

b) 16 h3 ♖f7. The inclusion of the moves h3
and ...h5 changes the dynamics of the position
as now White is going to have to take on g4.
This means that the h-file will be opened so
that is where Black's rook is heading. 17 a5 ♗f8
18 c6 ♖h7 (if Black takes on c6 then White will

have the possibility of ♘d5 as well as dangerous queenside pawns) and now:

b1) 19 b5 b6! 20 axb6 cxb6 is very interesting strategically. Black has allowed White a massive passed pawn on c6 but in return the queenside is totally blocked. Of course an endgame won't be fun for Black but before the endgame there is the middlegame! But make sure you don't consider playing in such a position until White has played the move b4-b5. If the pawn were back on b4 White would have use of the b5- square, especially for his knight, and things would not be so easy for Black.

After 20...cxb6 the game Hausner-Dolmatov, Bundesliga 1993 continued 21 ♖a3 ♕c7 22 ♘d3 g4 23 fxg4 hxg4 24 hxg4 ♕g7! 25 ♗xb6 ♕h6 with a strong attack for Black.

b2) 19 cxb7! (an improvement) 19...♗xb7 20 b5 (20 a6 ♗c8 21 ♘b5 is too slow on account of 21...g4!) 20...♗c8 21 b6 (White sacrifices a pawn to open the queenside) 21...axb6 22 axb6 ♖xa1 23 ♕xa1 cxb6 24 ♕a8 g4 (24...♗e7!? would prevent White's next move) 25 ♗a6 ♘e7 26 ♗h4 ♖h6 27 ♗xf6 ♖xf6 28 ♗xc8 ♘xc8 29 ♘b5 ♖f7 30 fxg4 hxg4 31 hxg4 ♕d7 32 ♕c6 ♕xg4 33 ♘f3 and White had some compensation for the pawn (I think the position is level), Stanec-Arakhamia, Vienna 1996.

c) 16 c6!? ♗h6 17 b5 b6 18 a5 g4 19 axb6 cxb6 20 fxg4!? hxg4 21 g3 with an unclear game, Korchnoi-Xie Jun, Marbella 1999. Korchnoi's sense of danger did not desert him. He realised that with the queenside closed drastic action was required on the kingside. Black, too, can now have a protected passed pawn on the 6th rank but her attack would also be blocked. Xie Jun preferred to hold back on ...f3 and eventually lost a complicated game.

15...cxd6 16 ♖c1 ♖f7

Black must defend his c7-square. Now 17 ♘b5 can just be met by 17...a6.

17 a4 ♗f8!?

Kasparov's new move. Previously Black had played 17...h5 to support g4 but Kasparov realised that if White plays ♘b5, as he wants to do, then Black does not actually need ...h5. He can just play ...g4 and if White plays fxg4 then ...♘xe4 destroys the white centre. Not only is Kasparov hoping to save time by omitting ...h5 but sometimes the attack can actually be

stronger with the pawn still at home. For example, after White accepts the sacrifice on g3 Black may be able to hit the bishop immediately with ...♘h5 (instead of ...h5-h4 and then ...♘h5 when White has a tempo) while a pawn on h4 can just get in the way of Black's queen. So ideally, Black would like to force through ...g4 without playing ...h5 but this is not always possible, especially if White leaves his knight on c3 to defend e4. Let's have a quick look at the old move 17...h5 as this is also not bad and there are some interesting thematic lines. White replies 18 a5 and now:

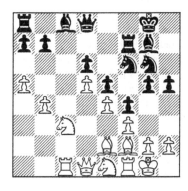

a) 18...g4 19 ♘b5 g3 20 ♗xa7! ♘h7 21 ♔h1 ♖xa7 22 ♖xc8! ♕xc8 23 ♘xa7 ♕d8 24 h3 should be compared with line 'a' in the notes to White's 15th move. There, with his rook on a1, White was unable to return the exchange with ♖xc8 and just got mated. This position after 24 h3 used to be considered good for White but in the latest game Black played 24...♘g5 followed by a sacrifice on h3 (White didn't accept) and the game ended in a draw.

b) 18...♗d7 19 ♘b5 ♗xb5 (one of the rare occasions Black is willing to give up his bishop) 20 ♗xb5 g4 21 ♔h1 g3 22 ♗g1 gxh2 23 ♗f2 is the main line of 17...h5. This is a well-known defensive tactic from White – he uses Black's pawn on h2 to shield his king. Black will now try and attack with ...h4, ...♘h5-g3 and very often he will throw in the move ...h3 to open the h-file. White will obviously try and breakthrough on the queenside. The game is very unclear and Black is supposed to start with 23...a6 in order to prevent White from advancing his own pawn to a6.

18 a5 ♗d7!

Kasparov is trying to tempt White into playing ♘b5. Piket obliges and becomes yet another victim of the champ's legendary preparation.

19 ♘b5?!

Afterwards White tried to rehabilitate this line with 19 ♔h1. This is a useful defensive move and it makes sense to play it before initiating complications on the queenside. One idea for Black is to play 19...♕e8 to stop ♘b5 (note that 19...a6 is bad as this concedes the b6-square) but 19...♖g7 is more direct. Now:

a) 20 ♘b5 g4 21 ♘xa7 g3 22 ♗b6 ♕e8! (to prevent ♗b5) 23 ♖c7 gxh2 24 ♖xb7 ♘h5 was very unpleasant for White, Burgess-Badea, Manchester 1990. Burgess confirms this in the book he co-authored (with John Nunn) on the Classical King's Indian.

b) 20 ♗b5 g4 21 ♗xd7 ♕xd7 22 fxg4 ♘xg4 23 ♘f3, D.Gurevich-Grünberg, New York 1991, was more solid but Black is still doing quite well after 23...♗e7. He plans to play ...♘h4 in order to exchange some of White's defensive pieces.

19...g4!

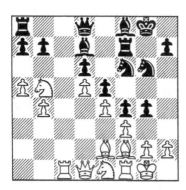

20 ♘c7?!

After 20 ♘xa7 g3 Kasparov gives the variation 21 ♗b6 ♕e7 22 ♔h1 ♘h5 23 ♘b5 gxh2 24 ♗f2 ♗xb5 25 ♗xb5 ♘g3+ 26 ♗xg3 fxg3 as clearly better for Black. In effect he is a king up! This didn't satisfy Black in the game Friesen-Lomineishvili, Rotterdam 1998. He decided to improve upon Kasparov's analysis and succeeded in spectacular fashion! Instead of 23...gxh2 the game went 23...♕h4 24 ♗g1 ♖f6

25 ♘c7 ♘e7 26 ♘xa8 gxh2 27 ♗f2 ♕xf2! with the point 28 ♖xf2 ♘g3+ 29 ♔xh2 ♖h6+ 30 ♔g1 ♖h1 mate. However, White could have defended with 26 ♘d3 as then after 26...gxh2 27 ♗f2 the queen sacrifice no longer works and on 26...♖h6 he can play 27 ♕e1. This is all very frightening for White but I'm not sure that he can't defend. Perhaps Kasparov was thinking of the proverb 'better a bird in the hand than two in the bush' as he recommended 23...gxh2.

Kasparov also gave 20 fxg4 ♘xe4 21 ♘c7 ♗a4 22 ♕xa4 ♖xc7 as White's best chance but there have been no takers for this variation.

20...g3!

I hope this move doesn't come as a surprise to you. We have seen it many times already.

21 ♘xa8?

This loses by force. Kasparov produced realms of analysis to show that Black is better after 21 hxg3 fxg3 22 ♗xg3 ♗h6!. We just have room for his main line. It runs 23 ♘xa8 ♘h5 24 ♗f2 ♘gf4 25 ♘d3! ♖g7! 26 ♘xf4 ♗xf4 27 g4! ♗xc1 28 ♕xc1 ♘f4 29 ♕e3 h5! with a clear advantage for Black.

21...♘h5!

Piket had probably been expecting 21...gxf2+ 22 ♖xf2 ♕xa8 when his rooks might become very active on the queenside. Kasparov's powerful continuation leads to the same position except with his knight on g3 instead of f6. We shall see what a difference this makes.

22 ♔h1

To avoid getting checkmated White must be in a position to meet ♕h4 with ♗g1. He can never play h3, of course, as Black just sacrifices the bishop on d7.

22...gxf2 23 ♖xf2 ♘g3+! 24 ♔g1 ♕xa8

Of course if White had taken the knight on his last move he would have been mated at once. There is still no time to take it as after 25 hxg3 fxg3 the queen just returns to d8 and Black has a winning attack.

25 ♗c4 a6!

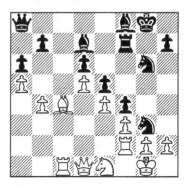

A beautiful little move which enables the black queen to occupy the most important diagonal on the board. The respective pawn chains mean that it is almost impossible for White to contest this diagonal.

26 ♕d3?! ♕a7 27 b5

White overlooks the threat but after 27...♕d2 Black would have won by 27...♗e7 and ♗h4.

27...axb5 28 ♗xb5 ♘h1!! 0-1

If people liked 25...a6 then they were in raptures over this. It was wonderful how Kasparov co-ordinated his queen and knight from the 21st move onwards. Piket resigned, as he will now be a whole piece down.

Game 3
Kaganskiy-Golod
Israel 1999

---

1 d4 ♘f6 2 ♘f3 g6 3 c4 ♗g7 4 ♘c3 0-0 5 e4 d6 6 ♗e2 e5 7 0-0 ♘c6 8 d5 ♘e7 9 ♘e1 ♘d7 10 ♗e3 f5 11 f3 f4 12 ♗f2 g5 13 ♖c1 ♖f6!?

The most common reply, at least in the past, to 13 ♖c1 is 13...♘g6 when play can easily transpose into one of the other lines. For example, 14 b4 ♘f6 15 c5 takes us into Game 2.

However, there is an interesting pawn sacrifice that enables 13 ♖c1 to stand alone as an independent line. After 13...♘g6 White can play 14 c5 (Kozul's idea again) 14...♘xc5 (14...dxc5 is worse) 15 b4 ♘a6 and now with either 16 ♘d3 or 16 ♘b5 he obtains reasonable compensation for the pawn (mainly because the knight is misplaced on a6). This line has become very theoretical and also leads to the sort of position we don't really want.

Therefore, I suggest that it is time to indulge in a spot of rook swinging. The possibility of playing ...♖f6 has already been mentioned several times in this chapter. Now it is time for this idea to take centre stage. It can be played against virtually all of White's 13th moves but most theoretical sources agree that this is one of the best moments to play 13...♖f6. That is because 13 ♖c1 puts less immediate pressure on the black queenside than some of the other moves and unlike 13 ♘d3, it does not contribute defensively either.

I have already touched upon the reasoning behind 13...♖f6 in the analysis of 13 ♘b5 in Game 1. A quick recap. The basic idea is to play ...♖h6 and ...♕e8 and if White fails to take the necessary defensive precautions then Black plays ...♕h5 and mates him. Take a look at the following examples that demonstrate some of the tactical possibilities available to Black. In the first two White was careless while the third features a classic panic reaction.

They all start after 13 ♖c1 ♖f6:

a) 14 ♘d3 ♖h6 15 b4 ♕e8 16 c5? ♕h5 17 h3 ♘xc5 (17...♖f6 also does the trick) 18 ♗xc5 ♗xh3 19 ♘f2 ♗xg2 20 ♘g4 ♕h1+ 21 ♔f2

♕h4+ 22 ♔g1 ♖h5 0-1 Borges Mateos-Pecorelli, Cali 2000. White is no mug but a member of the strong Cuban national team.

b) 14 b4 ♖h6 15 c5 a6 16 ♘a4 ♕e8 17 ♔h1 ♔h8 18 cxd6 (the prophylactic ♗g1 should have been played at some point) 18...cxd6 19 ♖c7 b5 20 ♘b2 ♘f6 21 a4 ♕h5 22 ♗g1 ♘fxd5! 23 ♖xc8+ (23 exd5 ♘f5 24 h3 ♘g3+ 25 ♔h2 ♗xh3 wins) 23...♖xc8 24 exd5 ♘f5 25 h3 e4 26 ♔h2 e3 27 ♘ed3 ♘h4 0-1 Opalic-Socko, Passau 1999.

c) 14 ♘d3 ♖h6 15 c5 ♕e8 16 g4 fxg3 17 ♗xg3 ♘f6 18 cxd6 cxd6 19 ♔f2 ♘g6 20 ♘e3 ♘f4 21 ♔d2 ♘6h5 22 ♔c2 ♗d7 23 ♔b1 ♖c8 24 ♗f2 ♘xe2 25 ♕xe2 ♘f4 26 ♘xf4 exf4 27 ♗xa7 ♖h3 28 ♗g1 g4 29 fxg4 ♖hxc3 30 bxc3 ♗b5 31 ♕b2 ♕xe4+ 0-1 Hoensch-Klundt, Bundesliga 1991.

How sad to have made it all the way to the queenside just to get mated there.

There are four basic defensive strategies against Black's attack:

1) White can play ♔h1 in order to meet ...♕h5 with ♗g1. If Black can then land with a knight on g3 that will be very nice but more often he ends up playing for g5-g4.

2) White can play ♘d3, ♗e1, and ♘f2 so that he can meet ...♕h5 with h3. Assuming that White arrives in time (i.e. he is not going to get blown away by a sacrifice on h3) then Black should switch strategies and play ...♖g6 (without ...♕h5) ...h5 and ...g4. White's queenside attack will be much slower as his knight and bishop are less actively placed.

3) White can play g4. In practice this tends to occur out of desperation when it is already too late, but if White played it on move 14, for example, it would be quite acceptable.

4) Once again White can sacrifice a pawn with 14 c5. You may not think of this as a defensive strategy but it does create a diversion. Black must deal with concrete problems on the queenside before he can contemplate an attack against the white king. I don't believe the sacrifice is so dangerous for Black in this particular position. See Game 4 for the details.

The three illustrative games are examples of White failing in his defensive efforts. Below we shall see what happens when White plays better.

14 b4

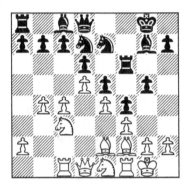

White prepares to play c5 and as I mentioned above playing it at once as a pawn sacrifice is possible and that is covered in Game 4.

The position after 14 ♘d3 ♖h6 featured in a couple of our quick wins for Black. After 15 c5 ♕e8 White should not play 16 g4 or 16 b4 (see above), nor 16 cxd6 which can be met by 16...♕h5!. Neither is there time for 16 ♗e1 but White could, conceivably, try 16 ♘b5 intending to meet 16...♕h5 with 17 h4. See the note to White's 16th move for analysis to a similar position. I don't know why White players avoid 16 ♔h1 in this position as 16...♕h5 17 ♗g1 ♘xc5 18 ♘xc5 dxc5 19 ♘b5 is good for White. Black should prefer 16...♘f6 with similar play to the main game.

Incidentally, the no-nonsense American Grandmaster Yermolinsky played 15 ♗e1 (after 14 ♘d3 ♖h6) so that he can defend with ♘f2 and h3 if need be. Yermolinsky-Gurcan, Istanbul Olympiad 2000 continued 15...a6 16 b4 ♘f6 17 ♘f2 ♖g6 18 c5 h5 19 h3 and now I like the idea of 19...♔h7 followed by ♘eg8-h6 and g4.

Before moving on it should be pointed out that Piket, one of ♖c1's main supporters, has played 14 g4 here. After 14...h5 play will be very similar to the 13 g4 line we are going to examine within the notes to Game 5.

14...♖h6 15 c5

I have switched the move order of the game so that we can look at some interesting stuff after 15 c5. The actual move order was 15 ♘d3 ♘f6!? 16 c5 ♕e8 17 ♔h1. Instead of 16 c5 White could have played 16 ♗e1 in order to meet 16...♕e8 17 ♘f2 ♕h5 with 18 h3. Black should play 17...♖g6 18 h3 h5 with a fairly standard King's Indian position.

15...♕e8!?

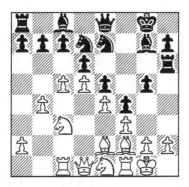

This is actually a new move, or at least a new move order that I have conjured up for the readers of this book. Everyone else gives 15...a6 in order to prevent ♘b5. However, there are drawbacks to playing ...a6. Firstly, it wastes a tempo and secondly, although it covers the b5-square, it weakens the b6-square. In Korchnoi-Nataf, Cannes 1998, the old war-horse tried to exploit this at once with 16 ♘a4!?. Now if the black knight moves from d7 White exchanges on d6 and invades on b6. And if the knight can't move it means that the whole of the black queenside is tied down. In the second of our three quick wins above we saw that Black has tactical ideas here as well but they only worked because White failed to take prophylactic action with ♗g1. The continuation of Korchnoi-Nataf was (after 16 ♘a4) 16...♕e8 17 ♔h1 ♕h5 (17...♘h8!?) 18 ♗g1 ♕h4 (threatening ♘f6-h5) 19 ♘d3 b5 (19...♘f6 20 ♕e1) 20 cxb6 axb6 21 ♕e1 with a slightly better game for White.

16 ♔h1

So what happens if White takes up the challenge and plays 16 ♘b5!?. Well, the answer is I don't really know but I'll share some of my thoughts with you. After 16...♕h5! 17 h4 (this suicidal-looking move is actually forced as 17 h3 loses to 17...♘f6 followed by ....♗xh3) Black can play either 17...♖g6 or 17...gxh4. When I started my analysis I assumed that Black could crush him with either move but White's position turned out to amazingly resilient:

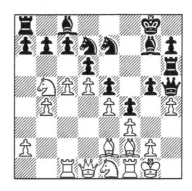

a) 17...♘g6 is an attempt to keep the h-file open. Now 18 ♘xc7 loses to 18...♘xh4 (threatening ...♘xf3+ or ...♘xg2 or ♘ anywhere), e.g. 19 ♗xh4 ♕xh4 20 ♘xa8 ♕h2+ 21 ♔f2 ♕g3+ 22 ♔g1 ♖h2! and there is nothing White can do about ...♕h4 and ...♖h1 mate. But White does have a defence: 18 g4! fxg3 19 ♗xg3. Now Black has to be careful. For example, 19...gxh4?? 20 f4! costs him his queen while after 19...♘xh4 20 ♘xc7 I can't see anyway through for Black. The best move is 19...♘f4 and after 20 ♘xc7 ♖g6. Black now threatens 21...gxh4 so White has to choose between 21 ♔h1 and 21 ♗xf4. I have analysed masses of variations and I still don't know what's happening. Let's just say the position is unclear. Perhaps that is unsatisfactory but the editor would have cut all the variations out anyway.

b) 17...gxh4 18 ♘xc7 h3 19 g4 fxg3 20 ♗xg3 (taking the rook is also possible; perhaps Black starts with 20...♕g5!? as 21 ♗xg3 ♕xg3+ ♔h1 ♖g6 is winning; I think White must play 21 ♔h1 when 21...h2 is fun and maybe good for Black but there are no guarantees) 20...h2+!? (20...♖g6 21 ♘xa8 ♕h4! wins for Black but I don't see anything good against 21 ♔h1!) 21 ♔h1 ♕h3 and now:

b1) 22 cxd6 ♕xg3 23 dxe7 ♘f6 24 ♘xa8 ♖g6! 25 ♖xc8+ ♔f7 and White gets mated after he runs out of checks.

b2) 22 ♘xa8 ♕xg3 23 ♘d3 ♖g6 24 ♖f2 ♘xc5!! (threatening ♗h3) 25 ♖xh2 ♘xd3 26 ♗xd3 ♗h3 and with ....♗h6 to follow Black has the advantage.

b3) 22 ♗f2! is best and after a few hours of unsuccessfully sacrificing my rook I finally settled for 22...♖b8. The position is totally unclear. Black's queenside has collapsed but so has White's kingside. There were many lines I looked at where White seemed to be doing quite well but then he suddenly got mated. I'll just point out that Black has no need to fear 23 cxd6 ♘g6 24 ♗xa7 as he has the reply 24...♘f4 and if White plays 25 ♗xb8 then he is mated after 25...♘h5!

To conclude, if you don't trust these variations then play 15...a6, but in my opinion it will take an extremely brave man to play 16 ♘b5.

16...♘f6!

White has defended against the threat of ♕h5 which he can now meet with 17 ♗g1. Black needs to feed some more pieces to the kingside if he's going to attack successfully there. It was possible to play 16...a6 but it is still unnecessary.

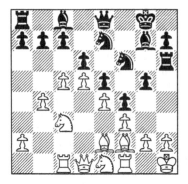

17 ♘d3

This time 17 ♘b5 looks much more plausible but it is in fact even worse than on the previous move. After 17 ♘b5 ♕h5 18 ♗g1 Black has the delightful move 18...♕h4!! Now if White plays 19 ♘xc7 then after 19...♘h5! he gets checkmated. The only way to prevent ...♘h5 is with the sad 19 g3 and after 19...fxg3 White must try 20 ♘xc7. The main line of my analysis then runs 20...♘g6! 21 ♘g2 (21 ♘xa8? ♕xh2+ 22 ♗xh2 ♖xh2+ 23 ♔g1 ♘f4 leads to mate) 21...♕h3 22 ♖e1 (22 ♘xa8 ♘f4 wins) 22...♘h5 23 ♗f1 gxh2 24 ♗f2 g4! with a powerful attack for Black (I think it wins by force).

17...♗d7

After my move order trip to uncharted territories we arrive back in the Kaganskiy-Golod

game after the text. Black has managed to prevent ♘b5 without having to resort to ...a6. His plan now is to break through on the kingside with ...g4. Note that 17...♘h5 would be met by 18 ♕e1.

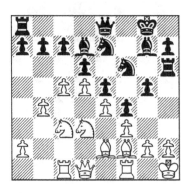

18 b5!?

Another game also reached this position and went 18 ♘b2 ♕g6 19 ♘c4 ♘h5 20 ♕e1 but Black could have played 19...g4!

18...b6 19 cxd6 cxd6 20 a4 ♔h8 21 ♕e1

White intends to play g4 to try and relieve some of the pressure on the kingside. Black could play 21...g4 himself but he only wants to play this when he has more forces available. As we shall see from the course of the game there is no need to stop White playing g4.

21...♕g6 22 g4 fxg3 23 ♗xg3 ♘h5 24 ♖g1 ♖f8 25 ♘d1 g4

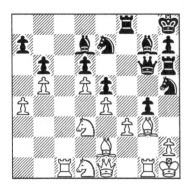

26 ♖c7?

White makes his first aggressive move for a long time and it's a mistake. The situation was less clear after 26 ♗h4! ♘f6 27 ♖g2.

26...gxf3 27 ♗f1 ♕e8 28 ♖xa7 ♗f6 29 ♕e3 ♘xg3+ 30 ♖xg3 ♕h5 31 ♕g1 ♗c8 32 ♘3f2? ♖g8 33 ♖xg8+ ♘xg8

Now we see what was wrong with White's 32nd move. It boxed in his own queen and the threat of 34...♖g8 now forces the knight to retrace its steps.

34 ♘d3 ♖g6 35 ♕e3 ♗h3 36 ♕e1 ♗xf1 0-1

Game 4
Vera-Nataf
Montreal 2003

---

1 d4 ♘f6 2 c4 g6 3 ♘c3 ♗g7 4 e4 d6 5 ♗e2 0-0 6 ♘f3 e5 7 0-0 ♘c6 8 d5 ♘e7 9 ♘e1 ♘d7 10 ♗e3 f5 11 f3 f4 12 ♗f2 g5 13 ♖c1 ♖f6 14 c5!?

The lines of the previous game are not a lot of fun for White so in the last year or two he has introduced a familiar pawn sacrifice in a new guise. It has to be said, though, that Black players seem to have come to terms with this particular version of the c4-c5 sacrifice quite quickly.

14...♘xc5

14...dxc5 15 ♘d3 b6 16 b4! cxb4 17 ♘b5 c5 18 dxc6 ♘xc6 19 ♖xc6! ♖xc6 20 ♘xb4 1-0 Kallio-Nordenbaek, Copenhagen 2003 is not the way to go.

15 b4 ♘a6

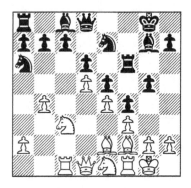

16 ♘d3

White can regain his pawn with 16 ♘b5 ♗d7 17 ♘xa7 but it is far from clear if that is a better continuation. For example, the game

Rotstein-Isonzo, Arco 2003 continued 17...♖g6 (18 ♗xa6 bxa6 19 ♕c2 ♘c8 20 ♘c6 ♕e8 is unclear) 18 a4 h5 19 h3 ♗h6 20 ♘c3 ♔h8 21 ♘b5 ♘g8 22 ♕c2 ♘f6 23 ♘xc7 ♘xc7 24 ♖xc7 g4! 25 fxg4 hxg4 26 hxg4 ♗xa4 27 ♕c4 ♗b5! 28 ♕xb5 ♕xc7 with a decisive advantage for Black.

16...♖h6

Black just gets on with his attack.

17 a4 ♕e8 18 ♔h1 ♗d7!

Up until here the two players had been following a game they played the previous year in Cuba. That went 18...♕h5 19 ♗g1 ♗d7 20 ♘a2 ♖c8 21 ♘f2 ♕e8 22 ♘g4 ♖g6 23 b5 ♘c5 24 ♗xc5 dxc5 25 ♖xc5 with advantage to White, Vera-Nataf, Havana 2002.

19 ♕b3 ♔h8 20 ♘b2

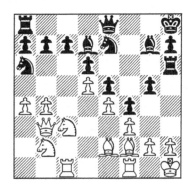

Nataf's improvement is quite clever. By delaying ...♕h5 for a couple of moves he has kept pressure on the a4 pawn and prevented White from repeating the strong plan he found in their previous game. But this is a good moment to launch the attack as the knight on d3, which often retreats to f2 to help in the defence of the king, has disappeared to the queenside

20...♕h5 21 ♗g1 g4 22 fxg4

White must capture on g4 as otherwise Black will win with ...g3, ...♕g5, ...♖xh2+ and ...♕h4.

22...♗xg4 23 ♗xg4 ♕xg4 24 ♘b5 ♗f6 25 ♘xc7?

25 ♕f3 looks better when Black can reply 25...♕d7.

25...♘xc7 26 ♖xc7 ♕e2! 27 ♖d1 ♕xe4 28 ♘c4

He probably has to play 28 ♕c4 but

28...♘f5 29 ♗f2 ♕xc4 30 ♘xc4 e4 is no fun for White.

28...♘f5 29 ♗f2 ♗h4! 30 ♗xh4 ♖g8!?

The simple 30...♘xh4 31 ♕h3 ♖g8 looks crushing as 32 ♖c8 is met by 32...♘f5.

31 ♕f3 ♕xf3 32 gxf3 ♖xh4

The attack is even stronger after the exchange of queens now that the g-file is open

33 ♖d2

Or 33 ♖xb7 ♘g3+ 34 ♔g2 ♘e2‼ 35 ♔h1 (35 ♔f1 ♖xh2) 35...♖h6! and Black has a mating attack

33...e4! 34 ♖f7 ♘g3+ 35 ♔g1 ♘e2+ 36 ♔f1 ♖g1+ 0-1

Sweet revenge for Nataf after his earlier defeat. The ball is now in White's court in this variation.

Game 5

Korchnoi-Xie Jun

Amsterdam 2001

---

1 d4 ♘f6 2 c4 g6 3 ♘c3 ♗g7 4 e4 d6 5 ♗e2 0-0 6 ♘f3 e5 7 0-0 ♘c6 8 d5 ♘e7 9 ♘e1 ♘d7 10 ♗e3 f5 11 f3 f4 12 ♗f2 g5 13 ♘d3

This move has a bad theoretical reputation based on some old games where Black dominated on the kingside. This reputation seems to be more or less justified but Korchnoi, at periodic intervals, has taken it upon himself to try and rehabilitate this line. Even he hasn't had great success. Although ♘d3 ensures that White can force through c5 without wasting a tempo on a pawn move such as b4, the knight

is not well placed here. It has few active possibilities and just tends to get in the way of the other pieces.

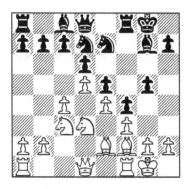

There is one other 13th move that has to be considered and that is 13 g4. The motivation behind such a move is to try and stop Black's kingside attack before it has even started. This move crops up from time to time in various variations of the King's Indian and is mainly played by players who are nervous about their king coming under fire. Immediately Black has an important decision to make. Should he capture en passant or not? Let's have a look at both options.

a) 13...fxg3 14 hxg3. The character of the position has now changed dramatically. With the disappearance of the pawn on f4 White now has more space for his pieces on the kingside. His king may look more exposed but there is much less long-term danger to it than before. In practice White scores heavily after Black exchanges on g3 but the move is not necessarily bad. After 14...♘g6 15 ♕d2 h5 16 ♘g2 a5 17 ♘a4 b6 18 a3 an interesting moment has arisen. Black has made some useful prophylactic moves on the queenside but now he has to decide whether or not to play 18...h4. This has the advantage of gaining control over f4 (White must reply g4) but at the same time concedes the f5-square to White. It also totally blocks up the kingside so Black can forget about any direct attack against the white king. In Savchenko-Fedorov, Nikolaev 1993 Black played 18...h4 and after 19 g4 ♘f4 20 ♔h2 ♘f6 21 ♘e3 ♗d7 22 ♘c3 a4 23 ♖fb1 he was very solid but had no active ideas at all. White's position must be slightly better.

In his notes to this game Savchenko suggested that 18...♘c5 is better. He gave the following line: 19 ♘xc5 bxc5 20 b4 axb4 21 axb4 ♖xa1 22 ♖xa1 cxb4 23 ♕xb4 g4 (this is one of the reasons for holding back with ...h4 – Black has more options on the kingside) 24 fxg4 ♗xg4 25 ♗xg4 hxg4 26 ♘e3 which he assessed as unclear. Burgess then chipped in with 26...♘f4 27 ♘f5 ♘h3+ 28 ♔g2 ♘xf2 29 ♔xf2 and said that White was better. 28...♘xf2 is a silly move. Black should play 28...♕d7 and then sacrifice the exchange on f5 with what appears to be adequate compensation.

b) 13...h5 is the alternative. Black allows White to keep his blockading pawn on g4 and plans to attack by transferring some major pieces to the h-file. He is in no rush to play hxg4 as this will just lead to exchanges on the h-file. He will only take on g4 when he has a decisive idea in mind. Black's attack requires a lot of build-up but White's queenside play is also more laboured than usual as he has to make sure that the g4 pawn has sufficient cover – a piece sacrifice there is likely to be devastating. Let's have a look at a game that went like a dream for Black. Jurga-Baecker, Germany 1995 continued 14 h3 ♖f6 15 ♔g2 ♖h6 16 ♖h1 ♔f7!? (Black clears the way for his queen to the h-file; another typical plan in such positions is to play ...♘g6 followed by ...♗f8-e7) 17 ♘d3 a6 (Black does not want ...♕h8 to be met by ♘b5) 18 b4 ♘f6 19 c5 ♗d7 20 a4 ♕h8 21 ♘c1? (this move is just ridiculous; White had to play 21 b5 with an unclear game) 21...♕h7! (now Black just triples on the h-file) 22 ♘d3 ♖h8. The

white kingside is about to cave in. Black threatens 23...hxg4 24 hxg4 ♖h2+ so White prevents this with 23 ♕g1 but after 23...♕g6! he is totally embarrassed as his rooks can no longer protect each other. After 24 b5 hxg4 White played the amazing 25 hxg4 just giving up his queen for a rook and resigned a few moves later. 25 fxg4 offers slightly more resistance when 25...♘xe4 is probably stronger than 25...♘xg4 (though both should win). This game may have given you the impression that Black wins by force against 13 g4 but this is certainly not the case. At least you know what you are aiming for now. This material should be studied in conjunction with Game 9 where g4 is played in a similar position.

13...♘f6

This is not thought to be the best moment to play the ...♖f6 plan, e.g. 13...♖f6 14 c5 ♖h6 15 cxd6 cxd6 16 ♘b5 is considered good for White.

14 c5 ♘g6 15 a4

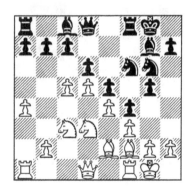

Korchnoi's attempts to give this line a new lease of life have centred around the advance of the a-pawn. While nearly everyone else concentrates on cxd6 Korchnoi often prefers c5-c6. First though, he likes to get a pawn to a5, having been scarred by his game with Kasparov (see below).

The alternative is 15 ♖c1 ♖f7 and now:

a) 16 ♖c2 was the choice in Taimanov-Najdorf, from the famous 1953 Candidates tournament in Zürich (made famous by Bronstein's excellent book on the tournament). After 16...♗f8 17 cxd6 cxd6 18 ♕d2 g4 19 ♖fc1 g3 20 hxg3 fxg3 21 ♗xg3 ♘h5 Black had a dangerous attack on the kingside.

b) 16 cxd6 cxd6 17 ♘b5 is the more direct approach but is well met by 17...g4! Now 18 fxg4 ♘xe4 is better for Black, 18 ♗xa7 loses to ♗d7, 18 ♘xa7 to 18...g3 and the rather desperate 18 g3 fxg3 19 hxg3 gxf3 20 ♗xf3 ♗h3 21 ♖e1 ♗h6 also led to trouble for White in Miladinovic-Georgiev, Belgrade 1988. Other moves allow Black his customary attack on the kingside. Here is a recent example: 18 ♕b3 g3 19 hxg3 fxg3 20 ♗xg3 ♘h5 21 ♗h2 ♗h6 22 ♖c2 a6 23 ♘c3 ♗e3+ 24 ♘f2 ♘gf4 25 ♘cd1 ♗d4 26 ♘e3 ♕g5 27 ♘eg4 ♗xg4 28 fxg4 ♘xe2+ 29 ♖xe2 ♕xg4 30 ♖e3 ♖af8 0-1 Saif-Timoshenko, Dubai 2000.

15...h5

Another idea is to prepare for ...g4 with 15...♔h8 16 a5 ♖g8. Korchnoi-Lanka, Linz 1997 now continued 17 cxd6 cxd6 18 ♘b5 g4 19 fxg4 ♘xe4 20 ♗xa7 ♗d7 21 ♗b6 ♕e7 22 ♘c7 ♖af8 with an unclear game.

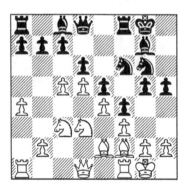

16 a5

In Korchnoi-Kasparov, Amsterdam 1991 White played 16 h3 ♖f7 17 c6 and was surprised by the reply 17...a5!. This game was such a bad experience for Korchnoi that never again did he allow c6 to be met by ...a5. Play continued 18 cxb7 ♗xb7 19 b4 ♗c8! 20 bxa5 ♗h6 21 ♘b4 (Kasparov considered 21 a6 to be unclear) 21...g4 22 ♘c6 (in the King's Indian the c6-square sometimes looks a more dangerous outpost than it really is; for example, here the knight attacks nothing) 22...♕f8 23 fxg4 hxg4 24 hxg4 ♗g5 25 ♗f3 ♕h6 26 ♖e1 ♘h4 27 ♗xh4 (White could have tried to evacuate his king with 27 ♔f1 but after 27...♘xf3 28 gxf3

♘xg4! 29 fxg4 f3 he is not going anywhere) 27...♗xh4 28 g5 ♕xg5 29 ♖e2 ♘g4 30 ♖b1 ♗g3 31 ♕d3 ♕h4 0-1. One of Korchnoi's worst defeats in this line. He usually gets at least a bit of counterplay.

16...g4

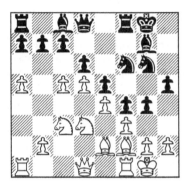

Sometimes Black has to work hard to achieve ...g4 – not this time. Perhaps Korchnoi just wanted to show that the ...g3 pawn sacrifice is not so dangerous for White if he just wants to make a draw.

17 c6

Korchnoi is going to accept the pawn on g3. This is better than 17 cxd6 cxd6 18 ♘b5 g3! 19 ♗xa7 ♘h7! 20 h3 (or 20 ♔h1 ♖xa7! – we have already seen this tactic before) 20...♕h4 and with ...♗xh3 to come Black had a decisive advantage in Larsen-Torre, Bauang 1973.

17...g3 18 hxg3 fxg3 19 ♗xg3 h4 20 ♗h2 ♘h5

It is much worse for Black to exchange on c6 as then White gets use of the d5-square. For example, if Black plays 20...bxc6 21 dxc6 and then continues as in the game with 21...♘h5 22 f4 ♘hxf4 23 ♘xf4 ♘xf4 24 ♗xf4 exf4 White now has 25 ♕d5+.

21 cxb7 ♗xb7 22 f4

Korchnoi has great experience in this line. He knows when it is time to defend on the kingside and when it is time to bail out. Without this move he would come under heavy pressure and if he doesn't play it now he might not get the chance again. There now follows a series of exchanges after which we suddenly find ourselves in an endgame.

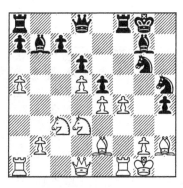

22...♘hxf4 23 ♘xf4 ♘xf4 24 ♗xf4 exf4 25 ♗g4 ♕g5 26 ♗e6+ ♔h8 27 ♖f3 ♗c8 28 ♖h3 ♗xe6 29 dxe6 ♖ae8 30 ♕e1 ♖xe6 31 ♕xh4+ ♕xh4 32 ♖xh4+ ♔g8

In the end Xie Jun had to work a little to hold the draw but at this particular moment Black is very comfortable. The remaining moves were: 33 ♖g4 c6 34 ♖c1 f3 35 gxf3 ♖xf3 36 ♘e2 ♖ff6 37 ♖xc6 ♖g6 38 ♖xg6 ♖xg6+ 39 ♔f2 ♗xb2 40 ♘f4 ♗d4+ 41 ♔f3 ♖f6 42 ♔g4 ♗e5 43 ♘d3 ♖f7 44 a6 ♗h2 45 ♖c8+ ♔g7 46 ♖b8 ♔f6 47 ♖b7 ♔e6 48 ♔h3 ♗g1 49 ♔g3 ♗e3 ½-½

Summary

This chapter includes some of the sharpest and most complex chess in the King's Indian. It is very heavily theoretical but there are some general rules and strategies that Black can follow to help him through the maze.

1) Black's main aim is to play ...g5-g4 as quickly as possible (though there is another idea where he plays ...♖f6-h6) and, assuming White doesn't take on g4, then ...g4-g3. As time is of the essence this advance usually has to be played as a pawn sacrifice. If White takes the pawn, and often he has no choice, then Black will follow up with moves such as ...h5-h4 (if the h-pawn has moved), ...♘h5-f4 and ...♗h6. Basically he takes over the dark squares on the kingside and gets a strong attack. Experienced White players may try and give the pawn back with f3-f4 to avoid suffocating on the kingside. The ...g3 pawn sacrifice usually persuades White to forget about his queenside attack and forces him to devote his energies to kingside survival.

2) If White meets ...g3 with h3 then Black will be looking to sacrifice his bishop on that square. If White just ignores the black pawn on g3 Black will usually try and force him into playing h3 (e.g. by threatening mate on h2) so that he can sacrifice his bishop. Usually Black is in no rush to play the move ...g3xh2 as White may be able to use Black's pawn as a shield for his own king. Sometimes an opponent's pawn can be better protection than one of your own as a piece cannot be sacrificed to remove it.

3) Black must guard his light-squared bishop most preciously as without it will be much harder to conduct a successful attack.

4) If White attacks any other piece on the queenside then Black's first reaction should be to see if he can ignore the threat and just get on with the kingside attack. Many a game has been lost by White wasting precious tempi capturing a rook on a8.

5) Apart from against 13 a4, where I am suggesting Black plays 13...a5, Black should leave the queenside alone and just concentrate on his kingside attack. Sometimes it is worth playing ...a6 to prevent White playing ♘b5, but Black should take care that this doesn't allow an even more serious invasion on b6.

6) Black's knight on d7 makes it harder for White to play c5. Although Black is itching to move this piece to f6 he should try and stay there until White has wasted a move preparing c5 (♘d3 or b4 for example).

CHAPTER TWO

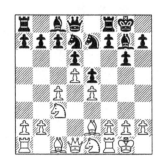

The Classical Variation: 9 ♘e1 ♘d7 without 10 ♗e3

---

1 d4 ♘f6 2 c4 g6 3 ♘c3 ♗g7 4 e4 d6 5 ♗e2 0-0 6 ♘f3 e5 7 0-0 ♘c6 8 d5 ♘e7 9 ♘e1 ♘d7

The old main line of the King's Indian is a mere shadow of its former self. Nowadays it is rarely seen and has been surpassed in popularity by all the other lines in the Classical during the last twenty years. I think it just became too theoretical for its own good and reached a sort of saturation point where everyone just decided to move on to pastures new. I can remember one frustrating experience as a young player where I had a club game sent for adjudication after 36 moves and we still weren't out of theory! Still, even if the lines are no longer so topical they are of great instructional value as they illustrate well the attacking and defensive ideas for each side.

White's main plan in these lines is to penetrate into the heart of the black position via the c7-square. In games 6-9 he starts with 10 ♘d3 in order to force through the advance c4-c5 and open the c-file for his major pieces. Once c5 has been achieved the knight is poorly placed on d3 so it usually retreats to f2 for defensive duty and White piles up his forces against c7. Black can usually prevent an invasion here with the help of moves like ...♘f6-e8 and ...♖f8-f7 and sometimes the interesting manoeuvre ...♗f8-e7-d8 or ...♗f6-d8 (see Game 7). With c7 so well protected White often turns his attention to the other vulnerable point in the black camp, a7. He will try and persuade Black to play ...a7-a6 as this weakens the b6-square

and gives White another possible entry point into the black camp. Very often Black will just let a7 go if it means gaining a tempo or two for the kingside attack (see Game 6). He has to be more careful about letting c7 go as this is not such a peripheral square. But Black's objective is not to hold the queenside for ever, as that would be almost impossible, but to just hold it together long enough for his attack on the kingside to become a potent force.

As in the previous chapter, Black's main idea is to break through on the kingside with ...g5-g4 and in the long run White will not be able to prevent this advance (unless he plays g2-g4 himself). Don't forget Black can always play it as a sacrifice the moment things start to go wrong on the queenside. Also, bear in mind that the black attack can afford to be a few moves behind the white attack as his prize is much the greater. A queenside attack may win material but a kingside attack can deliver mate!

In Games 9 and 10 we examine a radical idea where White breaks the rules by advancing g2-g4 in front of his own king. The thinking behind this is explained below.

Game 6
Miles-Sax
London 1980

---

1 d4 ♘f6 2 c4 g6 3 ♘c3 ♗g7 4 e4 d6 5 ♗e2 0-0 6 ♘f3 e5 7 0-0 ♘c6 8 d5 ♘e7 9

♘e1 ♘d7 10 ♘d3

For 10 f3 f5 11 g4 see Game 10.

10...f5 11 ♗d2

Unless White is planning to block the kingside with g4 he normally waits for Black to play ♘f6 before playing f3. This gives Black the chance to make the positional mistake 11...f4 which is strongly met by 12 ♗g4!. Also after 11 f3 f4 Black may be able to derive some benefit by leaving his knight on d7 for a while in order to hold up c5. It probably doesn't make all that much difference but 11 ♗d2 is considered the more accurate move order.

Very rarely White plays 11 exf5. This leads to equal play after both 11...gxf5 12 f4 ♘g6 13 ♗e3 exf4! 14 ♘xf4 ♘xf4 15 ♗xf4 a6 (preventing ...♘b5-d4) 16 ♕d2 ♕f6 17 ♖ae1 ♘e5 and 11...♘xf5 12 f3 ♘f6 13 ♘f2 c6 14 ♘fe4 ♘xe4 15 ♘xe4 ♕b6+ 16 ♔h1 ♗d7.

However, in general in the King's Indian Black meets exf5 with ...gxf5 in order to keep control of the e4-square.

11...♘f6

In the 1990's it become quite fashionable for Black to play an early ...♔h8, either here or on the next move. The idea (apart from freeing g8 for the knight on e7) is to adopt a more flexible set-up, not rushing with ...f4 and reserving the option of challenging White on the queenside with c6 or exchanging in the centre with ...fxe4. Unfortunately we don't have the space to cover this as well as the main line and I consider it more important to look at the main line, if only to develop your King's Indian culture!

12 f3 f4

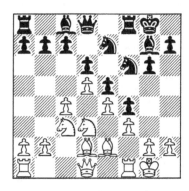

So the stage is set. Black closes the centre in anticipation of an attack against the white king. This is the real starting point of the variation and in a tournament game this position would usually be reached after just a couple of minutes play.

13 c5 g5 14 cxd6

White has little to gain in delaying this exchange on d6. There is a speculative sacrifice, 14 ♖c1 ♘g6 15 ♘b5 a6 (Black should take the piece as 15...♖f7 16 ♗a5 is awkward) 16 cxd6 axb5 17 dxc7, although the current view is that it is doubtful White has enough compensation after 17...♕e8.

14...cxd6 15 ♖c1

15 ♘f2 is equally popular and this is the subject of Game 8.

15...♘g6 16 ♘b5

White plans to invade on c7. Black must prevent this.

16...♖f7

You will see this move time and time again

throughout our coverage of the Classical King's Indian. The rook now both defends along the second rank and can move to g7 or h7 where it can play an important role in the assault on the white kingside.

17 ♕c2 ♘e8

It may seem like a concession for Black to retreat the knight but that is not the way to look at. In fact it's only because this knight on e8 does such a wonderful job of holding up the White queenside attack that Black can play in this fashion at all. It is possible for Black to attack at once with 17...g4 but the position after 18 ♘c7 gxf3 19 gxf3 ♗h3 20 ♘e6! is considered favourable for White.

18 a4

Note that 18 ♘xa7 fails to 18...♕b6+. White needs to play a4 so that he can meet 18...a6 with 19 ♘a3 and not have to worry about Black playing ...b5.

18...h5 19 ♘f2 ♗f8

19...♗d7!? is the subject of the next game.

20 ♘xa7

This little tactical trick should be familiar to the King's Indian player. In this position it is no longer considered to be very dangerous for Black and, as we shall see, he even has two satisfactory replies.

The alternative is to play 20 h3 when traditionally Black has played 20...♖g7 21 ♕b3 ♘h4 and tried to force through ...g4 as quickly as possible. The theoretical verdict here is that White has slightly the better chances. One of the problems is that if Black plays ...g4 too soon the white major pieces can swing along the third rank (after lots of exchanges on g4 this

will be open) and create threats against the black king. Remember it has no pawn cover left. Therefore, I suggest that after 20 h3 Black plays 20...♗d7!? and after White's most likely reply 21 ♕b3 we have transposed into Roeder-Hebden (the next game).

Black can use the move order of this game if he wants to give White the chance to play 20 ♘xa7. Otherwise just play 19...♗d7.

20...♗d7!?

This leads to a full-blooded struggle where Black will hope to make White pay the price on the kingside for his queenside greed.

The alternative 20...♖c7 leads by force to a drawish endgame, e.g. 21 ♗a5 ♖xc2 22 ♗xd8 ♖xe2 23 ♘xc8 ♖xa4 24 ♘d3 g4 25 ♖f2 ♖e3 26 ♘e1 ♖a8 27 ♖fc2 ♖b3 28 ♔f2 ♖a2 29 ♖b1 ♔f7 30 ♔e2 ♗e7 31 ♘xe7 ♘xe7 32 ♘d3 ♖a8 33 ♗xe7 ♔xe7 and Novikov-Glek, Lvov 1985 soon ended peacefully.

21 ♘b5 ♖g7 22 h3 ♘h4 23 ♕b3 ♔h8!

Black's plan is, of course, to play ...g4. He could have done so at once but he first decides to remove his king from the same diagonal as White's queen. This is a very sensible precaution. Why, you may ask, is it so important to get the king off the same diagonal as White's queen? After all, isn't it just blocked by a pawn on d5? Yes, true, but when Black commits himself to the kingside attack with ...g4 he will need to support this action by returning his knight from e8 to f6. This will allow White to play ♘c7 and subsequently ♘e6. A knight on e6 is hard for Black to live with and he will probably have to take it. White will recapture with dxe6 and with the black king on g8 he might be threatening a nasty discovered check by e6-e7. The tempo Black will have to spend to prevent this could cost him the game in such a sharp situation. The tempo is much better spent now before the hand to hand fighting starts and when White has only relatively quiet moves at his disposal.

24 a5

Black would have played ...g4 against virtually any White move, e.g. 24 ♖c3 g4 25 fxg4 ♘f6 26 ♕d1 hxg4 27 hxg4 ♘h5! gave Black a strong attack in Frias-Wilder, New York 1984.

24...g4! 25 fxg4

Or 25 hxg4 hxg4 26 ♘xg4 ♘f6! with the usual attacking chances.

25...hxg4 26 hxg4 ♘f6 27 ♘c7 ♘xg4 28 ♗xg4

After 28 ♘xa8 ♘e3 29 ♗xe3 ♖xg2+ 30 ♔h1 ♕g5 Black has a decisive attack.

28...♗xg4 29 ♘xg4 ♖xg4

30 ♖f2?

The key line is 30 ♗e1! f3 when Black is losing after 30...♖xg2+ 31 ♔h1 but 30...f3! 31 ♖xf3 ♕g5 leads to very unclear play. Perhaps it is a draw, e.g. 32 ♖g3 ♕xc1 33 ♖xg4 ♕xe1+ 34 ♔h2 ♖c8 35 ♘e6 ♖c1 36 ♘xf8 ♕h1+ 37 ♔g3 ♕e1+ 38 ♔h2 ♕h1+ etc.

30...♕g5 31 ♕h3 ♖g3 32 ♕h1

After 32 ♕xg3 ♕xg3 33 ♘xa8 f3 34 ♖c8 ♔g7 35 ♖c3 ♕g4! Black should be winning.

32...♖c8! 33 ♗e1

33 ♘e6 loses to 33...♖xc1+ 34 ♗xc1 ♕g4! 35 ♘xf8 ♖xg2+ 36 ♖xg2 ♕d1+ 37 ♔h2 ♘f3+.

33...♘h6 34 a6 bxa6 35 ♖c6 ♖g8 36 ♖xd6 f3 37 ♖xa6

There goes the black queenside. Not too

traumatic.

37...♖xg2+ 38 ♖xg2 ♕e3+ 39 ♗f2 ♖xg2+ 40 ♕xg2 fxg2 0-1

Game 7
Roeder-Hebden
Bern 1992

1 d4 ♘f6 2 c4 g6 3 ♘c3 ♗g7 4 e4 d6 5 ♗e2 0-0 6 ♘f3 e5 7 0-0 ♘c6 8 d5 ♘e7 9 ♘e1 ♘d7 10 ♘d3 f5 11 ♗d2 ♘f6 12 f3 f4 13 c5 g5 14 cxd6 cxd6 15 ♖c1 ♘g6 16 ♘b5 ♖f7 17 ♕c2 ♘e8 18 a4 h5 19 ♘f2 ♗d7!?

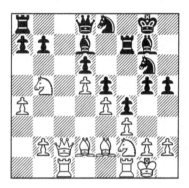

The previous game saw all out attack by the two sides on their respective wings. The text is a slightly more cautious move. Black still has every intention of crashing through on the kingside but this time he is also willing to take defensive measures on the queenside if he believes he has time for them.

20 ♕b3 ♗f8

Considering that in the main game Hebden adopted a plan with ...♕d8-b8, ...♗e7 and ...♗d8 it is certainly worth considering 20...♗f6!?, which has the intention of transferring the bishop from g7 to d8 in two moves instead of three. Still, it's not totally clear to me that this is an improvement as although 20...♗f6 gains a tempo it is less flexible. A typical continuation now would be 21 ♖c2 ♕b8 22 ♖fc1 ♗d8 and I refer you to the notes in the main game for a discussion of such positions.

In Neverov-Vokac, Bled Olympiad. 2002 White tried instead 21 ♗b4 but Black was able to solve the position tactically: 21...♗e7 22 ♖c2 a6 23 ♘a3 g4! 24. fxg4 hxg4 25 ♗xg4 ♗xg4 26 ♘xg4 ♕b6+ 27 ♔h1 a5 28 ♘h6+ ♔g7 29 ♘xf7 ♕xb4 30 ♕h3 ♔xf7 31 ♕f5+ ♔g7 32 g3 fxg3 (32...♘f6 is a safer continuation and after 33 gxf4 ♕xe4+ 34 ♕xe4 ♘xe4 35 fxe5 dxe5 36 ♖c7 ♖d8 a draw is the most likely outcome) 33 ♕f7+? (better was 33 ♖g1! as the text leaves e4 unprotected) 33...♔h6 34 ♘c4 ♘g7! (now White can't avoid the disastrous simplification that arises when Black plays ♖f8) 35 ♕f3 ♖f8 36 ♕d3 ♖xf1+ 37 ♕xf1 ♘h5 with a decisive advantage for Black who went on to win the game.

21 h3

White usually needs to play this move at some point but it wasn't forced just yet. He could have started by doubling his rooks on the c-file. Normally he does this with 21 ♖c3 or 21 ♖c2, but in the latest top class game to reach this position, Kozul-Radjabov, Sarajevo 2003, White opted for the strange 21 ♖c4!?. Play continued 21...a6 (21...♖g7!?) 22 ♘a3 (normally the knight quickly re-emerges on c4 after it is kicked back to a3, but with his rook there Kozul must have other ideas) 22...♖g7 (of course Black is getting ready to play ...g4; all he needs to do is to hold his queenside together long enough for his own attack to get out of the starting blocks – then White can have it all) 23 a5 ♘f6 24 ♕b6 ♕e8 25 h3 (25 ♕xb7 ♗b5 26 ♕b6 is not just the exchange but a queen after 26...♖b8) 25...g4 26 fxg4 hxg4 27 hxg4 ♘h4 28 ♖c7 ♕g6 29 ♗e1 (with the idea of playing ♗xh4 in certain variations; also, it would be very risky for White to start taking queenside pawns here, no matter what your computer programme may say) 29...♖h7! (Radjabov switches the attack to the h-file now that the move ♗e1 has hemmed in the white king) 30 ♕b3! (the queen rushes back to defend along the third rank as Black wins after 30 ♕xb7 ♕h6! 31 ♘h3 ♘xg2) 30...♘xe4 (Radjabov settles for the important central pawn) 31 ♕d3 ♘g3! 32 ♖xb7 and now instead of 32...e4?, Black should have played 32...♗f5! when 33 ♖xh7 (33 gxf5 ♘xe2+ 34 ♕xe2 ♕xg2 mate) 33...♗xd3 (33...♔xh7) 34 ♗xd3 ♔xh7 35 ♗xg6+ ♘xg6! gives him a much better endgame.

21...♕b8!?

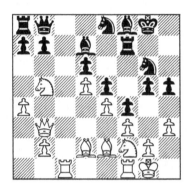

White's idea is to double rooks on the c-file and play ♘c7. Black can stop this by chasing the knight with a6 but he is reluctant to do this too soon because the manoeuvre ♘a3-c4-b6 may hurt. He can also remove the knight with ♗xb5 but as you already know Black hates parting with this bishop. There is a much more imaginative solution to the problem of White invading on c7. Black has played ♕b8 to enable the manoeuvre ♗e7-d8. After this White can forget about entering the black position via c7. In fact it becomes quite difficult for White to make any sort of progress at all on the queenside. The black bishop is extremely well placed on d8. On the kingside it had no active play at all but now it is just a short distance away from the diagonal of its dreams (g1-a7). Once Black takes control of this diagonal the white king will start to feel very uncomfortable. White normally does everything in his power to prevent this happening.

A word about the black queen. It may look horribly passive on b8 but it too has visions of activity on the g1-a7 diagonal. The sequence ...a7-a6 followed by ♕a7 is not unusual in this position. The queen is not as effective as the bishop on this diagonal as White may be able to arrange ♗e1 and ♗f2 to kick it off. Still, that takes time. Have a look at Game 2 (Piket-Kasparov) to see how dangerous this idea can be.

22 a5

White understands Black's plan and starts by taking control of the b6-square. It is less good for him to double rooks at once. For example, after 22 ♖c2 ♗e7 23 ♖fc1 ♗d8 24 a5 (to stop ♗b6) 24...a6 25 ♘a3 b5! (Olcayoz-Grivas, Mangalia 1992) White, if he wants to see move 30, dare not capture en passant. But if he can't do this that means his queenside play has come to an abrupt halt. Black is better as he will eventually force through ...g4. Grivas prepared this advance in the same way as Hebden, i.e. ...♖g7 followed by ...♘h8-f7-h6.

22...♖g7

As there is no immediate need to cover c7 Black takes a time out to improve his rook. Remember that ...g5-g4 is still his long-term ambition. In Krush-Fedorowicz, Somerset 1998 Black did play 22...♗e7 and after 23 ♘a3 ♗d8?! 24 ♗b5 White had achieved the positionally desirable exchange of light-squared bishops. The basic rule here is that when White plays ♘a3 Black replies with a6 to prevent this exchange. White will then try to play ♘c4-b6 and Black should be able to arrange his pieces so that he can meet this with ♗xb6 and White has to take back with the pawn. For example after 23 ♘a3 a6 24 ♘c4 Black plays 24...♗b5! to pin the knight on c4 and next move he plays 25...♗d8.

23 ♖c3?!

Perhaps not the best square for the rook as in interferes with the defence of the pawn on a5. Instead 23 ♖c2 ♗e7 24 ♖fc1 ♗d8 25 ♘a3 (Georgiev-Sahovic, Lvov 1984) 25...a6! 26 ♘c4 ♗b5 is fine for Black.

23...♗e7 24 ♖a1 ♗d8 25 ♖cc1

Black was threatening 25...a6 26 ♘a3 ♗xa5.

25...♘h8!?

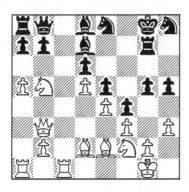

If one was playing without a plan then it

would be easy to play something like 25...♘h4. The problem is, then what? It is much better to reposition the knight to h6 so that Black can force through ...g4. It is also interesting that Hebden refrained from 25...a6 26 ♘a3 b5. Perhaps because in this position White can play 27 ♘c2 followed by ♘b4-c6, whereas in the similar position in the notes to move 22 he was nowhere near ready to play this manoeuvre.

26 ♘a3 a6!

Preventing ♗b5 – we already know this rule.

27 ♘c4 ♗b5 28 ♔f1 ♘f7 29 ♗e1 ♘h6 30 ♘b6 ♗xb6 31 axb6 ♗xe2+ 32 ♔xe2 ♕d8 33 ♘d3 g4

It wasn't such a bad idea for White to evacuate his king to the centre but Black's kingside play still gives him the initiative.

34 hxg4 hxg4 35 ♗f2 ♘f7

The knight is redundant on h6 once g4 has been achieved but as we shall see there is plenty of work for it elsewhere.

36 ♖h1 g3 37 ♗e1 ♕g5 38 ♗a5

White chooses this square for his bishop as he's planning an exchange sacrifice with ♖c7.

38...♕g6 39 ♖ac1 ♘g5

Black is now threatening to sacrifice a piece on e4.

40 ♖c4 ♖h7 41 ♖xh7 ♕xh7 42 ♖c7

White was probably looking forward to a dangerous passed pawn on the 7th rank after Black took the rook but Hebden had prepared a beautiful riposte...

42...♘xf3!!

Now 43 ♔xf3 ♕h5 mate and 43 gxf3 ♕h2+ followed by ...g2 are out of the question so White takes the queen.

43 ℤxh7 ♘d4+ 44 ♔e1 ♘xb3

Black wins a piece as he attacks both the rook and bishop. The remaining moves were:
45 ℤxb7 ♘xa5 46 ℤa7 ℤb8 47 b4 ♘c4 48 b7 ♔f7 49 ♘c5 dxc5 50 bxc5 ♔e7 51 c6 ♘c7 52 ♔e2 ♔d6 0-1

Game 8
Andruet-Spassov
Sofia 1990

---

1 d4 ♘f6 2 c4 g6 3 ♘c3 ♗g7 4 e4 d6 5 ♘f3 0-0 6 ♗e2 e5 7 0-0 ♘c6 8 d5 ♘e7 9 ♘e1 ♘d7 10 ♘d3 f5 11 ♗d2 ♘f6 12 f3 f4 13 c5 g5 14 cxd6 cxd6 15 ♘f2

In the previous games we saw White playing 15 ℤac1 followed by ♘b5. This time he is not in such a rush to play ♘b5 but prefers a slower set-up with ♕c2 and ℤfc1. He will then bring the queen's rook into play by a4 and ℤa3. If possible he will then continue with ♘b5 and ℤac3. If Black doesn't take action before this happens he will find himself in serious trouble.

15...h5 16 h3 ♘g6 17 ♕c2 ℤf7

The main drawback to White's system is that the knight on f6 doesn't have to retreat to e8. This means that Black can play a quick ...g4 and he should do so even if it means sacrificing a pawn. The text is a useful move as the rook is more active on the second rank but it is also possible to play ...g4 at once. For example 17...g4 18 fxg4 hxg4 19 hxg4 ♘e8 (Black plans to activate his bishop with ...♗f6-h4) and now:

a) 20 ℤfc1 ♗f6 21 ♗e1 ♗h4 22 ♘b5 ♗d7 23 ♕b3 ♗g3 24 ♘h1 ♕b6+ 25 ♗f2 ♗xf2+ 26 ♘xf2 f3 27 gxf3 ♘f4 28 ♗f1 ♘xe2 0-1 Resende-Van Riemsdijk, San Jose 1995.

b) 20 a4 ♗f6 21 ♘h3 ♗h4 22 ♘d1 ℤf7 23 ♘df2 ℤh7 (23...♗g7!?) 24 ℤa3 ♘f6 25 a5 ♗d7 26 ♕d1, Moehring-Uhlmann, Halle 1981, and now 26...♘e8 is supposed to be unclear.

18 ℤfc1

Sometimes White plays 18 a4 and Black usually replies 18...♗f8. However, I don't see why he can't play 18...g4 19 hxg4 hxg4 20 fxg4 ♘e8 with similar play to the main line.

18...g4

Formerly Black used to play 18...a6 to prevent ♘b5. After 19 a4 most games continued:

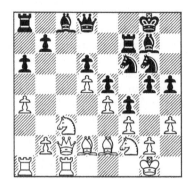

a) 19...♗f8 20 a5. Now White is threatening ♘a4-b6 so Black must react before it's too late. 20...b5 21 axb6 ♕xb6 looks tempting to get the queen on the dangerous diagonal but after 22 ♘a4 ♕a7 23 ♗a5! it is White who takes control. Instead Black took to playing 20...g4 21 fxg4 hxg4 22 hxg4 and only then 22...b5. However, a large number of games established that 23 axb6 ♕xb6 24 ♘a4 ♕a7 25 ♗a5! ℤb8 26 g5! was in White's favour. This is why Black is sacrificing a pawn with ...g4 immediately – to steer clear of this position.

b) But there is an intriguing new development in this line. In Kekelidze-Baklan, Batumi 2002 Black preferred 19...♘h4 20 a5 g4 and after 21 fxg4 (maybe 21 hxg4 hxg4 22 fxg4 is better) he didn't take back on g4 as players had done unsuccessfully in the past, but sacrificed another pawn with 21...f3!. Now:

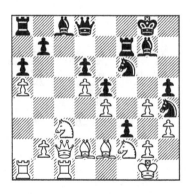

b1) According to Kostakiev (annotating for *ChessBase*) the critical position is reached after 22 gxf3 ♘h7! 23 ♕d3 ♘g5 24 ♗xg5 ♕xg5 25

♖ab1 ♗d7 26 ♔h1 which he assesses as slightly better for White. The one thing that is certain is that this is not the critical position! How could it be with that move 25 ♖ab1 included. It is, perhaps, the most pointless move of all time. But even after White improves on this (the immediate 25 ♔h1 or 25 ♘a4 are given by Andrew Martin) his position remains highly suspicious. His kingside and dark squares are riddled with weaknesses and any King's Indian player worth his salt should be happy to play such a position in return for a couple of weak backward pawns.

b2) 22 ♗g5!? is considered unclear by Baklan.

b3) The game continued 22 ♗xf3 ♘xg4!? (a fascinating piece sacrifice but 22...♘xf3+ 23 gxf3 ♘h7 also deserves consideration) 23 hxg4 (maybe White should decline the offer, e.g. after 23 ♗xg4!? hxg4 24 ♘xg4 ♗xg4 25 hxg4 ♕c8 26 ♗g5 ♕xg4 27 ♖xh4 ♕xh4 Black has good compensation for the pawn but perhaps no more) 23...♘xf3+ 24 gxf3 ♕h4 when it was not easy to see how White can defend his king-side

b31) The game finished: 25 ♘cd1 ♕g3+ 26 ♔f1 ♗d7 27 ♗e3 ♖xf3 28 ♖a3 ♗b5+ 29 ♔e1 hxg4 (Black has fantastic compensation for his piece: in fact the white position is already beyond redemption) 30 ♖b3 ♖af8 (30...♕g1+ 31 ♔d2 ♗h6! wins in more spectacular fashion) 31 ♖xb5 ♖xe3+ 32 ♘xe3 ♕xe3+ 33 ♔f1 g3 34 ♖b3 ♖xf2+ 35 ♔g1 ♕h6 36 ♕c8+ ♔h7 0-1

b32) 25 ♘h1 ♖xf3 26 ♗e1 ♖f1+!! is a crushing blow.

b33) 25 ♔g2 ♗xg4! (25...hxg4 26 ♖h1) 26 ♘xg4 hxg4 is dangerous according to Martin and winning for Black according to Fritz, who tends to be quite trustworthy in such positions. Baklan examines the possibility of White trying 26 f4 here and gives 26...exf4 27 ♖h1 (maybe 27 ♕d3) ♕g3+ 28 ♔f1 ♗d4 29 ♗c1 ♖g7! 30 ♔e1 ♕g2 31 ♖f1 ♕h3 32 ♕d3 ♖g3 33 ♕d4 ♕xf1+ 34 ♔d2 ♖g2 35 ♘cd1 ♖c8! and Black wins.

So, certainly food for thought. I didn't want to recommend this as the main line as experience is so limited but keep an eye out for future developments (or maybe create them yourself).

19 fxg4 hxg4 20 hxg4 ♘e8!

Black's plan is the same as in the notes to move 17, i.e. to play ...♘f6-h4 and hopefully develop a strong attack against the white king.

21 a4

The logical way to develop the queen's rook. On the third rank it will be well placed for both defence and attack.

21...♗f6 22 ♖a3 ♗h4 23 ♘cd1

White meets the immediate threat of 23...♗xf2+ and plans to use both his knights to defend his king.

23...♗g3

Freeing the h4-square for the queen.

24 ♖c3

White's play in this game was too ambitious. Another game Sosonko-Hellers, Wijk aan Zee 1986 also reached this position and there White preferred the more prudent 24 ♘h3 ♕h4 25 ♘df2 ♘f6 26 ♕d1 ♗d7 27 a5 ♖af8 and after 28 ♗e1 the players agreed to a draw. Black obviously has good play for the pawn. A well-timed ...f3 is the way to continue the attack.

Perhaps even immediately but it's difficult to work out the consequences. It is worth pointing out what could have happened if White had played 28 ♗b4. Black just replies 28...♖h7 as 29 ♗xd6? runs into 29...♗xf2+ 30 ♘xf2 ♕h2+! 31 ♔f1 ♕h1+ 32 ♘xh1 ♖xh1+ 33 ♔f2 ♘xe4+ 34 ♔f3 ♖xd1 35 ♖xd1 ♘xd6 with a decisive advantage for Black.

24...♗d7 25 ♗b5?

This move is asking for trouble. White is planning to invade on c8 but it is too slow. The bishop was needed for defence, especially against the advance ...f4-f3 which is now going to hurt in many variations.

25...♗xb5 26 axb5 ♕h4 27 ♘h3

27 ♖c8 ♕h2+ 28 ♔f1 f3! is winning.

27...♘f6 28 ♖c8+?

Perhaps 28 g5 was a better try. A possible variation is 28...♘g4 29 ♖c8+ ♖xc8 30 ♕xc8 ♘f8! and ...f3 is again on the cards.

28...♖xc8 29 ♕xc8+ ♔g7 30 ♘df2 ♗xf2+! 31 ♘xf2 f3!

The threats include 32...♕g3 and 32...♘xe4 33 ♘xe4 f2+. White is lost.

32 ♕f5 ♘xe4! 33 ♕xf7+

33 ♕xe4 loses to 33...♕g3!.

33...♔xf7 34 ♘xe4 ♕xg4 35 ♖c7+ ♘e7 36 ♘g5+ ♔g6 37 ♘xf3 ♘xd5 38 ♖xb7 e4 39 ♖b8 ♔g7 40 ♖b7+ ♔f6 0-1

Game 9
Fioramonti-Cvitan
Geneva 1995

---

1 d4 ♘f6 2 c4 g6 3 ♘c3 ♗g7 4 e4 d6 5 ♘f3 0-0 6 ♗e2 e5 7 0-0 ♘c6 8 d5 ♘e7 9 ♘e1 ♘d7 10 ♘d3 f5 11 ♗d2 ♘f6 12 f3 f4 13 g4

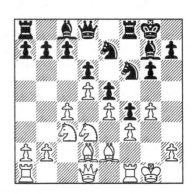

We have seen in the preceding games how all Black's kingside play revolved around playing the move ...g4. If he didn't play this move there was no attack. So White's logic is easy to understand. All he needs to do is stop Black from playing g4 and let the queenside attack decide the game in his favour. However, whilst it is true that the move g4 slows down Black's attack one can't advance a pawn two squares in front of one's own king without creating weaknesses and new targets. The most important factors in the position for Black now are the h-file, the possibility to sacrifice on g4 and the weakness of White's h4-square.

1) The h-file: Black will start by playing g5 and ...h5 when White will have to play h3. Black is now in a position to open the h-file, by playing ...hxg4, at a moment of his choosing. It is usually disastrous for White to touch any of his pawns there.

2) Sacrifices on g4: Black should always keep maximum pressure on the g4-square. Sacrifices here take two forms. In the first he just keeps taking on g4 and ends up with two pawns and a strong attack for a piece. In the second scenario Black sacrifices on g4 and when White plays fxg4 he plays an annoying ...f4-f3.

3) The h4-square: the h4-square is a serious weakness in the white camp especially with the white king on g2 and a black knight on g6 (as is almost always the case). White has to keep this square covered with his bishop but again, at a moment of his choosing, Black may be able to

force White to give up his bishop for a knight. The sequence ...♘h4+, ♗xh4, ...gxh4 is not always in Black's favour as the h-file becomes blocked but there are occasions when it is strong. For example, Black has a bishop on d8 that is ready to take over the g1-a7 diagonal once White's bishop (usually on f2) has disappeared.

You would be right to conclude from the above points that White has to be careful. The problem for him in this variation is that many of his pieces are tied down. He usually needs a rook on the h-file to prevent a Black invasion there, a bishop on f2 to cover h4 and a bishop on e2 and a queen on d1 to defend g4. He must take great care in how he conducts his queenside attack as opening the queenside prematurely may allow Black to lure some of these pieces away from their defensive duty.

13...g5

There are a couple of alternatives of dubious value that deserve a quick look.

a) 13...fxg3 doesn't look so bad and the position after 14 hxg3 is probably just slightly better for White but in practice Black has scored terribly here – just 25% according to my database. A typical continuation is 14...c6 (14...♘h5 15 ♔g2) 15 ♗e3 h6 16 ♔g2 g5 17 ♘f2 cxd5 18 cxd5 ♘g6 19 ♖h1 ♖f7 20 a4 with good play for White, Lutz-Fedorowicz, Porz 1988. It's very difficult for Black to do anything.

b) 13...h5 14 g5! ♘h7 15 h4 ♘xg5 (this is forced as otherwise the kingside has been totally sealed up and Black will die a slow death on the queenside) 16 hxg5 ♘f5 (taking the knight leads to perpetual check; 16...♘xd5 is less good as although Black gets more pawns the white pieces become more active) 17 ♖f2 ♕xg5+ 18 ♖g2 ♘g3 19 ♘f2 ♕f6 20 ♗f1 and White's position is to be preferred but Black is not without his chances. This is the sort of line which might not be quite sound at grandmaster level but worth a punt at club level.

14 ♗e1

Although this move is not essential just yet, White can't get by without covering the h4-square so he usually plays ♗e1 straight away. Instead, Gelfand-Kasparov, Reggio Emilia 1991 went 14 b4 h5 15 h3 ♔f7!? (in the main game Black plays differently but this plan of getting a

rook to the h-file as quickly as possible is an interesting alternative) 16 ♗e1 ♖h8 17 ♔g2 ♘g6 (another idea is ♖h6 and ♕h8) 18 c5?! (18 ♗f2 was better) 18...hxg4 19 hxg4 ♘h5! 20 ♖h1 (20 gxh5 ♖xh5! is simply too dangerous for White) 20 ♖h1 ♘g3! 21 ♗xg3 fxg3 and the weak dark squares around the white king give Black good compensation for the pawn that is about to drop off.

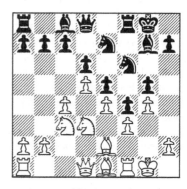

14...h5 15 h3 ♘g6 16 ♗f2

In the main game White, rather greedily, went after the black a-pawn. He never even managed to get in the important advance c4-c5 which most White players would play either now or on the next move. After 16 c5 ♖f7 we have a couple of interesting examples:

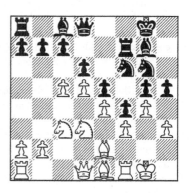

a) 17 b4 ♗f8 18 ♔g2 ♗e7 19 ♗f2 ♕f8! (see main game for explanation) 20 ♘b5 ♗d8 21 a4 (21 cxd6 cxd6 22 ♘xa7 is no good as after 22...♖xa7 23 ♗xa7 b6 the bishop is trapped and White is going to die on the dark squares; in general White is reluctant to exchange on d6 as it might let Black activate his dark-squared bishop) 21...♗d7 22 ♘c3 ♗e7 23 ♘b5 ♗d8 24 ♘c3 a6 (Black decides to play for a win and is immediately rewarded by an error from White) 25 b5? axb5 26 ♖b1 (after 26 axb5 ♖xa1 27 ♕xa1 the white queen has been dragged away from the defence of f3 so Black can play 27...hxg4 28 hxg4 ♘xg4! 29 fxg4 f3+) 26...bxa4 27 ♖xb7 a3! 28 c6 a2!? 29 ♖a7 (after 29 ♘xa2 hxg4 30 hxg4 Black has a choice of tactical continuations such as 30...♗xg4 31 fxg4 ♖xa2 or 30...♖xa2 31 cxd7 ♘xe4! when 32 fxe4 fails to 32...♖xe2! 33 ♕xe2? f3+) 29...♘h4+! 30 ♔g1 ♖xa7 31 ♗xa7 hxg4 32 hxg4 (after 32 cxd7 both 32...gxh3 and 32...g3!? ensure Black of a strong attack but he could have avoided these complications by exchanging earlier on g4) 32...♗xg4! 33 fxg4 f3 34 ♖xf3 (34 ♗xf3 ♘xe4!) 34...♘xf3+ 35 ♗xf3 ♘xe4? (Black takes the wrong pawn. 35...♘xd5! would have won easily) 36 ♗xe4 ♖f1+ 37 ♕xf1 ♕xf1+ 38 ♔xf1 a1♕+ 39 ♔g2 ♕xc3 (39...♕xa7 comes to the same; Black's combination has resulted in an endgame with an overwhelming material advantage – queen and pawn against two pieces – but unfortunately for him his king and bishop are eternal prisoners to the pawn chain and it is impossible to make any progress) 40 ♗e3 ♕c2+ 41 ♘f2 ♕e2 42 ♗a7 ♔f8 43 ♔g3 ♕a6 44 ♗e3 ♕e2 ½-½, Gyimesi-Cvitan, Chiasso 1994.

b) If White is worried about Black ever re-capturing with the bishop on d6 then he may exchange straight away. Bareev-Belotti, Aosta 1989 continued 17 cxd6 cxd6 18 a4 ♗f8 19 ♔g2 ♗e7 20 ♖c1 ♕f8! (Black adopts the Cvitan set-up) 21 a5 ♗d8 22 b4 ♗d7 23 ♗f2 ♘h4+!? 24 ♗xh4 gxh4 25 ♘f2 ♕e8 26 ♗d3 ♖g7 27 ♔h2 and now Black should have played 27...a6 and followed up with ...b6 in order to try and take control of the g1-a7 diagonal. Bareev considers the position to be better for Black.

16...♖f7 17 a4 ♗f8 18 ♔g2

White needs to be in a position to meet ...♖h7 with ♖h1.

18...♗e7 19 a5 ♕f8!

I like these multi-purpose moves. The two most important points are that it frees d8 for the black bishop and creates x-ray pressure down the f-file. For example, if White now carelessly moved his queen Black would be able

to sacrifice a piece on g4 and regain it with ...f3+. Additional points to ...♕f8 are that it brings the queen nearer to the h-file (...♕h6) and it also controls the c5-square. That may not be so important here but it was useful in the Gyimesi-Cvitan game given in the notes above.

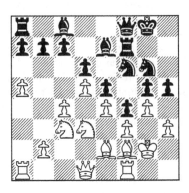

20 ♘b5 ♗d8 21 ♘xa7?

A mistake. 21 c5 is better with an unclear game after 21...a6. See the 16th move notes for examples of similar positions.

21...hxg4 22 hxg4 ♗xg4! 23 a6

23 fxg4 ♘xe4 is similar but the text at least obtains the c6-square for the knight.

23...bxa6 24 fxg4 ♘xe4 25 ♘c6

The point of the combination is that the white bishop must stay defending h4, e.g. 25 ♗g1 loses to 25...f3+ 26 ♗xf3 ♘h4+.

25...♘xf2 26 ♘xf2

White quietly returns the piece. 26 ♖xf2 e4 may be even worse

26...f3+ 27 ♔g1 fxe2 28 ♕xe2 ♘f4 29 ♕e4 ♕h6

It is surprising that White is able to put up any resistance at all but Black needs his queen-side pieces to play their part in the attack as well.

30 ♖a3! ♖h7 31 ♖e1 ♕h2+ 32 ♔f1 ♗f6 33 ♖ee3 ♖f8 34 ♖g3 ♗h8 35 ♖af3 ♖hf7 36 b3 ♗g7 37 ♘b4

Black can improve his position no further. When this occurs it's time to look for the knockout blow.

37...♘g6! 38 ♖h3?!

It looks tempting to trap the queen but Black obviously had something in mind when he allowed this. 38 ♘bd3 would, perhaps, offer more resistance although Black should win in the end. Starting with 38...♘h4 looks like a good idea.

38...♕xh3+! 39 ♖xh3

39 ♘xh3 ♖xf3+ 40 ♔e2 (40 ♔g2 ♘h4+ wins) 40...♖xh3 is hopeless for White (I know he can take the knight but it's still hopeless after 41 ♕xg6 ♖h6!).

39...♖xf2+ 40 ♔e1?!

40 ♔g1 is a slightly better chance. The simplest for Black is to play an ending after 40...♘h4 41 ♘d3 (41 ♖xh4 gxh4 offers no hope) 41...♖g2+ 42 ♕xg2 ♘xg2 43 ♔xg2 which he should win comfortably enough after the reply 43...e4.

40...♖f1+ 41 ♔d2 ♖8f2+ 42 ♔c3 ♖e1!

A wonderful move. Black finally breaks the blockade and the King's Indian bishop has the final say.

43 ♖e3

Or 43 ♕xe1 e4 mate.

43...♖xe3+ 44 ♕xe3 e4+ 0-1

Game 10
Pinter-Nunn
Thessaloniki Olympiad 1988

1 d4 ♘f6 2 c4 g6 3 ♘c3 ♗g7 4 e4 d6 5 ♗e2 0-0 6 ♘f3 e5 7 0-0 ♘c6 8 d5 ♘e7 9 ♘e1 ♘d7 10 f3 f5 11 g4

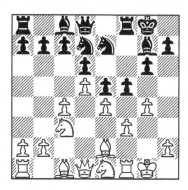

So another system where White tries to block up the kingside. I sometimes wonder why these guys are playing the Classical. If you don't like your king coming under fire then play the Fianchetto Variation. This particular version of White playing g2-g4 was very popular in the 1980's but White eventually concluded that there was too much tension in the position for g2-g4 to be successful. They then started to wait for Black to play ...f4 before playing g4 and that is what we have just seen.

11...♔h8

This flexible move was chiefly responsible for the demise (partial) of 11 g4. The main idea is to improve the position of the knight on e7 by playing ...♘g8. This introduces the possibility of playing ...♗h6 or ...♘gf6. The knight on d7 may be able to occupy the other good square on c5. Before 11...♔h8 became fashionable Black would often play 11...♘f6 but he struggled for equality.

Before moving on, note that 11...f4? would be a serious mistake as after 12 h4! Black won't be able to create any play at all on the kingside. If he ever plays ...g5 then White replies h5 and if he plays ...h5 White replies g5. The rule in this line is for Black to only consider playing f5-f4 when White has a bishop on e3.

12 ♘g2

This is one of three moves that White usually chooses from (others also occur from time to time). The idea behind 12 ♘g2 is to play h4 so that if Black tries to exchange his 'bad' bishop by playing ...♘g8 and ...♗h6 he just gets kicked back by g5. Once White has played h4 then Black will no longer be able to contemplate playing ...f5-f4 as then there will be no hope of active play on the kingside. As we shall see Black has a better plan whereby he creates pressure against the white centre. The alternatives:

a) 12 ♗e3 ♘g8 13 ♕d2 f4 (I won a couple of games with 13...a6 but ...f4 is probably more accurate) 14 ♗f2 h5! 15 h3 (15 h4? g5!) 15...♖f7 16 ♔g2 ♗f6 17 ♘d3 ♖h7 18 ♖h1 ♗h4! with a good game for Black, Jacimovic-Vukic, Kastel Stari 1988. Black's position is better than in Game 3 as he has managed to avoid playing ...g5. This means it is easy for him to exchange or activate his dark-squared bishop and also he will be able to use the g5-square for his pieces. For example a queen on g5 creates a lot of additional pressure against g4.

b) 12 ♘d3 ♘g8 13 ♔h1 a5 (13...a6 is a more flexible alternative) 14 ♖g1 ♖f7 15 g5?! (a strange choice as this pawn gets cut off and becomes weak; 15 ♗d2 was better when White could justify his previous two moves by the fact that 15...♗h6 is now met by 16 g5) 15...f4 16 ♗f1 ♗f8 17 b3 ♗e7 18 ♘b5 b6 19 ♗h3 ♘c5 20 ♗xc8 ♘xd3 21 ♕xd3 ♕xc8 22 ♕f1 h6! 23 gxh6 g5 with good play for Black, Vaganian-Uhlmann, Niksic 1978.

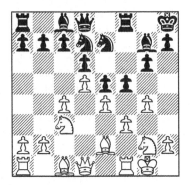

12...a5

Black secures c5 for his knight, a particularly good square now that White can no longer play ♘d3. With f6 earmarked for the other knight Black hopes to create strong pressure against e4.

13 h4 ♘c5 14 ♗e3 ♘g8

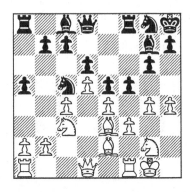

15 ♖b1

As 15 g5 f4 16 ♗f2 h6 leads to the opening of the kingside in Black's favour White turns his attention to the queenside. His long-term plan will be to try and expel the knight from c5 with a3 and b4. This position has been reached on a number of occasions and White nearly always played a different move. Here are a couple of examples:

a) 15 ♖c1 ♕e7 (Black could also play 15...♗d7 so as to meet 16 a3 with 16...a4) 16 a3 fxg4 17 fxg4 ♖xf1+ 18 ♔xf1 ♘f6 19 ♗f3 ♗d7 20 b4 axb4 21 axb4 ♘a4 with a comfortable game for Black, Markowski-Dolmatov, Polanica Zdroj 1993.

b) 15 ♕d2 b6 (Black must have spent some time considering 15...fxg4 16 fxg4 ♘f6 as 17 ♗xc5 is the only way for White to avoid losing a pawn) 16 exf5 gxf5 17 g5 f4 18 ♗xc5 bxc5 19 ♘e4 ♘e7 20 ♗d3 ♘f5 was the dubious plan selected by White in Chernuschevich-Rowson, Bratislava 1993. White has the e4-square and a stack of weaknesses in his camp which the black knight on f5 is ideally placed to exploit.

15...♗d7

Black is in no rush to play 15...♘f6 because of the variation 16 exf5 gxf5 17 g5! ♘h5 18 f4 when his bishop on c8 is no longer an active piece.

16 b3 b6 17 a3?! a4! 18 b4 ♘b3

White's inaccurate 17th move has enabled Black to take over the initiative on the queenside. White's next move is played to prevent Black from playing ...♘d4.

19 ♘b5 ♘f6 20 exf5 gxf5 21 ♘c3

White probably didn't enjoy retreating after having just played ♘b5 but he had to stop Black from playing ...e4 followed by ...f4. His intention when he took on f5 must have been 21 g5 but he now saw that 21...f4! 22 gxf6 ♗xf6 23 ♗f2 ♖g8 is a powerful piece sacrifice that is likely to end with his king getting checkmated.

21...e4! 22 g5 ♘h5 23 fxe4

Black is attacking the knight on c3 but White responds by attacking the black knight on h5.

23...f4!? 24 ♗d2 ♘xd2 25 ♕xd2 ♕e8 26 ♗f3 ♘g3 27 ♖fe1 ♗e5

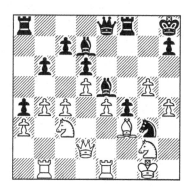

Black has sacrificed a pawn for total dark square control. His blockade of e5 reduces White to passivity. This ...e4, fxe4, ...f4 motif is an important theme in the King's Indian and other examples can also be found in the book.

28 ♘e2 ♘xe4!? 29 ♗xe4 f3 30 ♘ef4 fxg2 31 ♘xg2 ♕h5

In chess in order to keep the advantage one may have to transform it into another sort of advantage. That is what has happened here. Now it's Black's two powerful bishops on an open board that give him his compensation for the pawn. The chance to attack the white king is the bonus that makes his position preferable.

32 ♕d3 ♗g4 33 ♖e3 ♕f7 34 ♕d2 ♕g7 35 ♖d3 ♖f7 36 ♖e1 ♖af8 37 ♘e3 ♖f4 38 ♘g2 ♖4f7 39 ♘e3 ♗h5 40 ♖f1?

White should have played 40 ♘g2 again with

some chances to hold this inferior position. Now he loses by force.

40...♖xf1+ 41 ♘xf1 ♖f4 42 ♕e1 ♗d4+ 43 ♔g2 ♕e5 44 ♘g3 ♗g4!

Black could win the queen with 44...♗f2 but he doesn't want to allow White to get a rook and a piece for it.

45 b5 ♗f2 46 ♕xf2 ♗h3+! 0-1

White resigned because of 47 ♔g1 ♕a1+!.

Summary

1) Black's main attacking idea is to play ...g5-g4. He usually prepares this advance slowly, with the aid of manoeuvres such as ...♖f7-g7, but once he feels things getting out of hand on the queenside then he should not delay and just play ...g5-g4. It can be used as a kind of panic button, although hopefully we won't find ourselves in that situation.

2) Black's main defensive task is to prevent White infiltrating on c7, at least until his own attack is strong enough for this to be a mere irritation. He usually does this with the help of a knight on e8, a rook on f7 and sometimes a bishop on d8.

3) In Games 9 and 10 White tries to block up the kingside by playing g2-g4. This certainly stops Black from breaking through with the traditional ...g5-g4 but Black still has some dangerous attacking ideas based on sacrifices on g4 and an invasion on the h-file.

4) The King's Indian bishop can do worse than take up residence on d8 in these lines. From there it performs important defensive duties as well as just being one small step away from the diagonal of its dreams (a7-g1).

CHAPTER THREE

The Classical Variation:
The Bayonet Attack 9 b4

1 d4 ♘f6 2 c4 g6 3 ♘c3 ♗g7 4 e4 d6 5 ♘f3 0-0 6 ♗e2 e5 7 0-0 ♘c6 8 d5 ♘e7 9 b4

Over the last eight or nine years the Bayonet Attack has been one of White's main success stories in the King's Indian. Prior to this 9 b4 was generally thought to be a poor relation to the main alternatives in this position, 9 ♘e1 and 9 ♘d2. It was rarely seen in top class chess. Strange, you may think, as 9 b4 is the obvious way for White to force through c4-c5 as quickly as possible. In this position the pawn structure dictates that White will attack on the queenside. The reason why the move was not trusted was that it allowed Black to play the active 9...♘h5, whilst after moves like 9 ♘e1 or 9 ♘d2 the black knight, in order to get out of the way of the f-pawn, would have to retreat. Attitudes began to change after White discovered the move 10 ♖e1 (in reply to 9...♘h5). The simple idea is to meet 10...♘f4 with 11 ♗f1. The bishop on f1 is very well place defensively and it turns out, that despite its active appearance, that the knight on f4 is quite poorly placed. There is nothing for it to attack and it can even get in the way of Black's kingside play. For example, the traditional pawn storm with ...f5-f4 is not possible with the knight on f4 and Black will also have to be constantly on the lookout for White playing ♗xf4 at a favourable moment. It took quite a while, and cost an awful lot of points, before Black players appreciated this. Meanwhile, everyone was playing 9

b4. The old main lines, 9 ♘e1 and 9 ♘d2, just disappeared. The results were overwhelmingly in White's favour. Even Gary Kasparov got his fingers burned and the Bayonet Attack was the main reason for his recent loss of confidence in the King's Indian (he didn't play it once in his world title match with Kramnik, who happens to be one of the main advocates of 9 b4). Many other King's Indian specialists, such as myself, settled for giving up 7...♘c6. A whole new system with 7...♘a6 was born (see Chapter 5) almost solely due to White's successes in the Bayonet Attack.

However, the tide finally appears to be turning. The main problem for Black was not the strength of the Bayonet Attack, but the fact that he was playing too ambitiously. The King's Indian attracts players who are looking for a sharp struggle. Instead of trying to prove equality they were trying to destroy the Bayonet Attack. They didn't realise that the best way to destroy the Bayonet Attack is to prove equality!. Once equality has been established White players are bound to turn their attention elsewhere. And that is exactly what has happened over the last two or three years. We now see a lot less of the Bayonet Attack and a lot more of the other variations in the King's Indian. We are also seeing less of 7...♘a6 as players such as myself are returning to the heart and soul of the King's Indian, 7...♘c6.

9...♘h5

Black has one other important move, 9...a5,

where there have also been interesting developments so if the lines I am recommending get into trouble (chess theory is not static), then I suggest you turn your attention to 9...a5

Now the material is split up as follows:

10 ♜e1 – Games 11-14.

10 g3 – Games 15 and 16.

10 c5 (and others) – Game 17.

Game 11
Malakhatko-Jenni
Istanbul Olympiad 2000

---

1 d4 ♘f6 2 c4 g6 3 ♘c3 ♟g7 4 e4 d6 5 ♘f3 0-0 6 ♟e2 e5 7 0-0 ♘c6 8 d5 ♘e7 9 b4 ♘h5 10 ♜e1 f5

There is no need for Black to put his knight offside on f4. Instead, he looks at the move ♘h5 in the same way he would look at ♘e8 or ♘d7 – as a means of clearing the way for Black's traditional King's Indian move f5. It is still better to play 9...♘h5 (as opposed to 9...♘e8, for example) as this induced White into wasting a tempo with ♜e1.

11 ♘g5

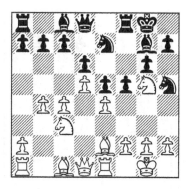

This is the critical test and the move that, originally, put many Black players off playing 10...f5. The knight is heading for e6. When it arrives there Black will have to give up his important light-squared bishop for it. In return he will have every chance to win the rather random white pawn that will appear on e6. Less critical alternatives are:

a) 11 ♘d2 ♘f6 12 c5 ♟h6 (this leads to simplification while 12...♚h8 13 f3 f4 is a more

ambitious try) 13 ♟d3 fxe4 14 ♘dxe4 ♘xe4 15 ♟xe4 ♟xc1 16 ♜xc1 ♘f5 17 ♕d2 ♘d4 18 ♘e2 ♘xe2+ 19 ♜xe2 ♟f5 20 f3 ♕f6 21 ♜c4 ½-½ Gelfand-Shirov, Wijk aan Zee 1998.

b) 11 c5 and now:

b1) 11...♘f6 12 ♟g5 ♘xe4 (12...h6 was played by Topalov) 13 ♘xe4 fxe4 14 ♘d2 h6 15 ♟xe7 ♕xe7 16 ♘xe4 ♟f5 was about level in Zontakh-Relange, Serbia 1998.

b2) 11...fxe4 12 ♘xe4 ♘f4 13 ♟xf4 ♜xf4 14 ♘fd2 dxc5 15 ♟c4 ♘xd5 16 ♘b3 c6 17 ♘bxc5 ♚h8, Kramnik-Gelfand, Novgorod 1996. White has compensation for the pawn but no more.

11...♘f6!

White was threatening 12 ♟xh5 so the knight has to move and this is the right square. There is a battle raging for control of the centre and the knight clearly exerts most influence on the centre from f6.

The variation 11...♘f4 12 ♟xf4 exf4 13 ♜c1 has been tested extensively in practice and appears to be slightly in White's favour.

12 ♟f3

White defends his centre with pieces and envisages the bishop on f3 becoming active when the long diagonal opens. He can also defend his centre with a pawn move. 12 f3 is the subject of Games 3 and 4.

12...c6

The tension in the centre increases dramatically after this move. Playing ...c7-c6 also gains space for Black on the queenside.

13 ♟e3

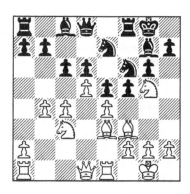

Note how White doesn't rush with ♘g5-e6. He's waiting for Black to spend a tempo and weaken his kingside with ...h7-h6 before carrying out his plan. 13 &e3 is Kramnik's move. It is an attempt to lure Black into playing 13...f4 after which White would calmly return home with 14 &c1. The move ...f5-f4 takes all the pressure off the white centre and White is quite happy to spend two moves to achieve this. Practice has demonstrated that Black should now instigate a forced series of exchanges to clarify the position.

Alternatives to 13 &e3 are considered in the next game.

13...cxd5 14 cxd5 h6 15 ♘e6 &xe6 16 dxe6 fxe4 17 ♘xe4 ♘xe4 18 &xe4 d5 19 &c2

19 &c5 dxe4 20 ♕xd8 ♖fxd8 21 &xe7 leads to the same ending we see in the 13th move notes in Game 12 (line 'b'), the only difference being that the white pawn is on b4 instead of b5.

19...b6

Black must stop White from playing &c5.

The position has settled down and is very difficult to assess. White has two active bishops, a safer king and a passed pawn on e6, which although likely to die, may seriously annoy Black in the process. In Black's favour is his strong centre and the fact that he is likely to emerge a pawn ahead. He must tread very carefully, though, as it will be easy to have a tactical accident as White's rooks and bishops pile pressure on the centre.

20 &a4?!

White comes up with the plan of parking his bishop on d7 in order to ensure the survival of his e6 pawn. Even if we leave aside the fact that

he is offering his b-pawn in the process, this is a rather dubious idea. The e6, d7 duo may look visually impressive but in reality the bishop is totally out of play on d7. This idea would only be dangerous if White could transfer his other bishop to the a3-f8 diagonal but this is very difficult to achieve. In fact the white pieces stuck in the black camp resemble prisoners of war more than anything else. It is so easy for Black to step around them. They are hardly even an inconvenience. All Black has to do is keep his knight on e7 to maintain the blockade.

In fact this line has been at the forefront of King's Indian theory and White usually chooses 20 ♕g4, a far more logical move which defends the e6 pawn and attacks g6. Initially Black was playing 20...♖f6?! but his pieces don't coordinate so well after that move. The strongest move is 20...e4! in order to take control of the dark squares (pushing the other central pawn, 20...d4, would be a positional disaster as it concedes control of the central light squares). Black is perfectly happy to exchange dark-squared bishops as White is then left with his passive bishop. Several games have continued 21 ♖ad1 ♕c7 22 &b3 ♖f5!.

This is an excellent move which defends the pawn on d5, prepares to double rooks on the f-file and cuts communications between the queen and the pawn on e6. What more could you ask? Practice has shown that White can only hope for equality in this position. A couple of examples:

a) 23 ♖d2 ♕c3 (Black should avoid 23...&c3 24 ♖c1 but Ponomariov has played 23...♖af8) 24 ♕d1 ♖d8 25 b5 ♕c8 26 &d4 &xd4 27

♖xd4 ♕c5 (note how Black can't play 27...♕xe6 because of 28 ♖dxe4!; in this line Black should always make sure, before capturing on e6, that White doesn't have such a tactic) 28 ♖e2 ♖df8 29 a4 ♖e5 30 h3 ½-½ Xu Jun-Ye Jiangchuan, Shanghai 2001.

b) 23 ♗d4 ♗xd4 24 ♖xd4 ♕c3 (24...♕e5!?) 25 ♕d1 ♖af8 26 ♖e2 ♕c7 27 g3 ♕c6 28 ♕c2 ½-½ Iskusnyh-Motylev, Russian Cup 1999. As in line 'a' Black cannot take on e6. If he had wanted to play on then 28...♖c8 suggests itself.

20...♕d6 21 ♗d7 ♕xb4 22 ♖b1 ♕h4!

Black plans a kingside attack.

23 f3 ♖f5!

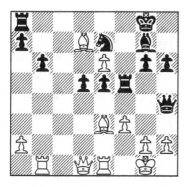

The black queen has a perfect square on f6 but if he is going to triple on the f-file he needs one rook in front of the queen. The rook on f5 also does a fine job protecting Black's e-pawn.

24 ♗f2 ♕f6 25 ♗g3 h5 26 h3 ♖f8 27 ♔h1 ♕g5 28 ♗h2 e4! 29 fxe4 ♖f2 30 ♖g1 dxe4

With White tied down to defending g2 and a ridiculous bishop on d7 the passed e-pawn is going to decide the game in Black's favour.

31 ♖b5 ♖8f5 32 ♕a4 e3 33 h4 ♕f6 34 ♕e4 e2 35 ♖b3 ♕d4 36 ♖e3 ♕xe4 37 ♖xe4 ♗c3 38 ♗d6 ♔f8 39 ♗h2 ♖d5 0-1

White lost on time but his position is hopeless. For example, 40 ♗g3 e1♕ 41 ♖gxe1 ♗xe1 42 ♖xe1 ♖xa2 43 ♖f1+ ♘f5 44 ♗c6 ♖d4.

Game 12
Shirov-Radjabov
Linares 2004

---

1 d4 ♘f6 2 c4 g6 3 ♘c3 ♗g7 4 e4 d6 5 ♗e2 0-0 6 ♘f3 e5 7 0-0 ♘c6 8 d5 ♘e7 9 b4 ♘h5 10 ♖e1 f5 11 ♘g5 ♘f6 12 ♗f3 c6 13 ♗b2

This hasn't been played too many times but may become more common after this game. We shall see. White's other tries:

a) 13 ♕b3 enjoyed a brief spell of popularity last year but Black seems to be able to deal with it relatively easily. He should avoid 13...cxd5 14 exd5! and whilst 13...♔h8 is quite playable the best line seems to be 13...h6 14 ♘e6 ♗xe6 15 dxe6 ♕c8 and now:

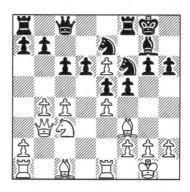

a1) The position after 16 c5 fxe4 17 cxd6 exf3 18 dxe7 ♖e8 19 ♗b2 ♖xe7 20 ♖xe5 ♕c7 21 ♖ee1 was reached three times in 2003. White has managed to keep his powerful pawn on e6 but at the cost of a seriously compromised kingside. I doubt we will be seeing much more of this from White. One example is Pelletier-Inarkiev, Istanbul 2003 which continued 21...fxg2 22 h3 ♖f8 23 ♗e3 ♘h5 24 ♖ae1 ♕f4 25 ♘d1 ♗xb2 26 ♕xb2 ♕f6 with advantage to Black.

a2) 16 ♖d1 ♖d8 (and not 16...♕xe6? 17 ♖xd6!) and now:

a21) 17 c5 is similar to the above except even worse: 17...fxe4 18 cxd6 exf3 19 dxe7 ♖xd1+ 20 ♕xd1 ♕xe6 21 ♕d8+ ♔h7 22 gxf3 (22 ♕xa8 ♕g4-+) 22...♕g8 23 ♕c7 ♕c4 24 ♗d2 ♖e8 and Black has a decisive advantage, Kallio-Kotronias, Batumi 2002.

a22) In Bacrot-Radjabov, Bled (Olympiad) 2002 the young French star preferred 17 b5. I must say that I have some difficulty in accepting that White has enough play for the pawn after 17...♕xe6 but I suppose Bacrot may think differently. At any rate he quickly reached a promising position after 18 ♗a3 ♔h8 19 bxc6 ♘xc6 20 exf5 gxf5 21 ♗d5! so I suggest that Black play 19...bxc6.

N.B. The very latest word: 17 b5 ♕xe6 18 bxc6 ♘xc6 19 exf5 ♕xf5 20 ♕xb7 ♘d4 21 ♗d5+ ♔h7 22 ♗e3 ♖ab8 23 ♕xa7 ♖b2 24 ♔h1 ♘g4 25 ♘e4 ♖f8 26 h3 ♘xe3 27 fxe3 ♘f3 28 ♘f6+ ♖xf6 29 ♗xf3 e4 30 ♖d5 ♕e6 31 ♗g4 ♕e8 32 h4 ♖ff2 33 ♗h3 ♕d8 34 h5 ♖xg2 35 hxg6+ ♔h8 36 ♕a5 ♖h2+ 37 ♔g1 ♕e8 38 ♗f5 ♖bg2+ 39 ♔f1 ♗a1 40 ♕a7 ♗g7 41 ♖xd6 ♖xa2 0-1 Bacrot-Radjabov, FIDE Wch KO, Tripoli (rapid) 2004. Keep an eye out for future developments.

b) 13 b5 cxd5 14 cxd5 (14 exd5 is no longer dangerous) 14...h6 15 ♘e6 ♗xe6 16 dxe6 fxe4 (16...♖c8!? is a more ambitious move which has been played by Ponomariov) 17 ♘xe4 ♘xe4 18 ♗xe4 d5 19 ♗a3 (this is why White played b5) 19...dxe4 20 ♕xd8 ♖fxd8 (don't take with the other rook as it will cost you an exchange) 21 ♗xe7 and now:

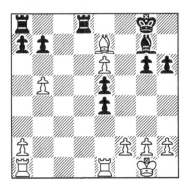

b1) 21...♖e8 22 ♗c5 ♖xe6 23 ♖xe4 a6! 24 b6 ♖c8 25 ♗e3 ♗f6 26 ♖d1 ♖d8 27 ♖b1 ♖c6 28 g4 h5 29 ♔g2 ♗f7 30 ♔f3 ♔e6 = Babula-Degraeve, Istanbul Olympiad. 2000 (½-½, 37). There have been quite a few other games which have been drawn in similar fashion. Some White players claim an edge in this ending because the pawn on e5 restricts the black bishop. This is true but the black rooks are active and his king closer to the centre. If there is an edge it is infinitesimal.

b2) 21...♖d5!? 22 ♖ad1 ♖xb5 23 ♗d8 ♖c8 24 ♖d6 ♖c6 25 ♖xc6 bxc6 26 h4 ♔f8 27 ♖c1

♔e8 28 e7 ½-½ Fressinet-Hebden, Lausanne 2001. This looks riskier for Black than 'b1' but Hebden assures me that Black has no problems at all and that this is an even easier route to equality than 21...♖e8.

It was with regard to lines such as this that I talked about Black been too ambitious. Many players avoided this line just because White could force such an ending. I don't see the problem. If it's a strong opponent then a draw with Black is fine and if they are weak just outplay them in the endgame.

13...h6

It is probably best not to give White the option of 13...cxd5 14 exd5!? here.

14 ♘e6 ♗xe6 15 dxe6 fxe4 16 ♘xe4

16 ♗xe4?! is not very convincing. Avrukh now suggests 16...♕b6!? with the trap 17 ♕xd6? ♕xf2+! 18 ♔xf2 ♘xe4+ in mind but 16...d5 is the most logical reaction. Bareev-Radjabov, Enghien-les-Bains 2003 continued 17 ♗d3!? e4 18 ♗f1 ♕b6 19 ♖b1 ♘h5 and now with 20 ♕d2 failing to 20...♖xf2! 21 ♕xf2 ♗d4 and 20 ♖e2 running into 20...♘f4, Bareev felt compelled to play the positionally repulsive 20 c5. After 20...♕c7 Black has a clear advantage although he eventually lost the game.

If White insists on playing this way then he should at least try 17 cxd5 cxd5 18 ♗c2 when 18...e4 is the best move.

16...♘xe4 17 ♖xe4

This is played with the intention of sacrificing the exchange. Instead, 17 ♗xe4 d5 18 cxd5 cxd5 19 ♗f3 (19 ♗c2 ♕b6 takes advantage of the fact that the bishop is on b2 rather than e3) 19...♕d6 20 ♕e2 e4 21 ♗xg7 ♔xg7 22 ♗g4

♖f4 23 g3 ♖f6 24 ♖ad1 (threatening to take on e4) 24...♕b6 leads to a roughly balanced game. White has retained his passed pawn on e6 but his bishop is reduced to a passive defensive role and Black has a strong pawn centre.

17...d5

On the available evidence, 17...♘f5 looks less risky. Dautov-Kindermann, Nussloch 1996 continued 18 b5 (White must soften up the black queenside otherwise he might lose his e6 pawn for nothing) 18...♖c8 19 ♖e2 ♖e8 20 bxc6 bxc6 21 c5 (the only real alternative available to White was to try ♕d1-a4 on one of the last few moves) 21...d5 22 ♗xe5 ♗xe5 23 ♖xe5 ♕f6 24 ♖e1 ½-½. The game seems about equal but of course Shirov may have a thing or two to say in the future about this line.

18 cxd5 cxd5 19 ♖xe5!

White must sacrifice an exchange to avoid a worse position, but obviously he has planned this all along.

19...♗xe5 20 ♗xe5 ♕b6 21 ♗b2!

The first new move of the game, although Shirov and his trainer Lanka had already looked at this position back in 1997. In previous games White had played 21 ♕d2 but after 21...♕xe6 (Radjabov had had this position before as well but played the less accurate 21...♔h7) 22 ♖e1, Black can equalise by returning the exchange, e.g. 22...♖xf3! 23 gxf3 ♘f5 24 ♗g3 ♕f7 25 ♖c1 ♖e8 26 ♖c7 ♖e7 27 ♖xe7 ♘xe7 28 ♕xh6 ♕xf3 29 ♗e5 ♕d1+ ½-½ Kallai-Barbero, Bern 1997.

21...♔h7!?

Radjabov is not tempted by either of the pawns that are on offer. Both 21...♕xb4 22 ♖b1! and 21...♕xe6 22 ♕d4 ♔f7 23 ♕g7+ ♔e8 24 ♕xh6 are better for White.

22 ♕e2

The best square for the queen. White threatens ♕e5 and avoids the type of exchange sacrifice we saw in the previous note. Black now, sensibly, closes the long diagonal.

22...d4 23 h4!

White switches his attack to the light squares. The idea is obviously to weaken the black king position with h4-h5.

To be honest, even if Black seems just about OK, this is not the sort of position I would like to play. Those bishops frighten me and the

17th move alternative certainly looks safer.

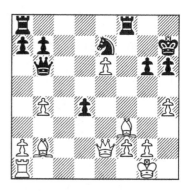

23...♖f6! 24 ♖e1 ♕xb4 25 a3

Black's fine defensive idea was to meet 25 h5 with 25...♖xf3! 26 gxf3 ♖g8 with good play. So Shirov drives back the queen to prevent this line. There is a lot going on just beneath the surface in top level chess.

25...♕d6! 26 h5! ♖af8 27 ♕e4 ♘c6

The d-pawn is more important than the g-pawn. The black king was hoping to take refuge behind the white pawn on g6 but Shirov has a fine sacrifice to prise him into the open.

28 hxg6+ ♔g7 29 ♗c1! ♕e7!

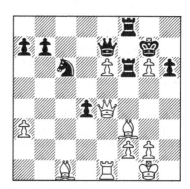

It's best to allow the sacrifice. With the e-pawn blockaded Black is now threatening to take on g6.

30 ♗xh6+! ♔xh6 31 ♕h4+ ♔xg6 32 ♗xc6!

Now the white rook gets to join in the fun.

32...bxc6 33 ♖e5! ♕xe6?

According to Shirov this is the only real mistake of the game. Instead 33...♖xe6! 34 ♕h5+ ♔g7 35. ♖g5+ ♕xg5 37 ♕xg5+ ♖g6 38 ♕xd4

♖f7! 39 g3 ♖fg7! leads to a position where White can make no progress.

All I can say is that if Black is equal in this line it is a lucky equality.

34 ♖xe6 ♖xe6 35 ♕g4+! ♔f7 36 ♕xd4

Now White is winning as Black cannot set up a fortress as in the previous note. The remaining moves were:

36...a6 37 g4 ♖g8 38 f3 ♖f6 39 ♔f2 ♖e8 40 ♕c4+ ♔g7 41 ♕xa6 ♖ef8 42 ♕d3 c5 43 a4 ♖a8 44 ♕c3 ♔g6 45 ♕xc5 ♖fa6 46 ♔g3 ♖xa4 47 ♕d6+ ♔f7 48 g5 ♖8a6 49 ♕d7+ ♔g6 50 f4 ♖a1 51 ♕d3+ ♔g7 52 ♕d4+ ♔g8 53 ♔g4 ♖1a2 54 ♕d8+ ♔g7 55 ♕c7+ ♔g8 56 f5 ♖a7 57 ♕d8+ ♔g7 58 f6+ ♔h7 59 ♕d3+ ♔h8 60 ♔f5 ♖a8 61 ♕h3+ ♔g8 62 ♔g6 ♖2a7 63 ♕e6+ ♔f8 64 ♕d6+ ♔g8 65 ♕d5+ ♔h8 66 ♕h1+ 1-0

Game 13

Zhu Chen-Ye Jiangchuan

Three Arrows Cup, Ji Nan 2003

---

1 ♘f3 ♘f6 2 c4 g6 3 ♘c3 ♗g7 4 e4 d6 5 d4 0-0 6 ♗e2 e5 7 0-0 ♘c6 8 d5 ♘e7 9 b4 ♘h5 10 ♖e1 f5 11 ♘g5 ♘f6 12 f3

In the previous games White defended his centre by 12 ♗f3 but this ultimately led to its destruction. Although White's active pieces gave him some compensation it was insufficient to claim any advantage. This time White prefers to defend his centre more solidly with a pawn. There are, however, certain drawbacks to 12 f3. The principal ones are that this solid pawn move doesn't combine very well with the double-edged ♘e6 that White is more or less committed to playing and that it weakens the dark squares around the white king.

12...♘h5!?

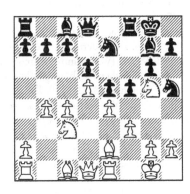

How can we explain such a move? Black plays 9...♘h5, 11...♘f6 and now 12...♘h5 again. I must admit that I didn't take this line very seriously at first but it has grown on me. The first point is that Black only played ♘f6 last move because he was forced to move the knight (White was threatening ♗xh5). With the h5-square available again it is certainly an option to return there. From h5 the knight has many interesting options, as you will discover from the games and notes that follow. The reason that Black can get away with moving his knight so many times is that White's last moves haven't really improved his position – b4, ♖e1, ♘g5 and f3 are just a collection of uncoordinated moves.

Before moving on a little word about the history of 12 f3. White players gave this variation up a few years ago because of the line 12...c6 13 ♗e3 ♗h6 as they couldn't find a satisfactory way to deal with the threat of ...f4. Due to 12 ♗f3's lack of success analysts returned to this position and discovered the threatened ...f5-f4 is not so serious after all. The position after 14 h4 cxd5 15 cxd5 f4 16 ♗f2 ♗xg5 17 hxg5 ♘h5 18 ♖c1 may actually be in White's favour (the knight on e7 is badly placed). It was after a couple of defeats here that Black went back to the drawing board and discovered 12...♘h5. Modern theory is in a permanent state of flux. Moves that get a '?' one day are rewarded with an '!' the next.

In the next game we shall take a look at an alternative for Black, 12...♔h8.

13 c5

White presses on with his queenside play and frees c4 for the bishop. There are a couple of alternatives worth looking at:

a) If White considers ...♘h5-f4 to be a threat then he can prevent it with 13 g3, although his results with this move have not been remarkable. The best reply is 13...♗f6!. Black wants to force ♘g5-e6 as it is difficult to live with this permanently in the air, and this is a much better way than 13...h6 as the g7-square is now available for the knight. 14 ♘e6 (White may try and improve on this in the future; 14 ♔g2 f4 15 ♘h3 doesn't inspire so he may have to try 14 exf5) 14...♗xe6 15 dxe6 f4. This keeps the centre closed and seriously reduces the threat from the white bishops. We now have:

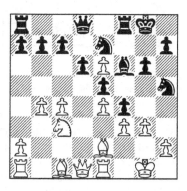

a1) 16 ♔g2 c6 17 ♕b3? fxg3 18 hxg3 ♘xg3! 19 ♔xg3 ♗h4+! 20 ♔g2 ♗xe1 21 ♗g5 ♗xc3 22 ♕xc3 ♘d5! 0-1 Berkvens-T.Paehtz, Bundesliga 2002. Short and sweet.

a2) 16 g4 ♘g7 17 ♕b3? (now when a black knight lands on d4 it is going to be with tempo: better is 17 c5 ♘c6 18 cxd6 cxd6 19 ♗c4 ♔h8 when Black will follow up with ...♘d4 and ...N(g)xe6; White has some compensation for the pawn but not quite enough as his king position is compromised) 17...♘c6 18 c5 ♔h8 19 ♗b2 ♘d4 20 ♕d5 ♘gxe6 21 cxd6 c6! (now White doesn't even get control over d5) 22 ♕c4 ♕xd6 (Black is a pawn up with a good position but White accelerates the end by opening the c-file and running into a little tactic) 23 b5 ♖ac8 24 bxc6 ♖xc6 25 ♕d3 ♘xe2+ 26

♕xe2 ♖xc3! 0-1 Quinn-Shirov, European Team (Leon) 2001.

b) 13 ♔h1 f4! (this would have been a bit slow after c5 but ♔h1 puts the black position under less pressure) 14 ♘e6 ♗xe6 15 dxe6 ♗f6 16 c5 ♗h4 (White's king can easily get into trouble here as ...♘g3+ check is in the air; that is why White decided to sacrifice material rather than play a move such as 17 ♖f1) 17 ♗c4 dxc5 18 ♘d5 (18 bxc5 ♕d4 is good for Black) 18...c6 19 bxc5 cxd5 20 exd5 ♕a5! 21 ♗b2 ♕xc5 22 ♗b3 ♗xe1 23 ♕xe1 ♖f5! 24 ♖c1 ♘g3+ 25 ♕xg3 (25 hxg3 ♖h5 mate) 25...♕xc1+ 26 ♗xc1 fxg3 and Black's huge material advantage easily defeated the passed pawns in Sargissian-Baklan, European Ch., Ohrid 2001.

13...♘f4 14 ♗c4

Or:

a) 14 ♕b3!? fxe4 15 fxe4 ♔h8 16 ♗xf4 exf4 17 ♖ad1 ♘c6!? 18 ♘f7+ ♖xf7 19 dxc6 ♖f8 was rather unclear in Pelletier-Smirin, Biel 2002;

b) 14 ♗xf4 exf4 15 ♖c1 ♗f6 16 ♘e6 ♗xe6 17 dxe6. If on move 11 Black had played 11...♘f4 instead of 11...♘f6 then a similar position would have been reached. The only difference is that here White has two extra moves, f3 and c5, and they don't improve his position. In fact, they harm it enough to change the assessment from better for White to fine for Black. A possible continuation: 17...dxc5 18 bxc5 ♗d4+ 19 ♔h1 ♗e3 with an unclear game.

14...♔h8 15 ♖b1!?

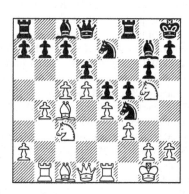

This new move was introduced in Bareev-Radjabov, Wijk aan Zee 2003. When asked in the press conference after the game if 15 ♖b1 was the result of home preparation Bareev gave the enigmatic answer, 'Sometimes you find an idea at the board, sometimes you find it at home'. Judging by his performance in Bareev-Baklan, FIDE World Championship (Moscow) 2001 (15 g3 h6 ½-½) I think you could safely bet the house on him having found this one at home.

Instead, 15 ♘e6 ♗xe6 16 dxe6 fxe4 17 fxe4 ♘c6! was reached a couple of times by the young Ukrainian talent Efimenko.

a) In Tukmakov-Efimenko, Lausanne 2001 he was just a pawn up for nothing after 18 ♗e3 ♘d4 19 ♖c1 dxc5 20 bxc5 ♘fxe6.

b) In Berkvens-Efimenko, Hengelo 2001 he emerged the exchange ahead after 18 cxd6 cxd6 19 ♘b5 ♕e7 20 ♕xd6 ♕g5 21 ♕d2 a6 22 ♘c7 ♘d4 23 ♔h1 ♖ac8 24 e7 ♕xe7 25 ♘d5 ♘xd5 26 ♗xd5 ♘c2. The reason this position is good for Black is that his knights are so active.

15...fxe4!?

This exchange looks more to the point than the mysterious 15...a6 that was played in Bareev-Radjabov. I suspect the main motivation behind 15...a6 was too simply play a move that Bareev wouldn't have considered too deeply in his preparation. For example, the most obvious-looking line for Black, 15...h6 16 ♘e6 ♗xe6 17 dxe6 fxe4 18 fxe4 ♘c6, would surely have been poured over in minute detail by Bareev and from a practical point of view must, therefore be avoided at all costs.

Still, after 15...a6 16 ♔h1 Radjabov could find nothing better than 16...h6 17 ♘e6 ♘xe6!? (in similar positions Black has usually taken with the bishop in order to preserve his active knight on f4, e.g. 17...♗xe6 18 dxe6 fxe4 19 fxe4 ♘c6) 18 dxe6 ♘c6 (the pawn on e6 has considerable nuisance value but if White loses the initiative Black will easily win it) 19 b5 (19 exf5! is best according to Bareev) 19...♘d4 (after 19...axb5 20 ♘xb5 Black can no longer play 20...♘d4 because of 21 ♘xd4 exd4 22 exf5) 20 bxa6 bxa6 21 ♗a3 ♖e8 22 ♗d5! with a difficult game for Black, 1-0 in 32.

16 fxe4

16 ♘cxe4 h6! just wins for Black while 16 ♘gxe4 ♘f5 is not an inspiring way for White to play.

16...♘exd5! 17 ♘xd5 ♕xg5 18 ♘xf4

It's interesting that Bareev originally said that

Black may try 15...♘exd5 16 ♘xd5 ♕xg5 but this is less good because of 17 ♗xf4 exf4 18 ♘xc7. By exchanging pawns first on e4 Ye has ruled this variation out as he can now meet 18 ♗xf4 exf4 19 ♘xc7 with 19...f3!.

18...exf4 19 cxd6 ♗g4

Black invites an endgame but 19...♗h3 was also possible.

20 ♕d5 ♕xd5 21 ♗xd5 cxd6 22 ♗xb7 ♖ab8 23 ♗d5 ♗d4+ 24 ♔f1 ♗d7

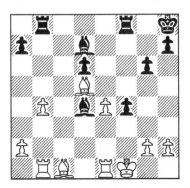

Black has a slight initiative in the endgame although a draw is by far the most likely result. The remaining moves were:

25 ♖d1 ♗b5+ 26 ♔e1 ♗e5 27 ♗b2 f3 28 ♗xe5+ dxe5 29 ♔f2 fxg2+ 30 ♔xg2 ♖f4 31 h3 ♖bf8 32 ♖d2 g5 33 ♖b3 g4 34 hxg4 ♖xg4+ 35 ♖g3 ♖gf4 36 ♖g5 ♗d7 37 ♖xe5 ♖g4+ 38 ♔h2 ♖h4+ 39 ♔g3 ♖g4+ 40 ♔h2 ♖h4+ 41 ♔g1 ♗h3 42 ♖g5 h6 43 ♖f2 ♖xf2 44 ♖g8+ ♔h7 45 ♔xf2 ♖xe4 46 ♗xe4+ ♗xg8 ½-½

Game 14

Ponomariov-Radjabov

Wijk aan Zee 2003

1 ♘f3 ♘f6 2 c4 g6 3 ♘c3 ♗g7 4 e4 d6 5 d4 0-0 6 ♗e2 e5 7 0-0 ♘c6 8 d5 ♘e7 9 b4 ♘h5 10 ♖e1 f5 11 ♘g5 ♘f6 12 f3 ♔h8!?

Just a few days after his defeat against Bareev, Radjabov suddenly finds the FIDE World Champion taking aim at him in the same variation. This is also a variation that Ponomariov knows well but from the Black side! So what is Radjabov to do? He may well have unearthed some improvements on his game with Bareev but he made the prudent choice of avoiding 12...♘h5 altogether. The reputation of 12...♔h8 suffered after Kramnik inflicted a heavy defeat on Ivanchuk, but it seems to be back on the map now.

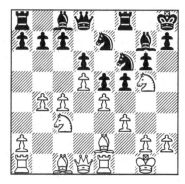

13 ♖b1!?

Could this be taking Bareev-inspired prophylaxis a step too far?

a) The above mentioned Kramnik-Ivanchuk, Monaco 2000 had gone 13 ♗e3 ♘e8 14 ♖c1 c6?! 15 c5! with a good game for White. But Black can do better than that. For example, in Pogorelov-Nataf, Reykjavik 2004 he met 13 ♗e3 with 13...♗h6!? not fearing 14 ♘f7+ ♖xf7 15 ♗xh6 as after he blocks it up with 15...f4 he is unlikely to miss his bishop too much. In the game Black soon obtained good attacking chances after the sequence 16 c5 ♘eg8 17 ♗g5 h6 18 ♗h4 ♖g7 19 ♗f2 g5 20 g4 fxg3 21 hxg3 ♘h5 22 ♔h2 g4 23 ♖h1 ♕g5 and 0-1, 51.

And please note the very latest example which followed the above game until move 15: 16 ♖c1 ♘eg8 17 ♗g5 ♖g7 18 g4 h5 19 h3 ♖h7 20 ♔g2 ♗d7 21 ♖h1 ♖c8 22 ♕g1 ♖a8 23 a4 ♕f8 24 a5 ♘h6 25 ♗h4 g5 26 ♗f2 a6 27 ♔f1 ½-½, Bacrot-Radjabov, FIDE Wch KO, Tripoli 2004.

b) Another possibility for White is 13 c5 when Black does best to play 13...h6 14 ♘e6 ♗xe6 15 dxe6 d5! 16 exd5 ♘fxd5 17 ♘xd5 ♕xd5 18 ♕xd5 ♘xd5 19 ♗c4 ♘xb4 20 ♖b1 ♘c6 21 ♗d5 when White had enough play to hold the balance in Rechlis-Avrukh, Israeli Team Ch. 2003.

13...h6 14 ♘e6 ♗xe6 15 dxe6 fxe4 16

fxe4 ♘c6 17 ♘d5 ♘g8!

Black obviously can't exchange on d5. This retreat is an interesting extra possibility offered by his 12th move. From g8 the knight controls the e7-square and now Black will want to play ...♘c6-d4 and then capture the pawn on e6 or drive away the white knight with ...c7-c6

18 ♗d3 ♘d4 19 ♕g4 g5!

And not 19...c6 20 ♕xg6! cxd5 21 exd5 when the weak pawn on e6 has suddenly turned into a monster. White has more than enough play for the piece here.

20 ♕h3

20 b5 must be worth considering to at least ensure that the b-file is opened after Black kicks the knight with c6 while Ftacnik suggests that 20 h4!? is an improvement

20...c6 21 ♘e3 ♕f6 22 ♘g4

It seems to me that within a couple of moves White finds himself a pawn down for not much. Even parking his knight on a better square looks insufficient though, e.g. 22 ♘f5 ♘xe6 (22...♕xe6 23 ♗xg5) 23 ♖f1 ♘f4 24 ♕g3 ♘e7 is good for Black.

22...♕e7

No need to allow 22...♕xe6 23 ♗xg5.

23 ♗e3 ♘xe6 24 g3 ♕d7 25 ♖f1 d5!?

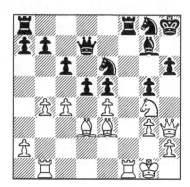

Not the sort of move one normally recommends when the opponent has the bishop pair but of course it all depends on the specifics. 25...♘d4 is the obvious and quieter alternative.

26 ♖f5?!

Radjabov examines numerous other moves in detail in his *Informator* notes. They are all probably better than the text but none of them good enough for equality.

26...dxc4?!

The immediate 26...♘d4 was stronger, one of the main points being that 27 ♗xd4 can be met by 27...dxe4!

27 ♗xc4 ♘d4 28 ♖xf8 ♖xf8 29 ♕h5 ♕d6 30 ♔g2 b5! 31 ♗f7 ♘c2 32 ♗c5 ♕d2+ 33 ♘f2

Or 33 ♔g1 ♘e1 34 ♘f2 ♘f6 35 ♕g6 ♘g4.

33...♘f6 34 ♕g6 ♘g4

Black has whipped up a vicious attack out of nowhere.

35 ♔g1 ♘ce3! 36 ♗xe3 ♘xe3 37 h4

37 ♕h5 g4.

37...♕e2 38 ♕h5 g4 0-1

White can't stop ...♕f3 and ...♕g2 mate. An effortless-looking victory although I'm sure it wasn't quite so easy in practice.

Game 15
Van Wely-Degraeve
Mondariz 2000

---

1 d4 ♘f6 2 c4 g6 3 ♘c3 ♗g7 4 e4 d6 5 ♘f3 0-0 6 ♗e2 e5 7 0-0 ♘c6 8 d5 ♘e7 9 b4 ♘h5 10 g3

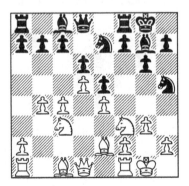

This is the old main line of the Bayonet Attack. White prevents ♘f4 at the cost of weakening his king position. As usual he plans to meet ...f5 with ♘g5 followed by ♘e6. Again Black will have to take this knight and White will recapture with dxe6. White appreciates that in the long run the pawn on e6 is doomed (though there are tricks that Black has to avoid) but he will hope to develop compensation, both on the light squares and because Black

often has to play awkward moves to collect the pawn. In recent times the main champion of 10 g3 has been the Dutch No. 1 Loek Van Wely. Even when the rest of the world switched to 10 ♖e1 he remained faithful to his pet variation. But something has happened recently. Suddenly Van Wely is playing a different system against the King's Indian in every game. 10 g3 is nowhere to be seen. As far as I can tell it is the two main games that I present here that have been the cause of Van Wely's disillusionment. It seems logical to use the lines that forced Van Wely to give up 10 g3 as the basis of our repertoire.

10...f5

In an ideal world Black would like to play h6 before f5 to prevent the white knight sortie into e6. The problem is that after 10...h6 11 ♘d2! White is threatening to take on h5 and Black has to retreat his knight before he can push his f-pawn (he can throw in 11...♗h3 12 ♖e1 first but it doesn't help).

11 ♘g5 ♘f6 12 f3

White must support the pawn on e4. Black has now tried many moves, but as I have already said, I am opting for the one that Van Wely has found the most unpleasant.

12...f4

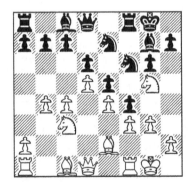

The direct approach. Black hopes to create threats against the white king. Until recently Van Wely thought that 13 ♔g2 was the best move and that is the subject of the next game. First we look at the line he tried in his last couple of games.

13 b5

The idea of this move is to prevent Black

from playing ...c6. Although the knight on g5 is heading for e6 White prefers to wait for Black to waste a tempo on h6 before completing his manoeuvre. Apart from 13 ♗g2 (next game) and 13 b5 White has also tried 13 c5 (13 gxf4 is too risky as it exposes the white king). John Nunn now likes the move 13...a5 (although he himself had a very unclear game against Curt Hansen which went 13...dxc5 14 ♗c4!?) which attempts to show that the advance c5 was premature. There have been very few games with this move. One of them was extremely entertaining. Larsen-Dittmann, Reykjavik 1957 continued 14 ♘b5 (White would like to play 14 a3 but this is impossible whilst 14 bxa5 is met by 14...dxc5 and 14 cxd6 by 14...♕xd6) 14...axb4 15 ♕b3 h6 16 ♘e6 (or 16 cxd6 cxd6 17 ♘e6 ♗xe6 18 dxe6 fxg3 19 hxg3 d5! with good play for Black) 16 ♘e6 ♗xe6 17 dxe6 fxg3 18 hxg3 dxc5 19 ♗e3 b6 (White has given up two pawns to maintain the jewel in his crown) 20 ♖ad1 ♕b8 21 f4 c6 22 fxe5 (unfortunately for White 22 ♘d6 loses to 22...♖a3!) 22...cxb5 23 ♗f4 (23 exf6 ♕xg3+) 23...♘h5 24 ♗xh5 gxh5. Could this be a unique pawn structure in the history of chess? The most relevant factor, though, is Black's extra piece. The remaining moves were: 25 ♖d7 ♖a3 26 ♕d1 ♕e8 27 ♕d6 ♕g6 28 ♕xe7 ♖xg3+ 29 ♔h2 ♖g2+ 30 ♔h1 ♖g4 31 ♔h2 ♖g2+ 32 ♔h1 ♕xe4 33 ♖g1 ♖f2+ 0-1.

13...fxg3 14 hxg3 h6! 15 ♘e6 ♗xe6 16 dxe6 ♕c8 17 ♘d5

Otherwise White loses the pawn on e6 for nothing.

17...♕xe6 18 ♘xc7 ♕h3!

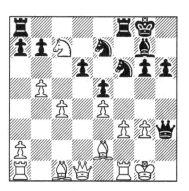

So we have come to the end of a long forced sequence set in train by Black's 13th move. This line was previously used as a means of agreeing a quick draw. Quite a few games have finished 19 ♘xa8 ♕xg3+ 20 ♔h1 ♕h3+ 21 ♔g1 ♕g3+ ½-½. This is a ridiculous line for White to play. Black has at least a draw and maybe more. Van Wely obviously has something else in mind.

19 ♖f2

This avoids the perpetual check as 19...♕xg3+ 20 ♖g2 just costs Black an exchange. Previously it was thought that Black had to play 19...♖ac8 and earlier in the year Van Wely had won a game against Golubev in precisely this line. After 20 ♖h2 ♕xg3+ 21 ♖g2 ♕h3 (21...♕h4 is unclear according to old theory but I'm sure Van Wely has something prepared here) 22 ♕xd6 ♖f7 23 c5 White was on top. The French Grandmaster Degraeve would have noted this game during his preparation and started searching for an improvement. His next move would have been a nasty surprise for Van Wely.

19...♘xe4!

Now the theoreticians have to rewrite the theory books.

20 ♖h2

White avoids the critical line 20 fxe4 ♖xf2 21 ♔xf2 ♖f8+ when Black has a dangerous attack for the sacrificed piece. Van Wely must have analysed this after the game, and judging by the fact that he is no longer playing this line, not liked what he saw. Here are a couple of possible continuations:

a) 22 ♗f3 ♕h2+ 23 ♔e3 ♕xg3 24 ♘e6 ♖f6 25 ♘xg7 ♔xg7 26 ♕h1 g5 27 ♕g2 ♕e1+ 28 ♔d3 ♘g6;

b) 22 ♔e3 (22 ♔e1 leads to the same position) 22...♕xg3+ 23 ♔d2 ♖f2 24 ♕b3 ♕g2 25 ♕e3 (25 ♕d3 ♘f5 26 exf5 e4 is also strong) 25...h5!. This last move both threatens ♗h6 and sets Black's most dangerous passed pawn in motion.

In both cases the black attack looks well worth the investment.

20...♕d7

Of course not 20...♕xg3+ 21 ♖g2 when Black loses his knight.

21 ♘xa8 ♘xg3!

The knight in the corner is going nowhere

and can be collected later. First Black takes a crucial kingside pawn. The white king is now guaranteed a rough ride.

22 ♗xh6 ♗xh6 23 ♖xh6 ♔g7 24 ♖h2 ♘ef5 25 ♔f2 ♖xa8

Black finally finds the time to take the knight. Despite having just one pawn for the exchange Black has the better game. There are excellent squares for his knights and his king is much safer.

26 ♗d3 ♕c7 27 ♗xf5 ♘xf5 28 ♕d3 ♖c8 29 f4?! ♕c5+ 30 ♔f3?

This loses quickly. 30 ♔g2 exf4 would have lost more slowly.

30...e4+! 31 ♕xe4 ♕a3+ 32 ♔g2 ♕b2+ 33 ♔f3 ♕c3+ 34 ♔g2 ♕b2+ 35 ♔f3 ♕xh2

Taking the other rook was even more convincing, e.g. 35...♕xa1 36 ♕xb7+ ♔f6 37 ♕xc8 ♕f1+ 38 ♔f2 (after 38 ♔e4 d5+ Black also wins the queen) 38...♕h3+ 39 ♔e2 ♘d4+ 40 ♔d2 ♕xc8.

36 ♕xb7+ ♔h6 37 ♕xc8 ♕g3+ 38 ♔e2 ♕e3+ 39 ♔d1 ♕d4+ 40 ♔c2 ♕xa1 0-1

Game 16
Van Wely-Fedorov
European Team Ch., Batumi 1999

---

1 d4 ♘f6 2 c4 g6 3 ♘c3 ♗g7 4 e4 d6 5 ♘f3 0-0 6 ♗e2 e5 7 0-0 ♘c6 8 d5 ♘e7 9 b4 ♘h5 10 g3 f5 11 ♘g5 ♘f6 12 f3 f4 13 ♔g2

White takes a time out to improve his king position. The invasion on h3 that we saw in the previous game is no longer possible.

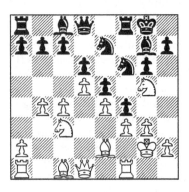

13...c6

This is a desirable move as after the sequence ♘e6, ...♗xe6, dxe6 White can no longer play ♘d5 (unless he sacrifices a piece as in the game). It also means that if White plays b5 Black can seal up the centre with ...c5. True, this concedes the d5-square after the subsequent exchanges on e6 but this is a price worth paying for blocking the position (see the notes to move 14). Black has a large number of alternatives. I'd just like to take a quick look at two.

a) 13...♘h5 is interesting but I don't want to recommend it as after 14 g4! ♗f6 15 ♘e6 ♗xe6 16 dxe6 ♘g7 17 c5 White has an improved version of Game 12. The only difference is that White has played ♔g2 instead of ♖e1 but this means that his king is much better placed. The position is still not too bad for Black but I don't want to give a line against 10 g3, a supposedly less dangerous move than 10 ♖e1, where Black ends up with a worse version of what he played against 10 ♖e1.

b) 13...♔h8!? (the black king is better off here than on g8; the only question is whether he should spend a tempo on this move right now) 14 c5 (other moves are less dangerous)14...h6 15 cxd6 (15 ♘e6 ♗xe6 16 dxe6 d5 17 exd5 ♘exd5 18 ♘xd5 ♘xd5 19 ♗c4 c6 is fine for Black; this is an important line to bear in mind as the ...d5 break is often a possibility after White has played c5) 15...♕xd6 (now 15...cxd6 16 ♘e6 ♗xe6 17 dxe6 d5 18 exd5 ♘exd5 19 ♘xd5 ♘xd5 20 ♗c4 is good for White as Black can't support his knight with c6) 16 ♘b5 ♕b6 17 a4 ♘fxd5! (Black needs a square for his queen as White was threatening a5) 18 exd5 hxg5 19 a5 ♕f6 20 ♘xc7 ♖b8 21 g4! Now in Van Wely-Nunn, Wijk aan Zee 1992 Black got into trouble after 21...♗d7 and the line was more or less discarded. Nunn points out, though, that both 21...♕d6 and 21...e4 give Black an equal game

14 ♕b3

Alternatively:

a) 14 b5 c5! 15 ♕d3 (15 ♘e6 ♗xe6 16 dxe6 ♘e8 17 ♘d5 ♘c7 18 ♘xc7 ♕xc7 is good for Black) 15...♘e8 (threatening ♘xd5) 16 ♘e6 ♗xe6 17 dxe6 ♕c8 18 ♘d5 ♕xe6. White doesn't have much play for the pawn as with the position blocked his bishops are ineffective. It will still be very difficult for Black to win as his extra pawn is the backward one on d6.

b) 14 c5 is very aggressive and probably best met by 14...h6 15 ♗c4!? (15 ♘e6 ♗xe6 16 dxe6 d5!) 15...hxg5 16 cxd6 ♔h7 17 dxe7 ♕xe7. If White now plays 18 d6 he is likely to end up losing the pawn (Black can start with 18...♕d7) whilst 18 g4 is met by 18...♕xb4 and other moves, such as 18 b5, by 18...g4 with good attacking chances for Black.

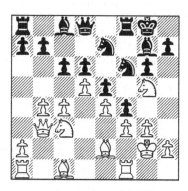

14...h6

When Black feels he is ready to face ♘e6 he plays this move; otherwise he just keeps on improving his position.

15 ♘e6 ♗xe6 16 dxe6 ♕c8 17 ♖d1 ♖d8

Avoiding the trap 17...♕xe6? 18 ♖xd6! ♕xd6?? 19 c5+ which costs Black his queen.

18 ♘d5!?

White was faced with the choice of letting his e6 pawn go for insufficient compensation or sacrificing a piece to ensure that it survives for the rest of the game. This sacrifice is known

from similar positions but normally White gets more direct play than he does here.

18...cxd5 19 cxd5 g5

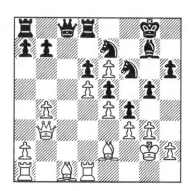

It is very hard to believe that White has enough for the piece. I'm sure Van Wely doesn't believe it either as it was after this game that he gave up 13 ♔g2. Still, as the game shows it is not easy for Black to make progress.

20 ♗d2 ♖f8 21 g4 h5 22 h3 ♘g6 23 ♖dc1 ♕b8 24 ♗e1 hxg4 25 hxg4 ♘e8 26 a4 ♗f6 27 a5 ♗d8 28 ♕a4 ♘f6 29 ♖a3 ♔g7 30 ♗f2 ♖h8 31 ♖ac3 ♗e7 32 ♖c7 ♖h6 33 ♕a1 ♕h8 34 ♖h1 ♘xg4!? 35 fxg4 f3+ 36 ♗xf3 ♘f4+ 37 ♔g1 ♖xh1+?!

Black got fed up with all the quiet manoeuvring and sacrificed a piece for an attack. Fedorov should have contented himself with perpetual check: 37...♘e2+! 38 ♔g2 (38 ♗xe2 ♖xh1+) 38...♘f4+ 39 ♔g1 ♘e2+. After his choice he was lucky to escape with a draw.

The remaining moves were: 38 ♗xh1 ♕h3 39 ♕d1 ♖h8 40 ♖xe7+ ♔g6 41 ♗f3 ♕h2+ 42 ♔f1 ♖c8 43 ♖f7 ♕h3+ 44 ♔g1 ♖c3 45 ♖xf4 gxf4 46 ♗g2 ♕h8 47 ♗e1 ♖c7 48 ♗f1 a6 49 b5 axb5 50 ♕b1 b4 51 ♕xb4 ♖h7 52 ♗g2 ♕f8 53 ♕a3 ♕b8 54 ♔f1 ♕c7 55 ♕c3 ♕d8 56 ♗f2 ♔g5 57 ♗f3 ♖h3 58 ♔g2 ♕h8 59 ♔g1 ♕d8 60 ♔f1 ♕e8 61 ♕b3 ♕c8 62 ♔g2 ♖h8 63 ♕b1 ♕c7 64 ♕e1 ♕c2 65 e7 ♔f6 66 e8♕ ♖xe8 67 ♕h1 ♔g7 68 ♕h4 ♖h8 69 ♕e7+ ♔g8 70 ♕d8+ ♔g7 71 ♕b6 ♕c1 72 ♗g1 ♕d2+ 73 ♕f2 ♕xa5 74 ♕c2 ♔g6 75 ♕d1 b5 76 ♗f2 b4 77 g5 ♕a2 78 ♗g4 b3 79 ♗f5+ ♔g7 80 ♕f1 ♖h5 81 ♕b5 ♖h2+ 82 ♔xh2 ♕xf2+ 83 ♔h1 ♕e1+ 84 ♔g2 ♕d2+ 85 ♔f1 ♕d1+ 86 ♔f2 ♕d2+ 87 ♔f1 ½-½

Game 17
Kamsky-Kasparov
New York (rapid) 1994

1 d4 ♘f6 2 c4 g6 3 ♘c3 ♗g7 4 e4 d6 5 ♘f3 0-0 6 ♗e2 e5 7 0-0 ♘c6 8 d5 ♘e7 9 b4 ♘h5 10 c5

So far we have seen lines where White takes the threat of ...♘f4 seriously. 10 ♖e1 enabled the bishop to drop back to f1 while 10 g3 prevented ♘f4 altogether. In this game we shall look at lines where White ignores the threat of ...♘f4. 10 c5, the subject of the main game is by far the most common of these lines while below we have a quick look at two of White's rarer alternatives:

a) 10 ♕b3 ♘f4 11 ♗xf4 exf4 12 ♖ad1 h6 (12...♗g4 is also worthy of consideration) 13 c5 g5 14 e5 g4 (14...dxe5 15 d6 is dangerous for Black) 15 exd6 cxd6 16 ♘d4 ♘f5! (Nunn's suggestion – we now follow his analysis) 17 ♘xf5 ♗xf5 18 ♘b5 ♗e5 19 ♘xd6 (or 19 cxd6 f3) 19...f3 and Black has a good game, e.g.

a1) 20 gxf3 ♕h4 21 h3 gxf3 (21...♗h2+ 22 ♔xh2 ♕xh3+ 23 ♔g1 g3 is a draw) 22 ♕xf3 ♗xh3 with good play for Black.

a2) 20 ♗xf3 ♗xd6 21 cxd6 gxf3 22 ♕xf3 ♗g6 and the three pawns are not as good as the piece.

a3) 20 ♗d3 ♕h4 21 h3 fxg2 22 ♗xf5 gxf1♕+ 23 ♔xf1 with advantage to Black

b) 10 ♘d2 ♘f4 11 a4 (on the immediate 11 ♗f3 Black achieves good play with 11...♘d3 12 ♗a3 a5; 11 a4 is designed to make the square a3

more comfortable for the white bishop) 11...f5 (if Black does not feel comfortable with the complications that follow he can play 11...♘xe2+ before playing ...f5) 12 ♗f3 g5 13 exf5 ♘xf5 14 g3 ♘h3+ (Black can also sacrifice a piece with 14...♘d4 but the latest evidence suggests it is unsound) 15 ♔g2 ♕d7! 16 ♗e4 (16 ♔xh3? ♘e3+ wins for Black) 16...g4 17 ♘b3 ♕e7 18 ♕d3 h5 with a double-edged position. The game Mannion-Smirin, Las Vegas 1997 should give you some idea of how Black can develop his game on the kingside: 19 c5 ♘f4+ 20 gxf4 exf4 21 f3 ♗e5 22 ♖a2 ♕g7 23 ♘d1 g3 24 ♖g1 gxh2+ 25 ♔xh2 ♘g3 26 ♖gg2 ♕g5 27 ♘f2 ♔h8 28 ♘d4 ♕h4+ 29 ♔g1 ♖f7 30 ♘e6 ♗xe6 31 dxe6 ♖g7 32 ♗b2 ♖ag8 33 ♗xe5 dxe5 34 ♘g4 ♕h1+ 35 ♔f2 hxg4 36 fxg4 ♖xg4 37 ♗f3 e4 38 ♕d4+ ♖4g7 0-1.

10...♘f4

10...h6 and 10...f5 are played from time to time but there is no reason to avoid the main line.

11 ♗xf4

11 ♗c4 is the only serious alternative. Bykhovsky-Avrukh, Beersheba 1996 now continued 11...♔h8 (Black is planning f5 so he needs to get his king off the sensitive diagonal; 11...♗g4 12 h3 ♗h5 13 ♖e1 ♔h8! leads to the same position) 12 ♖e1 ♗g4 13 h3 ♗h5! 14 ♗f1 (White defends h3 in order to threaten g3 or g4) 14...f5 15 ♗xf4 (neither 15 exf5 e4 nor 15 g3 fxe4 16 ♘xe4 ♘xh3+ are playable) 15...exf4 16 ♖c1 a5 17 a3 axb4 18 axb4 ♗xf3 19 gxf3 (19 ♕xf3 ♖a3 20 ♕d3 f3! is good for Black) 19...fxe4 20 ♖xe4 ♘f5 with advantage to Black.

11...exf4

12 ♖c1

White can also defend the knight with his queen.

a) 12 ♕b3 can be met by 12...h6 as 13 ♖ad1 would then transpose to line 'a' to White's 10th move, but 12...♗g4 is also a good move. Black wishes to take the knight on f3 so that he can have total control over e5. Shneider-Gufeld, Helsinki 1992 continued 13 ♖ad1 ♗xf3 14 ♗xf3 g5 (this is a key move in a number of variations; Black intends ♘g6-e5 when his knight would be extremely powerful) 15 ♗h5 ♘g6 16 ♗xg6 hxg6 17 ♘b5 ♖e8 18 ♖fe1 a6 19 ♘a3 g4 20 ♘c4 ♗e5 with advantage to Black.

b) 12 ♕d2 ♗g4 13 ♖ac1 ♗xf3 14 ♗xf3 g5 15 ♗g4 ♘g6 16 ♖fd1 ♕e7 17 cxd6 cxd6 18 ♖e1 a6 19 a4 ♖ae8 20 ♔f1 ♘e5 21 ♗f5 f3 22 g3 g4 and White was in trouble in Larsen-Gligoric, Lugano 1970.

12...a5!?

More common is 12...h6 followed by ...g5 and ...♘g6, but this is a good moment to challenge White's supremacy on the queenside. The main points in 12...a5's favour are that it develops the rook on a8 and that Garry Kasparov plays it!

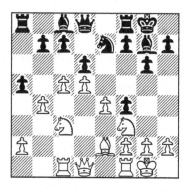

13 cxd6

A more solid continuation is 13 a3. Tukmakov-Smirin, Elenite 1993 then continued 13...axb4 14 axb4 f5!? (14...♗g4 and 14...h6 also come into consideration) 15 ♖e1 ♗xc3 16 ♖xc3 fxe4 17 ♘g5 f3 18 gxf3 exf3 19 ♗xf3 ♘f5 20 ♘e6 ♗xe6 21 dxe6 ♕f6 22 ♕d2 ♘e7 23 cxd6 cxd6 24 ♖d3 d5 ½-½.

13...cxd6 14 ♘b5

White is willing to give up his pawn on b4 in

order to get a rook to the 7th rank.

14...♗g4 15 ♖c7 axb4 16 ♕d2

16 ♕b3 can also be met by 16...♗xf3 with similar play.

16...♗xf3! 17 ♗xf3 ♗e5

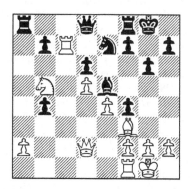

18 ♖xb7?!

According to my database this position has been reached twice and both times White has played this inferior move. Inferior because it leads, without a fight, to a prospectless position where White might be able to hang on for a draw or he might not. 18 ♖fc1 is better after which all White's pieces, bar one, are actively placed. The problem is this one, the light-squared bishop, has very little indeed to look forward to. It is completely smothered by the central pawns that are fixed on light squares. In fact White would be better off if he simply removed these pawns from the board. Black also has a poorly placed piece, the knight on e7, but this at least has the potential to become a wonderful piece (see the main game if you don't believe me). After 18 ♖fc1 the plan of ...g5 and ...♘g6 is rather slow so Black should initiate complications with the aim of exchanging his passive knight for White's active one. Here are a few plausible variations: 18...♖a5!, and now:

a) 19 ♖xb7 ♕a8 20 ♕xb4 (20 ♖cc7 ♖xa2 is good for Black while 20 ♖xe7 ♖xb5 is also rather unpleasant for White) 20...♕xb7 21 ♕xa5 ♖a8 22 ♕b4 (22 ♖c7 ♕b8! is worse) 22...♖xa2 with an edge for Black.

b) 19 ♕xb4 ♖xa2 20 ♖xb7 ♖b2 21 ♕a3 ♕a8! 22 ♖xe7 (22 ♕xa8 ♖xa8 23 ♘xd6 looks like a nice combination but 23...♖c2! is the refutation) 22...♖xb5 and Black is better because his bishop has a juicy target on f2 whilst White's has nothing to attack.

18...♕a5 19 ♘d4 ♕xa2 20 ♕xa2 ♖xa2 21 ♖xb4 ♖fa8

In Herndl-Kindermann, Austrian League 1996 Black immediately played 21...♗xd4 and after 21...♗xd4 22 ♖xd4 g5 23 ♖b4 (23 ♗h5 is better) ♘g6 24 ♗g4 ♘e5 25 h3 ♖fa8 he also ended up triumphing on the dark squares. The remaining moves were: 26 ♖b6 ♖8a6 27 ♖xa6 ♖xa6 28 ♖b1 ♖a4 29 ♗f5 h5 30 f3 ♔g7 31 ♖c1 ♔f6 32 ♖c3 ♘c4 33 ♗d7 ♖a1+ 34 ♔f2 ♖a2+ 35 ♔g1 ♘e3 36 g4 h4 37 ♖c7 ♖g2+ 38 ♔h1 ♖g3 39 ♗e8 ♖xh3+ 40 ♔g1 ♖xf3 41 ♖xf7+ ♔e5 42 ♖e7+ ♔d4 43 e5 ♖g3+ 44 ♔h2 f3 0-1

22 ♗g4

After 22 ♘c6 ♘xc6 23 dxc6 ♖c2 White will lose his passed pawn but can at least activate his bishop by 24 ♗d1 ♖xc6 25 ♗b3. Kindermann's 21...♗xd4 would have avoided this possibility.

22...♗xd4 23 ♖xd4 g5

Black now threatens to achieve a strategically won game by the manoeuvre ...♘g6-e5. We have already seen an example of this in the Kindermann game above. White could have played 24 ♗h5 to prevent ...♘g6 but then Black would have calmly improved his position with ...♖b8 and ...♔g7-f6. Kamsky decides to allow the knight into e5 and instead pins his hopes on breaking up the Black pawn structure. With best play the position may be a draw but it is very unpleasant to defend.

24 h4 gxh4 25 ♔h2 ♘g6 26 ♔h3 ♖b2 27 ♗f5 ♘e5 28 ♔xh4 h6 29 ♗h3 ♔g7 30 ♖dd1 ♖aa2 31 f3 ♘g6+ 32 ♔g4 ♔f6 33 ♖b1 h5+!

Suddenly the white king finds itself in a mating net.

34 ♔xh5 ♖a8! 35 ♔g4 35...♖h8 36 g3 ♖h2

White stopped the mate but at the cost of his bishop.

37 ♖h1 ♖8xh3 38 ♖xh2 ♖xh2 39 gxf4 ♖g2+ 40 ♔h3 ♘xf4+ 41 ♔h4 ♘e5 42 ♖b7 ♔d4 43 ♖xf7 ♔e3 0-1

Summary

1) The Bayonet Attack, or more specifically the 10 ♖e1 variation, has become one of the most important lines in the King's Indian. Games 11-14 are, therefore, of particular importance.

2) The manoeuvre ♘g5-e6 occurs very often. This leads to an unbalanced game with positions that are hard to assess. White will obtain the bishop pair and a passed pawn on e6, which though doomed in the long run, has considerable nuisance value. Black will aim to safely round up the pawn and then consolidate his position. Often White will play ♘g5 and then the knight will then remain suspended there for a few moves. This is because White is waiting for Black to waste a tempo and weaken his kingside with ...h6 before completing the journey to e6. In the end Black usually forces the issue as it is more unpleasant to play with the threat of ♘e6 hanging over him than it is for the move to actually happen. The old proverb 'the threat is stronger than the execution' is very relevant here.

3) Black must take great care when taking the pawn on e6 that White hasn't prepared a tactical refutation. For example, within the notes to Game 11 we see ...♕xe6 running into a sacrifice on e4 while in Game 12 there is an example of ♕xe6 running into ♖xd6. Black must take extra care when his king is on g8 and White has a queen or bishop on b3.

4) When White plays c5 after ♘g5-e6 has happened then the first thing Black should examine is whether he can play the move d5 or not. If White plays c5 with the knight still on g5 then Black may be able to play h6, ♗xe6 and d5.

5) Game 17 features a different sort of game where White meets ♘f4 by playing ♗xf4 and then clears the long diagonal to limit the influence of Black's dark-squared bishop. A key manoeuvre for Black in this line is ...♗g4xf3 in order to gain complete control over e5. His bishop may settle here but it is an ideal outpost for his knight. The usual route from e7 is via g6 after Black has played g5.

CHAPTER FOUR

The Classical Variation: 9th Move Alternatives

---

1 d4 ♘f6 2 c4 g6 3 ♘c3 ♗g7 4 e4 d6 5 ♘f3 0-0 6 ♗e2 e5 7 0-0 ♘c6 8 d5 ♘e7

In this chapter we shall examine the alternatives to 9 ♘e1 and 9 b4. That means 9 ♘d2 and 9 ♗g5. The first two games deal with 9 ♘d2 and the third game concentrates on 9 ♗g5 with some of the rare 9th move options mentioned in the notes.

9 ♘d2

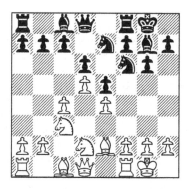

With 9 ♘d2 White is taking prophylactic action against Black's kingside attack. He will now be able to defend his centre, if need be, by playing f3. But the move also has an aggressive side and the knight on d2 is looking forward to playing an important role in the queenside attack. Once White has played c5 it will be able to occupy the fine square on c4. From there it attacks the crucial d6-square and will give added

strength to the advance b4-b5-b6 which White likes to carry out. In fact after 9 ♘d2 very few Black players are willing to get involved in a direct race. Against 9 ♘e1, for example, Black just gets on with game not minding too much that White's attack is a bit further along the line than his. The point is that his prize at the end is much greater – the white king – and is worth suffering a bit for. But in this 9 ♘d2 line, if Black decides to get involved in such a race he can easily end up with his queenside decimated whilst his own attack is still just a glint in its mother's eye.

To show you what I mean, take a look at Beliavsky-Solak, Europe Ch., Saint Vincent 2000. After 9 ♘d2 play continued 9...♘d7 10 b4 f5 11 f3 (White can also play 11 c5!? at once) 11...♘f6 (now 11...f4 would certainly be met by 12 c5) 12 c5 f4 13 ♘c4 g5 14 a4 (a strong case can also be made for 14 ♗a3)14...♘g6 15 ♗a3 ♖f7 16 b5 ♘e8?! 17 a5 ♗f8 18 ♘a4 h5 19 b6 ♗d7 20 bxc7 ♕xc7 21 a6 bxa6 22 c6 ♗c8 23 ♘ab2 ♖g7 24 ♘d3 ♘h8 25 ♘f2 ♘f7 26 h3. Beliavsky's last four moves really rubbed the salt in Black's wounds. Instead of going for the kill on the queenside he adopts the same defensive set-up we saw in Chapter 2, with the difference that instead of White just having attacking chances on the queenside Black has already been wiped out in that part of the board. The remaining moves were: 26...♘h6 27 ♖b1 ♕d8 28 ♗b4 ♘f6 29 ♖b3 a5 30 ♗xa5 ♕e8 31 c7 ♕g6 32 ♖b8 g4 33 hxg4 hxg4 34 ♖xa8 ♗d7 35

c8♕ ♗xc8 36 ♖xc8 g3 37 ♘h3 ♘f7 38 ♗b4
♘g5 39 ♗xd6 ♕h5 40 ♗xf8 ♘xh3+ 41 gxh3
♕xh3 42 ♗xg7+ ♔xg7 43 ♖c7+ ♔g8 44 ♖f2
gxf2+ 45 ♔xf2 ♕h4+ 46 ♔g2 1-0.

Okay, Black could have defended better but I'm sure you get the picture.

So that means that if we are not going to challenge White to a race we have to take some action to slow down his attack on the queenside. An added benefit of this strategy is that if Black can prevent White from playing c5 the knight on d2 can end up looking quite stupid.

The most radical way to prevent c5 is for Black to play it himself. However after 9...c5 White has new targets on the queenside and by playing ♖b1 and b4 he is able to develop the initiative. The main line after 9...c5 runs 10 ♖b1 (10 dxc6 bxc6 11 b4 is also interesting) 10...♘e8 11 b4 b6 12 bxc5 bxc5 13 ♘b3 f5 14 ♗g5! with an edge for White, e.g. 14...h6 15 ♗xe7 ♕xe7 16 ♘a5.

I suggest that Black plays 9...a5!. This will be no great surprise to those of you already familiar with this position as it is the main line. The point is that even after White plays a3 he is still in no position to play b4 because of the pin on the a-file. Therefore he needs another move (usually ♖b1) in order to be able to play b4. Playing ...a5, therefore, saves Black a tempo. Even this might not be sufficient for Black to get involved in a straight race, but as we shall see he no longer needs to. In some of the material below he actually challenges White for supremacy on the queenside. This usually means playing ...c6 and Black is aided by the fact that after a well-timed ...axb4 he can take control of the a-file. Having said this, Black's primary objectives are still on the kingside and one of the reasons for playing ...c6 is to slow down, or make less effective, the white attack on the queenside. After 9...a5 10 a3 I suggest that Black plays 10...♘d7 in order to prepare ...f5 and this is covered in games 18 and 19 below.

Game 18
Lputian-Dolmatov
Rostov 1993

---

1 d4 ♘f6 2 c4 g6 3 ♘c3 ♗g7 4 e4 d6 5 ♘f3 0-0 6 ♗e2 e5 7 0-0 ♘c6 8 d5 ♘e7 9 ♘d2 a5 10 a3 ♘d7

In the early 1990's, before the Bayonet Attack took over, this line was the main battleground in the King's Indian. Black retreats his knight in order to play ...f5, and chooses the d7-square (as opposed to e8) in order to hold up c5 for as long as possible.

The main alternative is 10...♗d7 which is not considered here but there is coverage in SOKID.

11 ♖b1 f5 12 b4 ♔h8

A semi-waiting move that has displaced all other moves. How did Black arrive at such a decision? Well, the two most obvious moves, 12...f4 and 12...♘f6 both have their drawbacks. 12...f4 allows White to play 13 ♗g4 while Black is also reluctant to move his knight from d7 just yet as it is holding-up White's c4-c5. Therefore, by a process of elimination Black arrives at 12...♔h8 (he could also flick in 12...axb4 13 axb4 and then make his decision but delaying this exchange cuts down slightly on White's options). Of course this is not just a waiting move. Black now has the g8-square available for manoeuvres such as ...♘g8-f6 and the king is safer in the corner, especially if ...c7-c6 is played.

13 ♕c2

In fact another reason behind Black's previous move was too pass the buck to White. He, too, has a difficult decision to make. The obvious way to support c5 is with 13 ♘b3, but the problem with this is that the knight will be misplaced once c5 has been played. After c5 White wants to play ♘c4. White normally chooses between the text and 13 f3, which is the subject of the next game.

13...♘f6

13...♘g8 was popular for a while but the position after 14 f3 (14 exf5 gxf5 15 f4 is also interesting) ♘gf6 15 ♗d3! has proved quite difficult for Black. The only way for Black to continue waiting is with 13...b6, but as I am going to recommend a line which involves playing ...c6 this is not possible for us.

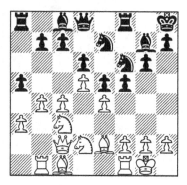

14 f3

This is the standard reaction to ...♘f6. If White doesn't play this move then Black may be able to equalise by exchanging on e4. For example, 14 ♗b2 fxe4 (14...c6!?) 15 ♘dxe4 (15 ♘cxe4 axb4 16 axb4 c6) 15...♘f5 16 ♘xf6 ♘d4 17 ♕d2 ♕xf6 should be fine for Black.

Last year I had to face the unusual 14 ♖d1 in Arlandi-Gallagher, Mitropa Cup 2003. Unfortunately my form in this tournament was abysmal (I can't think of worse, that's for sure) and I didn't react well. 14 ♖d1 is obviously directed against Black's ...c7-c6 but after a long (and I mean long) think I went ahead and played 14...axb4 15 axb4 c6 only to end up with the slightly worse position after 16 c5 fxe4 17 ♘dxe4 ♘xe4 18 ♘xe4 ♗f5 19 ♗d3. I soon blundered and lost.

Looking at the position in the cold light of day it is possible to exchange at once on e4 (as I suggested against 14 ♗b2) or, perhaps, more to the point, start to advance on the kingside. 14...g5 looks like a good move.

14...axb4

In some of the games below the exchange on b4 occurred later but for simplicity's sake I

will assume that Black exchanged now. Anyway, this is probably the right moment to exchange to avoid the possibility of being surprised by White taking on a5.

15 axb4 c6!?

With the centre still tense Black is not yet committed to an all-in assault on the white king. The text fights for some space on the queenside and prevents White from playing c5. True, after an eventual exchange on d5 Black will have performed a task that White normally undertakes – opening the c-file – but he will have also avoided the most dangerous lines where White keeps his pawn on c5 supported by a knight on c4. Then White will have the additional possibilities of c5-c6, b5-b6 or simply to exchange on d6 at a moment of his choosing. Let's have a look at a few examples where Black left the queenside to fend for itself.

a) 15...f4 16 c5 g5 17 ♘b5 (17 ♘c4 is more accurate when Black should play 17...g4) and now:

a1) 17...♘e8? 18 ♘c4 ♘g8 19 ♗b2 ♘gf6 20 ♖a1 ♖b8 21 ♘a7 ♗d7 22 c6 bxc6 23 ♘a5! and White's attack is already decisive.

a2) Instead of passively defending on the queenside Black should have countered with 17...dxc5 18 bxc5 c6!. Ftacnik-Nunn, Groningen 1988 concluded 19 d6 cxb5 20 dxe7 ♕xe7 21 ♖xb5 g4 22 ♗b2 gxf3 23 ♗xf3 ♘g4 24 ♗xg4 ♗xg4 25 ♘f3 ♖fc8 ½-½.

b) 15...g5!? enables Black to combine both pawn and piece play on the kingside and was the choice of the then World Champion in Vaganian-Kasparov, Manila Olympiad 1992. Play continued 16 c5 ♘g6 17 ♘c4 (17 exf5

♘f4 18 ♗c4 dxc5 19 bxc5 g4 is good value for a pawn) 17...♘f4 18 cxd6 cxd6 19 ♗e3 g4 20 ♗b6 ♕e7 21 exf5 ♘xe2+ 22 ♘xe2 gxf3 23 ♖xf3 ♘xd5 with a very complex position. The game eventually ended in a draw.

These lines look like decent alternatives to 15...c6.

16 ♔h1

One of the other points of 15...c6 is that ...♕b6+ becomes a possibility. It is a sensible precaution for White to remove his king from the exposed diagonal. Let's have a look at the alternatives:

a) 16 ♘b3 fxe4 (I once played 16...♘h5 which is also interesting) 17 fxe4 cxd5 18 cxd5 ♕b6+ 19 ♔h1 ♗d7! (after 19...♕xb4 20 ♗e3 the queen is in trouble) 20 ♘a5?! (20 ♕d3 is better as by overprotecting the f1-square White would have avoided the fate that befell him in the game) 20...♘g4! 21 h3 ♖xf1+ 22 ♗xf1 ♖f8 23 ♗g5? (and here White should have tried 23 ♕e2) 23...♘f2+ 24 ♔h2 ♘xh3! and Black wins the queen after 25 gxh3 ♖f2+ and the king after 25 ♗xe7 ♕g1+ 26 ♔g3 ♗h6! 27 ♗xf8 (there is no defence) 27...♕e3+ 28 ♔h2 ♗f4+ with mate next move. In Lputian-Piket, Wijk aan Zee 2000, White played 25 ♗b5 but his position was hopeless after 25...♘xg5 26 ♗xd7 ♖f4

b) 16 dxc6 ♘xc6 (this is the right way to recapture; 16...bxc6 17 b5! is better for White) 17 ♘b5 ♘h5!? (the solid 17...fxe4 18 ♘xe4 ♘xe4 19 fxe4 ♖xf1+ 20 ♗xf1 ♘d4 21 ♘xd4 exd4 soon led to a draw in M.Gurevich-Ye Jiangchuan, Comtois 1999) 18 ♖d1 ♕h4! 19 ♘f1 (19 ♘xd6? loses to 19...♘d4 20 ♕d3 ♘f4) 19...fxe4 20 ♕xe4 ♘f4! 21 ♗xf4 (after 21 ♘xd6 ♗f5! 22 ♘xf5 gxf5 23 ♕e3 ♖a2 Black has dangerous threats, e.g. 24 ♖d2 ♗h6! 25 ♖xa2 ♘h3+ 26 gxh3 ♖g8+ 27 ♔g3 ♗xe3 28 ♗xe3 f4 29 ♗f2 fxg3 30 hxg3 ♖xg3+ 31 ♗xg3 ♕xg3+ 32 ♔f1 ♘d4 and the powerful combination of queen and knight leave White fighting for a draw) 21...exf4 22 ♘xd6? (this loses; 22 g3 is a better chance) 22...♗f5! 23 ♘xf5 gxf5 24 ♕c2 (White can't keep d4 under control as 24 ♕d5 is met by 24...♖ad8) 24...♗d4+ 25 ♖xd4 (25 ♔h1 ♕f2) 25...♘xd4 26 ♕b2 ♕f6 with a winning position for Black, Nemet-Gallagher, Zürich 1994.

16...f4

Back to basics. Black closes the centre and

prepares to attack on the kingside. This line is a speciality of Dolmatov and he has been playing it successfully for almost a decade now.

17 dxc6

In a more recent Dolmatov game White tried 17 ♕b3, but eventually ended up getting crushed on the kingside. Here are the moves: 17...cxd5 18 cxd5 g5 19 ♘c4 h5 20 ♗d2 g4 21 ♖a1 ♖b8 22 ♘b5 ♘e8 23 ♖fc1 ♘g6 24 ♗f1 ♗f6 25 ♘a7 ♗d7 26 b5 ♗h4 27 ♗e1 ♗xe1 28 ♖xe1 ♘h4 29 fxg4 hxg4 30 ♘d2 ♖f7 31 ♖e2 f3 32 ♖e3 fxg2+ 33 ♗xg2 ♘g7 34 ♗f1 ♕g5 35 ♕d3 ♖f2 36 ♗e2 ♕h5 37 ♘f1 ♖bf8 38 ♖e1 ♘f3 0-1 Ulibin-Dolmatov, Calcutta 1999.

17...♘xc6

Dolmatov has always played this but the alternative capture is also worthy of consideration. In fact after 17...bxc6 18 b5 g5 we have transposed into some analysis by the French grandmaster and King's Indian expert Igor Nataf (he gives the move order 16...g5!? 17 dxc6 bxc6 18 b5 f4). He fancies Black's chances in this position. A sample variation: 19 bxc6 (19 b6 ♖b8) ♘xc6 20 ♘b5?! g4 21 ♕d3 g3! 22 ♕xd6 ♕e8 23 ♘c7 ♕h5 24 h3 ♗xh3! and Black wins.

18 ♘b5

This both covers the d4-square, thereby stopping Black from playing ...♘d4, and targets the weak pawn on d6.

18...♕e7

Dolmatov calmly completes his development, not rushing prematurely into a kingside attack. Before attacking he must ensure that his weakness on d6 has sufficient protection. Later, when his attack is further along the road he may be able to jettison this pawn but for the moment it's best to consolidate.

19 ♖d1 ♗e6 20 ♘f1

White assigns his knight to defensive duty. An alternative was 20 ♘b3 when Ruban-Dolmatov, Novosibirsk 1993 continued 20...♖fd8 (20...♘xb4 21 ♕d2) 21 ♕d2 ♗f8 and instead of 22 ♘a3 Ruban claims that White could have obtained the better game by 22 ♘a5 g5 23 ♘xc6 bxc6 24 ♘c3. This is debatable and, as Nunn points out, Black can even play 24...d5.

20...♖fd8 21 ♗d2 g5 22 ♗e1 ♗f8!

A very logical move. Black needs to defend d6 but it is best to do so with his passive bishop rather than his active queen. Swapping the position of the bishop and queen will improve the fortunes of both.

The immediate 22...g4 would have been a mistake on account of 23 ♗h4!

23 ♗f2 ♕g7 24 g4

A panicky reaction which doesn't stop Black's attack. 24 ♖d2 is better according to Dolmatov.

24...h5 25 h3 ♕h7

25...♕h6! is more accurate as 26 ♘c7 loses to 26...hxg4. White would have to play 26 ♔g2 when after 26...♖d7 Black has an improved version of the game.

26 ♔g1 ♖d7

Black's long-term plan is to mate White down the h-file. With this pawn structure the sacrifice of a piece on g4, to break up the king's defences, becomes almost inevitable at some point.

27 ♘h2 hxg4 28 hxg4 ♕h3 29 ♗f1 ♕h6

30 ♗e1 ♗e7!

White has managed to defend along the second rank, so with no immediate breakthrough Black just improves his position a bit more. There are two ideas behind ...♗e7. The first is that the possibility ♗d8-b6 is now in the air and the second is simply to clear the way for the queen's rook to reach the kingside.

31 ♖b2 ♔g7 32 ♕g2 ♖c8

Not only is White suffering on the kingside but his queenside pawns are also weak. He would have more chances of organising a defence if he could push his b-pawn back one square.

33 ♗e2 ♘d8! 34 ♕f1 ♘f7 35 ♗c3? ♗d8!

White's last move was a mistake as he can no longer prevent the King's Indian bishop getting to the lethal g1-a7 diagonal.

36 ♖bd2 ♗b6+ 37 ♔h1 ♗xg4! 38 ♘xd6

The simple point behind the sacrifice was that 38 fxg4 loses to 38...♘xe4.

38...♖xd6! 39 ♖xd6 ♖h8 0-1

White resigned as the only way to prevent mate, 40 ♕g2, loses the queen to 40...♗h3.

Game 19

Ljubojevic-Kasparov
Linares 1993

---

1 d4 ♘f6 2 c4 g6 3 ♘c3 ♗g7 4 e4 d6 5 ♗e2 0-0 6 ♘f3 e5 7 0-0 ♘c6 8 d5 ♘e7 9 ♘d2 a5 10 ♖b1 ♘d7 11 a3 f5 12 b4 ♔h8 13 f3

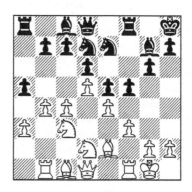

A more forthright move than the 13 ♕c2 of the previous game. What are the advantages of

13 f3 over 13 ♕c2? Well, firstly, it's not clear where the white queen belongs yet. In some lines it may even be better off on its original square so it is quite logical to first play a move, f3, that White can rarely do without. Secondly, by solidly defending the e4 pawn, White is taking prophylactic action against ...♘d7-f6. The point is that White normally has to meet this move with f3, thereby giving Black time to play the lines with ...c6 that we saw in the previous game, whereas now, with f3 already played, White can meet ♘f6 with c5. There are also certain drawbacks to playing f3 so soon. Firstly, it weakens the dark squares on the kingside before it is essential to do so, and secondly, it allows Black to play f4 and immediately start his kingside attack (White no longer has ♗e2-g4). The main way for Black to try and exploit the dark squares is the manoeuvre ...♘g8-f6-h5-f4. In fact, Black has played 13...♘g8 in countless games but it was eventually discovered that after 14 ♕c2 ♘gf6 15 ♗d3! the attack to the f-pawn means that Black has nothing better than to play 15...f4. The manoeuvre ♘g8-f6 now turns out to be useless as the f4-square is no longer available. In fact, the black knights are just stepping on each other's toes and the knight on f6 would actually be better off back on e7. The point is that after Black plays f4 and g5 it would then have a very nice square on g6. Therefore, I am suggesting that Black meets 13 f3 by immediately blocking the centre.

13...f4

There is one potential drawback to Black declaring his hand (he is going to pawn storm) on the kingside so soon. That is that, with the centre blocked, White may be able to sacrifice a pawn to accelerate his own queenside attack. However, as we shall see in the concrete variations below, Black appears to be able to deal with this.

And what about the plan with ...c6 that Black adopted in the previous game? Well, that is not so effective here as White has saved an important tempo with his queen. In fact, not only has White saved the tempo he spent on ♕c2 but, against the ...c6 idea, the queen is probably even better placed on d1. Remember the lines where White had to worry about ...♘d4 attacking the queen? There were also

occasions when the queen on d1 would have attacked the pawn on d6.

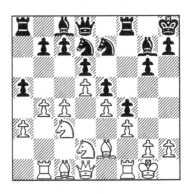

14 ♘b3?!

You have already learnt from the 13th move notes to the previous game that this is a rather feeble move. Let's take a look at some of the alternatives.

a) 14 ♘b5 is often suggested but rarely played. The idea is to prepare c4-c5 by making the sacrifice too dangerous to accept. Black has the choice between getting on with his kingside play or taking further precautions on the queenside.

a1) 14...b6 15 c5!? bxc5 16 bxc5 ♘xc5 17 a4 occurred in Vladimirov-Temirbaev, Alma-Ata 1989. Black now played 17...g5?! and eventually lost (only this move is given in NCO). In his notes Vladimirov says (according to Nunn) that after 17...c6 18 dxc6 ♘xc6 19 ♘c4 ♘d4 20 ♘cxd6 White would only be marginally better. It is my experience that when players annotating one of their nice games give a variation in the notes which is only marginally better, it is not better at all! Where is White's advantage here? I don't see it. Can he even maintain the balance after 20...♘xa4!? I'm not so sure. For example, after 21 ♗a3 ♗a6 22 ♕a4? loses to 22...♘e2+ 23 ♔h1 ♘g3+!!.

a2) 14...g5 15 c5 axb4 16 axb4 ♘f6 17 ♕c2 ♘e8 (the usual response when White is threatening to invade on c7) 18 ♘c4 h5 19 ♗b2 ♘g6 20 ♖a1 ♖xa1 21 ♖xa1 ♗d7 22 ♘a5 ♕b8 23 ♔h1 g4 with chances for both sides, Lukacs-Xie Jun, Budapest 1992.

b) In the late 1980's and early 1990's there were quite a few games that went 14 c5 axb4 15 axb4 dxc5 16 bxc5 ♘xc5 17 ♘c4. The open lines on the queenside gave White good compensation for the pawn. Black then made the important discovery that he should refrain from the exchange on b4. For example, after 14...dxc5 15 bxc5 ♘xc5 Black can meet 16 ♘c4 with 16...a4 when it is not easy for White to generate threats. Black even has outposts of his own on b3 and d4. In Hernandez-Frolov, Havana 1991 White preferred 16 a4 but Black had a little trick prepared against this: 16...♘e6! with the point that 17 dxe6 ♕d4+ 18 ♔h1 ♕xc3 is good for him and that if the knight is not taken it will hop into d4. After 16...♘e6 the game continued 17 ♗a3 ♘d4 18 ♗c4 g5 19 ♘e2 c6!? 20 d6 ♘g6 with good play for Black. There is no need to worry about White grabbing an exchange with 21 d7 as in return Black will have two pawns and a grip on the dark squares.

c) 14 ♘a4 is a rather crude way to support the advance c5 and Dr. Nunn believes that this decentralising move is best met by 14...axb4 15 axb4 c6.

d) 14 ♕c2 also prepares the advance c5. Black can try and hold it up with 14...b6 but he can also get on with his kingside attack, e.g. 14...g5 15 c5 axb4 16 axb4 ♘f6 (it's too dangerous to take the pawn with the queen on c2) 17 ♘c4 h5 (17...♘g6!?) 18 ♗a3 (18 ♘b5 ♘e8 transposes to 'a2' while 18 b5 is another try) 18...g4 19 cxd6 cxd6 20 b5 ♖xa3! (rather than defending passively with 20...♘e8 Black gives up the exchange to kill off the white attack – now it's his turn) 21 ♘xa3 g3 22 b6 (White is reluctant to play h3 as he knows that Black will be able to sacrifice a piece there one day but he

won't be able to resist for ever) 22...♘g6 23 ♘cb5 ♘h7 24 ♖fc1 ♕h4 25 h3 ♗xh3! 26 gxh3 ♘g5 27 ♗f1 ♘xf3+ 28 ♔h1 ♘g5 (the f and g-pawns are enormous) 29 ♘xd6 f3 30 ♘f5 ♖xf5 31 exf5 ♘xh3 32 ♗xh3 ♕xh3+ 33 ♔g1 f2+ 34 ♕xf2 gxf2+ 35 ♔xf2 ♕xf5+ and Black soon won, Harestad-Rasmussen, Copenhagen 1996. A very typical King's Indian attack.

14...axb4 15 axb4 g5

16 ♗d2?

White opts for the rather leisurely plan of invading down the a-file. It is too slow. In a previous game, Dreev-Shirov, USSR 1988, White was also in trouble after 16 c5 ♘f6 17 ♗d2 ♘g6 18 c6 b6 19 ♖e1 ♖g8 20 ♘d2 h5 21 ♘b5 g4. It is clear that after one inaccurate move (14 ♘b3?!) that the situation is already becoming critical for White on the kingside. Kasparov believes the only chance is to try and block it up with 16 g4.

16...♘g6 17 ♖a1 ♖xa1 18 ♕xa1 ♘f6 19 ♕a7

Now it's too late to block the kingside as after 19 g4 fxg3 20 hxg3 ♘h5 21 ♔g2 ♘gf4+! 22 gxf4 gxf4 Black has a crushing attack.

19...g4 20 fxg4

White can't allow the pawn to advance to g3.

19...♘xg4 21 h3

The pawn on h3 will turn out to be a fatal weakness. White could have tried 21 ♗xg4 ♗xg4 though after 22 ♕xb7 ♘h4 Black's attack is decisive according to Kasparov.

21...♘h6

The main reason for retreating here, as opposed to f6, is to stay out of the queen's way.

22 ♗e1 ♖g8 23 ♘d2 ♗f6!

Clearing the g-file and preparing to play ♗h4. Once the dark-squared bishops are exchanged it will become easy for Black on the kingside.

24 ♔h1

The last chance to put up any resistance was offered by 24 ♘f3. Black should still play 24...♗h4!

24...♗h4 25 ♘f3 ♗xe1 26 ♘xe1

After 26 ♖xe1 ♘h4 27 ♖g1 ♘xf3 28 ♗xf3 ♕h4 the game will also be decided by Black sacrificing his bishop on h3.

26...♘h4 27 ♖f2 ♕g5 28 ♘f3 ♘xf3 29 ♗xf3 ♗xh3 0-1

Ljubo, as he's commonly known, had seen enough. A possible finish: 30 ♕xb7 ♗xg2+ 31 ♖xg2 (31 ♗xg2 f3) 31...♕h4+ 32 ♔g1 ♕e1+ 33 ♔h2 ♖xg2+ 34 ♗xg2 ♕g3+ 35 ♔h1 f3 36 ♕c8+ ♘g8 and Black wins. The expression 'taking candy from a baby' seems quite appropriate in relation to this game.

Game 20
Lukacs-Rajlich
Budapest 2001

---

1 d4 ♘f6 2 c4 g6 3 ♘c3 ♗g7 4 e4 d6 5 ♘f3 0-0 6 ♗e2 e5 7 0-0 ♘c6 8 d5 ♘e7 9 ♗g5

This is White's 4th most common move after 9 ♘e1, 9 b4 and 9 ♘d2. As we shall see it is not without danger for Black. There are a few others which occur from time to time. We shall just take a quick look at them.

a) It has been quite a while since 9 ♗d2 was in fashion. 9...♘h5 is considered to be the main line but as there are quite a few tricky sidelines there for Black to avoid we are going to concentrate on 9...♘e8. This line gained fame in the 1971 Candidates quarter-final match between Taimanov and Fischer which the American won 6-0. Apart from the main line 10 ♖c1, White can play 10 ♘e1 f5 11 ♘d3 ♘f6 transposing to Chapter 2 or 10 b4 f5 11 ♕b3 ♘f6 12 exf5 gxf5 13 c5 ♔h8 14 cxd6 cxd6 15 ♖ac1 ♗d7 16 a4, Korchnoi-Geller, Moscow 1971, and now instead of 16...♘g6 17 ♗b5! which was slightly better for White, 16...a6 would have kept the bishop out and maintained the balance.

After 10 ♖c1 f5 (10...c5 11 dxc6 bxc6 12 b4 ♘c7 13 b5 d5 also offers good chances of equality) we have:

a1) 11 ♘g5 h6 12 ♘e6 ♗xe6 13 dxe6 ♕c8 14 c5 (14 ♕b3 c6 15 f4 exf4 16 ♗xf4 g5 17 ♗g3 f4 18 ♗f2 ♕xe6 19 ♕xb7 is unclear) 14...♕xe6 15 cxd6 cxd6 16 ♘b5 ♕d7 17 ♗b4 ♘c6 18 ♗xd6 with an edge for White, Geller-Minic, Skopje 1968. This is what most theoretical sources give but as Nunn points out, 16...♕d7 is a strange move. Why doesn't Black grab another pawn? After 16...fxe4 17 ♗b4 ♖c8! it is not immediately obvious how White is going to win back his pawns.

a2) 11 exf5 gxf5 12 ♘g5 h6 13 ♘e6 ♗xe6 14 dxe6 ♕c8 15 ♕b3 c6 16 ♗h5 ♕xe6 17 ♕xb7 ♘f6 18 ♗e2 ♖fb8 19 ♕a6 ♖xb2 is quite good for Black, Taimanov-Fischer, Vancouver (m/1) 1971.

a3) 11 ♕b3 b6 (Black prevents c5) 12 exf5 gxf5 13 ♘g5 h6 (13...♘f6 14 f4 h6 15 fxe5 dxe5 16 c5 ♘fxd5 17 ♘xd5 ♘xd5 18 cxb6 axb6 19 ♖c6 ♔h8 is the famous 3rd game of the Taimanov-Fischer match; Taimanov claimed that 20 ♕h3 would have been very good for White but subsequent analysis shows that Black can hold the balance with 20...♖f6!) 14 ♘e6 ♗xe6 15 dxe6 ♕c8 16 ♘d5 ♕xe6 17 ♘xe7+ ♕xe7 18 c5+ ♔h8 19 cxd6, Taimanov-Ma.Tseitlin, USSR 1973. In the game Black chose 19...♘xd6 and after 20 ♖c6 ♖ad8 21 ♖fc1 ♖d7 22 ♗b4 White had pressure for the pawn. Perhaps it was better for Black to play 19...♕xd6 20 ♖fd1 c5. The bishop pair still gives White compensation but Black has a solid position.

b) 9 ♔h1 is a strange idea of Larsen that was also played a lot by the late Tony Miles. It is a sort of waiting move which frees the g1-square for use by White's pieces. The variations 9...♘d7 10 g4! ♔h8 11 ♖g1 and 9...♘h5 10 ♘g1 ♘f4 11 ♗f3 f5 12 g3 illustrate a couple of White's ideas. After 9...♘e8 it is not so easy for White to justify his king move. Sulava has tried 10 ♖g1 (Black replies 10...f5 of course) while Miles preferred 10 ♘e1 f5 11 exf5 (11 f3 f4 would be like Chapter 2 except that White has wasted a move on ♔h1) 11...♘xf5 (11...gxf5 12 f4 ♘g6 is also playable) 12 ♘f3 ♘f6 13 ♗d3 ♘d4 14 ♘xd4 exd4 15 ♘e4 ♘xe4 16 ♗xe4 ♕h4 17 ♕c2 ♗f5 18 ♗xf5 ♖xf5 and Black's active pieces compensated for his slightly inferior pawn structure, Miles-Tirard, Cappelle la Grande 2000.

c) 9 a4 shocked the chess world when it was introduced in the game Korchnoi-Kasparov, Barcelona 1989. The move appears to be antipositional as after 9...a5 it will be more difficult for White to open the queenside. 9...a5 was indeed Kasparov's choice and after 10 ♘e1 ♘d7 11 ♗e3 f5 12 f3 ♘c5 (Black can also transpose to Game 6 by 12...f4 13 ♗f2 g5 but Kasparov wants to take advantage of White's strange move order) 13 ♘d3 b6 14 b4 ♘xd3 15 ♕xd3 axb4 16 ♘b5 ♔h8! (in order to improve the position of the knight on e7) 17 ♕b3 ♘g8 18 ♕xb4 Kasparov played the move 18...♘f6 and eventually won but afterwards he said that 18...fxe4! 19 fxe4 ♖xf1+ 20 ♖xf1 ♗h6! 21 ♗f2 ♘f6, with advantage to Black, was more precise.

Later White tried to rehabilitate this line by replacing 11 ♗e3 with 11 ♘d3. After 11...f5 12 f3 (12 exf5 gxf5 13 ♖a3, Larsen-Gabriel, Bad Homburg 1998, should be met by 13...f4 according to GM Daniel King) 12...♔h8!? (it's not so bad for Black to block the position with 12...f4 here as White's bishop is less actively placed; in that case White would try to open the queenside with b3, ♗a3 and b4 while Black would get on with the kingside attack) 13 ♗e3 b6 14 b4 ♘g8!? (14...axb4 15 ♘xb4 ♘c5 is supposed to be about equal) 15 bxa5 ♖xa5 16 ♘b4 ♗b7 17 ♘b5 ♗h6 with a satisfactory position for Black, Bergsson-Steffansson, Reykjavik 1990.

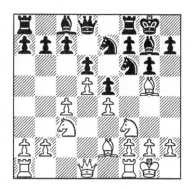

9...♘h5

White's basic idea when playing 9 ♗g5 is to deploy both his queen's bishop and king's knight actively. Thus, after 9...♘d7 or 9...♘e8 White plays 10 ♘d2 f6 (or 10...f5 11 f3 f4 12 ♗h4) 11 ♗e3 f5 12 f3 with the ideal set up for a queenside attack. His bishop is active on the g1-a7 diagonal and his knight on d2 is ready to come to c4 after White has played c5. There are two main ways for Black to disrupt White's plan. The first is to play 9...♘h5 as now 10 ♘d2 is met by 10...♘f4. That is the subject of our main game. The other is the most principled reaction, 9...h6. White now has to give up his bishop (the bishop is not well place on h4 and 10 ♗e3 is well met by 10...♘g4) but in return he will force through c5 quicker than usual. After 10 ♗xf6 ♗xf6 11 b4 Black can play for ...f5 at once or he can delay this until he has his pieces on their optimum squares.

a) 11...♗g7 12 c5 f5 13 ♘d2 fxe4 (Black is too far behind to play for an attack) 14 cxd6 (14 ♘c4 ♗f5 and 14 ♘dxe4 ♘f5 15 ♗g4 h5 16 ♗h3 a6 are thought to be OK for Black) 14...cxd6 15 ♘cxe4 ♘f5 16 ♘c4 (the white knights are ideally placed) 16...b5 17 ♘a5 ♕h4 18 ♕d3 ♘d4 19 ♘c6 ♗f5 20 f3 with an edge for White, Baikov-Odeev, USSR 1991.

b) 11...♗g7 looks slow but Black wants to play improve his minor pieces with ...♘g8 and ...♗e7 (or maybe ...♗g5). The knight on g8 will then be well placed to jump into f6 after Black has played f5 and the bishop on e7 will force White to come to an early decision on how he is going to conduct his queenside attack. 12 c5 ♘g8 and now:

b1) 13 a4 ♗e7 14 c6 (14 cxd6 is met by 14...♗xd6!) 14...bxc6 (better than 14...b6 as now Black gets more room for his pieces) 15 dxc6 f5 16 ♗c4 (on 16 ♘d2 Black should play 16...♗g5) 16...♘f6 17 ♗d5 (on 17 ♘d2 Black can contemplate 17...d5!?) 17...f4 (17...♘xd5 18 ♘xd5 fxe4 19 ♘d2 ♗f5 20 ♕e2 is supposed to be very good for White, but I'm not so sure; e.g. 20...♗e6 21 ♕xe4 ♗g5 looks like an interesting battle between knights and bishops while on 22 ♖fd1 Black can take the two knights with a roughly level game) 18 ♘d2 g5 (the pawn sacrifice 18...f3!? is an option) 19 ♕b3, Vlaskov-Umanskaya, St Petersburg 1994, and now Black should play 19...♕e8 20 b5 ♕g6 in order to prevent White from exchanging bishops with 21 ♗e6. This now runs into 21...♘xe4!

b2) There are various other alternatives thought to be less critical than 13 a4, e.g. 13 ♘d2 ♗e7 14 c6 bxc6 15 dxc6 ♗g5 =; 13 ♖c1 ♗e7 14 ♕b3 ♘f6 (14...f5 looks like the obvious move) 15 cxd6 cxd6 (15...♗xd6) 16 ♘d2 ♘e8 17 ♘c4 ♗g5 18 ♖c2 f5 with equal chances, Ftacnik-Kolev, Budapest 1993; 13 ♕c2!? ♗e7 14 ♘b5 ♗g4 15 ♘fd4 ♗xe2 16 ♘xe2 a6 17 ♘a3 a5 18 b5! dxc5 19 ♘c4 ♗d6 20 b6 cxb6 21 ♖ab1 gave White good compensation for the pawns in Pelletier-Polzin, Bundesliga 2000. Black should be able to do better than this. 14...f5 looks critical.

10 ♘e1

As previously stated 10 ♘d2 ♘f4 is quite good for Black but in the early days of this system White used to play 10 g3. This is now considered harmless because of 10...h6 11 ♗d2 ♗h3 (the immediate 11...f5 is also good enough

for equality) 12 ♖e1 f5 13 ♘h4 ♘f6 14 exf5 g5 15 ♘g6 ♘xg6 16 fxg6 ♗f5 17 ♗f3 ♕e8! followed by ♕xg6 with a level game.

10...♘f4 11 ♘d3 ♘xe2+

11...♘xd3 12 ♕xd3 f5 13 f3 f4 14 ♗h4 is quite promising for White.

12 ♕xe2 h6

This is what nearly everyone plays, but perhaps there is no need to chase the bishop away. According to established theory 12...f5 should be met by 13 f4 (after 13 exf5 both 13...gxf5 and 13...♗xf5 lead to a roughly equal struggle) 13...h6 14 ♗xe7 (after 14 ♗h4 exf4 White will have to take on e7 anyway) 14...♕xe7 15 ♖ae1 c6!? (15...fxe4 16 ♘xe4 exf4 17 ♘xf4 ♗f5 18 g4! may lead to a slightly better endgame for White) 16 exf5 ♗xf5 17 fxe5 dxe5 18 ♘e4 cxd5 19 cxd5 ♖ad8 20 d6! ♕d7 21 ♘df2, Cvetkovic-Simeonidis, Ano Liosia 1998, with an edge for White. But 19...♖ad8 is a clear mistake which allows White to hold onto his d-pawn. After 19...♕d7! Black has no problems.

13 ♗d2

13 ♗e3 has been a speciality of Pelletier. He just wants to have a traditional queenside attack versus kingside attack race with his bishop well placed on the g1–a7 diagonal. However, I believe the game Pelletier-Fedorov, European Team Ch., Plovdiv 2003 has dented his confidence in this variation. After 13...f5 14 f3 Fedorov produced the novelty 14...g5! This is more flexible than 14...f4 against which Pelletier had already won several games. Play continued 15 c5 ♘g6 16 ♖fc1 ♖f7 17 ♖c2 (17 exf5 ♗xf5 is level according to Pelletier) 17...♘f4 (this is the main reason that Fedorov held back with f5-f4; he can now exchange of the knight that often just gets in the way of the other black pieces) 18 ♕d2 ♘xd3 19 ♕xd3 g4! 20 fxg4 (otherwise Black takes on f3, and perhaps also on e4, opening up even more lines on the kingside) 20...f4 21 ♗f2 ♗xg4. Black has already achieved a great deal on the kingside – he has a positional advantage to go with his attacking chances – before the white queenside attack has even got out of the starting blocks. He went on to win the game.

13...f5

I'm giving this as the main line even though it looks untrustworthy. That is because we are going to re-write existing theory. Unfortunately, though, not in Black's favour. The alternatives:

a) 13...g5 prevents White from playing f4. Now 14 h4? g4 15 f4 gxf3 16 ♕xf3 f5 was good for Black in Oll-Shirov, Tilburg 1992, so White usually plays 14 g4 to prevent Black from playing f5. After 14...♘g6 15 f3 ♘f4 16 ♗xf4 exf4 17 ♘d1 c6 18 ♗c3 White probably has a very faint edge as with such a blocked pawn structure it is better to have a knight than a bishop.

b) 13...c6!? and now:

b1) 14 f4 exf4 (14...f5 is all right for Black according to Nunn) 15 ♗xf4 cxd5 16 cxd5 f5 is unclear because 17 e5 can be met by 17...g5 18 exd6 ♘g6 19 ♗e3 ♖e8.

b2) 14 ♖ac1 f5 15 f3 and now Ftacnik gives 15...g5 16 ♘f2 ♘g6 17 g3 as unclear.

14 f4 exf4

14...fxe4 15 ♘xe4 ♘f5 16 fxe5 (16 ♗c3!?) 16...dxe5 17 ♗c3 but Nunn suggests that Black try 15...b5.

15 ♘xf4 g5 16 ♘h5

16 ♘e6?! ♗xe6 17 dxe6 f4 18 g3 ♘g6 19 gxf4 ♗xc3! 20 bxc3 gxf4 21 ♔h1 ♕f6 22 ♖g1 ♔h7 was good for Black in Blees-Klarenbeek, Heraklio 1993.

16...♗d4+ 17 ♔h1 f4 18 g3

18...♗h3 19 gxf4! is a powerful exchange sacrifice.

18...fxg3 19 ♖xf8+ ♕xf8

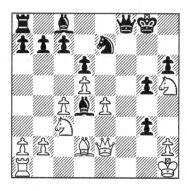

20 ♘b5!

A very interesting moment. Previously White used to play 20 ♖f1 and, quite understandably, it was thought that Black had to move his queen. As 20...♕e8 21 ♖f6 (or 21

♘b5) appears very dangerous for Black the main line ran 20...♕d8 21 ♕f3 ♗h3 22 ♕f7+ ♔h8 23 hxg3 ♗xf1 24 ♗e3! ♗e5 (24...♗xe3?? 25 ♕g7 mate) 25 ♘f6 ♗xf6 26 ♕xf6+ ♔g8 27 ♕e6+ ♔f8 28 ♕xh6+ ♔e8 when both 29 e5 and 29 ♕h5+ lead to a draw but no more.

But then GM Nataf suggested a very interesting improvement for White: 21 ♘b5!? ♗h3 22 ♘xd4! g2+ 23 ♕xg2! ♗xg2+ 24 ♔xg2. White has just two pieces for the queen but with moves such as ♘e6, ♘f6+ and ♗c3 about to swamp Black he has a massive attack. Nataf suggested that Black might be able to try 21...♗xb2 but this appears to lose to 22 ♕f3! (see Line 2 in next note).

Why, then, you may ask have I awarded 20 ♘b5 an '!' if 20 ♖f1 is so strong. The reason is that in a game between Prakash and Konguvel (Nagpur 1999) Black met 20 ♖f1 with the amazing novelty 20...♗h3!. White must take the queen but after 21 ♖xf8+ ♖xf8 it turns out that he cannot hold on to his own queen. In the game Prakash played 22 ♘xg3 and after 22...♖f2 23 ♕xf2 ♗xf2 24 ♘d1 ♗d4 25 ♗e3 ♗xe3 26 ♘xe3 ♗f7 27 ♔g1 ♔g6 he had to fight hard to avoid defeat. 22 hxg3 may have been better, though here too 22...♖f2 regains the queen. So that's why White was in need of an improvement and why 20 ♘b5 is deserving of an '!'

20...♕f2!

The bishop on d4 is attacked but it's too dangerous for Black to move it:

a) 20...♗b6 and now 21 ♖f1 ♗h3 22 ♖xf8+ ♖xf8 23 ♘xg3 ♖f2 24 ♕xf2 ♗xf2 25 ♘xc7 is good for White (though it is still complicated after 25...♘g6) but the simple 21 hxg3 looks very strong. The black kingside is in trouble with the bishop off the long diagonal.

b) 20...♗xb2 21 ♖f1 ♕d8 22 ♕f3 ♗h3 23 ♕f7+ ♔h8 24 ♖f6 wins for White. This was not possible in the similar variation in the previous notes (20...♕d8) as with the bishop on d4 Black could play 24...g2 mate here.

21 ♕xf2

And not 21 ♘xd4?? g2 mate!

21...♗xf2 22 ♘xc7!

The right pawn to take. In Prakash-Konguvel, Indian Ch. 2000 (yes, them two again) White played 22 hxg3? and after 22...♗b6 23

♗c3 a6 24 ♘d4 ♔f7 25 ♔g2 ♔g6 26 ♖h1 ♗d7
Black was better and eventually won.

22...♗h3! 23 hxg3

Of course not 23 ♘xa8?? g2 mate.

23...♖c8

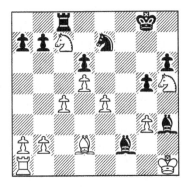

24 ♔h2?!

This seems good enough for an edge but the critical line must be 24 ♘b5 ♖xc4 25 ♔h2! Now Black would love to keep his powerful bishop but its obvious retreat squares are mined. Both 25...♗g4 and 25...♗d7 lose to 26 ♘f6+. That leaves:

a) 25...♗c8. Now White has many tempting continuations, e.g. 26 ♘xd6 ♖c2 27 ♘xc8 ♘xc8 28 ♖c1! ♖xd2 29 ♖xc8+ ♔f7 30 ♔h3 and the central passed pawns should prove decisive; or 26 ♗c3 ♗c5 27 b3 ♖xc3 28 ♘xc3 ♗d4 29 ♖c1 ♗g4 30 ♘b5 ♗e5 31 ♘xd6! ♗xh5 32 ♘xb7 and White should win.

b) 25...g4 locks the bishop on h3 out of the game. White should not play 26 ♘xd6? on account of 26...♖c2 but both 26 ♖c1 and 26 ♗c3 are good for him. Note that Black can't play 26...♖xe4 because this too loses to 27 ♘f6+. What an annoying creature that knight on h5 is.

c) 25...♖c2 26 ♔xh3 ♖xd2 27 ♘xd6 is also very good for White.

If these variations prove correct then the whole line seems unsound for Black. He should choose one of the alternatives suggested earlier.

24...♖xc7

The only way to keep the bishop was 24...g4 (don't forget his retreats are mined) but 25 ♘xb5 ♖xc4 transposes to line 'b' above, which was good for White.

25 ♔xh3 ♖xc4 26 ♗c3

White retains some advantage as his pieces are more active.

26...♗d4 27 ♖f1?!

Was it really necessary for White to allow his queenside pawns to be weakened 27 ♗xd4 ♖xd4 and now either 28 ♖c1 or 28 ♖f1 look more natural.

27...♗xc3 28 bxc3 g4+ 29 ♔g2 ♖xc3 30 ♘f6+ ♔h8 31 ♘xg4 ♖c2+ 32 ♔h3 ♔g7 33 ♘f6 ♖xa2 34 ♘e8+ ♔g6 35 ♘xd6 ♖e2 36 ♖f4 b6 37 ♘f7 ♔g7 38 ♘d8 ♘c8 39 ♘e6+ ♔g6 40 ♖f8 ♘d6 41 ♘f4+ ♔g7 42 ♖d8 ♘f7 43 ♘h5+ ♔h7 44 ♖d7 ♔g8 45 ♖xa7 ♘g5+ 46 ♔g4 ♘xe4 47 ♔f3 ♘c3 48 ♘f6+ ♔f8 49 ♖c7 ♖e1 50 ♘h7+ ♔g8 51 d6 ♖f1+ 52 ♔g2 ♖d1 53 d7 b5 54 ♘f6+ ♔f8 55 ♖xc3 ♔e7 56 ♖c8 ♖d2+ 57 ♔h3 1-0

So although the main line of 9...♘h5 now seems quite good for White there are, between moves 9 and 14, plenty of alternatives in the notes that Black can choose from. Take your pick.

Summary:

1) Not so long ago 9 ♘d2 became the main line of the whole King's Indian with many of the world's top players taking part in a theoretical battle that raged here during the late 1980's and early 1990's. Those days have gone and now it is lying relatively dormant but who knows what the future holds for this rich variation.

2) Black should not challenge White to the usual direct kingside attack v queenside attack race as White is clear favourite in this line. The reason for this is that the knight on c4 is incredibly powerful. Instead Black should take precautions on the queenside (9...a5, maybe ...c7-c6 at some point) whilst still, of course, pursuing his ultimate aim of delivering checkmate to the white king.

3) 9 ♗g5 is in my opinion an underrated line where Black has to be quite careful. It is very easy to slip into a bad position if you are unfamiliar with its nuances as many Black players are. The existing theory is also quite poor and some of it has been re-written in Game 20. It's worth taking a close look at this game, not only for its theoretical value but because it also includes some fascinating variations.

CHAPTER FIVE

The Classical Variation: 7...♘a6

---

1 d4 ♘f6 2 c4 g6 3 ♘c3 ♗g7 4 e4 d6 5 ♘f3 0-0 6 ♗e2 e5 7 0-0 ♘a6

If the main lines with 7...♘c6 are too sharp or too theoretical for you then this chapter is your refuge. 7...♘a6 has completely displaced the old traditional lines such as 7...♘bd7 and 7...exd4 as Black's main alternative to 7...♘c6. The line simply didn't exist until the early 1990's but its popularity grew as many players became weary of suffering in the Bayonet Attack. It was also part of a general revolution in King's Indian thinking as Black started to play ♘a6 in many lines where he had not done so previously (Four Pawns Attack for example).

In SOKID I asked the question, 'Isn't the knight badly placed on the edge?' and I answered myself as follows: 'On a superficial reading of the position the knight is indeed badly placed on the edge of the board. The move would appear to go against the basic chess principles of controlling the centre. However, once we look a little more closely we can see that this is not the case. White will not be able to hold the tension in the centre for ever and at some point he is either going to take on e5 or play d5. In both cases the knight on a6 is poised to jump into c5, one of its best squares in the King's Indian. On other occasions Black, himself, may relieve the central tension by playing ...e5xd4 and here, too, the square c5 becomes available to the knight. If for some reason Black is unable to play ...♘c5 then there is an alternative method of bringing it back into

play: ...c7-c6 followed by ...♘c7 and ...♘e6. The move 7...♘a6 is also more flexible than the old 7...♘bd7 line as it doesn't interfere with the development of the rest of Black's queenside.'

White's most popular response to 7...♘a6 is 8 ♗e3 and that is tackled in Games 21-25. This position is important as whilst you may prefer the variation 7 0-0 ♘c6, I am also recommending that Black meets the Gligoric System, 7 ♗e3, with 7...♘a6 which then transposes here after 8 0-0. Nowadays the vast majority of Games reach the positions examined in Games 23-25 where I examine both the old (if we can call anything old here) 11...h6 and the new 11...f6. Both seem viable.

In Games 26 and 27 we look at the main alternative 8 ♖e1 (others are briefly mentioned in the Game 21 notes). Black's main choice here is whether to exchange on d4 or encourage White to block the centre with d5. The former (Game 27) often leads to a drawish position while the latter (Game 26) can lead to a dour struggle.

Game 21
Rogers-Gallagher
Bundesliga 1997

---

1 d4 ♘f6 2 c4 g6 3 ♘c3 ♗g7 4 e4 d6 5 ♘f3 0-0 6 ♗e2 e5 7 0-0 ♘a6 8 ♗e3

Otherwise:

a) 8 dxe5 dxe5 9 ♕xd8 ♖xd8, as usual, offers White nothing.

b) 8 d5 ♘c5 is considered in Game 29.

c) 8 ♗g5 has earned a few supporters. That is because the variation 8...h6 9 ♗h4 ♕e8 10 ♗xf6 ♗xf6 11 c5! is quite unpleasant for Black. It is much simpler to play 9...g5 10 ♗g3 (10 dxe5 ♘h5 will transpose) 10...♘h5 when 11 d5 transposes into a harmless variation of the Petrosian and 11 dxe5 ♘xg3 12 hxg3 dxe5 is level.

d) 8 ♖e1, the main alternative, is covered in Games 26 and 27.

8...♘g4

Disruption is the name of the game. White should not be allowed to develop his forces harmoniously without a struggle.

9 ♗g5 ♕e8

In the early days of this variation Black often played 9...f6 but this was discarded because of the continuation 10 ♗c1 c6 11 h3 ♘h6 12 c5!.

10 h3

10 dxe5 is the subject of Games 22-25.

10...h6! 11 ♗c1

Also:

a) 11 ♗h4 exd4 12 ♘xd4 ♘f6 and now:

a1) 13 ♗f3 ♘h7 14 ♖e1 ♘g5 15 ♗xg5 hxg5 16 ♕d2 c6 17 ♖ad1 ♕e7 18 ♗g4 ♗xg4 19 hxg4 ♗e5 was about level in Nakamura-Perelshteyn, Bermuda 2003. This is similar to the main game.

a2) 13 ♖e1 g5 14 ♗g3 ♘xe4 15 ♗d3 ♘xc3 16 bxc3 ♕d8 and it's doubtful that White has enough play for the pawn, Groszpeter-Gallagher, San Bernardino 1990 (I won quite easily).

b) 11 hxg4 hxg5 (11...exd4!?) 12 dxe5 dxe5 13 ♘xg5 ♕e7 14 ♘h3 c6 gives Black more than enough compensation for the pawn.

11...exd4! 12 ♘xd4 ♘f6 13 ♗f3

White has a choice of evils and settles for defending the e-pawn in this manner. The problem with 13 f3 is that having already played h2-h3 this would leave the kingside full of holes.

13...♘h7!

It is because of this fine move that White players nearly always play 10 dxe5 these days. That in itself can be considered a small feather in Black's cap as White would prefer to maintain the status quo in the centre.

14 ♖e1

White players are reluctant to play the ugly 14 h4 but it seems as good as anything else. The position after 14...♕e7 15 g3 c6 is probably about equal.

14...♘g5

A strong case could also be made for starting with 14...♕e5!?, e.g. 15 ♗e3 ♘g5 16 ♕d2 c5! (but not 16...♗xh3 17 ♗e2!) looks quite good while 15 ♘b3 ♘g5 16 ♗g4 ♗xg4 17 hxg4 ♕e6 18 ♕e2 ♖ae8 was at least equal for Black in Lassila-Yrolja, Finnish Team Ch. 2002

15 ♗g4 ♗xg4 16 hxg4 ♘c5 17 ♗xg5!?

After the game the Australian grandmaster Ian Rogers made an interesting comment. He said he couldn't decide whether to play 17 f3 or 17 ♗xg5 but settled on the text as King's Indian players tend to overestimate the importance of the dark-squared bishop (well, we certainly respect it). In other words he was trying to provoke me into playing recklessly for a win. Well, he succeeded but to be honest I considered the position to be about level around here.

17...hxg5 18 ♕d2 c6 19 ♖ad1 ♖d8 20 ♘f3 ♕e6!

Searching for counterplay on the queenside rather than defending the position passively

21 ♕xg5 ♕xc4 22 ♕h4 ♘e6 23 ♖e3 ♖fe8!

It's crucial to give the king a square on f8.

24 g5?! d5!

Black must break out in the centre before White plays ♘h2-g4.

25 ♘d2?

It's only after this move that White is in real trouble. 25 ♘h2? d4 26 e5 dxc3! 27 ♕xc4 ♖xd1+ 28 ♘f1 cxb2 is not good either but 25 exd5! ♕xh4 26 ♘xh4 ♘xg5 27 ♖xe8+ ♖xe8 28 dxc6 bxc6 29 ♘f3 should lead to a slightly worse but tenable endgame for White.

25...♕b4 26 ♖h3 ♕xb2!

It's just a check on h7, nothing to worry about.

27 exd5 cxd5 28 ♘db1 ♕b6 29 ♖hd3 ♘c7

Black has won a pawn and now he has to defend for a few moves

30 ♘d2 ♕c6!

Preventing ♘e4.

31 ♖c1

31 ♘de4 fails to 31...dxe4 32 ♖xd8 ♗xc3.

31...d4 32 ♘e2 ♕a6! 33 ♘f4 ♘d5 34 ♖f3 ♘c3! 35 ♖h3

Or 35 g3 ♘e2+ 36 ♘xe2 ♕xe2 37 ♕f4 ♖e7 and wins

35...♘e2+! 36 ♘xe2 ♕xe2 37 ♖c7

This loses but so does everything else.

37...♕xd2! 38 ♕h7+ ♔f8 39 ♖xf7+

39 ♖f3 ♕e1+ 40 ♔h2 ♕e5+

39...♔xf7 40 ♖f3+ ♔e6 41 ♕xg6+ ♔d7

0-1

White resigned as the checks will run out in a few moves.

1 d4 ♘f6 2 c4 g6 3 ♘c3 ♗g7 4 e4 d6 5 ♘f3 0-0 6 ♗e2 e5 7 0-0 ♘a6 8 ♗e3 ♘g4 9 ♗g5 ♕e8 10 dxe5 dxe5 11 ♘d2

11 h3 is the subject of the next three games.

11...f6!?

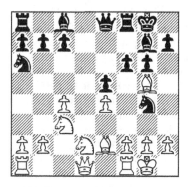

The latest fashion and it is now beginning to look like Black's most reliable move. In fact it looks like the majority of White players are just giving up 11 ♘d2 because of it. The older line is 11...h6 12 ♗h4 ♘f6 13 ♘d5 with Black now having the choice between 13...g5 and the queen sacrifice 13...♕d8 14 f4 ♘xd5.

12 ♗xg4

I don't like this anti-positional move. White needs his bishop to cover the sensitive dark squares. However, 12 ♗h4 doesn't appear too dangerous for Black either, e.g.

a) 12...♘h6 13 a3 c6 (13...♘c5 14 b4 ♘e6 15 ♘b3 c6 is similar) 14 b4 ♘c7 15 ♘b3 ♘f7 16 ♕c2 (16 ♖a2!?) 16...♘e6 17 ♖ad1 ♘d4! 18 ♕b2 (18 ♘xd4 exd4 19 ♖xd4 g5 20 ♗g3 f5 and Black threatens both ...♗xd4 and ...f4) 18...♘xb3 19 ♕xb3 ♗e6 with a level game, Huzman-Gallagher, Crete (rapid) 2002.

b) 12...h5 13 a3 ♗e6 (probably better than 13...c6) 14 b4 ♖d8 and Black can follow up with ♘a6-b8-c6 and hopefully into d4.

12...fxg5

At first glance the pawn structure may look favourable for White but the reality is different.

Not only is there the usual hole on d4 for White to worry about (remember Black can play c6 to cover d5) but the f-file has also been opened for Black's rooks. In addition, having doubled g-pawns means that Black will be able to use the front one aggressively without weakening his own king position. Black's pawn structure is very dynamic and it might only begin to turn in White's favour in a static endgame position.

13 ♘b3

13 a3 ♘c5 14 b4 ♗xg4 15 ♕xg4 ♘e6 16 c5 h5 17 ♕e2 ♘d4 18 ♕c4+ ♔h7 19 a4 g4 20 ♘b3 c6 with good play for Black, Sasikiran-Thipsay, Nagpur 2002. Still there was no need for 21 ♘e2?? ♕f7! after which Sasikiran resigned.

13...c6 14 ♗xc8 ♖xc8 15 ♕d6

15 ♕d2 ♕e6 16 ♕xg5 ♕xc4 is supposed to be about level but I would prefer to play 15...g4 with similar play to the main game.

15...♖f7 16 ♖ad1 ♕e8!

Black's last two moves show that the white queen is redundant on d6 and there is nothing better for her than to beat a hasty retreat

17 ♕d2

17 ♖d3?? ♗f8 and 17 ♘c5?? ♗f8 are not recommended.

17...g4!

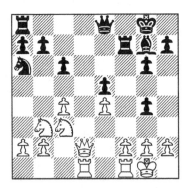

The white knights are passive and it is much easier for Black to improve his position than White. For example, he can move his queen to e7 or e6, double rooks on the f-file, advance his h-pawn, activate his bishop on g7 and bring his knight on a6 to the tasty outposts in the centre and on the kingside. White, meanwhile, has no easy plan

18 ♕e2 ♕e6 19 ♘a4 ♗f8 20 c5

White is dreaming of playing ♘a5-c4 but this will remain just a dream as the c5 pawn is in need of protection.

20...♗e7 21 f3!?

A slightly panicky reaction due to dissatisfaction with his game. He didn't want to sit there doing nothing while Black built up his position.

21...gxf3 22 ♖xf3 ♖xf3 23 ♕xf3 ♕c4!

This is the problem with f3: the queen was needed on e2 to prevent this invasion. I suppose White could have played 23 gxf3 but that is just awful.

24 ♖d7

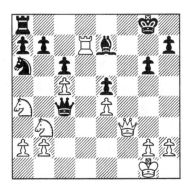

White was relying on this move whilst I actually thought that the best chance was 24 ♕g4!. After 24...♗xc5+ 25 ♘axc5 ♘xc5 26 ♘xc5 ♕xc5+ 27 ♔h1 ♕c4 28 b3 ♕f7 29 h3 ♖e8 Black has an extra pawn but will have to overcome considerable technical difficulties.

24...♗xc5 + ?

Based on an oversight otherwise I would have played 24...♖e8! as 25 ♕g4 ♕xa4 26 ♕e6+ ♔f8 27 ♕xe5 and now 27...♗xc5+ is an ending with an extra pawn but 27...♕xb3!! is a killer as 28 axb3 ♗xc5+ regains the queen with an extra piece, while after both 28 ♕h8+ and 28 ♕f4+ Black can interpose his queen to block the check.

25 ♘axc5?

The obvious knight, but the wrong one! I had seen the variation 25 ♘bxc5! ♘xc5 26 b3 ♕c1+ 27 ♖d1 ♕c2 but stopped my analysis here, not noticing that 28 ♖f1! leads to a roughly level game.

25...♘xc5 26 ♘xc5 ♖f8!

The point.

27 ♕d1

The only move. 27 ♕d3 ♕xc5+ 28 ♔h1 ♕c1+ 29 ♕d1 ♖f1+, 27 ♕b3 ♖f1 mate and 27 ♘d3 ♖xf3 28 gxf3 ♕xa2 all win for Black.

27...♕xc5+ 28 ♔h1 ♕c2!

A neat way to force the exchange of queens. Black would be unable to win with queens on as his king is too exposed.

29 h3 ♕xd1+ 30 ♖xd1 ♖f7 31 ♖d8+

Otherwise ...♔f8-e7.

31...♔g7 32 ♔g1 ♔f6 33 ♖a8 a6 34 ♔f2

Falling for my trap but 34 ♖d8 is met by 34...♖d7 and other moves by 34...♔e6.

34...♔e7+ 35 ♔e3 ♖f8 36 ♖a7 ♖b8! 0-1

A rather sad end to the white rook.

Game 23
Van Wely-Gallagher
Biel 2000

---

1 d4 ♘f6 2 c4 g6 3 ♘c3 ♗g7 4 e4 d6 5 ♘f3 0-0 6 ♗e2 e5 7 0-0 ♘a6 8 ♗e3 ♘g4 9 ♗g5 ♕e8 10 dxe5 dxe5 11 h3 h6

11...f6!? (Game 25) is currently fashionable.

12 ♗d2

The position after 12 hxg4 hxg5 has already been discussed in the 10th move notes to Game 21 (Line 2).

12...♘f6 13 ♗e3 ♕e7!

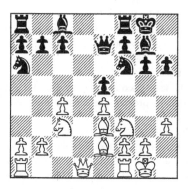

Black has tried many moves in this position (and so have I) but over the last few years the text has firmly established itself as the most respectable. That is because it makes it difficult for White to play c4-c5. In the next game you will discover that 14 ♘d5 is not terribly worrying for Black whilst in this game we shall look at the other main line where White advances his queenside pawns.

14 a3 c6 15 b4 ♘h5

Black's previous two moves have solidified and co-ordinated his position. Now he is ready for the standard ...♘h5-f4 manoeuvre. Black's move order is quite important. The text is preferable, for example, to 15...♖d8 16 ♕c2 ♘h5 when 17 ♖fd1 gives White chances of an edge.

16 ♖e1

The other move White plays here is 16 c5 and now Black should avoid both 16...♘c7, which allows 17 ♕d6, and 16...♘f4, which is better for White after 17 ♗xa6, in favour of 16...♖d8! 17 ♕c1 ♔h7 with about equal chances. Black is no longer worried about ♗xa6 because of the passive white queen on c1 (it normally goes to a4 after ♗xa6 to attack the weak pawns).

16...♘f4 17 ♗xf4

A double-edged move. The solid 17 ♗f1 is played more often and now:

a) Many Black players play 17...♕f6 and then 18 ♖a2! ♖d8 19 ♖d2 may indeed be slightly better for White.

b) But 17...♖d8! is a much better and after 18 ♕c2 it is probably best to play 18...♘e6 (18...♕f6 is also interesting) and then into d4. For example, 19 ♖ad1 ♘d4 20 ♗xd4 exd4 21 ♘a4 c5! looks like an edge for Black.

17...exf4 18 e5 ♗f5

Black must stop ♘e4. Of course 18...♗xe5 runs into a pin after 19 ♗d3.

19 c5 ♘c7!

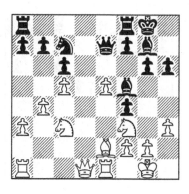

Better than the 19...♖ad8?! that was played in Gallagher-Nunn, Bundesliga 2003 (yes, I was also most surprised to find myself on the other side of this variation). The reason Nunn refrained from 19...♘c7 was 20 ♕d6 but after 20...♖fe8 he failed to appreciate that 21 ♖ad1 is just met by 21...♗xe5 while 21 ♗c4 ♖ad8 22 ♕xe7 ♖xe7 23 ♘e4 ♗xe4 24 ♖xe4 g5 is comfortable for Black.

20 ♗c4 ♖ad8 21 ♕c1 ♘e6

Black would like to exchange off the knight on f3 (by playing either ♘g5 or ♘d4) which is doing a good job protecting the white centre and kingside.

22 ♘e4

22 ♗xe6 fxe6 23 ♕xf4 ♗xh3 is nothing to worry about.

22...♗xe4 23 ♖xe4 ♘g5! 24 ♘xg5 ♕xg5 25 ♕e1 ♖fe8 26 e6 ♔h7!

Now the draw is inevitable.

27 ♖d1 ♖xd1 28 ♕xd1 fxe6 29 ♖xe6 ♖xe6 30 ♗xe6 ♕e5 31 ♗c8 b6 32 cxb6 axb6 33 ♕c1 ½-½

Game 24
Knott-Gallagher
British Ch., Torquay 2002

---

1 ♘f3 d6 2 d4 ♘f6 3 c4 g6 4 ♘c3 ♗g7 5 e4 0-0 6 ♗e2 e5 7 0-0 ♘a6 8 ♗e3 ♘g4 9 ♗g5 ♕e8 10 dxe5 dxe5 11 h3 h6 12 ♗d2 ♘f6 13 ♗e3 ♕e7 14 ♘d5

The most obvious move which some theoretical sources claim gives White an edge

14...♕d8!

Certainly not the horrible 14...♘xd5 15 cxd5 after which the pawn structure is very much in White's favour. There is no need to take the knight. it is much better to drive it away with ...c7-c6. Meanwhile, Black is threatening to take the pawn on e4.

15 ♘xf6+

Alternatively:

a) 15 ♕c1 ♔h7 (15...♘xe4 16 ♗xh6 is quite risky for Black) 16 ♖d1 ♘xe4! 17 ♘b6 axb6 18 ♖xd8 ♖xd8 gives full compensation for the queen. Therefore, in Wells-Gallagher, Bundesliga 1999 White tried 17 c5 and after 17...♗d7 18 c6 bxc6 19 ♗xa6 cxd5 20 ♖xd5 c6 21 ♖d1 ♕c7 22 ♕c4! f5 23 ♖ac1 he probably had just about enough compensation for the pawn (½-½ in 49 after many adventures).

b) 15 ♕c2 c6 16 ♘xf6+ ♕xf6 17 ♖fd1 ♕e7 is very comfortable for Black. I annotated my nice game with Tukmakov in SOKID so I'll just give the moves here. Play continued (after 17...♕e7) 18 c5 (the rather pathetic 18 ♕d2 ♔h7 19 ♕d6 occurred in Gofshtein-Tkachiev, Paris (rapid) 2001 and White managed to hold the ending with some difficulty) 18...♘c7 19 b4 ♔h7 20 a4 f5 21 b5 fxe4! ♘d5 23 ♘xe4 ♗f5 24 ♖a3 ♖ad8 25 f3 ♘xe3 26 ♖xe3 ♖xd1+ 27 ♗xd1 ♖d8 28 bxc6 bxc6 29 ♗e2 h5! 30 ♗d3 ♗h6 31 ♖e1 ♖d5 32 ♔h1 ♕h4 33 ♖e2 ♕d8! 34 ♗c4 ♖d1+ 35 ♔h2 ♕d4! 36 ♖f2 ♖c1! 37 ♕b3 ♗xe4 38 ♗g8+ ♔h8 0-1 Tukmakov-Gallagher, Basle 1999.

15...♕xf6 16 c5 ♘b8

The knight is repositioning itself on c6 and it must take this route as 16...♘b4? 17 ♕d2 costs a pawn.

17 b4

17 ♕b3 ♘c6 is about level so the text is designed to prevent the knight from settling on the c6-square

17...a6!?

A novelty I found over the board. At first I wanted to play 17...♘c6 18 b5 ♖d8?! (the immediate 18...♘d4 is better) 19 ♕c1 ♘d4 but I wasn't too happy with the position after 20 ♘xd4 exd4 21 ♗xh6 d3 22 ♗xg7 ♔xg7 23 ♗f3. I realised, though, that the possibility to open the a-file would make all the difference to this variation so that is how I found 17...a6.

18 a4

18 ♕a4 ♘c6 19 b5 ♘d4 20 ♗xd4 exd4 21 bxa6 ♕f4! is fine for Black.

18...♘c6

19 b5

A year later in Al.Spielmann-Gallagher, French League 2003 I reached the same position again. Play continued 19 ♖b1 ♔h7!? (19...♖d8 20 ♕c1 ♘d4 21 ♘xd4 exd4 22 ♗xh6 is good for White) 20 ♕c1 ♕e7 (now Black is ready to play ...f7-f5 against quiet moves; I didn't want to play ...♘c6-♘d4 until White pushed me and 20...♗e6? 21 ♘g5+! hxg5 22 ♗xg5 is a typical trap for this variation that Black has to avoid) 21 b5 axb5 22 axb5 ♘d4 23 ♗xd4 exd4 24 ♗d3 and although the position isn't quite as tremendous for Black as I first thought (open a-file, c3-square, bishop pair and weakness on c5) he is at least not worse. I eventually won in 54 moves.

19...♖d8

It was also possible to exchange on b5 and a1 before playing ...♘c6-d4.

20 ♕c1?

Knott was going for the variation I gave in the 17th move notes (which he told me afterwards had been recommended somewhere as good for White) but doesn't appreciate how the position of the a-pawns has changed everything. He should have played 20 ♕c2 with an unclear/equal game after 20...♘d4 21 ♗xd4 exd4 22 bxa6 bxa6 23 ♖ad1.

20...♘d4 21 ♗xd4

Now he realised that his intended 21 ♘xd4 exd4 22 ♗xh6 is just good for Black after 22...♗xh6 23 ♕xh6 d3 because of the pin on the a-file. Note that on 24 e5 Black doesn't play

24...♕xe5 because of 25 ♗xd3! ♖xd3 26 ♖ae1!, but instead 24...♕e7! 25 ♗f3 axb5 26 axb5 ♖xa1 27 ♖xa1 ♕xe5 with a clear advantage.

21...exd4 22 e5 ♕e7 23 bxa6

White tries to avoid opening the a-file (23 ♕c2 axb5 24 axb5 ♖xa1 25 ♖xa1 ♗f5 is excellent) but runs into a powerful pawn sacrifice.

23...d3!

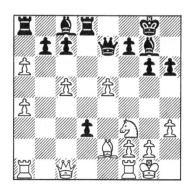

24 axb7 ♗xb7 25 ♗d1 d2!?

Maybe it would have been simpler to just play 25...♗xe5 as 26 ♖e1 is impossible on account of 26...♗xf3 followed by 27...d2.

26 ♕a3

My idea was to meet 26 ♘xd2 with 26...♗xg2 (and not 26...♗xe5 27 ♖e1 ♗h2+ 28 ♔f1 ♗xg2+ 20 ♔xg2 ♕xe1 30 ♘f3! when White escapes into an ending) 27 ♔xg2 ♕g5+ and 28...♖xd2 which is very good for Black. After the text it is time to cash in and take the exchange that is on offer. Black has a decisive advantage. The remaining moves were:

26...♗a6 27 ♕e3 ♗xf1 28 ♔xf1 ♖a5 29 ♖a2 ♕xc5 30 ♖xd2 ♖xd2 31 ♕xd2 ♗xe5 32 ♕xh6 ♕c4+ 33 ♗e2 ♕xa4 34 g3 ♕e4 35 ♕d2 ♖a3 36 ♕d8+ ♔g7 37 ♕e7 ♖a1+ 38 ♔g2 ♕xe2 39 ♕xe5+ ♕xe5 40 ♘xe5 ♔f6 0-1

Game 25
Grooten-Motylev
Hoogovens 2003

---

1 d4 ♘f6 2 c4 g6 3 ♘c3 ♗g7 4 e4 d6 5 ♘f3 0-0 6 ♗e2 e5 7 ♗e3 ♘a6 8 0-0 ♘g4 9 ♗g5 ♕e8 10 dxe5 dxe5 11 h3 f6!?

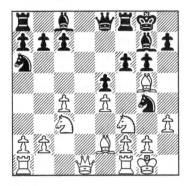

This move has become more and more popular over the last couple of years and it is certainly more fashionable than 11...h6 at the moment. Somewhat surprising, as White has never proved anything against 11...h6. Probably this line just suits the style of King's Indian players better.

12 ♗d2 ♘h6 13 ♗e3

White's main idea in this line is to play c4-c5 which he very often follows-up with ♗xa6 to cripple Black's queenside pawn structure. In the early days of the variation they played the text in order to prepare c4-c5 until some bright spark realised that 13 c5 could be played immediately as a pawn sacrifice. For a while Black players just took White at their word and declined the offer. But this wasn't altogether satisfactory as the tempo saved on 13 ♗e3 was enough to make life unpleasant. But then some even brighter spark worked out that Black could take on c5 after all. Let's take a look:

13 c5 ♘xc5! 14 ♕c1 ♘f7 15 ♘d5 ♘e6 and:

a) It was assumed that White had some advantage after 16 ♘xc7 ♘xc7 17 ♕xc7 until Black discovered 17...♘d8!. This excellent move allows the black pieces to find new squares that suit the altered structure. The knight is going to c6, the rook to f7 and the bishop to e6 and everything will co-ordinate. A couple of the latest examples:

a1) 18 ♗c4+ ♗e6 19 ♖ac1 ♖f7 20 ♗xe6 ♕xe6 21 ♕c4 ♕xc4 22 ♖xc4 ♘e6 23 ♖fc1 ♖d7 24 ♔f1 ♔f7 25 ♔e2 ♗f8 26 a4 b5 27 axb5 ♖b8 28 g3 ♖xb5 29 ♗c3 ♖db7 30 ♖a1 ½-½, Eljanov-Efimenko, Ukrainian Team Ch. 2004.

a2) 18 ♖fc1 ♗e6 19 ♗e3 ♖f7 20 ♕c3 ♘c6 21 b4 ♖d7 22 b5 ♘d8 23 a4 ♘f7 24 ♘d2 f5 25 f3 ♘d6 with an active game for Black (½-½ in 64 moves), Volkov-Nakamura, FIDE World Ch., Tripoli 2004.

b) The other critical line is 16 ♗b4 after which 16...c6 17 ♗xf8 (17 ♘e7+ ♔h8 18 ♘xc8 c5 is a key line when 19 ♗xc5 ♖xc8 20 ♗xf8 ♖xc1 21 ♗xg7+ ♔xg7 22 ♖axc1 ♘d6 is at least equal for Black) 17...♕xf8 18 ♘e3 ♘d6 19 ♕c2 leads to an unbalanced position with roughly equal prospects. Of course I would prefer to play Black but fully accept that this is because of my King's Indian bias. In fact, I don't even consider Black to be material down here as I work to the rule of thumb that dark-squared bishop + pawn = at least rook in a typical King's Indian middlegame. Let's take a look at a couple of examples:

b1) 19...f5 has occurred in a couple of Shabalov games. In the first, Shabalov-Perelshteyn, Vermont 2003 he played 20 ♘c4 but after 20...fxe4 21 ♘fxe5 ♘d4 22 ♕d2 c5 23 f4 ♗e6 24 ♘e3 ♖d8 25 ♕e1 ♘6f5 Black had the better game. So in Shabalov-Movsesian, Bermuda 2004 he was ready with an improvement, the interesting 20 exf5 gxf5 21 ♗c4!?. Normally one worries when the opponent has the bishop pair but here Shabalov is trying to destroy the knight pair. His idea worked well after 21...♔h8 22 ♗xe6! ♗xe6 23 ♖ad1 as Black's knight on d6 is unstable. Better, as Avrukh has pointed out, would have been the continuation 21...♘xc4 22 ♕xc4 (22 ♘xc4 e4) 22...♔h8 23 ♖ad1 e4 24 ♘e1 ♘f4 with a good game.

b2) In Mikhalevski-Oratovsky, Israeli Team Ch. 2004 Black chose 19...♘f4. He also wanted to take the white bishop but without opening the position. After 20 ♖fd1 ♘xe2+ 21 ♕xe2 ♗e6 22 ♕d3 ♘f7 23 ♘c4 ♕b4!? 24 b3 ♗f8 25 ♖ac1 a5! 26 ♕c3! ♕b5 27 a4 ♕b4! 28 ♕xb4 ♗xb4 Mikhalevski considers the position to be about level. That seems like a reasonable assessment.

13...c6 14 c5

14 a3 ♘f7 15 b4 ♕e7 is very comfortable for Black. In Barkhagen-Gallagher, Stockholm 2003 I actually went on to lose this position but only because I was lulled into a false sense of security. After 16 ♕b3 f5 17 ♖ad1 f4 18 ♗c1 ♘c7 19 c5 ♘e6 20 ♘b1! (White continues to go backwards – but correctly so) 20...b6 (20...♘d4 21 ♘xd4 exd4 is fine for Black) 21 cxb6 axb6 22 ♗b2 I now started my downhill trip with 22...♔h8 when 22...c5! would have been about equal.

14...♘f7

Black can just play 14...♘c7 here if he is concerned about 15 ♗xa6.

15 ♘d2!?

White usually plays 15 ♗xa6 bxa6 16 ♕a4 but recently he has not fared well after 16...♖b8!.

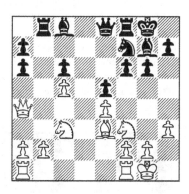

This little rook move is a significant improvement on the previously played 16...f5 as now the rook will be able to swing to the kingside or centre via the b7-square. A couple of examples:

a) 17 b3 f5 18 exf5 gxf5 19 ♖fe1 ♖b7! 20 ♖ad1 ♖e7 21 ♕h4 ♗e6 22 ♘g5 ♘xg5 23 ♗xg5 h6 24 ♗c1 ♔h7 25 ♖d6 ½-½ Savchenko-Damljanovic, Halkidiki 2002. If anything Black has an edge after 25...♖xd6 26 cxd6 ♕g6 27

♖d1 ♖f7.

b) 17 ♘d2?! f5! 18 exf5 gxf5 19 ♖fe1 ♗e6 20 f4 ♖xb2 21 ♘c4 ♗xc4! 22 ♕xc4 exf4 23 ♗xf4 ♕d8 24 ♗d6 ♖c2! 25 ♖e3 f4! 26 ♖f3 ♕g5 27 g4 h5! 28 ♖e1 (28 ♗xf8 hxg4 29 h4 ♕xh4 30 ♕xf4 ♗d4+! 31 ♕xd4 ♕h2+ 32 ♔f1 ♕h1+ 33 ♕g1 ♕xf3+ 34 ♔e1 ♕xc3+ 35 ♔f1 ♕xa1 mate) 28...hxg4 29 ♗e7 gxf3+ 30 ♗xg5 f2+ 31 ♔f1 fxe1♕+ 32 ♔xe1 ♖xc3 33 ♕xf4 ♘e5 34 ♕e4 ♘f3+ 35 ♔d1 ♘xg5 36 ♕xc6 ♖d8+ 37 ♔e2 ♘f3 38 ♕e6+ ♔h8 39 ♔f2 ♖d2+ 0-1 Volkov-Volokitin, Halkidiki 2002. An excellent attacking game from another fine young talent.

15...f5 16 f3 ♕e7

16...f4 17 ♗f2 g5 had been played before after which White can play ♘c4-d6. The text is much better, targeting the c-pawn and making it more difficult for White to carry out this plan, at least if he is intent on refraining from ♗xa6.

17 ♖c1 f4 18 ♗f2 ♖d8 19 ♕e1 ♗e6

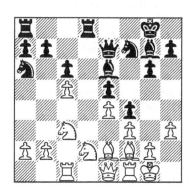

20 ♗xa6

A rather damning indictment on White's play. He did everything to avoid this move and ends up playing it anyway.

20...bxa6 21 ♕e2 h5 22 ♖fd1 g5 23 ♔f1

A clear sign that things are not going according to plan. The open centre is no sanctuary for the white king, so presumably he was just looking to free g1 for the bishop.

23...g4 24 hxg4 hxg4 25 ♕xa6

25 fxg4 ♘h6 won't be fun for White.

25...♕f6!?

Black transfers his queen to the h-file whilst indirectly defending the pawn on c6.

26 ♔e2?!

He should have at least gone straight to e1.
26...g3 27 ♗g1 ♕h6 28 ♔e1 ♕h1 29 ♕f1 ♘g5 30 b3 ♖d3!!

Wonderful! Black plans to increase the pressure by doubling on the d-file taking advantage of the fact that the knight on d2 can't move because it must prevent a crushing sacrifice on f3. But isn't the rook simply en prise?

31 ♕xd3

31 ♘db1 ♘xf3+ 32 gxf3 ♖xf3 is the crushing sacrificed I mentioned.

31...♕xg2!!

Another great move. The g2 pawn is more important than the bishop.

32 ♕f1 ♕h1

Threatening ♗h3.

33 ♔e2 ♗h3 34 ♕e1 ♖d8!

Making sure that the white king cannot evacuate the danger zone via d3.

35 ♗f2

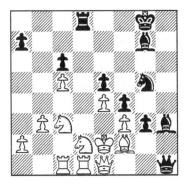

The last chance was 35 ♘cb1 in order to shore up the defences of f3. However, after

35...♕g2+ 36 ♗f2 ♘e6 37 ♖c4 (or 37 ♕g1 ♘d4+ 38 ♔e1 gxf2+ 39 ♕xf2 ♕h1+ 40 ♘f1 ♗f6) 37...♘d4+ 38 ♖xd4 exd4 39 ♔d3 gxf2 40 ♕h1 ♕g3 Black should still be winning.

35...♖xd2+! 36 ♕xd2 ♕xf3+ 37 ♔e1 ♕h1+ 38 ♔e2 ♕f3+ 39 ♔e1 ♕g2 40 ♕d8+ ♔h7 41 ♔d2 gxf2 42 ♖f1 ♘f3+ 43 ♔e2 ♘d4+ 0-1

As 44 ♔d2 ♕g3 and 44 ♔d3 ♕xf1+ 45 ♖xf1 ♗xf1+ 46 ♔d2 ♘f3+ 47 ♔c1 ♗h3 are both totally hopeless.

A tremendous game from one of Russia's numerous rising stars.

Game 26
Soffer-Mittelman
Israeli Team Ch. 2003

---

1 c4 ♘f6 2 ♘c3 g6 3 e4 d6 4 d4 ♗g7 5 ♗e2 0-0 6 ♘f3 e5 7 0-0 ♘a6 8 ♖e1

A quiet, prophylactic continuation. White decides to reinforce his e-pawn and await developments.

8...c6

This move has several points. It covers the d5-square and opens a path to the queenside for the black queen. It also allows Black to meet d4-d5 with ...c6-c5 without having to worry about White capturing en passant, as well as giving him the chance to exchange on d5 as he does in the main game.

8...♕e8 is a major alternative. After 9 ♗f1 ♗g4 10 d5:

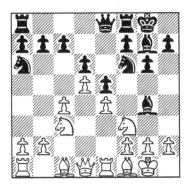

a) 10...♘b4 has occurred countless times. Black now threatens 11...♗xf3 as 12 ♕xf3 will cost White an exchange and 12 gxf3 wreck his kingside pawn structure. White usually defends against this with 11 ♗e2 and Black smugly plays 11...a5, his little trick having gained the time to improve his fortunes on the queenside. It seems to me, however, that after 11 a3! ♗xf3 12 gxf3 Black has paid to high a price for the damage he has inflicted on White's kingside. Can he really get away with giving White the moves a3 and b4 for free, not to mention parting with the precious light-squared bishop. P.Nielsen-De la Riva, Bled Olympiad 2002 suggests not. Play continued 12...♘a6 13 b4 ♘d7 (to hold up c4-c5) 14 ♗e3 f5 15 ♖c1 ♖f7 (It is surprisingly difficult for Black to create threats on the kingside. If, for example, he plays ...f5-f4 then White just drops his bishop back to d2 and there is no obvious way for Black to continue. Note that the light-squared bishop will be able to deploy itself very actively on h3. Paradoxically, the white king seems safer on an open g-file than in the more traditional lines.) 16 ♘a4 ♘b6 17 ♘b2 ♘d7 18 c5 dxc5 19 bxc5 f4 20 c6 fxe3 21 cxb7! exf2+ 22 ♔xf2 ♖b8 23 ♗xa6 ♖f6?! 24 d6? (Nielsen's powerful play has netted him a clear advantage but now he couldn't resist a further combination that turned out to be a false trail. If he had seen one move further he would have settled for 24 ♕a4 and would most likely have won the game.) 24...♖xd6 25 ♕xd6 cxd6 26 ♖c8 ♘c5! 27 ♖xe8+ ♖xe8 28 ♗c4+ ♔f8 29 ♗d5 ♘xb7! (White loses the pride and joy of his position. Perhaps Nielsen had only considered 29...♖b8 when 30 ♖b1! saves the pawn.) 30 ♘d3 (30 ♗xb7 ♖b8 31 ♘c4 ♖xb7 32 ♘xd6 is equal) 30...♘c5 31 ♘xc5 dxc5 32 ♖b1 (White has enough activity to compensate for the missing pawn) 32...♖f6 33 ♔e2 ♔g7 34 a4 c4 35 ♗xc4 ♖e7 36 a5 ♖c7 37 ♔d3 ♗e7 38 ♗d5 ½-½.

b) I have played 10...♘h5 myself a couple of times but I'm not totally convinced by it. After 11 h3 there is:

b1) 11...♗xf3 12 ♕xf3 f5 13 exf5! gxf5 14 ♗e2 ♘f6 15 ♗d3! (better than 15 ♕xf5 ♘xd5) 15...f4 (15...♘c5 16 ♗xf5 e4 17 ♕g3; 15...e4 16 ♕xf5) 16 ♗f5 with some advantage to White, I.Sokolov-Gdasi, Antwerp 1995.

b2) 11...♗d7 is, perhaps, the more natural continuation when Black has been doing fine

after 12 ♖b1 ♘c5 13 b4 ♘a4 14 ♘xa4 ♗xa4. I am a little concerned, however, about the untested 12 a3 as now 12...♘c5 13 b4 ♘a4 can be met by 14 ♘b5!. This was not possible with the rook on b1 because of ...♗xb5 followed by ...♘c3.

So Black probably should meet 12 a3 with 12...f5 when White can play 13 b4 locking the knight on a6 out of the game. Maybe the Black position isn't so bad but its definitely first blood to White.

9 ♗f1

On 9 ♖b1 Black should probably exchange in the centre. After 9...exd4 10 ♘xd4 ♖e8 11 ♗f1 (11 ♗f3 can be met 11...♘g4 and 11 f3 by 11...♘h5) 11...♕b6 12 ♘a4 (12 h3?! ♘c5 is good for Black) 12...♕a5! the game is level according to Dautov who backs up his claim with the following analysis: 13 f3 (13 b4? ♘xb4 14 ♗d2 c5 15 ♘b5 ♘xe4 16 a3 ♗g4!) 13...d5! 14 b4 (14 cxd5 ♘xd5!=; 14 ♗d2 ♕d8 15 cxd5 ♘xd5!=) 14...♕d8! 15 cxd5 ♘xd5 16 ♗xa6 ♘c3! 17 ♘xc3 ♗xd4+ 18 ♗e3 ♗xc3=.

9...♗g4

9...exd4 is Game 27.

10 d5

Black's last move was designed to force this advance and White doesn't really have a choice. Exchanging on e5 would be too feeble and the move he would like to play, 10 ♗e3 runs into 10...♗xf3 11 ♕xf3 ♘g4! 12 ♕xg4 exd4 13 ♗g5 f6 14 ♗d2 f5! 15 ♕h3 dxc3 16 ♗xc3 ♗xc3 17 ♕xc3 fxe4 18 ♖xe4 ♘c5 19 ♖e2 ♕f6 with a level game, Portisch-Cramling, Marbella 1999.

10...cxd5!?

It's not so common for Black to exchange on d5, but as it was the choice of Shirov it is certainly worth taking seriously. Let's take a look at some of the alternatives.

a) 10...♘b4 is the move Black has played the most. We have already seen this idea in the analysis of 8...♕e8 (see above). This time 11 a3 ♗xf3 12 gxf3 is not good for White because he doesn't have the same queenside initiative as in the previous example. Instead he usually plays 11 ♗e2 and after 11...a5 he has played a large number of moves but 12 ♗g5 h6 13 ♗e3 seems to give him the best chance of an edge.

b) Blocking the centre with 10...c5 is Black's second most popular choice. After 11 h3 ♗d7

White, again, often plays 12 ♗g5 h6 13 ♗e3. Black would much prefer not to have played the move ...h7-h6 as he may well feel the weakness of g6 after he has played ...f7-f5.

c) Therefore, recently quite a few Black players have started playing 10...♘e8.

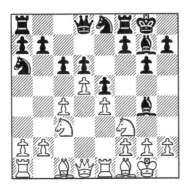

The idea is still to defend on the queenside with ...c6-c5 (this ♘a6 and pawn on c5 combination is one of the toughest set-ups for White to breakdown) and attack on the kingside with ...f7-f5, but with this move order White no longer has the annoying ♗g5. Here are a couple of examples from my own practice:

c1) Gelfand-Gallagher, Biel 2000 went 11 h3 ♗d7 12 dxc6!? (an attempt to punish Black for his move order) 12...bxc6!? (12...♗xc6 13 ♖b1 ♘ac7 14 b4 b6 is a more solid continuation) 13 ♗g5 f6 14 ♗e3 c5! (preventing White from playing c4-c5 and although Black has ceded control of the d5-square he will be hope to manoeuvre a knight of his own into d4) 15 ♘d5 ♘ac7 16 b4 (16 ♘xc7 ♕xc7 17 ♕d5+ ♔h8 18 ♕xa8 ♗c6) 16...♘e6 17 ♖b1 ♔h8 18 ♘d2 (18 ♕c1!?) 18...f5 19 exf5 gxf5 20 f4 cxb4 21 ♖xb4 ♗c6 22 ♘f3 ♕a5 23 ♖b1 ♘8c7! and now best play is 24 ♗d2 ♕c5+ 25 ♗e3 ♕a5 with a draw, but Gelfand preferred to gamble with 24 fxe5 dxe5 25 ♘e7 even though he is close to lost after 25...♗e4! From a sporting point of view his decision was entirely vindicated as he won due to my time trouble errors.

c2) In Akesson-Gallagher, Gausdal 2001 White chose not to attack the bishop and started queenside operations at once. After 11 ♖b1 c5 12 a3 I still felt the need to retreat my bishop with 12...♗d7 before playing ...f7-f5 as I

didn't want to have to give it up for the knight, e.g. 12...f5 13 h3 fxe4 14 hxg4 exf3 15 gxf3 seemed in White's favour to me. White now produced the interesting 13 g3 f5 14 ♗h3 and I agreed to an exchange of light-squared bishops with 14...f4 as I thought I would have good attacking chances against his king. His monarch did eventually perish after a tough and interesting manoeuvring game: 15 ♗xd7 ♕xd7 16 ♔g2 h6 17 h3 g5 18 ♘h2 ♘f6 19 g4 ♖f7 20 ♗d2 ♗f8 21 ♕a4 ♕c8 22 f3 ♗e7 23 ♖h1 ♗d8 24 ♗e1 ♔g7 25 ♗f2 ♗b6 26 ♖hc1 ♘b8 27 ♕d1 ♘bd7 28 ♘a4 ♕c7 29 ♕g1 ♖c8 30 ♘f1? (White needed his rooks to stay in touch with the kingside) 30...h5 31 ♘d2 hxg4 32 hxg4 ♖h8 33 ♕d1 ♘f8! 34 b4 ♕d7 35 bxc5 ♘xg4! 36 fxg4 f3+ 37 ♘xf3 ♕xg4+ 38 ♗g3 ♖h3 0-1

11 cxd5 ♘e8 12 ♗e2

This is directed against 12...f5 which is now unplayable on account of 13 ♘g5. A couple of other examples:

a) 12 h3 ♗d7 13 a4 h6 14 ♘d2 f5 15 ♘c4 ♘c5 16 exf5 gxf5 17 ♗e3 b6 18 b4 ♘b7 19 ♖c1 f4 20 ♗d2 ♘f6 21 ♗e2 ♗f5 22 ♗f3 ♔h8 with excellent chances on the kingside for Black, Haritakis-Khamatgaleev, Ikaros 2002.

b) 12 ♗xa6 bxa6 13 ♕d3 ♗c8 14 ♘d2 f5 15 ♘c4 f4 16 a4 ♕h4 17 ♗d2 g5 18 f3 g4 19 fxg4 ♗xg4 with good play for Black, Candela-Comas Fabrego, Burgos 2003.

White's play can no doubt be improved on in these examples but they do serve to demonstrate typical plans for Black.

12...♗d7 13 a3 ♘ac7 14 ♕b3 b5

Black defends actively on the queenside.

15 ♗g5 f6 16 ♗d2 f5

17 ♖ac1

A new move. In Ftacnik-Shirov, Bundesliga 2001, White played the unconvincing 17 ♘g5 ♕e7 18 ♘e6 and after 18...♘xe6 19 dxe6 ♗xe6 20 ♕xb5 ♘f6 Black's superiority in the centre gave him an edge.

17...♘f6 18 ♘g5 ♔h8 19 ♗d3 ♗h6 20 ♕b4

20 ♘f7+ ♖xf7 21 ♗xh6 fails to 21...♘g4 while 20 ♘e6 ♘xe6 21 ♗xh6 ♘c5 22 ♕d1 ♖f7 is rather unclear.

20...♘g4 21 f3 ♘e6!?

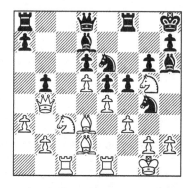

My first reaction was that this must be a misprint, but no it really is a playable move. It's all based on ...♕d8-b6+ and smothered mate ideas. Another interesting possibility is 21...a5 22 ♕xd6 ♖f6 23 fxg4 ♖xd6 24 ♘f7+ ♔g7 25 ♘xd8 ♗xd2 26 ♘b7 ♗xc1! (26...♖b6 27 ♘c5 ♗c8 28 exf5±) 27 ♘xd6 ♗xb2 28 ♘cxb5 ♘xb5 29 ♗xb5 ♗xa3 with equality.

22 fxg4

Or 22 dxe6 ♕b6+ 23 ♗e3! ♘xe3 24 ♔h1 with unclear play.

22...♘xg5 23 ♗xg5 ♕b6+! 24 ♔h1 ♗xg5 25 ♖c2 a5 26 ♕b3 fxg4 27 ♗xb5 ½-½

To be honest, I'm not sure what Black should play on move 10 (or move 9, see next game) as I keep changing myself. You'll have to make your own mind up.

Game 27
Gelfand-Markowski
Polanica Zdroj 1998

---

1 d4 d6 2 ♘f3 ♘f6 3 c4 g6 4 ♘c3 ♗g7 5 e4 0-0 6 ♗e2 ♘a6 7 0-0 e5 8 ♖e1 c6 9 ♗f1 exd4

The reason that 8 ♖e1 is less popular than 8 ♗e3 is because of this move. The most that White can hope for is a faint edge in a rather dry position and it is unlikely that he can even achieve that.

The reason that 9...exd4 is not even more popular amongst Black players is that it is very hard for Black to play for a win in this line.

10 ♘xd4 ♘g4 11 h3

White's choice is limited because of Black's kingside threats. He has tried 11 ♘f3 and 11 ♖e2 but both of these are still well met by 11...♕b6.

11...♕b6

Only Mark Hebden has punted 11...♘xf2 12 ♔xf2 ♕b6 but that was 15 years ago and I haven't seen him do it again.

12 hxg4 ♕xd4

12...♗xd4 is considered inaccurate as after 13 ♗e3 White gets to exchange bishops. Still, it's not that bad for Black.

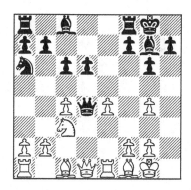

13 ♕f3

White has tried quite a few moves here. Let's have a look at some of them:

a) 13 g5 is played quite often when Black can choose between 13...♘c5 and the endgame after 13...♕xd1 14 ♖xd1 ♗e5 where I see no advantage for White. For example,

a1) 15 ♗e3 ♘c5 16 f3 ♗e6 17 ♖ac1 a5 18 ♖c2 a4 19 ♔f2 f6 20 gxf6 ♖xf6 21 ♗d4 g5 (Hoelzl-Naumann, Austrian Team Ch. 2003) and if anyone is better here it's Black

a2) 15 ♘a4 (White is simply getting out of the way of a possible capture on c3 by Black)

15...♘b4!? 16 a3 (16 f4 ♗g4) 16...♘c2 17 ♖a2 ♘d4 18 b4 b6 19 ♗e3 ½-½ Huzman-Comas Fabrego, Istanbul 2003.

b) 13 ♕e2 ♕e5 14 ♗e3 ♕e7 (or 14...♘c5 15 f3 a5) 15 ♖ad1 ♖e8 16 f3 ♘c5 17 ♕d2 ♗e5 18 ♗f2 ♘e6 19 g3 g5 with a level game, Ostenstad-Trygstad, Fredrikstad 2003.

c) 13 ♗e3 gives Black the choice between 13...♕e5 and 13...♕xd1 14 ♖axd1 ♗xg4 15 f3 ♗e6 16 ♖xd6 ♖fe8 with a roughly level endgame.

13...♕e5

The queen doesn't belong in the middle of the board so she starts to make her way back to her ideal home on e7.

14 g5

14 ♗f4 ♕e7 15 ♕g3 ♗e5 16 g5 f6 is similar and perhaps slightly easier for Black.

14...♕e7 15 ♕g3 ♘c5 16 ♗f4 ♗e5 17 ♖ad1 f6!

Gelfand had aimed for this position as White had already won it several times after poor play from Black. The text seems to be the best.

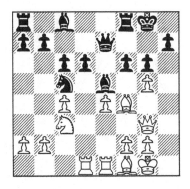

18 gxf6 ♖xf6 19 ♗xe5 ♕xe5 20 b4 ♕xg3?

A serious error although it is not easy to appreciate that without seeing Gelfand's idea. Instead, 20...♘d7! maintains the balance, e.g.

a) 21 ♕xe5 ♘xe5 22 c5 dxc5 23 bxc5 b5.

b) 21 ♕e3 can be met by 21...a5 22 a3 (22 b5 ♘c5) 22...g5 with no problems for Black.

c) 21 c5 ♕xg3 22 fxg3 ♘e5! 23 cxd6 ♗g4 24 ♗e2 ♗xe2 25 ♖xe2 ♖d8 and, as Gelfand says, White may have an extra pawn but the advantage is with Black as he controls the centre.

21 fxg3 ♘d7 22 e5!!

An excellent move that liberates the white

army. Black has a potentially nice position but he is lagging in development and not ready for an open centre. That is why it was so costly to release the blockade of e5, even if it was only supposed to be momentarily.

22...dxe5

Or 22...♘xe5 23 ♘e4 ♖f8 24 ♘xd6 with a clear advantage to White.

23 ♘e4 ♖f7 24 c5 ♔g7 25 ♗c4 ♖e7 26 a4 ♖e8?

26...b6 offered more resistance.

27 ♖f1 ♖e7 28 ♖d2 b5 29 axb5 cxb5 30 ♗d5 1-0

Summary:

1) For those of you who prefer a strategical battle to a theoretical battle then 7...♘a6 is an excellent alternative to the main lines. I know as I have played it a lot myself in the last few years. It was virtually unknown a decade or so ago but has now developed into one of the major systems of the King's Indian.

2) After 8 ♗e3 Black, as long as he played carefully, was doing fine in the older lines with ...h7-h6 (13...♕e7!) but that wasn't enough for some players and new lines with ...f7-f6 have been developed. Black has also started out fine there and whilst I feel pretty confident in the 11...f6 of Game 22 I would say that the jury is still out on the 11...f6 of Game 25.

3) 8 ♖e1 is less popular but slightly more unpleasant for the typical King's Indian player to face. That is because he may be reluctant to enter into the solid equalising lines of Game 27. I am not saying that Black is worse in Game 26, just that it feels like we are playing Black.

CHAPTER SIX

The Classical Variation
White's 7th Move Alternatives

In this chapter we examine White's alternative tries to the extremely natural 7 0-0.

Classical 7 d5

1 d4 ♘f6 2 c4 g6 3 ♘c3 ♗g7 4 e4 d6 5 ♘f3 0-0 6 ♗e2 e5 7 d5

The Petrosian System is the name given to the variation where White blocks the centre and follows up with 8 ♗g5. It is named after one of the all time greats, the 1963-69 World Champion Tigran Petrosian. Vladimir Kramnik also played this variation extensively in his formative years. The wily Armenian, as Petrosian was often called, was famous for his deep, strategic, and often negative play. His philosophy was to stop the opponent's threats before they even thought of them. The reason he played ♗g5 against the King's Indian was to prevent Black

from moving his knight on f6 and playing ...f5. Black can still arrange ...f5 but only by playing some awkward-looking moves or making positional concessions.

Black's two main replies to 7 d5 are 7...a5 and 7...♘bd7 and then after 8 ♗g5 we have entered the main lines of the Petrosian System. I am, however, suggesting that we take two of Petrosian's main characteristics – his wiliness and his prophylactic nature – and use them against his own system. By playing 7...♘a6 Black renders the Petrosian System harmless as he has a relatively simple way to equalise against 8 ♗g5. I am amazed at how many White players are totally ignorant of this line which we cover in Game 28. So if White is going to refrain from 8 ♗g5 what does he play instead? Well, he has several options and these are covered in Games 29 and 30. Still, they are not the most dangerous lines in the King's Indian. This is because with his 7th move White made a slight concession by blocking the centre without getting anything in return (such as a tempo, for example).

Game 28
Golod-Gallagher
Zürich 2003

---

1 d4 ♘f6 2 c4 g6 3 ♘c3 ♗g7 4 e4 d6 5 ♘f3 0-0 6 ♗e2 e5 7 d5 ♘a6!?

I shall not be covering the main line 7...a5 in

this book but for those of you who prefer that it is examined in SOKID. As I mentioned above the text is a relatively unusual move that seems to neutralise the Petrosian System.

8 ♗g5

There are three main alternatives. 8 0-0 and 8 ♘d2 are covered in Game 29 whilst 8 ♗e3 transposes to the Gligoric System (7 ♗e3) and that is covered in Game 30.

8...h6 9 ♗h4

Obviously it doesn't make sense for the bishop to go back to e3 now as White can't meet 9...♘g4 with 10 ♗g5.

9...g5 10 ♗g3 ♘xe4!

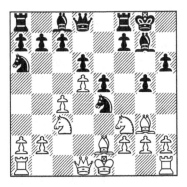

Tactical ideas based on ...♘xe4 followed by ...f5 and ...f4 are quite well known in the King's Indian but they are usually not so good as White often ends up with a powerful blockade of the e4-square. This time it is different as although White may still be able to blockade e4 it is of a more fragile nature.

11 ♘xe4 f5 12 ♘fd2

The first decision White has to make is whether to part with a knight or the bishop on g3. Although the text is the most common I believe it is slightly more accurate to give up the bishop on g3 which can easily become a problem piece for White. Therefore 12 ♘c3 f4 and now:

a) 13 ♘e4 ♗f5 14 ♘fd2 ♘c5! (White is now forced to weaken his position in order to maintain the blockade of e4) 15 f3 fxg3 16 hxg3 g4 17 ♕c2 c6! 18 fxg4 ♗g6 19 ♗d3 cxd5! 20 ♘xc5 e4 21 ♗xe4 dxe4 22 ♘e6 ♕b6 23 ♘xf8 ♖xf8 with a clear advantage for Black, Olsen-Kindermann, Reykjavik 1998.

b) 13 ♘d2! is an improvement for White as his pieces co-ordinate better with knights on c3 and e4 than on d2 and e4. Now I would dearly love to play 13...e4 but on close inspection it doesn't seem adequate. Therefore, 13...♘c5 14 ♘de4 and now I think Black should play 14...♗f5 15 ♗d3 fxg3 (it is also possible to delay this capture, e.g. 15...♘xd3 16 ♕xd3 a6) 16 hxg3 ♘xd3+ 17 ♕xd3 and now I like 17...a6 best. For the time being White has a relatively secure blockade of e4 but his position is somewhat unwieldy as if the blockade is ever broken he will be in trouble. 17...a6 is a semi-waiting move which prepares the possible advance ...b7-b5. What is Black waiting for? Well, he's waiting to see where the white king is going. If White plays 18 0-0-0 then 18...b5 looks good whilst if White plays 18 0-0 then 18...♕e8, intending ...♕g6 looks like a good idea. And if White plays 18 f3, intending to follow up with g3-g4, then Black should play 18...g4! himself. The one thing he should never do is exchange off his light-squared bishop for one of the knights. I consider the position to be dynamically balanced.

12...fxe4 13 ♘xe4 ♗f5 14 ♗d3

Or 14 ♘c3 ♘c5 15 0-0 a5 (I spent a long tome thinking about 15...e4 and it is certainly playable as well) 16 f3 e4 17 fxe4 ♗xe4 18 ♗f2 ♕e7 19 ♗d4 ½-½ Rahman-Gallagher, British Ch. (Edinburgh) 2003. Another easy game with Black against a grandmaster.

14...g4!

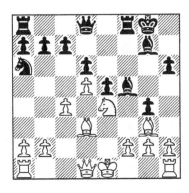

This is the key move as White is going to have to weaken his kingside to save his bishop on g3.

15 0-0 h5 16 f3 ♗xe4! 17 ♗xe4 ♘c5 18 ♕e2

White would prefer to keep his bishop but this means lifting the blockade of e4. After 18 ♗c2 e4! 19 ♗xe4 (19 fxg4 ♖xf1+ 20 ♕xf1 ♕g5!? looks better for Black) 19...♘xe4 20 fxe4 ♗xb2 21 ♖b1 ♖xf1+ 22 ♕xf1 ♗d4+ 23 ♔h1 ♕g5 Black had some advantage in Jacimovic-Maki, Pula 1997.

18...♘xe4

18...h4 19 ♗e1 ♘xe4 20 fxe4? ♖xf1+ 21 ♔xf1 ♕f6+ 22 ♔g1 ♖f8 eventually led to a Black victory in Wildig-Hebden, Nuneaton 1999 but 20 ♕xe4 just transposes to the notes below.

19 ♕xe4

19 fxe4 ♕g5 is good for Black.

19...gxf3 ½-½

Accompanied by a draw offer (early morning game) which my opponent accepted.

I expected the game to continue along the following lines: 20 ♗h4! (20 ♖xf3 ♖xf3 21 ♕xf3 ♕g5 is pleasant for Black) 20...♕e8 21 ♖xf3 ♖xf3 22 gxf3 (22 ♕xf3 e4 23 ♕e2 ♕e5 24 ♖e1 ♖e8 25 b3=) 22...♕f7 23 ♔f2 ♖f8 24 ♖g1 ♕f5 25 ♕xf5 ♖xf5 26 ♔e2 ♔f7 with equality.

19...h4 may look like a tempting alternative but just weakens Black's position. After 20 ♗e1 ♖f4 21 ♕g6!? White is certainly not worse.

To sum up, I like this way of playing against the Petrosian System. White players, even grandmasters, seem to be quite unfamiliar with it and it is very easy for White to end up in a poor position. The only critical variation seems to be line 'b' in the 12th move notes as my

suggested way for Black to play is still untested.

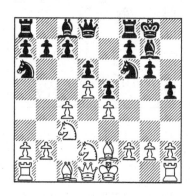

Game 29
Legky-Gallagher
French League 2001

1 d4 ♘f6 2 c4 g6 3 ♘c3 ♗g7 4 e4 d6 5 ♘f3 0-0 6 ♗e2 e5 7 d5 ♘a6 8 0-0

8 ♘d2 has some supporters. I imagine they justify this ugly move along the following lines: OK, I don't like 8 ♗g5 and 8 ♗e3 and I'm not that keen on 8 0-0 as this just transposes into an old and relatively harmless line after 8...♘c5 9 ♕c2 a5 (see main game). So why not overprotect the e-pawn before Black attacks it. Now ♘a6-c5 is out of the question because of the reply b2-b4. That means it won't be so easy for Black to bring his knight on a6 into the game. And if Black follows his most obvious plan of playing for ...f7-f5 with 8...♘e8 then we can exploit the fact that we haven't castled yet by playing 9 h4!.

And what should Black think on seeing such a move: What? ♘d2. Surely that can't be any good with his bishop still on c1. OK, I see what he wants but we don't have to fall in with his plans. In fact I have a few interesting ideas of my own which may highlight the drawbacks of 8 ♘d2.

Firstly 8...♗h6 is quite possible and a lot depends on the assessment of the pawn sacrifice 9 h4 ♘c5 10 h5 ♗xd2+ 11 ♕xd2 ♘fxe4 12 ♘xe4 ♘xe4 and now either 13 ♕h6 or 13 ♕e3.

The move I like the most, however, is 8...h5.

Now there is no need to worry about White

advancing on the kingside (we got there first) and we can play ...♘f6-h7 followed by ...f7-f5. And take a look at the white position, What move do you feel like playing now? ♘d2-f3, perhaps.

Here are a few examples of how play can develop after 8...h5!?:

a) 9 a3 c5 (it's best to stop b2-b4) 10 ♘f3 ♘h7 11 h4 f5 (Black can delay this in favour of 11...♘c7 has Hebden has done in the past) 12 exf5 ♗xf5 13 ♗e3 e4 14 ♘g5 ♘xg5 ½-½ Komarov-Sakaev, St Petersburg 1997.

b) 9 ♘b3 c5 10 ♗g5 ♕e8 11 ♘d2 ♘h7 12 ♗e3 h4 13 ♘f3 ♕e7 14 g3 h3 with a good King's Indian for Black, Lawton-Hebden, Swansea 1995.

c) 9 h3 ♘h7 10 g4 hxg4 11 hxg4 ♗f6! 12 ♘f1 ♗g5 13 ♗e3 ♕f6 14 a3 c5 15 dxc6 bxc6 16 ♕d2 ♘c5 17 ♖d1 ♖d8 18 ♘g3 ♗f4 with an edge for Black, Stojanovic-Arsovic, Belgrade 2002

8...♘c5 9 ♗g5!?

Quite a controversial move as White is willing to give up his important bishop in return for a few tempi on the queenside.

The old, old main line, rarely seen today, runs 9 ♕c2 a5 10 ♗g5 h6 11 ♗e3 when Black has a wide choice of playable moves. It's not easy to suggest one (even for myself) so I'll take a look at a few of the most interesting lines:

a) 11...♘g4 12 ♗xc5 dxc5 13 h3 ♘f6 14 ♘xe5 ♘xd5 15 cxd5 ♗xe5 16 f4 ♗d4+ was played by Fischer and is obviously a very critical variation. However, it is rarely seen as most Black players deem it to be unnecessarily risky. It is already unclear where White should put his

king.

b) 11...♘h5!? 12 g3 ♗h3 13 ♖fe1 b6 (13...f5!? 14 ♘h4 leads to sharp play) 14 ♘d2 ♘f6 (the solid choice, 14...f5 is still sharp) 15 f3 ♘h7 16 ♘d1 ♗d7 17 ♘f2 f5 18 exf5 gxf5 19 f4 ♕f6 with a comfortable game for Black, Piket-Hernandez, FIDE Wch KO, New Delhi 2000

c) 11...b6 (in many lines it's useful to have the knight on c5 properly defended) 12 ♘d2 ♘h7!? (12...♗g4 and 12...♗g4 are more common) and now:

c1) 13 a3?! f5 14 f3 a4! 15 ♗xc5 bxc5 16 ♘xa4 h5! (a typical King's Indian sacrifice: Black has excellent attacking chances on the weakened dark squares around the white king) 17 ♘c3 ♗h6 18 ♖ae1 h4 19 ♘d1 ♘f6 20 ♖f2 ♗d7 21 ♘b1 ♘h5 22 ♘bc3 ♗f4 23 ♗d3 ♗g3! (Nunn relates how the teenage Anand took all of five seconds to choose this course of action) 24 hxg3 hxg3 25 ♖d2 ♕h4 26 ♘e2, Palatnik-Anand, New Delhi 1986. Black has a winning attack and the best way to continue was 26...♔g7 in order to play ...♖h8 and bring the rook into the attack. The moves ...♕h1+ and ...♘f4 are likely to be played at some point as well.

c2) 13 b3 is a better move. White spends a tempo to avoid the positionally undesirable continuation of the previous note. The game Naumkin-Gleizerov, USSR 1986 now continued 13...f5 14 f3 f4 15 ♗f2 g5 16 a3 ♘a6 17 ♕b1 h5 18 b4 g4 19 ♔h1 g3 20 hxg3 fxg3 21 ♗xg3 h4 with good compensation for Black.

9...h6 10 ♗xf6 ♕xf6

I prefer recapturing with the queen as after 10...♗xf6 Black will have little choice but to return the bishop to g7, whilst after the text the queen has the option of dropping back to e7. Which square is better for the queen is unclear, at least to me, as can be seen from the fact that I once played ...♕d8 and the other time ...♕e7.

11 b4 ♘d7 12 ♘d2

I had never faced this line before and then I had to face it twice in a relatively short period of time. The plan I used successfully against Legky I had already found over the board in Kraai-Gallagher, Bundesliga 1999. In that game White played 12 ♖c1 and play continued 12...♕d8 13 ♘d2 h5!? 14 ♘b3 ♗h6 15 ♖c2

♘f6 16 c5 ♘g4! 17 h3 ♘f6 18 ♘a5 ♘e8 19 ♗b5?! ♘g7 20 ♘c4 a6 21 ♗a4 h4 22 ♘e2 ♘h5 23 ♖c3 b5! 24 cxb6 cxb6 25 ♗c6 ♖a7 26 a4 f5 27 exf5 gxf5 28 ♔h1 ♗g7 with a large advantage for Black which I eventually converted.

12...♕e7 13 ♘b3 h5!

Of course Black can also play ...f7-f5 but the text just felt right to me. With his opposite number departed the dark-squared bishop needs to be activated. Control of squares in the white camp such as c1 and d2 may also prove annoying for White.

14 a4 ♗h6 15 a5 ♘f6 16 c5 ♘g4!

The idea is to encourage White to create a weakness by playing h2-h3. That is well worth a couple of tempi.

17 h3

Could Black have ignored the knight? Well, certainly not if he wants to win the game. For example, 17 c6 bxc6 18 dxc6 ♘xh2 19 ♔xh2 ♗f4+ 20 ♔g1 ♕h4 21 g3 ♗xg3 22 fxg3 ♕xg3+ 23 ♔h1 and Black has a draw or may even play on with 23...♕xc3!?

17...♘f6

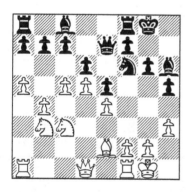

Now I wanted to play ♘h7-g5 and sacrifice something on h3.

18 c6 ♖b8! 19 b5 b6 20 axb6 axb6 21 ♖a3

White has just one target to aim at on the queenside – c7. I had spent ages trying to work out whether he could cause any trouble with ♖a7, followed by ♘c3-a2-b4-a6 but concluded that my kingside attack was too quick for this lengthy manoeuvre. Legky must have reached a similar conclusion and opted for a more defensive rook move.

21...♘h7 22 ♘d2?

That was a nice surprise. White is trying to clear the third rank so that his rook defends the vulnerable h3-square but this was not a good way to go about it.

22...♗xh3!

23 ♘cb1

Legky preferred to take his chances in the middlegame rather than the bad ending after 23 gxh3 ♕g5+ 24 ♔h1 ♕xd2 25 ♕xd2 ♗xd2.

23...♗c8 24 ♕a4

White is hoping to cause trouble with ♕a7.

24...♗f4 25 ♖d1

25 ♕a7 loses to 25...♗g4 26 f3 ♕h4!.

25...♔g7

I feel sure there was a nice point to this move – I just can't remember it. Maybe I was just waiting for White's next move. It certainly didn't help his cause.

26 ♗f1?

He had to try 26 ♘f1 though Black should still be winning.

26...♗g4! 27 ♘f3

27 f3 loses to 27...♕h4 and after 27 ♖e1 Black can, at the very least, play 27...h4. My only worry in this position was that the rook could get trapped on b8 due to the lack of squares for the bishop on the c8-h3 diagonal. Once the move ...h5-h4 has been played then the bishop will just be able to drop back to h5 if attacked.

27...♘g5 28 ♗e2 ♖a8! 29 ♕xa8 ♖xa8 30 ♖xa8 ♘xe4

30...♘xf3+ 31 ♗xf3 ♗xf3 32 gxf3 ♕g5+ 33 ♔f1 h4 is also good but the text is crushing.

31 ♔f1 h4 32 ♖a3 h3 33 g3?! ♗xg3 34 fxg3 ♘xg3+ 35 ♔f2 ♘xe2 0-1

Classical 7 ♗e3 (Gligoric System)

1 d4 ♘f6 2 c4 g6 3 ♘c3 ♗g7 4 e4 d6 5 ♘f3 0-0 6 ♗e2 e5 7 ♗e3

The coverage of the Gligoric System will be light in this book as I am recommending that Black play 7...♘a6. White now usually plays 8 0-0 which takes us into Chapter 5. The only real alternative is 8 d5 and that is covered in Game 30 below. I will just take a quick look at the main 7th move alternatives for Black.

a) 7...♘g4 is probably the most important. It leads to very complex strategical play with positions that are rather difficult to handle for both sides. After 8 ♗g5 f6 there is:

a1) 9 ♗h4 ♘c6 (9...g5 10 ♗g3 ♘h6 is the other main line) 10 d5 ♘e7 11 ♘d2 ♘h6 12 f3 g5 (12...c5 has been played a lot but White seems to have an edge here after 13 dxc6 bxc6 14 b4) 13 ♗f2 f5 14 c5 and now Black usually chooses between 14...♘g6 and 14...g4. The play is sharp but the practical results seem to be slightly in White's favour.

a2) 9 ♗c1 ♘c6 10 0-0 (10 d5!?) f5. Black has played many moves here but the text seems to offer the best chance of a level game. I shall now take a quick look at I.Sokolov-Shirov, FIDE Wch KO, Las Vegas 1999. It should be of interest mainly to those of you who do not wish to meet 7 0-0 ♘c6 8 ♗e3 with the accurate but boring 8...♖e8! (see Chapter 1), preferring instead to mix it up with 8...♘g4 9 ♗g5 f6 10 ♗c1 f5 and a direct transposition here. The game continued 11 ♗g5 (11 d5 ♘e7 12 ♘g5 ♘f6 is thought to be okay for Black: it is similar to material we have already looked at in the

Bayonet Attack chapter) 11...♕e8! (11...♗f6 12 ♗xf6 ♘xf6 13 exf5 ♗xf5 14 d5 ♘e7 15 ♘g5 is a little better for White) 12 dxe5 (12 d5 can be met by 12...♘e7 or 12...♘d8, intending ♘d8-f7) 12...dxe5 13 h3 (13 ♘d5 ♕f7=) ♘f6 14 ♗d3 ♗e6 15 ♖e1 ♕f7 16 c5? (16 ♗xf6 ♗xf6 17 ♘d5=) 16...♘d7 17 ♗b5 ♘d4! 18 ♗xd7 ♗xd7 19 ♘h4 ♗c6 20 ♘g5 ♕f6! (Black threatens to win a piece with ...h7-h6 and there is no good discovered attack with the knight) 21 exf5 gxf5 22 ♘e2 ♖ad8 23 ♘xd4 ♖xd4 24 ♕h5? h6 0-1

b) 7...h6!? was a favourite of John Nunn who raised its profile by using it against top class opposition. The idea is to play ...♘f6-g4 but without allowing ♗g5. The main line runs 8 0-0 ♘g4 9 ♗c1 ♘c6 10 d5 ♘e7 11 ♘e1 f5 12 ♗xg4 fxg4 with a most unusual kingside pawn structure. Black will now play ...g6-g5 and ...♘g6-f4 while White will seek his fortune on the queenside. Most theoretical sources agree that White has slightly the better chances.

c) 7...exd4 is not such a bad move as Black is often able to create counterplay by a quick ...c7-c6 and ...d6-d5. For example, 8 ♘xd4 ♖e8 9 f3 c6 10 ♕d2 (10 ♗f2!?) 10...d5 11 exd5 cxd5 12 0-0 ♘c6 13 c5 ♖xe3!? is the famous exchange sacrifice that first occurred in Karpov-Kasparov, New York 1990 (11th game of the world championship match).

Game 30
Berkes-Jobava
European Team Ch., Plovdiv 2003

---

1 d4 ♘f6 2 c4 g6 3 ♘c3 ♗g7 4 e4 d6 5 ♘f3 0-0 6 ♗e2 e5 7 ♗e3 ♘a6!? 8 d5

Most White players accept the invitation to transpose to Chapter 5 by playing 8 0-0.

8...♘g4

8...♘c5?! 9 ♘d2 would allow White his ideal set-up but 8...♘h5 looks like a plausible alternative. At any rate Black must play actively.

9 ♗g5 f6 10 ♗h4 h5!?

I myself have favoured 10...♘h6 in this position, winning one very nice game against Smirin and losing a rather less nice one against Korchnoi. However, most other grandmasters seem to prefer the text and as they always seem to win with Black in this variation I am beginning to see their point of view.

11 ♘d2 c5

This is a standard defensive reaction in such positions. It will now be much harder for White to make progress on the queenside and there will be occasions when Black can take over the initiative there as well. For example, if White castles queenside then Black may be able to organise the advance ...b7-b5 to open lines against his king. In the most recent game played in this line, however, Black delayed the advance ...c7-c5 for some time. Volkov-Nakamura, FIDE World Ch., Tripoli, 2004 went 11...♗d7 12 h3 ♘h6 13 g4 hxg4 14 hxg4 ♕e7 15 ♘f1 ♘f7 16 ♘e3 ♗h6 17 ♗d3 ♔g7 18 ♕e2 ♖h8 19 0-0-0 c5 20 a3 ♘c7 21 ♔b1 a6 with good play for Black. He went on to win in 65 moves.

12 a3

White, rather half-heartedly I feel, begins to prepare b2-b4.

In Razmyslov-Matamoros, Coria del Rio 2004 he played an over-ambitious pawn sacrifice: 12 h3 ♘h6 13 g4 hxg4 14 hxg4 ♘f7 15 g5?! ♘xg5 16 ♗xg5 fxg5 17 ♘g4 ♘b4 18 ♗e2 (a slightly embarrassing retreat) 18...♖f4 19 a3 ♘a6 20 ♕b3 ♘c7 21 ♖h2 ♖h4 22 ♘f3 ♖xh2 23 ♘xh2 ♕f6 with a clear plus for Black.

12...♕e8

Black prefers to wait for h3 before retreating his knight as 12...♘h6 can be met with 13 f3.

13 h3

On 13 ♘b5 Black just plays 13...♕e7 and follows-up with ...♘a6-c7.

13...♘h6 14 g4

This kingside advance is a favourite amongst White players although it seems to me that the opening of the h-file actually favours Black.

14...hxg4 15 hxg4 ♘f7 16 ♕b3 ♕e7

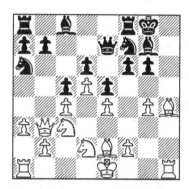

Now Black is ready to play the three key moves, ...♗g7-h6, ...♔g8-g7 and ...♖f8-h8 that ensure he won't have to face any serious threats on the kingside.

We already saw this same manoeuvre above in Volkov-Nakamura.

17 ♘d1 ♗h6 18 ♕h3 ♔g7 19 ♘e3 ♖h8

With his grip on the kingside dark squares Black has at least equality in this position.

20 ♕g2 ♗d7 21 0-0-0 ♘c7 22 ♖dg1

Perhaps White should sacrifice a pawn with 22 g5!? He doesn't get anything concrete in return, just some open lines. A possible continuation could be 22...g5 ♗xg5 23 ♖dg1 ♖ag8 24 ♘f3 ♗xe3+ 25 fxe3 ♔f8 and White has some compensation.

22...♗f4 23 ♔b1 ♘g5 24 ♗xg5 fxg5 25 ♖xh8 ♖xh8 26 ♖h1 ♖xh1+ 27 ♕xh1 ♗xe3 28 fxe3 ♘e8 29 ♘f1 ♘f6 30 ♘h2 ♕d8

Black has a strategically won game but one could have expected some tough resistance from White. Instead he committed suicide and lost in a few moves.

31 ♗f3 ♕h8 32 ♕g1 ♗a4 33 b4 b5 34 ♔b2 bxc4 35 ♔c3 cxb4+ 36 axb4 a5 37 bxa5 ♕b8 0-1

Classical 7 dxe5 (Exchange Variation)

1 d4 ♘f6 2 c4 g6 3 ♘c3 ♗g7 4 e4 d6 5 ♘f3 0-0 6 ♗e2 e5 7 dxe5 dxe5 8 ♕xd8 ♖xd8

I have written many scathing words on this variation in the past. I won't repeat them all here but just say that most of the players who play this variation are playing 'scared chess' and are just looking to draw the game. Make them work for this draw.

After the almost universal choice 9 ♗g5 I am still recommending that Black play the old main line 9...♖e8. In Game 31 we take a look at 10 ♘d5 (I have very little to add to what I wrote in SOKID here) and Game 32 features 10 0-0-0.

Game 31
Salgado-Gallagher
L'Hospitalet 1992

---

1 d4 ♘f6 2 c4 g6 3 ♘c3 ♗g7 4 e4 d6 5 ♘f3 0-0 6 ♗e2 e5 7 dxe5 dxe5 8 ♕xd8 ♖xd8 9 ♗g5

White now threatens to win material with 10 ♘d5.

9 ♘xe5? is just a mistake. After 9...♘xe4! 10 ♘xe4 ♗xe5 Black has the better game after both 11 ♗g5 ♖d4! and 11 0-0 ♘c6. His forces are more effectively placed and the d4-square makes a nice home for any number of Black pieces.

9...♖e8

9...c6 is a more modern line which can lead to initially sharp play but can also fizzle out easily. 9...♖f8 is also a good move but I prefer to stick with the old reliable variation that was played by Bobby Fischer and that I have been recommending for years.

10 ♘d5

10 0-0-0 is the subject of the following game.

10...♘xd5 11 cxd5 c6!

An essential move as Black doesn't want to be left with a weak pawn on an open file.

12 ♗c4

12 d6?! would just leave the pawn weak and isolated deep in the enemy camp. It would be most likely to drop off.

12...cxd5 13 ♗xd5 ♘d7!

13...♘c6 and 13...♘a6 have also been played but against these moves White does have the chance of a nagging edge. Black now threatens to gain the bishop pair by ...♘d7-f6.

14 ♘d2!

The only way to maintain equality. By defending his e-pawn White renders the ...♘f6 idea harmless. A mistake that White plays quite often is 14 ♖c1?!. What could be more natural than to put the rook on an open file? The problem is that after 14...h6 15 ♗e3 (15 ♗h4 g5 16 ♗g3 ♘f6 is also good for Black) 15...♘f6

White would be in trouble if he allowed ...♘xd5. That means he has to go in for 16 ♗b3 ♘xe4 17 ♖c7 ♗e6 18 ♗xe6 ♖xe6 19 ♖xb7 ♖a6 20 a3 ♘d6! when Black has an edge because he has a mobile central pawn majority and White has still not completed his development. This position was reached in Teschner-Fischer, Stockholm 1962. The young Bobby failed to win but other players, including myself, have since registered the full point in this ending.

14...♘c5

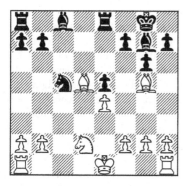

15 ♘c4?!

A slight mistake as it allows Black some tricks based on ...♘xe4, while the knight may also get booted by ...b7-b5 at some point. White is also not out of the woods after 15 0-0 ♗e6 16 ♗xe6 ♖xe6 (16...♘xe6 17 ♗e3 ♘d4 18 ♘b3! should be a draw). Mark Hebden has won this position a couple of times against grandmasters.

The best move is 15 0-0-0! and after 15...♘e6 (not 15...♘d3+ 16 ♔b1 ♘xf2 17 ♖df1! and White wins but 15...♗e6 is again a possibility) 16 ♗e3 ♘f4 17 ♗xf4 exf4 both 18 ♔b1 ♗e6! 19 ♗xe6 ♖xe6 20 f3 f5! and 18 f3 ♗e6 19 ♘b3 ♗xd5 20 ♖xd5 f5! lead to equality. Note how in both cases Black plays ...f7-f5 to activate his rooks.

15...♗f8

This keeps the knight out of d6 and also transfers the bishop to a more active post. There is not much life on the long diagonal.

16 0-0-0

On the last move castling queenside was best. Now it is rather risky.

Alternatively, the position after 16 0-0 ♗e6 17 ♗xe6 ♖xe6! may appear dead drawn at first sight but a closer inspection will reveal a sizeable initiative for Black here. His rooks are more active, White's bishop is offside on g5 and the knight on c4 will soon be hit by ...b5. Acebal-Gallagher, Candas 1992 continued 18 f3 b5 19 ♘e3 h6 20 ♗h4 ♘d3 21 ♘d5 ♖c8 22 b3 ♖c2 23 ♖fd1 ♘b4! 24 ♘xb4 ♗xb4 25 ♗f2 a6! 26 a3 ♗d2! (White is totally paralysed and can only watch while Black calmly improves his position by bringing the king to the centre and playing ...f5) 27 ♗c5 a5 28 ♔f1 ♖c6 29 b4 a4 30 ♖ab1 ♔g7 31 ♖a1 f5 32 ♔g1 ♔f6 33 ♖f1 ♔e6 34 ♖f2? (this loses material but passive defence would also have lost) 34...♗6xc5! 35 exf5+ gxf5 36 ♖xd2 ♖xd2 37 bxc5 ♖c2 0-1.

16...♗e6 17 ♔b1 ♖ac8

17...♘xe4 18 ♗xe4 ♗xc4 19 ♗xb7 ♖ab8 is fine for Black but I wanted more. I saw a sneaky way to improve this line.

18 ♗e3?

Thank you very much. White falls for the trap. He should have played 18 ♖he1 when 18...♗xd5 19 exd5 should be slightly better for Black as White's d-pawn is more likely to turn out weak than strong.

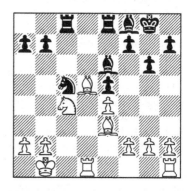

18...♘xe4! 19 ♗xe4 ♖xc4 20 ♗xb7 ♖b8 21 ♗d5 ♗f5+ 22 ♔a1 ♖c2

Now White reached for his bishop to bring it to b3 when he suddenly spotted my trick: 23 ♗b3 ♖xb3! 24 axb3 ♖c6! and there is no way to stop ...♖a6 mate. The only chance to resist was 23 ♖b1 (although Black wins after 23...♗c5 24 ♗xc5 ♖xc5 25 ♖bd1 ♖c2) but White just picked up his other bishop and played...

23 ♗xa7? ♖bxb2 24 ♗e3 ♗b4 25 g4 ♗c3! 0-1

Now that's what I like to do to people who exchange queens in the King's Indian.

Game 32
O.Moor-Ekstroem
Zürich 2002

---

1 d4 ♘f6 2 c4 g6 3 ♘c3 ♗g7 4 e4 d6 5 ♗e2 0-0 6 ♘f3 e5 7 dxe5 dxe5 8 ♕xd8 ♖xd8 9 ♗g5 ♖e8 10 0-0-0

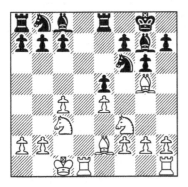

This is played considerably less often than the 10 ♘d5 of the previous game although it is not inferior. It is just equally harmless. It usually leads to a lengthy manoeuvring game.

10...h6

Black can also play 10...♘a6 here when:

a) 11 ♘xe5 has usually been met by 11...♘c5 with a roughly level game after 12 ♗xf6! ♗xf6 13 f4 c6 14 b4 ♗xe5 15 fxe5 ♘d7 16 e6 ♖xe6 17 ♗g4 ♖e7 18 b5 ♔g7, Haik-Spassky, French Ch. 1991. However, Uhlmann, a lifelong devotee of this line recently played 11...♘xe5!? 12 ♖d8+ ♖e8 (12...♘e8 13 f4 ♖e6 14 ♗g4 is supposed to be good for White although I wouldn't bet the mortgage on this verdict in view of 14...♖b8!) 13 ♗xf6 ♖xd8 14 ♗xd8 ♗xc3 15 bxc3 ♗h3 16 ♖d1 ♗xg2 and he went on to win this rather unbalanced endgame in Wronn-Uhlmann, Dresden 2002. Food for thought.

b) If White doesn't take on e5 then we should see similar play to the main game. A recent example is 11 ♘d2 c6 12 ♘b3 ♘c7 13

f3 ♘e6 14 ♗e3 ♗f8 15 a3 b6 16 ♖d2 ♗a6 17 ♔b1 ½-½ Akobian-Yermolinsky, Agoura Hills 2004.

11 ♗e3

White can also play 11 ♗h4 but it doesn't really change the character of the game.

11...c6

There is no need for Black to complicate life with 11...♘g4 12 ♘d5 ♘a6 13 c5. The text emphasises that Black has control over his d5-square whilst there is a big hole on White's d4-square. This can turn out to be an important positional advantage.

12 h3

I don't believe that Black should play ...♘f6-g4 even if given the chance. For example, the position after 12 ♘e1 ♘g4 13 ♗xg4 ♗xg4 can, no doubt, be assessed as level but Black has given White the chance to rid himself of what usually turns out to be the worse minor piece.

After 12 ♘e1 the game Ludden-Nijboer, Amsterdam 1997 went instead 12...♗e6 13 ♘c2 ♗f8 14 f3 a6!? 15 ♖d2 b5 16 b3 ♘bd7 17 ♖hd1 ♖ec8 with a slightly better position for Black. White has no entry squares for his rooks on the d-file and Black eventually took over the initiative on the queenside. Normally in such positions Black plays with ...a7-a5 in order to secure the c5-square but Nijboer's plan looks more dynamic.

12...♗f8

I shall repeat my comment from the previous game – there is not much life on the long diagonal.

13 ♘d2 ♗e6 14 g4 ♘bd7 15 f3 a6!?

The player conducting the black pieces in

this game is an experienced international master but a newcomer to our favourite opening. His King's Indian career took off after he borrowed a copy of SOKID from me during the last Olympiad and then didn't want to give it back at the end (this may even have been his debut game). Note how he sticks religiously to the Nijboer plan that was mentioned in that book.

16 ♘b3 ♖ec8 17 h4 b5 18 ♔b1 h5 19 g5 ♘e8

I suppose it is easy to say with hindsight but White, by advancing his kingside pawns for no particular reason, has just laid the seeds of his own defeat. The weakness of the pawn on h4 will cost him the game.

20 ♗f1 ♘d6 21 ♘a5 ♖ab8 22 ♗a7 ♖a8 23 ♗g1 ♖ab8 24 ♗a7 ♖a8 25 ♗g1 ♘xc4!

Ekström had obviously also taken on board the following advice given in SOKID, 'On no account should the wimps who play this variation be given a draw until every last possibility has been exhausted. Perhaps they will achieve their objective, if they play extremely well, but they should at least be made to suffer.'

26 ♘xc4 bxc4 27 ♘a4 ♖ab8 28 ♗h3 ♗xh3 29 ♖xh3 ♖c7 30 ♖h2 ♗e7!

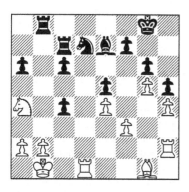

Better than 30...♖b4 31 ♖hd2!. Black is now ready to walk his king back to the centre and the f8-square becomes available for the knight.

31 ♖hd2 ♖bb7 32 ♗f2

Now if White tries 32 ♖c2 ♖b4 33 ♖cd2 Black can play on with 33...♘f8!.

32...♔f8 33 ♗e1!

Covering the b4-square so that White can meet 33...♕e8 with 34 ♖c2.

33...♘c5 34 ♘xc5

White can also play 34 ♖d8+ ♗xd8 35 ♘xc5 ♔e8 36 ♘xb7 ♖xb7 37 ♖d1 although it is not a cast iron draw after 37...♖d7 38 ♖xc4 ♖d1+ 39 ♖c1 ♖xc1+ 40 ♔xc1 f6!.

34...♗xc5 35 ♖d8+?!

35 ♗g3! looks better when 35...♗e7 (35...♗d4 36 ♖xd4) 36 ♖c1 looks close to equality.

35...♔e7 36 ♗c3 ♖d7! 37 ♖1xd7+ ♖xd7 38 ♖c8

The point is of course that after 38 ♖xd7+ ♔xd7 39 ♗xe5 ♗f2 the pawn on h4 drops. Now the endgame is very difficult for White. The remaining moves were:

38...♔d6 39 ♗e1 ♗d4 40 ♔c2 ♖b7 41 b3 a5 42 ♖d8+ ♔e7 43 ♖c8 c5 44 ♖a8 cxb3+ 45 axb3 c4 46 bxc4 ♖b2+ 47 ♔d1 ♖b3 48 ♗xa5 ♖xf3 49 ♗b4+ ♔d7 50 c5 ♖b3 51 ♖a7+ ♔c6 52 ♗e1 ♖f3 53 ♔e2 ♖f4 54 ♗g3 ♖xe4+ 55 ♔f3 ♖g4 56 ♖e7 ♗xc5 0-1

Summary:

1) 7...♘a6 is an excellent move against someone hoping to play the Petrosian System. In my experience very few White players know anything about this slightly unusual move and even if they do it still looks like a comfortable game for Black.

2) The Gligoric System (7 ♗e3) can be one of the toughest lines for Black to face. I suggest that we sidestep this line by playing 7...♘a6 (that move again) after which White has nothing better than 8 0-0 and a transposition into Chapter 5.

3) I used to face the Exchange Variation all the time but ever since I started to slag it off in public people have stopped playing it against me. The endgame is, of course, just equal but make sure you play it on till the very end as the sort of person who plays this variation is liable to crack at some point. They are, with some exceptions of course, psychologically weak.

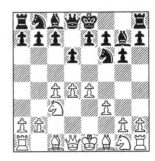

CHAPTER SEVEN

The Sämisch

1 d4 ♘f6 2 c4 g6 3 ♘c3 ♗g7 4 e4 d6 5 f3 0-0

Our coverage of the Sämisch, a variation named after the German grandmaster Fritz Sämisch, starts after the moves 1 d4 ♘f6 2 c4 g6 3 ♘c3 ♗g7 4 e4 d6 5 f3 0-0 although it is the move 5 f3 which characterises the variation. What are the ideas behind this non-developing move?

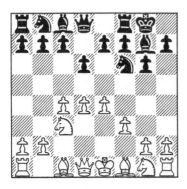

1) It defends e4 so creates a secure and stable centre.

2) With his centre so stable White can start an attack on the kingside. ♗e3, ♕d2, ♗h6 as well as g2-g4 and h2-h4 are typical moves when White wishes to carry out this plan. On other occasions White may attack on the queenside. The Sämisch is a flexible variation which does not commit White to any particular course of action. In fact, in the line that I am going to

recommend for Black, 6...c5, White will often look to break through in the centre.

3) The move f3 secures the square e3 for White's bishop. It can now take up residence there without having to worry about ...♘g4.

The move f3 also has certain drawbacks, the main one being that the price for this strong centre is clumsy kingside development. There is also some potential for trouble on the dark squares that were weakened by f3.

How does Black combat this popular variation? Well there are three main methods.

1) He can strike in the centre in Benoni fashion with c5

2) He can strike in the centre in traditional King's Indian fashion with 6...e5

3) He can delay his central strike in favour of queenside play. The most common way to do this is the Panno variation with 6...♘c6.

I covered all these methods in SOKID but in this book I have decided to base the repertoire around Plan 1, striking in the centre with c5. This also happens to be Black's most popular choice as it gives him the best chance of exploiting the weakened dark squares in the white camp.

Recent Developments in the Sämisch

In the diagram position White usually chooses between the moves 6 ♗e3, 6 ♗g5 and 6 ♘ge2. The fact that he even thinks about his 6th move is a relatively new phenomenon. In the past he always used to play 6 ♗e3 because this was thought to prevent Black from playing 6...c5. True, Black can still play the move but it loses a pawn and an impressive-looking white performance from Karpov in the mid 1970's had convinced everyone that the sacrifice was unsound. The general feeling was that c5 needed further preparation and that Black had to prepare the advance with either 6...b6 or 6...②bd7. But both of these moves have their drawbacks (b6 wastes a tempo and d7 is not always the best square for the knight in these lines and it also allows White to play ②h3-f2) and they never really caught on. So until the early 1990's Black generally met 6 ♗e3 with either 6...e5 or 6...②c6. But there then occurred a revolution that changed the whole landscape of the Sämisch. Certain Black players started playing 6...c5 again and it became clear that the lines which were supposed to cause serious problems for Black were actually quite harmless. A theoretical debate on the merits of the pawn sacrifice raged for a number of years but Black eventually emerged triumphant (i.e. he proved equality). White players simply stopped accepting the pawn sacrifice. Most of them gave up the Sämisch and played another variation but others decided to try their luck in the Benoni positions that arise when White meets ...c5 with d5. Results here were also mixed and then White players began to realise that e3 might not be the ideal square for their bishop in these variations. And why were they still playing 6 ♗e3 anyway? The main reason for the move, to stop c5, was clearly redundant. So many White players switched to 6 ♗g5 as they considered the position after 6...c5 7 d5 to be a slight improvement on 6 ♗e3 c5 7 d5, whilst others preferred 6 ②ge2 keeping all the options open for the bishop. Nowadays the three moves (6 ♗e3, 6 ♗g5 and 6 ②ge2) are regularly seen in international chess. I am suggesting that Black meets them all with 6...c5 and the Benoni positions that arise from each are of course quite similar (and there are even quite a few transpositions from one line to another). I shall cover each variation in turn although the lion's body of theory is still concentrated on 6 ♗e3. The players who accept the pawn sacrifice may be few and far between today but it is still essential to have a thorough understanding of why

you're opening repertoire involves immediate transposition into an endgame a pawn down. Otherwise things could possibly get rather embarrassing.

6 ♗e3

Gambit Accepted

1 d4 ②f6 2 c4 g6 3 ②c3 ♗g7 4 e4 d6 5 f3 0-0 6 ♗e3 c5!

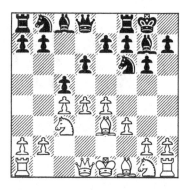

I have already explained much about this move above but I shall just stress that this is the most positionally desirable way for Black to combat the Sämisch and it was only because it lost a pawn that it took so long to become popular. Once it became clear that the endgames a pawn down were fine for Black King's Indian players flocked to this variation in their droves after years of suffering in the other variations of the Sämisch.

7 dxc5 dxc5 8 ♕xd8

Others:

a) For a while White tried to make the line 8 e5 ②fd7 9 f4 work but this has virtually disappeared from practice now. It is essential that Black immediately challenges White's grip in the centre. This is done by 9...f6 and after 10 exf6 he should offer the c-pawn again with 10...②xf6! and after 11 ♕xd8 ♖xd8 12 ♗xc5 play 12...♗f5!. The most important factor in the position is that White, having played c4 and f4, has no pawn control over the important central squares e4 and d4. This was borne out quite splendidly by the continuation of Campos Moreno-Mortensen, European Club Championship 1991: 13 ②f3 ②e4! (the point of ...♗f5 is revealed; the knights are removed from the long diagonal to increase the scope of Black's bishop on g7) 14 ♘xe4 ♗xe4 15 ♗a3 ♘c6 16 ♗e2 ♘d4 17 ♘xd4 ♗xd4 when Black's bishops simply radiate power. He should have won this ending but White managed to escape with a draw.

b) A few players have taken the c-pawn without exchanging queens. But this is rather risky, for example 8 ♗xc5 ♘c6 and now the following are possible:

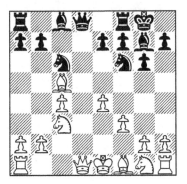

b1) 9 ♗e3 ♘d7! 10 ♖c1 (Dlugy was later successful with 10 ♘ge2 ♘de5 11 ♘f4 ♘a5!? 12 ♕a4 but after 12...♗d7 13 ♕b4 ♖c8 Black has good compensation) 11 ♘h3 ♖d8 (the drawback of retaining the queens can be seen clearly here; whilst the black queen is aggressively posted on a5, White's is struggling to escape the black rook's line of fire) 12 ♘f2 (best, according to Burgess, is 12 ♘f4 with an unclear game) 12...♘c5 13 ♗d2 ♗xc3! 14 bxc3 ♗e6 15 ♕c2 ♘e5 16 ♗f4 ♘xc4 17 ♗e2 g5! 18 ♗xg5 ♘d3+ 19 ♗xd3 ♕xg5 and Black has a winning position, Dlugy-Gelfand, Baleares 1989.

b2) 9 ♘ge2 ♕a5 10 ♗e3 ♖d8 11 ♕c1 ♘h5 12 ♔f2 f5 13 exf5 ♘b4 14 ♘g3, Graf-Zulfugarli, Dubai 2003, and now in this position I like the straightforward continuation 14...♘xg3 15 hxg3 ♗xf5 best with good play for the pawn.

b3) The inventive grandmaster Jacob Murey has tried to solve the problem of Black's active queen on a5 by getting their first with 9 ♕a4!?. However, the position after 9...♘d7 10 ♗f2 ♗xc3+!? 11 bxc3 ♕a5 12 ♕xa5 ♘xa5 13 0-0-0

♘e5 looks at least equal for Black.
8...♖xd8 9 ♗xc5 ♘c6

Don't worry if you are rather confused by the fact that Black has lost a pawn and allowed the queens to be exchanged. It took the cream of world chess about 50 years to understand this position. If you are unfamiliar with this position feel free to be a little sceptical. I suspect that the more you look at the variation the more it will grow on you.

Anyway, here is an attempt to define exactly what compensation Black has for the pawn? Well, firstly, the long diagonal has been opened and the King's Indian bishop has a very bright future. Secondly, Black has a decent lead in development. He has four pieces in play to two of White's. Furthermore, the presence of a pawn on f3 seriously hinders the development of White's kingside which will, at best, be laborious. Thirdly, White has a big hole on d4 as well as several other squares on the queenside which Black's knights will be eager to occupy. A fourth factor is that the white king can easily find itself exposed to enemy fire. All these points put together would be worth far more than a pawn if it wasn't for the fact that White has one big trump of his own – the possibility to play ♘d5.

We shall now examine the main lines through a couple of recent games (recent by the standards of this variation anyway). Game 33 features 10 ♗a3 as well as a few other 10th move possibilities whilst in Game 34 we shall see White playing the immediate 10 ♘d5, the move which was once thought to be the refutation of 6...c5.

Game 33
Fritz 6-Har Zvi
Israeli Team Ch. 2000

My apologies for presenting the game of a computer but with so few humans willing to accept the pawn sacrifice these days this was the most thematic recent game I could find. What is incredible is that Israeli league teams are allowed to have a computer in their side. I hope that they are soon banned.

1 d4 ♞f6 2 c4 g6 3 ♞c3 ♝g7 4 e4 d6 5 f3 0-0 6 ♝e3 c5 7 dxc5 dxc5 8 ♛xd8 ♜xd8 9 ♝xc5 ♞c6 10 ♝a3

What is the point of this bishop move? Well, one of Black's main ideas is to play ...♞d7. The knight is not doing very much on f6 so it often retreats to d7 in search of a new home (c5 or e5 for example). In doing so it also gets out of the way of the bishop on g7. ♝a3, therefore can be considered a prophylactic retreat so that the bishop on c5 will no longer be attacked if Black plays ...♞d7. White chose the a3-square in order to protect the pawn on b2. He is still planning to play ♞d5.

Let's have a quick look at some of the lesser played alternatives.

a) 10 ♜d1 was quite popular at one point but after the hammering it took in Razuvaev-Shirov, Bundesliga 1992 it more or less disappeared. Play continued 10...♜xd1+ 11 ♞xd1 (11 ♔xd1 might be an improvement though Black is at least equal after 11...♞d7 12 ♝a3 ♝xc3 13 bxc3 ♞de5) 11...♞d7! 12 ♝a3 a5! (preparing

...♞b4; this idea is going to become familiar to you) 13 ♞e3 (White did manage to survive a more recent game after 13 ♞e2 ♞b4 14 ♝xb4 axb4 15 ♞c1 but it was hardly a good advertisement for the first player) 13...♞b4 14 ♞h3 ♞c5 (I don't see how White can hold his queenside together) 15 ♞f2 e6 16 ♝e2 b6 17 ♜fd1 ♞xa2 18 ♞c2 ♝a6 19 ♝xc5 bxc5 20 ♞a3 ♞c1! 21 ♞b5 ♜b8 22 ♝f1 a4 23 ♔d2 ♞b3+ 24 ♔c2 ♜d8 25 ♞bc3 ♜d2+ 26 ♔b1 ♞a5 27 g3 a3 28 bxa3 ♝xc4 29 f4 ♝b3 0-1

b) 10 ♞ge2 ♞d7 and now White has a choice of bishop moves:

b1) 11 ♝a3 ♞de5 12 ♞f4 e6 13 ♜d1 ♜xd1+ 14 ♞xd1 a5!, intending ...♞b4, gave Black good play in Murey-Degraeve, Cappelle la Grande 1993.

b2) 11 ♝e3 ♞de5 12 ♞f4 ♞b4 13 ♔f2 (13 ♜d1 fails to the nice variation 13...♞xf3+! 14 gxf3 ♝xc3+ 15 bxc3 ♞c2+ 16 ♔e2 ♜xd1 17 ♔xd1 ♞xe3+ with a clear advantage for Black) 13...♝e6! 14 ♞cd5 (14 ♞xe6 fxe6 is good for Black) 14...♝xd5 15 ♞xd5 (15 cxd5 ♜dc8) 15...♞c2 16 ♜c1 ♞xe3 17 ♔xe3 ♝h6+ 18 f4 e6 19 ♞c3 g5! 20 g3 ♞g6!, Gunawan-Gelfand, Minsk 1986 and Black wins the pawn on f4 as 21 f5 g4+ picks up the rook on c1 and 21 ♞e2 allows 21...gxf4 22 gxf4 e5.

10...a5!

Black has a much quieter system where he plays moves such as 10...b6 and ...♝b7 and relies on long-term pressure. The text takes the fight to White at once by introducing the possibility of ...♞b4.

11 ♜d1

White almost always plays this move. 11 ♞d5 ♞xd5 12 cxd5 ♞b4 13 0-0-0 e6! was fine for Black in the game Beliavsky-Nunn, Amsterdam 1990.

11...♝e6

This is better than exchanging on d1 as that would only help the white king to a better home on the queenside, e.g. 11...♜xd1+ 12 ♔xd1 ♞b4 13 ♞ge2 b6 14 ♞c1 e6 15 ♞a4 ♞d7 16 b3 ♝a6? (after 16...♝b7 the situation would have been far from clear as 17 ♝b2 could then have been met by 17...♞e5! 18 ♞xb6 ♜d8+ 19 ♔e2 ♝h6!) 17 ♝b2! with a clear advantage for White, Graf-Nunn, Manila 1992.

12 ♞d5 ♞b4!

This excellent discovery of Shirov was basically the death knell of White accepting the gambit in top class chess. That doesn't mean that Black is better after ...♘b4, just that White has no hope of obtaining an advantage. When that happens the theoreticians move away en masse in search of fresh pastures.

In earlier games Black had played 12...♗xd5 13 cxd5 ♘b4 but 14 ♗b5! ♘c2+ 15 ♔f2 ♘xa3 16 bxa3 e6 17 d6 e5 18 ♘e2 ♗f8 19 d7 ♗xa3 20 g4! was shown to be good for White in the game Kramnik-Nunn, Manila Olympiad. 1992.

The logic behind 12...♘b4 is not difficult to understand. Black has a massive lead in development so he seeks to complicate the game before White can consolidate. There is also the little matter of ...♘c2+ on the cards, which will deprive White of his dark-squared bishop and ruin his pawn structure.

13 ♘xe7+

White accepts the challenge. 13 ♗d3 is also possible when 13...♗xd5 14 cxd5 ♘xd3+ 15 ♖xd3 e6 leaves Black with full compensation for the pawn. If White plays d6 (with or without ♗e7) Black will round up the pawn while White is trying to get his kingside out.

Lines that White should definitely avoid are 13 ♘xb4 ♖xd1+ 14 ♔xd1 axb4 15 ♗xb4 ♖xa2 and 13 ♗xb4?! axb4 14 ♘xb4 ♘d7! 15 ♖d2 ♘c5 as in both cases his position is on the verge of collapsing.

13...♔h8 14 ♖xd8+

White can also keep rooks on the board and play 14 ♘d5. After 14...♘c2+ 15 ♔f2 ♘xa3 16 bxa3 b5! (the standard idea to break White's grip on d5) there is:

a) 17 ♘h3 (17 cxb5 ♘xd5 18 exd5 ♗xd5 must be good for Black) 17...♖ac8 18 ♗e2 bxc4 19 ♘hf4 ♘xd5 20 ♘xd5 ♗xd5 21 ♖xd5 ♖xd5 22 exd5 ♗d4+ 23 ♔g3 c3 with a clear advantage to Black, Bigler-Har Zvi, Biel 1993.

b) 17 a4!? is an interesting novelty from Rowson or, more likely, from his computer programme. I almost played this move myself a few years ago after Fritz kept telling me it was good for White but in the end I didn't really believe it promised anything. At any rate it is certainly an improvement on the above variation. The point of 17 a4 is to try and force Black to capture on c4 before he would like to. Is White better after 17...bxc4 18 ♗xc4 ♖ac8 19 ♗b3 ♗xd5 20 exd5 ♗f8? I'm not sure he is but in the game Rowson-Kotronias, Hastings 2003/04 Black preferred 17...bxa4 which does at least keep open the option of winning the game. After the further moves 18 ♘e2 ♖ab8 19 ♘c1 ♖b2+ 20 ♗e2 ♖c8 21 ♘e7 ♖e8 22 ♘d5 ♖c8 23 ♘e7 Rowson suddenly decided to take a draw by repetition. He could have played on with something like 23 ♔e3 but it wouldn't be risk free.

14...♖xd8 15 ♘d5

White is two pawns up but miles behind in development. He will now try and complete his development under the cover of his one good piece, the knight on d5. If Black takes the knight then White will recapture cxd5 and obtain a strong passed pawn. The centre would still be blocked so White should have enough time to get his pieces out before anything serious can happen to him. Black has another plan. He is going to undermine the defenders of this knight so that it won't be able to maintain its dominant position in the centre.

By the way, the position after 15 ♗xb4 axb4 16 ♘d5 ♖a8 17 ♘xb4 ♘d7! is promising for Black despite his three-pawn deficit!

15...♘c2+!

Black starts with the obvious move. Once he takes on a3 White will only be able to claim, at most, a one and a half pawn advantage.

16 ♔f2

16 ♔d2 was the choice in the prototype game, Kramnik-Shirov, Bundesliga 1992. After 16...♘xa3 17 bxa3 b5! (the star undermining move) 18 ♘h3 a draw was agreed in view of the variation 18...bxc4 19 ♗xc4 ♘xd5 20 exd5 ♗xd5 21 ♗xd5 ♖xd5+. I would be tempted to continue a little with Black as his strong bishop looks more important than the useless extra a-pawn.

16...♘xa3 17 bxa3 b5!

Again this undermining move. White's control of d5 is soon to be history. Kramnik has also suggested the more ambitious 17...♘d7 if Black is playing for a win. The idea is to take control of the dark squares.

18 ♘h3 ♖c8

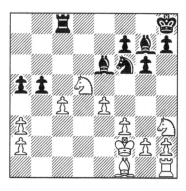

18...bxc4 19 ♗xc4 ♖c8 20 ♗b3 a4! is also good enough for equality.

The move played by Har Zvi, 18...♖c8, was analysed by Shirov in the notes to his game with Kramnik. He now gave the variation 19 ♘hf4 bxc4 20 ♘xe6 fxe6 21 ♘b6 ♘xe4+! 22 ♔e3 ♖c6 23 ♔xe4 ♖xb6 24 ♗xc4 as level. At first I was not so sure as White's pieces look more active. However Black has a strong continuation 24...♖c6 25 ♗b3 a4! when White can't

take the pawn and so must retreat his bishop to a passive square. White could have played 25 ♖c1 but then his bishop would be pinned and after an exchange of rooks (all White can play for now) the game would be completely drawn.

The computer program playing White is not interested in such a variation. Despite the advances made in computer play they still tend to be very materialistic. It was too much for Fritz to resist the chance to go three pawns up in an ending.

19 ♘xf6? ♗xf6 20 cxb5 ♖c2+! 21 ♔e3 ♖xa2

White's problem is that once a3 drops Black's a-pawn will be tremendously strong as it receives great support from the bishops. White's extra pawn on the kingside is virtually irrelevant in such a position.

22 f4 ♗d8!

Excellent chess. From b6 the bishop will firmly blockade White's passed pawn and also menace the white king.

23 ♗d3 ♗b6+ 24 ♔f3 ♖xa3 25 ♖d1 a4!

As the saying goes, passed pawns have to be pushed.

26 ♘f2?! ♖b3! 27 ♖b1 a3 28 ♖xb3 ♗xb3 29 ♗b1 a2 30 ♗xa2 ♗xa2

The rest of the game is a simple technical exercise for the grandmaster playing Black. A knight and two pawns are rarely a match for two bishops and certainly not here.

31 ♘g4 ♔g7 32 ♘e3 ♔f6 33 g4 ♔e6 34 g5 ♗xe3 35 ♔xe3 ♗c4 36 b6 ♗a6 37 ♔d4 ♗b7 38 ♔e3 ♔d6 39 ♔d4 ♔c6 40 h3 ♔xb6 41 h4 ♔c7 42 ♔e5 ♔d7 43 ♔d4 ♔d6 44 ♔d3 ♔c5 0-1

Game 34
Graf-Guseinov
Dubai 2003

1 d4 ♘f6 2 c4 g6 3 ♘c3 ♗g7 4 e4 d6 5 f3 0-0 6 ♗e3 c5 7 dxc5 dxc5 8 ♕xd8 ♖xd8 9 ♗xc5 ♘c6 10 ♘d5 ♘d7!

It was the discovery of this possibility that alerted Black to the fact that 6...c5 might be a good way to meet the Sämisch. After the game Karpov-Barle, Ljubljana-Portoroz 1975, which went 10...♘xd5 11 cxd5 ♗xb2 12 ♖b1 ♗c3+ 13 ♔f2 with advantage to White, the general consensus was that 6...c5 was a dubious pawn sacrifice. During the next ten years only a few die-hards tried it but after the discovery of 10...♘d7! just about everyone jumped on board.

11 ♗xe7

White gives up his important bishop, in the hope that his knight will prove to be dominant on d5.

After 11 ♘xe7+?! it is doubtful whether White can even maintain the balance, e.g. 11...♘xe7 12 ♗xe7 ♗xb2! 13 ♖b1 (the position after 13 ♗xd8 ♗xa1 is very promising for Black as he is able to co-ordinate his forces quicker than White. For example, 14 ♘h3 ♗c3+ 15 ♔d1 ♗e5 16 ♘f2 ♘b6 17 ♘d3 ♗d4 18 ♘c1 ♘a4 19 ♗a5 ♗e6 20 ♘b3 ♗e5 21 ♘d2 b6 22 ♗b4 a5 23 ♗a3 ♘c3+ 24 ♔c2 ♘xa2 and Black was well on top in James-Wells, Irish Open 1993) 13...♗c3+ and now possible are:

a) 14 ♔d1 ♖e8 15 ♔c2 ♗g7 16 ♗d6 ♘e5! 17 g3? ♗d7! 18 ♖xb7 ♗c6 19 ♖b4 a5! (by offering the b-pawn Black gains time to start a dangerous attack: note how he steered clear of 19...♘xf3? 20 ♘xf3 ♗xe4+ 21 ♗d3 ♗xf3 which wins his two pawns back but also solves the problem of White's undeveloped kingside for him) 20 ♖b6 ♖ed8 21 c5 (after 21 ♗xe5 ♗a4+! 22 ♔b2 ♗xe5+ 23 ♔a3 ♗c2 the white king is in a mating net) 21...♗a4+ 22 ♔b1 ♘d7! 23 ♖b5 and now instead of 23...♘xc5?! (which also won) Black should have just played 23...♗xb5 24 ♗xb5 ♘xc5! 25 ♗xc5 ♖ac8 when White can't move his bishop from c5 on pain of checkmate.

b) It is not an improvement for the king to head to the kingside as after 14 ♔f2 ♗d4+ 15 ♔g3 (15 ♔e1 ♖e8) 15...♖e8 16 ♗g5 ♘f6! it comes under fierce attack. Gil-Howell, Gausdal 1986 didn't last long: 17 ♘h3 ♘h5+ 18 ♔h4 ♔g7! 19 g4 h6 20 ♗xh6+ ♔xh6 21 gxh5 f5! 22 ♔g3 fxe4 23 ♗g2 gxh5 24 f4 ♖g8+ 25 ♘g5 h4+ 0-1 as it is mate next move.

11...♘xe7 12 ♘xe7+ ♔f8 13 ♘d5

13 ♘xc8? ♗xb2 14 ♖b1 ♗c3+ 15 ♔f2 ♗d4+ 16 ♔e1 ♖axc8 and Black has an extremely dangerous initiative. 17 ♖xb7 fails to 17...♗b6.

13...♗xb2 14 ♖b1

14 ♖d1 has been played a few times. After 14...♘c5 (14...♘b6!?) 15 ♘e2 both Timman-J.Polgar, Paris (rapid) 1992 and Brenninkmeier-Troyke, Groningen 1992 continued 15...♗d7 16 ♘ec3 ♖ac8 17 ♗e2 ♗e6 18 ♔f2 and now Polgar played 18...♗c6 and Troyke 18...♖d6 but against either move White could have obtained a good game with 19 ♖b1! Black should proba-

bly have retreated his bishop before it got cut off on b2, e.g. 15...♗g7 16 ♘ec3 ♗d7 17 ♗e2 ♖ac8 18 ♔f2 ♗e6 19 ♔e3 ♖d6 and White hasn't really gained by having his rook on d1 as opposed to b1.

14...♗g7

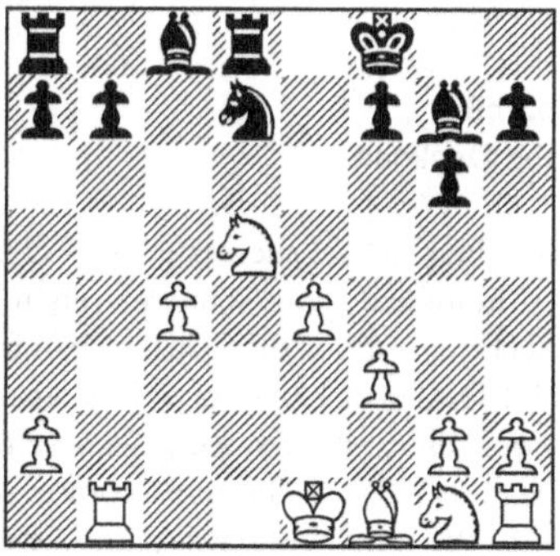

For his pawn Black has an extremely strong dark-squared bishop and a couple of weak white pawns on the queenside to take aim at. He also has a fine outpost on c5 for a knight. True, White also has a strong knight on d5 but Black is often able to play around this piece. The knight on d5 will only be taken if Black has a concrete follow up in mind (such as an invasion to the 7th rank. There has to be a good reason to allow White to straighten out his pawn structure with cxd5. I suspect the position is dynamically balanced but in practice Black has done well. It is quite notable that even Karpov or Korchnoi have struggled to make anything out of the extra pawn.

15 ♘h3

The text gets the Karpovian seal of approval, but there are a number of alternatives:

a) 15 ♘e2 ♘c5 16 ♘ec3 (16 ♘c1 ♗e6 17 ♘d3 transposes to the note to move 17 in the main game) ♗d7 (16...♗e6 17 ♗e2 ♗xc3+ 18 ♘xc3 ♘d3+ is given as equal by Hazai) 17 ♗e2 ♖ac8 18 0-0 ♖c6! (transferring the rook to the a-file is a standard way for Black to increase his pressure in this line) 19 ♖fd1 ♖a6 20 f4 ♗xc3 (Black rids himself of his bishop before e5 renders it redundant) 21 ♘xc3 ♖a3 22 ♖bc1 ♖c8 23 e5 ♗e6 and Black had full compensation for the pawn in Wells-Lamoureux, Oakham 1993.

b) 15 g4. This immediate action on the kingside doesn't solve White's problems. The game Levitt-Watson, London 1990 continued 15...b6 16 g5 ♗b7 17 h4 ♖ac8 18 f4 (White looks as if he possesses one of the loosest positions of all time) 18...♘c5 19 e5 ♗xd5 20 cxd5 ♖xd5 with advantage to Black.

c) 15 h4 has the intention of bringing the rook on h1 into play as quickly as possible. The most logical reaction is 15...♘c5, meeting 16 h5 with 16...g5 and 16 ♘h3 with 16...♗e6. In Ehlvest-Gelfand, Polanica Zdroj 1997 Black preferred 15...♘b6 and after 16 h5 ♗e6 17 ♘h3 ♖ac8 18 ♘g5 ♗xd5 19 cxd5 ♖c2 20 ♗d3 ♗c3+ 21 ♔f1 ♖d2 22 hxg6 hxg6 23 ♗e2 ♖xa2 an extremely unclear position had been reached which Black eventually won in 63 moves.

15...♘c5 16 ♘f2 ♗e6 17 ♗e2

17 ♘d3 ♖ac8 18 ♗e2 (after 18 ♘xc5 ♖xc5 19 ♖xb7 ♖a5 Black will win the pawn on a2 and gain a powerful passed a-pawn; with 19 ♖b3! however White should be able to achieve a draw) 18...b6 (18...♘a4 is another possibility) 19 0-0 ♘b7!? (19...♘xd3 20 ♗xd3 ♖c5 is another idea) 20 ♖fc1 ♘a5 21 ♖b4 ♖c6 22 ♖c2? (a tactical oversight; after 22 ♔f1 ♖dc8 23 ♘3f4 ♗h6 24 g3 ♖c5 Black has strong pressure for the pawn) 22...♗xd5 23 exd5 ♖xd5! 24 cxd5 ♖xc2 25 ♔f1 ♔e7 and Black was better in Georges-Gallagher, Zürich 1994 as his queenside pawns are more dangerous than the white d-pawn.

17...♖ac8 18 0-0 b6

Black decides to manoeuvre his knight to a5 in order to exert maximum pressure on the white c-pawn (as he did in Georges-Gallagher above). The other main idea, which we have already seen in line 'a' in the 15th move notes, is to quickly transfer the rook to the a-file. For example, 18...♖d6 19 ♖fd1 ♖a6 20 ♖d2 ♖a3 was fine for Black in Korchnoi-J.Polgar, Roquebrune 1992.

19 ♖fe1

Graf may have been concerned about Black playing ...f5, which is another one of his typical ideas in this position. However, Black must time this advance well and he is often better off holding it in reserve until he has tied White down on the queenside.

19...♘b7 20 ♖ec1 ♗h6 21 ♖d1

Obviously not 21 ♖c2 ♗xd5 22 exd5 ♖xd5

21...♘a5 22 ♖b4 ♖c5

Preparing to double on the c-file. Graf was obviously not feeling too comfortable as he now elected to return the pawn without alleviating any of the pressure.

23 f4?! ♗xd5 24 exd5

24 ♖xd5 might be better.

24...♗xf4 25 ♘e4 ♖c7 26 ♔f2

26 d6 just loses a pawn.

26...♘b7?

A desirable move but tactically flawed. Instead 26...f5 27 g3 ♖e7! 28 gxf4 (28 ♘c3) 28...♖xe4 29 ♔f3 ♖de8 30 ♗f1 ♘b7 leaves Black with a clear positional advantage which may well prove sufficient to win the game.

27 ♖a4?!

White misses his chance: 27 c5! bxc5 28 ♘xc5 ♘xc5 29 ♖xf4 looks like a draw.

27...♘d6 28 ♘f6

I wouldn't wish the long term suffering involved after 28 ♘xd6 ♗xd6 on anyone but it may be a better chance.

28...♗e5! 29 ♘xh7+

29 ♘g4 ♗g7 just leaves the knight horribly placed.

29...♔g7 30 ♘g5 ♗f6! 31 c5

If the knight moved (or is captured after 31 h4) then 31...♘e4+ followed by 32...♘c3 picks up an exchange.

31...bxc5 32 ♘f3 c4

Black has a decisive advantage as his pieces, including the respective passed pawns, are far superior to their counterparts. He eventually translated this superiority into a mating attack. The remaining moves were:

33 ♖c1 c3 34 ♗d3 ♘c8 35 ♖c4 ♖b7 36 g4

♖b2+ 37 ♔g3 ♘b6 38 ♖c7 ♘xd5 39 ♖xa7 ♘e3 40 ♗e4 g5 41 h4 ♖g2+ 42 ♔h3 ♖xg4 43 ♗c2 gxh4 44 ♗b3 ♖g3+ 45 ♔h2 ♖xf3 46 ♖xf7+ ♔h6 47 ♔h1 ♖h3+ 48 ♔g1 ♖g8+ 49 ♔f2 ♖g2+ 0-1

An impressive performance from Black. It is not an easy task to despatch the German no. 1 in such fashion.

6 ♗e3 c5
Gambit Declined

Due to their lack of success in the Gambit Accepted more and more White players turned to the Benoni positions that usually arise from the Gambit Declined. I shall now look at the various possibilities through these games. The first two feature 7 ♘ge2, the most common move, whilst in the third White just plays the immediate 7 d5.

Game 35

Bogdanovski-Kempinski

Halkidiki 2002

1 d4 ♘f6 2 c4 g6 3 ♘c3 ♗g7 4 e4 d6 5 f3 0-0 6 ♗e3 c5 7 ♘ge2 ♕a5!?

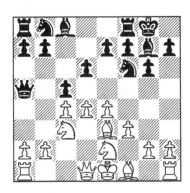

A very tricky move. The normal continuation is 7...♘c6 8 d5 ♘e5 9 ♘g3 and we have entered a heavily analysed variation. The point of the text is to wait for 8 ♕d2 before playing 8...♘c6. This transposes into a similar variation which is normally reached via the move order 7...♘c6 8 ♕d2 ♕a5. But most White players discarded this line, long ago, in favour of 8 d5.

It seems that the inclusion of the queen moves is not unfavourable for Black. In Game 36 we shall take a look at this line while here we shall examine the 8th move alternatives for White.

8 d5

The only other possibility (apart from 8 ♕d2) is 8 ♘c1 and this is a good moment for Black to exchange in the centre. After 8...cxd4:

a) 9 ♗xd4 (a strange choice) 9...♘c6 10 ♘b3 ♕d8 (I suppose Black could also have swung his queen over to the kingside) 11 ♗e3 ♗e6 12 ♖c1 ♘e5 13 ♘d5 ♗xd5 14 cxd5 e6 (Black must play actively as if White can complete his development before anything nasty happens to him his space advantage and bishop pair will give him the edge) 15 dxe6 fxe6 16 ♗e2 (on 16 ♕d2 Black can play 16...d5) 16...♘xe4! (I certainly approve of that one) 17 fxe4 ♕h4+ 18 ♔d2 ♕xe4 19 ♖c3 ♕xg2 (why is Black distracted by this pawn: after 19...d5! I consider him to be clearly better) 20 ♔c1 ♖ac8 21 ♖e1 ♖xc3+ 22 bxc3 ♖c8 23 ♗d4 ♕xh2 24 ♔b1 ♕g2 25 ♘d2 ♕d5 ½-½ Bischoff-Stellwagen, Pulvermuehle 2004.

b) 9 ♘b3 is more logical. Now I recommend the queen sacrifice 9...♕xc3+ 10 bxc3 dxe3. Only joking! I would love to but Black can't have enough here after 11 ♕d3. But Dautov has pointed out that 9...♘h5 10 ♘xd4 ♘c6 gives Black an easy Maróczy type position. There are no practical tests but a possible continuation could be something like 11 ♕d2 (11 ♗e2 ♕h4+ is quite irritating for White after both 12 g3 ♕h3 and 12 ♗f2 ♕g5) 11...♘xd4 12 ♗xd4 ♗e6 and now:

b1) White could try and embarrass the black queen with something like 13 h4 ♖fc8 14 c5 (or 14 b4 ♗xc4 15 g4 ♘xg4 with plenty of play for the piece) but then 14...♖xc5! 15 g4 (obviously Black has more than enough play for the exchange if White takes on c5) ♘xg4 16 fxg4 ♗xg4 should not be worse for Black and looks like fun to play.

b2) 13 ♘d5 is the solid choice when either capture on d5 leads to a balanced game, e.g. 13...♘xd5 14 ♗xg7 ♔xg7 15 cxd5 ♗d7 or 13...♗xd5 14 cxd5 ♘d7 15 ♗xg7 ♔xg7 16 ♗b5 ♘f6 with equality. These Maróczy type positions can be unpleasant for Black but only when there are more minor pieces on the board

and he has space problems.

8...b5!

The correct response to White's premature closing of the centre. Black now gets a good version of the Benko Gambit.

9 cxb5 a6 10 ♘g3

10 ♘c1, heading for b3, is the move that White would like to play but this has the drawback of leaving the rook on a1 undefended. So what, I hear you say. But it does matter. After 10...♘xe4! 11 fxe4 ♗xc3+ 12 bxc3?! ♕xc3+ Black wins.

Perhaps the sad-looking 10 b6 is White's best move when Black should probably just reply 10...♕xb6.

10...axb5 11 ♗xb5 ♗a6 12 ♗xa6 ♘xa6 13 0-0 ♘d7

Black has more pressure than usual in the Benko, mainly because the knight on g3 is out of the game. Kempinski now quickly polished off some pretty inept play from White.

14 ♖c1 ♘e5 15 ♕e2 c4!

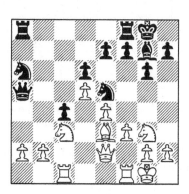

The d3-square is the advanced base camp that will enable Black to destroy the white position.

16 a3 ♘d3 17 ♖c2 ♘ac5 18 ♘d1 ♕b5 19 ♗d2 ♘a4

19...♘b3 followed by ...♘d4 also looks good.

20 ♗c3 ♘xc3 21 ♘xc3 ♕b3 22 ♘d1 ♖ab8 23 f4

White finally plays an active move but it just offers Black an additional target.

23...e6! 24 dxe6?!

Understandable, as otherwise Black will just exchange on d5 and pick up the weak white pawn on that square, but after the text White loses his f-pawn.

24...fxe6 25 ♖f3 ♘xf4! 0-1

White resigned as the f-pawn is just for starters, e.g. 26 ♕d2 and 26 ♕f2 both lose to 26...♘h3+! whilst 26 ♖xb3 ♘xe2+ 27 ♘xe2 cxb3 is obviously hopeless as well.

Game 36
Lehtivaara-Gallagher
Neuchâtel 2004

---

1 d4 ♘f6 2 c4 g6 3 ♘c3 ♗g7 4 e4 d6 5 f3 0-0 6 ♗e3 c5 7 ♘ge2 ♕a5 8 ♕d2 ♘c6

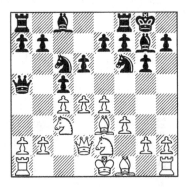

This game may be hot off the presses but we have now reached a position which I covered extensively in my 1995 book on the Sämisch. I shall be drawing quite heavily on this material for a couple of reasons:

a) Hardly anybody bought the book (probably my best one as well, at least from a technical

point of view) so it is a shame to waste such material.

b) It is still very relevant as there have been very few games in this line in the intervening years.

9 d5

Obviously White is not forced into this advance but other continuations promise nothing:

a) 9 dxc5 (this anti-positional capture is usually only good when it wins a pawn, and even then...) 9...dxc5 10 ♘d5 (otherwise the white queen is just exposed on the open file) 10...♕xd2+ (10...♘xd5 11 ♕xa5 ♘xe3! is a typical and strong queen sacrifice but 11 cxd5 ♘b4 12 ♘c3 is less clear) 11 ♗xd2 ♘d7! followed by ...e6 with an easy game for Black. Note that this is stronger than winning a pawn with 11...♘xd5 12 exd5 ♗xb2 13 ♖b1 ♘e5 14 ♘c3! when White has the advantage.

b) 9 0-0-0 is most simply met by 9...cxd4 10 ♘xd4 ♘xd4 11 ♗xd4 ♗e6 12 ♔b1 ♖fc8 13 b3 a6 and in view of his king position, it's probably safest for White to liquidate into an equal ending with 14 ♘d5 ♕xd2 15 ♖xd2 ♗xd5 16 cxd5 ♘d7 17 ♗xg7 ♔xg7 18 ♗e2 a5.

Another decent possibility for the more ambitious Black player is 9...a6 10 ♔b1 e6! and now:

b1) 11 d5 exd5 12 ♘xd5 ♘xd5 13 cxd5 ♕xd2 14 ♗xd2 ♘e5 with a pleasant game for Black;

b2) 11 ♗h6 b5 12 ♗xg7 ♔xg7 13 dxc5 b4!? (there is nothing wrong with 13...dxc5 e.g. 14 ♘c1 ♖d8 15 ♕e1 ♖xd1 16 ♕xd1 ♘d4) 14 ♘d5 exd5 15 cxd5 dxc5!? 16 dxc6 ♗e6 with good attacking chances for Black, Gheorghiu-

M.Piket, Lugano 1989.

b3) 11 dxc5 dxc5 12 ♘c1 ♖d8 13 ♕f2 ♖xd1 14 ♘xd1 (Schneider-Hazai, Espoo 1988) and now Hazai gives 14...♖d8 15 ♘c3 b6 as Black's best. White would struggle to claim equality in this position.

9...♘e5 10 ♘c1

With the black queen on a5, the text makes more sense than 10 ♘g3. At any rate, its what everybody plays. That's what I wrote 9 years ago. We do now have an interesting example of 10 ♘g3. Dautov-Kempinski, Munich 1997 continued 10...a6 11 f4?! (11 ♗e2 looks more solid) 11...♘ed7! (there is no need for Black to get involved in 11...♘eg4 12 ♗g1 as after the text White has serious problems with his centre) 12 h3 (Dautov points out the variation 12 ♗e2 h5! 13 0-0 b5 14 cxb5 h4 15 ♘h1 axb5 16 ♗xb5 when the standard King's Indian trick 16...♘xe4! leaves White in bad shape) and now Black should have played 12...b5! 13 cxb5 h5 14 bxa6 h4 15 ♘ge2 ♗xa6 with excellent compensation for the pawn.

10...a6

Black prepares to play ...b5.

11 ♗e2

White has also played 11 a4, intending to meet 11...♗d7 with 12 ♖a3 when Black can no longer play ...b5. Therefore it is best to counter in the centre at once with 11...e6. This occurred in Spassky-J.Polgar, Budapest (m/3) 1993 and Black achieved good play after 12 ♖a3 exd5 13 cxd5 ♘h5! 14 ♗e2 f5 15 exf5 gxf5 16 ♗h6 ♕b4 17 ♗xg7 ♘xg7 18 f4 ♘c4 19 ♗xc4 ♕xc4 20 a5 ♗d7 21 ♘1e2 and now, according to Nikitin (Spassky's second in the match), the most accurate continuation was 21...♘h5!, immediately improving the position of the worse placed piece. After 22 0-0 ♘f6 23 ♖f3 ♖ae8 Black would have a good game.

11...♗d7

11...b5 looks premature but 11...e6 is a possible alternative.

12 f4?!

Lehtivaara, who was unfamiliar with the position, became nervous about the potential tactics on the queenside and decided to change the course of the game (I was playing very quickly but in reality I was struggling to remember stuff during his thinking time).

12 a4 was the choice in Kramnik-Gelfand, Linares 1993. After 12...♕b4 it is dubious to play 13 ♘1a2 on account of 13...♘xc4! 14 ♕d3 when Black has the choice between an interesting queen sacrifice, 14...♘xe3!? 15 ♘xb4 ♘xg2+ 16 ♔f2 ♘f4, or an ending with an armada of passed pawns after 14...♘xb2 15 ♕c2 (15 ♘xb4 ♘xd3+ 16 ♘xd3 ♘xe4!) 15...♗xa4 (15...♘xd5!?) 16 ♘xb4 bxc2 17 ♘xc2 ♘d7.

Therefore Kramnik defended c4 with 13 b3 and now:

a) 13...♘fg4 is the move crying out to be played, but unfortunately it's unsound: 14 ♘1a2! ♘xe3 15 ♘xb4 ♘xg2+ 16 ♔f2 cxb4 17 ♘a2 ♘h4 18 f4 f5! 19 ♔g3 g5! is given as unclear by Kramnik, and I would like to add the following possible continuation: 20 fxg5 (20 fxe5 ♗xe5+ 21 ♔f2 fxe4+) 20...fxe4 21 ♔xh4 (21 ♖af1 ♘eg6! 22 ♗g4 ♗e5+ 23 ♔h3 ♘f3 wins for Black) 21...♖f3! 22 h3 ♖af8 23 ♖ag1 ♖8f4+ 24 ♖g4 (24 ♕xf4 ♘g6+!) 24...♖xg4+ 25 hxg4 ♘g6+ 26 ♔h5 ♘f4+ 27 ♔h4 ♘g2+ 28 ♔h5 ♗e8+ 29 g6 ♗xg6+ 30 ♔g5

I shall claim the diagram position as my study. Black mates with 30...♘f6+! (the immediate 30...♔f7 allows 31 ♖xh7!) 31 ♔h6 ♔f7!! 32 ♗xf3 ♗g7+ 33 ♔g5 h6+ 34 ♖xh6 ♗f6 mate. Chess can be a beautiful game.

However, Kramnik provides the cold shower: 17 ♔xg2! bxc3 18 ♕xc3! and whilst Black is not completely lost, he doesn't have anything like as much play as in some of the other typical Sämisch queen sacrifices.

b) 13...♘xf3+ 14 ♗xf3 ♘xe4 15 ♘xe4 ♕xd2+ 16 ♔xd2 ♗xa1 is interesting but probably in White's favour as Black will just create weaknesses if he advances his pawns.

c) 13...e6 was played in the game. It continued 14 ♘1a2 ♕a5 15 dxe6 (15 0-0 exd5 16 cxd5 b5 was not to White's liking so he decides to grab a pawn) 15...♗xe6 16 ♕xd6 ♘fd7 17 ♔f2!? (17 0-0 may appear more natural, but sometimes it can be useful to have the bishop on e2 protected and, in the case of an ending arising, f2 is somewhat nearer the centre than g1) 17...♘c6 18 ♖ac1 ♘d4 19 b4 ♕b6 (19...♕d8!? could be an attempt to punish White for his 17th move) 20 ♕xb6 ♘xb6 21 bxc5 ♘xe2 22 ♘xe2 and now Gelfand played 22...♘xc4?! and went on to lose but Kramnik has pointed out that 22...♘xa4! would have given Black a very comfortable game, e.g. 23 ♘f4 ♖fc8 24 ♘d5 ♗f8! 25 ♘ab4 a5 26 ♘d3 ♘xc5 27 ♘xc5 ♗xc5 28 ♖b1! is equal.

Before getting back to the Lehtivaara-Gallagher game it's worth pointing out that the attempt to trap the black knight in the centre with 12 h3? b5 13 b3? just loses material to 13...♘e8! or 13...♘h5! (I once played 13...♘fg4?? but still won).

12...♘eg4 13 ♗g1 b5 14 ♗f3

Of course 14 h3 is met by 14...b4, but now with e4 defended White is threatening to play h3. I looked at several interesting continuations but probably failed to find the most precise move order.

14...♘h5

Black should just play the immediate 14...♗h6! when it is difficult to suggest a good move for White.

15 ♘1e2

15 h3 ♘g3 was the idea.

15...♗h6! 16 ♗xg4

Of course the point of ...♗h6 is to make the e5-square available for the black knight. White probably has nothing better than this capture, which wouldn't have helped much if I'd played 14...♗h6 as then Black could recapture with the knight.

16...♗xg4 17 ♗e3 ♗xe2

I was already running short of time (it doesn't take much at 36 moves in 1.5 hours) so opted for what I though was going to be a slightly better ending. My opponent surprised me, however, with...

18 ♔xe2?!

A brave man but he should have played 18 ♘xe2.

18...♘f6

18...f5 is good but I had another idea in mind. Of course the immediate threat is 19...b4.

19 ♔f3

No choice as 19 e5 ♘g4 is good for Black.

19...♘d7!

The knight is heading for b6 and the c4-square. I am trying to force White to exchange on b5 and open lines rather than playing bxc4 myself, which may win a pawn but reduces Black's possibilities of active play.

20 g4?!

The gung-ho approach turns a difficult situation into a desperate one.

20...♘b6 21 cxb5

21 ♘b1 ♘xc4 is just a clear pawn.

21...♘c4 22 ♕e2 axb5 23 ♘d1

After 23 a4 ♕b4! 24 axb5 the quiet 24...♗g7 is probably the most unpleasant for White.

23...♗g7 24 h4 e6! 25 h5

25 dxe6 fxe6 is equally hopeless.
25...exd5 26 exd5 ♖ae8

26...♖fe8 is also good but I wanted to vacate a8 for the queen and had seen that there was a simple way to deal with White's attack.
27 ♕h2

Or 27 hxg6 fxg6 28 ♕h2 h6.
27...g5! 28 h6 ♗xb2! 29 ♖b1 ♕a8!

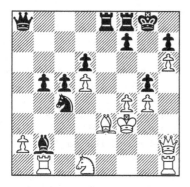

30 ♖xb2 ♕xd5+ 31 ♔g3

Or 31 ♔f2 ♘xb2 32 ♘xb2 ♖xe3 33 ♔xe3 ♖e8+ and Black mates.
31...♘xe3 32 ♕d2 ♕xh1 0-1

Game 37
Mihajlovic-Kovacevic
Yugoslav Ch. 1996

---

1 d4 ♘f6 2 c4 g6 3 ♘c3 ♗g7 4 e4 d6 5 f3 0-0 6 ♗e3 c5 7 d5

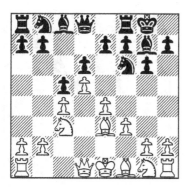

This is the least played of White's seventh move options as the most that he can really

hope for after 7 d5 is transposition to another variation (there are several possibilities). White normally waits for ...♘c6 before playing this advance in order to play similar positions but with a black knight already committed to the double-edged e5-square. Play can transpose but it is up to Black whether or not he wishes to move his knight to e5.

You may also compare this position to the one after 6 ♗g5 c5 7 d5 and you will notice that with the bishop more actively deployed on g5 Black usually feels the necessity to weaken his kingside with h6. The bishop then retreats to e3 and White can hope to gain a tempo, in comparison with this variation, as at some stage Black is going to have to deal with the threat to his h-pawn.
7...e6 8 ♕d2

Less common moves are:
a) 8 dxe6 ♗xe6 9 ♗d3 ♘fd7! with a good game for Black.
b) 8 ♘ge2 exd5 9 cxd5 ♘bd7 10 ♘g3 is similar to Game 38 but with White already having committed his bishop to e3.
8...exd5 9 cxd5 a6

One of the standard ways for Black to seek active play in these Benoni positions is to advance on the queenside with ...b5. White nearly always prevents this by playing a4 but, on balance, it is in Black's favour to have the moves ...a6 and a4 included. There are a few positions where ♘b5 could be annoying and Black still has the possibility to play ...b7-b5 as a Benko-style pawn sacrifice.
10 a4 ♖e8

A good alternative is 10...h5 transposing into

Game 42.

A less good alternative is 10...♘bd7 as this allows White to develop his king's knight favourably to h3. The knight will then settle on f2 from where it can keep an eye on a number of important squares, as well as not clogging up the kingside as it does on e2.

A good rule of thumb for Black in these lines is don't play ...♘bd7 until White has played ♘e2.

11 ♘ge2

White should give up on the idea of ♘h3, as he hasn't got a good alternative to the text, e.g.

a) 11 ♗e2 ♕c7 12 ♗d1 ♘bd7 13 ♘h3 ♘e5 and Black threatens ...♘c4

b) 11 a5 b5 12 axb6 ♕xb6 13 ♗d3 ♘bd7 14 ♘h3 ♘e5 15 ♘f2 ½-½ in Schneider-Szvia, Budapest 1991, even though Black already has the upper hand.

c) 11 ♗d3 ♘bd7 12 ♘h3 ♘e5 and exchanges nearly always suit Black in the Benoni structure.

11...♘bd7

11...♕a5 12 ♖a3 is not a favourable development for Black.

12 ♘c1

The knight has to move again to allow White to complete his development. The question is where does it go? Here are a couple of alternatives:

a) 12 ♘g3 h5 13 ♗e2 h4 14 ♘f1 ♘h7 leads to an inferior version, for White, of Game 39. The inclusion of the moves ♕d2 and ♖e8 should be slightly in Black's favour.

b) 12 ♘d1 is a typical move from White in such positions.

His idea is to achieve the ideal set-up for his knights by playing ♘ec3 and ♘f2. Note how this has takes four moves (not counting the original ♘c3) with the knights whilst if Black had played ...♘bd7 before White played ♘ge2 then by ♘h3-f2 White gets the same set-up having played only two knight moves. Now you can appreciate why Black shouldn't rush with ...♘bd7 (see above). The downside to 12 ♘d1 is that it does nothing to speed up White's rather sluggish pace of development.

Here is an example where things didn't go too well for Black: 12...♘e5 13 ♘ec3 ♕a5?! 14 ♗e2! (White is right not to fear ...b5, and concentrates on development in order to be able to counter in the centre as quickly as possible) 14...b5 15 0-0 ♘fd7 16 ♘f2 ♘c4 17 ♗xc4 bxc4 18 f4 ♖b8 19 e5 dxe5 20 ♘fe4 ♕b6 21 f5!, Meulders-Douven, Holland 1991. White has obtained a powerful attacking position by employing a standard Benoni trick, e5, ...dxe5, f5, which blocks the long diagonal and thereby restricts the black bishop, while vacating the e4-square for White's knights.

I think that Black's troubles in this game can be traced back to 13...♕a5. I would prefer to prepare for ...b5 with 13...♗d7 14 ♗e2 ♖b8 with what appears to be a reasonable game for Black. Alternatively, Black could also consider 13...♘h5 with the idea of striking in the centre with ...f5.

See also Game 42 for an example of the same plan from White.

12...♘e5 13 ♗e2

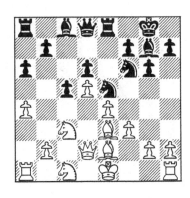

13...♘h5!?

Black gets ready to play ...f7-f5. The alternative is to play for b5 with 13...♗d7 14 0-0 ♖b8 when White should play 15 a5. Now, in practice, Black has played both 15...♗c8 and 15...♕c8, neither of which I like, as well as the pawn sacrifice 15...b5. I believe Black has reasonable compensation after 16 axb6 ♖xb6 17 ♖xa6 ♖xa6 18 ♗xa6 ♕a5 19 ♗e2 ♖b8 but I would still prefer to play for ...f5 than give up a pawn. Note that Black also has 13...h5!? followed by ...♘h7 as another means of preparing f5.

14 0-0 f5 15 f4 ♘d7!?

Interesting decision. Black allows his kingside pawns to be shattered just as in Game 40. 15...♘g4 16 ♗xg4 fxg4 also looks quite playable and quite difficult to assess.

16 ♗xh5 gxh5 17 e5

Even if he wanted to take on f5 White couldn't because of the tactical response 17...♖xe3! 18 ♕xe3 ♗d4 (a standard trick in these positions).

17...dxe5 18 ♘d3 b6

Black prefers to keep control of d4, e.g. 18...c4 19 ♘xe5 ♘xe5 20 fxe5 ♗xe5 21 ♗d4 looks good for White.

19 fxe5 ♘xe5 20 ♘xe5 ♗xe5 21 ♗g5 ♕d6 22 ♗f4 ♗xf4 23 ♖xf4 ♗d7 24 ♖af1 ♖e5

It's one of those positions that looks as though it should be good for White but somehow isn't (Black controls the centre and has a mobile queenside majority). In fact it may even be better for Black. At any rate he won pretty quickly.

25 ♖4f3 b5 26 ♖g3+ ♔h8 27 axb5 axb5 28 ♘e2 h4 29 ♖d3 b4 30 ♘f4 ♗b5 31 ♖c1 ♗xd3 32 ♕xd3 ♖e4 0-1

6 ♘ge2

Game 38
Dreev-Bologan
Shanghai 2001

1 d4 ♘f6 2 c4 g6 3 ♘c3 ♗g7 4 e4 d6 5 f3 0-0 6 ♘ge2

This time White delays the development of his queen's bishop. He will decide later where it should go (if anywhere) and first concentrates on the king's knight. This is often a problem piece for White in the Sämisch as the move f3 has deprived it of its natural home. It takes more than one move to develop the knight as it can't stay on e2 where it clogs up the rest of the white kingside. The knight is heading for g3 in order to restrain (or is it to encourage) Black's kingside play. As we shall see this knight is not in for a quiet life. The main exponent of this line is the Russian grandmaster Dreev who features in our two games. It was, therefore, most interesting to do battle with him this year in Gibraltar in a variation which I have played with both colours (see next game). Black has the usual assortment of replies but I see no reason to differ from our chosen response to White's other 6th moves.

6...c5 7 d5 e6 8 ♘g3

8 ♗g5 transposes to Game 41.

8...exd5 9 cxd5 h5!?

Quite often Black flicks in the moves 9...a6 10 a4 before deciding on his plan of action. However, in conjunction with a quick ...h5 it is better to delay these moves. The reason will be seen later. The knight on g3 makes a tempting target for the h-pawn. It has just spent two moves getting there and it is soon to be on the move again. Of course there is some risk involved in advancing the h-pawn but if Black wants to play ...f5 it is necessary to first kick the knight from g3.

In Game 40 I examine an alternative for Black, 9...♘h5!?

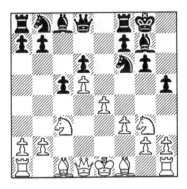

10 ♗g5

For the time being White stops Black from playing ...h4. The other move that White plays with about equal frequency is 10 ♗e2. See Dreev-Gallagher (Game 31).

10...♕b6

Black normally breaks such pins by playing ...h6 but with the pawn on h5 that is no longer possible. He must resort to other means to break the pin. The b6-square is not an ideal home for the queen but developing it here gains Black a tempo by attacking the b2 pawn.

11 ♕b3

This is a speciality of Dreev. The comments to ...♕b6 are equally applicable to ♕b3. This is not a good square for the queen but White gains time by offering an exchange. In this position White has the sounder structure (pawn majority in the centre, weakness on d6 to aim at) so Black must seek his chances in dynamic play. As the most dynamic piece is the queen Black should keep them on the board.

11 ♕d2 is also possible when Black would just reply 11...♘h7. Note that 12 ♗h6 (12 ♗h4 is best met by 12...♘d7) is not possible because after an exchange of bishops Black takes on b2. If the pawns had already been on a6 and a4

then White would be able to play a4-a5 after ♘h7 and when the black queen retreats to c7 then he could indeed play ♗h6 in order to exchange off the bishops. That is why Black is delaying the move ...a6 in this variation.

11...♕c7! 12 ♗e2 a6

13 0-0

An interesting moment. Most players would play 13 a4 without much thought but Dreev decides to allow Black to play ...b5 as he will then hope to undermine the queenside with a subsequent a4. Black probably does best to delay ...b5 for the time being and get on with his kingside play, as Bologan did in the game. In fact Dreev had already reached this position more than once. The first time, against Topalov, Elista Olympiad. 1998 he did play 13 a4 and wasn't very successful. Play continued 13...♘h7 14 ♗e3 ♕e7 15 0-0 ♘d7 (Black avoids the immediate ...f5 as White has a little trick that wins a pawn: 15...f5 16 ♗xc5 dxc5? 17 d6+ ♕f7 18 ♗c4 costs Black his queen) 16 f4 ♗d4 17 ♗f2 h4 18 ♘h1 g5 (this is a standard idea in such positions; Black will now take control of the e5-square which will make a fine outpost for a minor piece and also ensure that White won't be able to smash through in the centre) 19 ♕d1 ♕f6 20 fxg5 ½-½.

13...♘h7 14 ♗e3 h4

The game Dreev-Tkachiev, Cap D'Agde 2000 went 14...♕e7!? 15 f4 h4 16 ♘h1 b5 17 ♘f2 ♘d7 18 ♗f3 g5 19 ♘e2 f5 with a very promising position for Black. Why is Dreev playing the same line again? Has he simply forgotten this game? And why has Bologan not played 14...♕e7? Well, Dreev, one of the world's top players, has certainly not forgotten this game. What has happened is that he has worked on it at home and found an improvement for White. Bologan avoids 14...♕e7 as he doesn't wish to become another victim of Dreev's homework.

15 ♘h1 f5 16 exf5

16 f4 ♗d4!? may well be the subject of a future game in this line.

16...♗xf5 17 ♗f2?!

The start of an over-ambitious plan. It is quite common for White to retreat his knight to the corner but very rarely does he leave it on this sad square for any length of time. 17 ♘f2 would have been more prudent.

17...g5 18 f4 gxf4 19 ♗xh4 ♗d4+ 20 ♘f2 ♘d7 21 ♔h1 ♘e5

Dreev was probably hoping to show that the pawn on f4 is weak but he has allowed the black pieces tremendous activity and anyway, the pawn can be defended easily enough.

22 ♘fe4 ♘g6 23 ♗f2 ♖ae8 24 ♗f3 ♘e5 25 ♕d1 ♘xf3 26 ♕xf3 b5 27 ♖ae1?

A blunder in a difficult position.

27...b4 28 ♗xd4 cxd4 29 ♘d1 ♗xe4! 30 ♖xe4 ♘g5 31 ♕g4 ♖xe4 32 ♕xg5+ ♕g7 33 ♕h5 d3 34 ♘f2 ♖e5 35 ♕d1 ♖xd5 36 ♘xd3 ♕g6 37 ♖f3 ♖e8 38 h3 ♖e3 39 ♖xf4 ♖exd3 40 ♕e2 ♖5d4 41 ♖f1 ♖h4 0-1

Game 39
Dreev-Gallagher
Gibraltar 2004

---

1 d4 ♘f6 2 c4 g6 3 ♘c3 ♗g7 4 e4 d6 5 f3

0-0 6 ♘ge2 c5 7 d5 e6 8 ♘g3 exd5 9 cxd5 h5 10 ♗e2

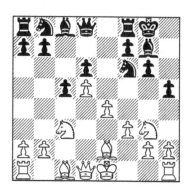

Until a few months ago I was responsible for running a King's Indian website for Chess Publishing. This involved a monthly update with analysis of the most recent King's Indian games. No doubt I was slightly biased in Black's favour but my successor, the Israeli grandmaster Mikhalevski (who plays the King's Indian about as often as Karpov) has taken things too far the other way. He called Black's last move, for example, 'unfortunate' and describes 10 ♗e2 as 'killing'. A slight exaggeration, I feel (by the way, his stuff on Chess Publishing is still quite interesting). 10 ♗e2 may or may not pose more problems for Black than other moves but it is certainly not killing.

10...♘h7

Black can also play 10...h4 11 ♘f1 ♘h7 but I preferred to avoid this move order as I once obtained a good game with White by playing 12 ♘e3.

11 ♗e3

Dreev doesn't fall for 11 0-0?? ♗d4+ 12 ♔h1 h4 when the customary h1-square is no longer available for the knight. But your opponents might do!

11...a6

Dreev's adversaries have been quite keen on playing 11...h4 12 ♘f1 f5 but since they all lost (Tkachiev, Radjabov and Obodchuk) I preferred another approach. In general I like to have more pieces developed when I play ...f5.

12 a4 h4

Black can also delay this move and play 12...♘d7 when 13 0-0 h4 14 ♘h1 f5 leads to a fairly typical sort of position. In fact this was reached in Dreev's next game in this line which was, rather amazingly, against Anatoly Karpov. The black side of the King's Indian is not a place where one expects to find Karpov but he acquitted himself rather well for his debut with the opening. Play continued 15 ♕d2 ♕f6 (Mikhalevski suggests 15...h3 16 g3 fxe4 17 fxe4 ♘hf6 18 ♗f2 ♘e5, which does look fine for Black, but Karpov prefers to force White to deal with the threat of ...f5-f4) 16 f4 (16 exf5 is the alternative when Black will recapture 16...gxf5 with a reasonable game) 16...fxe4! 17 ♗f2 ♕e7 18 ♘cxe4 ♘df6 19 ♘xf6+ ♕xf6 with an unclear game (½-½, 70 after Karpov messed up a completely winning position)

13 ♘f1 ♘d7

Topalov played 13...f5 here against Dreev and he lost too. My comment from move 11 is still applicable.

14 ♗f2!

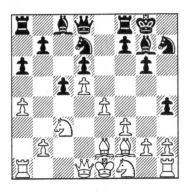

A novelty, which in my opinion White needed quite badly. My preparation for this game had homed in on this position, and with this move order, as the best way to create problems for White in this line. This position had been reached previously in the game Korchnoi-Xie Jun, Roquebrune 1998 which continued 14 ♘d2 f5 15 exf5 gxf5 16 f4 ♘df6 17 h3 (White wants to rule out ...♘g4 possibilities) 17...♕e7 18 ♔f2 ♖e8 19 ♘c4 ♖b8 20 a5 b5 21 axb6 and now Black should have just recaptured with 21...♖xb6! as after 22 ♘xb6 ♕xe3+ 23 ♔f1 ♕xf4+ 24 ♗f3 ♘e4 she would have had a very strong attack.

14...f5 15 exf5 gxf5 16 f4

The point of Dreev's novelty is to bring the knight back into play via e3. But first he prevents Black from playing ...f4.

16...♖e8!?

This leads to fascinating complications but just a few weeks after our game in Malakhatko-Damljanovic, Montenegro 2004 Black played more solidly with 16...♕f6. The idea is to meet 17 ♘e3 with ♕h6! So Malakhatko changed plan and played 17 ♘d2 but after 17...♕h6 18 0-0 ♕xf4 19 ♗xc5 ♕h6 20 ♗f2 ♘e5 (20...h3!?) Black had good squares for his pieces. Mikhalevski suggests 18 ♘c4 as an improvement, the point being that after 18...♕xf4 White has 19 ♗e3. He gives 18...♖b8 19 a5 b5 20 axb6 ♘xb6 21 ♘a5 ♕xf4 22 ♘c6 as best and claims an edge for White here. I'm not so sure but it is a definite improvement on 18 0-0.

17 ♘e3 ♗d4

The logical follow-up.

18 ♘xf5!?

When he played this almost instantly I started to get worried but relaxed a little when he took over an hour on his 20th move. I was planning to meet 18 ♘c4 with 18...♗xf2+ 19 ♔xf2 ♘b6 20 ♘e3 ♕f6 with a satisfactory game. The queen may even jump into d4 in the near future.

18...♗xf2+ 19 ♔xf2 ♖f8!

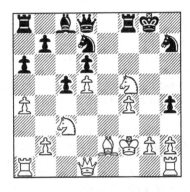

Better than 19...♕f6 when 20 g4! hxg3+ 21 hxg3 ♖xe2+ (21...♕xf5 22 ♗d3) 22 ♕xe2 ♕xf5 23 ♕e6+!? (23 ♕e8+ ♘df8 24 ♖ae1 is an alternative) 23...♕xe6 24 dxe6 ♘df6 25 ♖ae1 b6 26 ♖h4! is not a lot of fun for Black.

20 g4!

After his marathon think Dreev opts for a

sacrificial attack. The main point behind Black's play is that after the solid 20 ♗d3, defending the knight and threatening ♕g4+, Black has the excellent reply 20...♘e5! with a good game. I suppose it may be possible to grab the d-pawn but Black has a strong initiative after 20 ♘xd6 ♖xf4+.

20...hxg3+ 21 hxg3 ♖xf5 22 ♖xh7!

Stronger than 22 ♗d3 ♘df6!

22...♔xh7 23 ♗d3 ♘f6?!

I thought this was forced as I have to prevent ♕h5+ but I missed a fascinating possibility here in 23...♕g5!. It seems that White has to play 24 ♕f3 and after the game we thought that both 24...♕g6 25 g4 ♘e5! 26 ♗xf5 ♘xg4+ 27 ♕xg4 ♗xf5 28 ♖h1+ ♔g7 29 ♕h4 ♔f7 and 24...♕g6 25 fxg5 ♖xf3+ 26 ♔xf3 ♘e5+ 27 ♔e3 ♘xd3 28 ♔xd3 ♗f5+ 29 ♔d2 ♔g6 led to roughly level positions.

24 g4

White regains the rook.

24...c4!

Avoiding 24...♕b6 25 gxf5! c4+ 26 ♔f2 cxd3 27 ♕h1+ ♔g7 28 ♖g1+ ♔f7 29 ♕g2! when White has a winning attack.

25 ♗xf5+ ♗xf5 26 gxf5 ♕b6+ 27 ♔f3 ♕xb2 28 ♕e1!

28...♖g8??

A sad conclusion to a wonderful game. I had seen that Black is losing after 28...♖e8 29 ♕h4+ and was about to try 28...♔h8 when I saw that it too lost in brilliant fashion to 29 ♖a2 ♕b3 30 ♖h2+ ♘h7 31 ♖xh7+ ♔xh7 32 ♕e7+ ♔h8 33 ♕f6+ ♔g8 34 ♕g6+ ♔f8 35 f6 ♕xc3+ 36 ♔g4. And then my flag was about to fall (I was down to 30 seconds a move for the rest of the game

by now) and I had to play something. The right move, 28...♕h2!, simply didn't occur to me. Now after 29 ♕e7+ ♔g8 30 ♕xf6 ♕h3+ 31 ♔f2 ♕h2+ White cannot escape the checks so his only winning try would be 29 ♕h1. Black shouldn't have too many problems in the ending though, e.g. 29...♕xh1+ 30 ♖xh1+ ♔g7 31 a5 (31 ♖b1 b5) 31...♖c8 32 ♖b1 ♖c5 33 ♖xb7+ ♔g8 34 ♖b6 ♘xd5 35 ♘xd5 ♖xd5 36 ♖xa6 c3=.

29 ♕e7+ ♖g7 30 ♖h1+! ♔g8 31 ♕d8+ ♔f7 32 ♕c7+ ♔f8 33 ♕c8+ 1-0

On account of 33...♘e8 34 ♖h8+ and 33...♔f7 34 ♕e6+.

Game 40
Svetushkin-Romero Holmes
Bled Olympiad 2002

1 d4 ♘f6 2 c4 g6 3 ♘c3 ♗g7 4 e4 d6 5 f3 0-0 6 ♘ge2 c5 7 d5 e6 8 ♘g3 exd5 9 cxd5 ♘h5!?

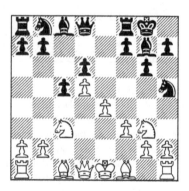

This crazy-looking move is the latest fashion but it does come with a health warning. Black allows his kingside pawn structure to be shattered so that he can play f5 and get active play for his pieces on the kingside as soon as possible. In the famous 1972 world championship match Fischer played ...♘h5 in a similar position and the chess world was shocked. In modern chess virtually anything goes but one should still be careful. There are many more positions where the rules can't be broken than there are exceptions.

10 ♘xh5 gxh5 11 ♗d3

Everyone plays this except Chris Ward who likes 11 ♗f4. He has reached the position after 11...f5 12 ♕d2 ♕f6 13 ♗g5 ♕g6 14 ♗d3 a couple of times. The unconvincing 14...♘a6 was played the first time but in the second game Black found a better plan: 14...fxe4 15 ♗xe4 (or 15 ♘xe4 ♗f5) 15...♗f5 16 0-0 ♘d7 17 ♖ae1 ♘e5 18 ♗f4 ♗xe4 19 ♖xe4, Ward-Snape, 4NCL 2001, and now Black should expand on the queenside with 19...b5! as 20 ♘xb5? fails to 20...♗xf3+! and 20 ♗xe5 ♗xe5 21 ♘xb5 ♖xf3! 22 ♖xf3 ♕xe4 is fine for Black.

11...♘d7!?

The latest twist. Black is getting clever with his move order. After the usual 11...f5 12 0-0

Black has tried:

a) 12...f4. This is what Black would really like to play if he could maintain the blockade whilst slowly transferring his pieces to the kingside. But he can't as White can play 13 ♘e2 ♗e5 14 g3!. It's still complicated but good for White.

b) 12...♘a6 when it seems that White does best to play 13 a3, preparing 14 ♕c2.

c) 12...♘d7 and now most White players favour the prophylactic 13 ♗c2 even though Black seems to be doing all right after 13...♗e5 14 ♘e2 ♘g6!?. For example, Khenkin-Reinderman, European Ch., Ohrid 2001 continued 15 exf5 ♗xf5 16 ♗xf5 ♖xf5 17 ♘g3 ♖f7 18 ♘xh5 ♗d4+ 19 ♔h1 ♕h4 20 f4 ♖e8. Quite a fitting position for this line One of the weak black pawns has dropped off but in return he has completed his development most harmoniously whilst White's queenside still languishes at home. White decides to return the pawn in order to rectify this. 21♗d2 ♗xb2 22

♖b1 ♗d4 23 ♖b3! (the point behind the sacrifice; White's rook will be very active on the open 3rd rank) 23...♕e7 24 ♘g3 ½-½.

I'm afraid that in this most unclear position the players chickened out and called it a draw. Most likely a great time scramble was looming. GM Stohl analysed this position and considered the chances to be about equal. Both sides have dangerous pawn majorities and although Black's king is more exposed he still has the more active pieces.

12 f4

In the two games I have where Black played 11...♘d7 White has replied both times with this double-edged move. I doubt it is better than 12 0-0 when Black can play 12...♘e5 13 ♗c2 f5 transposing into line 'c' in the previous note.

12...f5

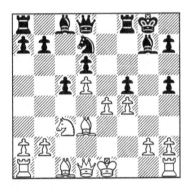

13 ♕xh5

A brave move. Instead 13 0-0 ♘f6 and now:

a) In Agrest-Kazhgaleyev, Nice 2000/01 White played the passive 14 h3 and Black soon obtained an excellent game: 14...fxe4 15 ♘xe4 ♘xe4 16 ♗xe4 ♕f6 17 ♔h1 ♗f5 18 ♗xf5 ♕xf5 19 ♗e3 ♖ae8 20 ♗g1 ♖e4 21 ♖b1 h4 22 ♗h2 ♖fe8. He has a positional bind and went on to win the game.

b) The critical line must be 14 e5 (14 exf5 ♘g4 looks fine for Black) when 14...♘g4 looks better than the immediate exchange on e5 (both for concrete tactical reasons and the fact that Black must be careful about opening lines for the white pieces with his king so exposed). Now 15 e6 would be a terrible blunder on account of 15...♗d4+ 16 ♔h1 ♕h4 17 h3 ♕g3! when White gets mated and 15 h3 dxe5! 16

hxg4 e4 17 g5 exd3 appears quite satisfactory for Black. Perhaps White has to settle for something like 15 ♕e2 and be content with some compensation for the pawn Black will now take on e5.

13...b5!?

One would expect nothing less from the imaginative Spanish grandmaster playing Black in this game. For those of you who relish a quieter life I don't see anything wrong with 13...♘f6, e.g. 14 ♕f3 fxe4 15 ♘xe4 ♗f5 16 0-0 c4 17 ♘xf6+ ♕xf6 18 ♗xf5 ♕xf5 with full compensation for the pawn.

14 exf5?!

After this there is no question that Black has an excellent game. The critical response appears to be 14 ♗xb5. I'm not sure what Romero had in mind apart from the general opening of lines in all sectors of the board. Perhaps he was going to try and win material with 14...♗xc3+ 15 bxc3 ♕a5 16 ♖b1! ♖b8 (not 16...♕xc3+ 17 ♗d2 ♕c2 18 ♖b3!) 17 a4 ♕xc3+ (I don't trust 17...a6 18 0-0! axb5 19 c4) 18 ♗d2 ♕c2 19 ♕g5+ ♔h8 20 ♖c1 ♕xe4+ and now 21 ♔f1 ♖g8 22 ♗c3+ ♘e5 23 ♗xe5+ dxe5 24 ♕f6+ ♖g7 25 ♕f8+ ♖g8 26 ♕f6+ is a draw while I'm not sure what is going on after 21 ♔d1!?

14...c4 15 ♗c2

Maybe 15 ♗e2 is better.

15...♖e8+ 16 ♔f2 ♗xc3! 17 bxc3 ♕b6+ 18 ♔f1 ♘f6 19 ♕h4 ♔f7!

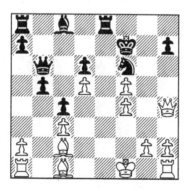

Of course everyone knows that a knight is the best defender for the king. With his bishops hemmed in by his own pawns White's only chance is to advance on the kingside.

20 g4 ♕c5! 21 ♖g1 ♕xd5 22 ♕h3 h5! 23 ♗a3

The wonderful point behind Black's last move is that 23 g5 loses to 23...♗xf5!! when 24 ♕xf5 allows 24...♕f3 mate and 24 ♗xf5 ♕d1+ 25 ♔g2 ♖e2+ 26 ♔h1 ♕d5+ is also the end.

23...hxg4 24 ♖xg4 ♖h8

With some very powerful play Romero has built up a winning position and now, with time no doubt extremely short he opted for a very good ending (obviously 25 ♕xh8 ♕f3+ 26 ♔e1 ♕xg4 is hopeless for White) instead of the even stronger 24...♗b7!. This threatens ♖h8 with a decisive attack and if White plays 25 ♖d1 then 25...♕f3+ wins material.

25 ♕g2 ♕xg2+ 26 ♖xg2 ♗b7 27 ♖e2 ♖ae8 28 ♖ae1 ♖xe2 29 ♖xe2 ♗f3 30 ♖f2 ♘g4! 31 ♖d2

31 ♖xf3 ♘xh2+ 32 ♔f2 ♘xf3 33 ♔xf3 ♖h3+ 34 ♔e4 ♖xc3 and Black wins.

31...♘xh2+ 32 ♔f2 d5

Black has a decisive advantage an went on to win as follows: 33 ♗c5 a6 34 ♗d1 ♗e4 35 ♗e2 ♖g8 36 ♗d4 ♗xf5 37 ♗h5+ ♔e6 38 ♗e5 ♗e4 39 ♗e2 ♖g2+ 40 ♔e3 ♗d3 41 ♗b8 ♗xe2 42 ♖xe2 ♘g4+ 43 ♔f3+ ♖xe2 44 ♔xe2 ♔f5 45 ♔f3 d4 46 cxd4 ♘f6 47 a4 b4 48 d5 ♘xd5 49 ♗e5 b3 50 ♔e2 ♘xf4+ 0-1

6 ♗g5

Game 41
Hauchard-Krakops
Cappelle la Grande 1997

1 d4 ♘f6 2 c4 g6 3 ♘c3 ♗g7 4 e4 d6 5 f3

0-0 6 ♗g5

I have already discussed earlier in the chapter why 6 ♗g5 became quite popular, but it has to be said that its popularity has declined slightly over the last few years as more and more White players prefer 6 ♘ge2. Against 6 ♗g5 I am remaining faithful to the Benoni set-up and suggest that Black plays 6...c5. Incidentally, if you decide to go your own way just make sure you don't play 6...e5?? as it loses immediately.

6...c5 7 d5 e6

8 ♕d2

Occasionally White plays 8 ♘ge2 and now 8...exd5 9 ♘xd5 ♗e6 10 ♘ec3 is a slightly improved version of the main game for White. Therefore, Black should play 8...h6 and exchange on d5 only after the bishop has dropped back to e3. Then play is likely to transpose elsewhere in the chapter.

For example, I reached the position after 8...h6 9 ♗e3 exd5 10 cxd5 a6 11 a4 ♘bd7 twice with Black against Kelecevic.

a) The first time went 12 ♕d2 ♘e5 13 ♘c1 (13 ♗xh6 ♘xe4) 13...♘h7! 14 ♗e2 f5 15 0-0 g5 16 exf5 ♗xf5 and Black was already better because of the misplaced knight on c1.

b) The second time went 12 ♘g3 h5 13 ♗e2 and now 13...h4 14 ♘f1 ♘h7 is Dreev-Gallagher and 13...♘h7 14 0-0 h4 15 ♘h1 f5 is Dreev-Karpov (this is what I played).

Incidentally, don't worry too much about all these confusing move orders. I get pretty confused myself! Just make sure you have a good understanding of the underlying plans.

8...exd5 9 ♘xd5

Because the knight on f6 is pinned White has the option of recapturing with the knight. An important difference but, as we shall see, Black should not lose any sleep over it.

The main line is 9 cxd5 and that is the subject of the next game.

9...♗e6 10 ♘e2 ♘c6!?

Black usually plays 10...♗xd5 so that White has to take back with a pawn. For example, Yusupov-Gelfand, Moscow 1992 continued 11 cxd5 ♘bd7 12 ♘c3 a6 13 a4 ♕c7 14 ♗e2 c4 15 0-0 b5 with an unclear game. The text seemingly allows White to maintain a knight on the important d5-square but Black has a tactical solution to the position.

11 ♘ec3 ♗xd5 12 ♘xd5 h6! 13 ♘xf6+

The first point is that after 13 ♗xh6? ♘xe4! 14 fxe4 ♕h4+ Black regains the piece with advantage.

13...♗xf6 14 ♗xh6 ♗xb2!

15 ♖b1

Black's idea was, of course, to meet 15

♕xb2 with 15...♕h4+. White tries to avoid this exchange but after Black's next move he has no choice but to acquiesce.

15...♗c3! 16 ♕xc3 ♕h4+ 17 g3 ♕xh6 18 ♕d2 ♕h5 19 ♗g2 ♘d4 20 0-0 b6

From a strategic point of view the position is very interesting. At first glance it looks as though Black is doing really well because he has a massive knight on d4 and White a passive bishop on g2. However, that is not the whole story. Black's pawn structure is slightly inferior and White may also be able to create play on the queenside by pushing his a-pawn. Black will also have to keep an eye out for e5 as this would open the position for the white bishop. He can prevent this easily enough by playing f6. The game is about level.

21 f4 ♖ae8 22 ♖be1 ♔g7 23 h3 f6 24 a4 ♖e7 25 a5 bxa5!? 26 ♕xa5 ♘c2 27 g4 ♕h8 28 ♖e2 ♘d4 29 ♖ef2 ♕h4

I'm slightly puzzled as to why Black didn't go here straight away.

30 ♕a6 ♖d7 31 e5 fxe5 32 fxe5 ♖xf2 33 ♖xf2 dxe5 34 ♕c8 ♕e7 35 ♗d5 ♖d8 36 ♕a6 ♖f8 37 ♖xf8 ♕xf8 38 ♕xa7+ ♔h6 39 ♔g2 ♘e2 40 h4 ♘f4+ 41 ♔g3 ♘e2+ 42 ♔g2 ♘f4+ 43 ♔g3 ♘e2+ ½-½

Game 42
Rufener-Gallagher
Bern 1997

---

1 d4 ♘f6 2 c4 g6 3 ♘c3 ♗g7 4 e4 d6 5 f3 0-0 6 ♗g5 c5 7 d5 e6 8 ♕d2 exd5 9 cxd5 a6 10 a4

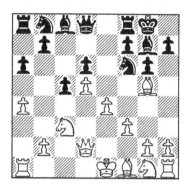

There are a few players who don't consider ...b5 to be a serious threat and just play 10 ♘ge2. The position after something like 10...b5 11 ♘g3 ♘bd7 12 ♗e2 c4 13 0-0 ♘c5 is highly complex with chances for both sides. I'll just say that, playing Black, I always feel more comfortable with the move ...b5 in than without it.

10...h6

It is desirable for Black to break the pin and this is the best moment to attack the bishop.

11 ♗e3

So what happens if White takes the pawn. After 11 ♗xh6 ♘xe4! 12 ♘xe4 ♕h4+ 13 g3 ♕xh6 14 ♕xh6 ♗xh6 15 ♘xd6 ♖d8 16 ♘xc8 ♖xc8 Black has full compensation. This conclusion was reached after a number of games including one where I was White. Funnily enough, if the a-pawns were still at home the position would be more promising for White. The point is that with the pawns on a2 and a7 White can castle queenside quite safely (first he has to play f4 to block out the bishop on h6) but now if he castles long Black will be able to start an attack with ...b5. That is the reason for not playing 9...h6 as then 10 ♗xh6 is certainly an option for White.

11...h5

Of course Black is not forced to move the pawn yet but at some point in the near future White is really going to be threatening to take it. Black will then have to choose between defending it with ...♔h7 (passive) or advancing it. I think it's best to move it at once as the other two natural moves, 11...♘bd7 and 11...♖e8 both have slight drawbacks

a) 11...♘bd7 allows White to play 12 ♘h3!

and after 12...♘e5 13 ♘f2. As I have already pointed out this is thought to be the ideal square for the king's knight in this line.

b) The drawbacks to 11...♖e8 are less obvious and this move is often played. However, with Black's main plan being to play for ...f5 it is not really clear yet if the rook is better on f8 or e8. There are also occasions when Black may retreat his knight from f6 to e8 (see Rogers-Gallagher in the notes below) so, all in all, 11...h5 feels the most accurate.

12 ♘ge2 ♘bd7 13 ♘d1

I refer you to the 12th move notes in Game 37 for a discussion of the ideas behind this.

An alternative for White is to play 13 ♘f4. This awkward-looking move is of a purely defensive nature. The idea is to prevent Black's active plan of ...♘h7 and ...f5. With the knight on f4 it will take an awful lot of arranging to play f5. In SOKID I annotated my nice win against Ian Rogers. Here, I'll just give the moves in brief:

13...♘e5 14 ♗e2 ♗d7 15 0-0 ♘e8 (15...b5!?) 16 ♖fb1 a5! (a most unusual way for Black to play in this line but it made sense to me to prevent b4 and leave the rooks looking rather silly) 17 ♘b5 ♗xb5 18 ♗xb5 ♘c7 19 ♗f1 ♕d7 20 ♖d1 ♔h7 21 h3 b6 22 b3?! f5! 23 exf5?! ♕xf5 24 ♖ac1?! ♖ae8 25 ♗b5 ♖e7 26 ♘e6? ♘xe6 27 dxe6 ♕xe6 28 ♗g5 ♘xf3+! 29 gxf3 ♗d4+ 30 ♔h1 (30 ♔g2 ♖xf3! 31 ♗xf3 ♕xh3+ 32 ♔f4 ♕g4 mate) 30...♖xf3 31 ♗f1 ♕e4! 32 ♔h2 (32 ♗g2 ♖xh3 mate) 32...♖ef7! 33 ♕g2 ♖f2 34 ♔h1 ♖xg2 35 ♗xg2 ♖f3! 0-1 Rogers-Gallagher, Lugano 1999.

13...♘e5 14 ♘ec3 ♖e8!?

You see what I mean about getting confused. I am not sure why I didn't play 14...♘h7 as I did in the game with Klauser (see below). Probably I thought I was following it. The main reason for playing ...♖e8 in such positions is that occasionally White can meet ...f7-f5 with f3-f4, attacking the knight on e5, followed by e4-e5 and after Black plays d6xe5 then ♗e3xc5, which is obviously stronger if it hits a rook on f8. However, that doesn't seem much of a threat here but it is worth bearing in mind for similar positions. Anyway, Klauser-Gallagher, Silvaplana 1997 had gone 14...♘h7 15 ♗e2 f5 16 0-0 ♗d7 17 ♘f2 ♕h4 18 exf5 gxf5 19 ♗f4 ♖ae8 20 ♖ae1 ♕f6 21 ♔h1 ♔h8 with an unclear position that I eventually won.

15 ♗e2 ♘h7 16 ♘f2 f5 17 exf5 gxf5

Although there are quite a few exceptions in general it is better to recapture with the pawn in order to keep control of e4.

18 0-0 ♕h4 19 ♖fe1?!

White got into trouble on the e-file so it is easy, with the benefit of hindsight, to criticise this move.

19...♗d7 20 ♗f4 ♖e7! 21 ♘h3?! ♖ae8

Black is threatening ...♘xf3+ so White decides to defend his rook on e1.

22 ♔f1 b5! 23 axb5 ♘xf3!!

I must have felt good playing that one.

24 ♗xf3

24 gxf3 ♕xh3+

24...♗xc3! 25 ♕xc3

25 ♖xe7 ♗xb5+ 26 ♗e2 ♗xd2 27 ♖xe8+ ♗xe8 28 ♗xd2 is hopeless for White.

25...♗xb5+

The point of 21...b5 is revealed. The check is

crushing as the white king cannot desert the rook on e1.

26 ♗e2 ♖xe2 27 ♖xe2 ♖xe2 28 ♕g3+ ♕xg3 29 ♗xg3 ♘f6 30 ♔g1 ♘e4 31 ♘f4 ♖xb2 32 ♘xh5

Black has a completely won endgame and I only wish that I could now write that I won after a few more moves. But I can't as I somehow contrived to draw! I must have just switched off after the beautiful combination. I can only hope the editor cuts out the remaining moves but in case he doesn't here they are.

32...a5 33 ♗f4 a4 34 ♘g3 ♘xg3 35 ♗xg3 ♖d2 36 ♗xd6 ♖xd5 37 ♗f4 c4 38 ♔f2 ♔f7 39 h4 ♔g6 40 g3 c3 41 ♖c1 ♖c5 42 ♗d6 ♖c4 43 ♔e3 c2 44 ♗f4 a3 45 ♔d2 ♗a4 46 ♖a1 ♗b3 47 ♔c1 ♖a4 48 ♗d6 ♖d4 49 ♗xa3 ♖d3 50 ♔b2 ♖xg3 51 ♗e7 ♔h5 52

♖f1 ♔g4 53 h5 ♗c4 54 ♖h1 ♖e3 55 ♗c5 ♖h3 56 ♖xh3 ♔xh3 ½-½

Summary

1) Black should meet the Sämisch with 6...c5. It is playable against all three of White's 6th move options.

2) The endgame a pawn down after 6 ♗e3 c5 7 dxc5 dxc5 8 ♕xd8 ♖xd8 9 ♗xc5 holds no fears for Black and very few White players accept the pawn in master chess nowadays. Most players are happier to play chess a pawn down with a good position than a pawn up with a bad position.

3) 6 ♗e3 c5 7 ♘ge2 ♕a5 is a very interesting, almost totally unknown move order, which encourages White to transpose into a variation that he discarded. I see no profitable way for White to avoid this transposition.

4) 6 ♘ge2 is probably the most difficult move order for Black to face but with precise play he can achieve a good game. 9...♘h5 (Game 40) is the more controversial way to play and we will have to see if it stands the test of time. 9...h5, despite the comments of Mikhalevski, is a much more respectable line.

5) In these Benoni positions Black would, primarily, like to expand on the queenside. As White usually prevents this his most common method of counterplay comes in the form of ...f5. Black cannot play this variation passively. If he does he will lose.

CHAPTER EIGHT

The Fianchetto Variation

1 d4 ♘f6 2 c4 g6 3 ♘f3 ♗g7 4 g3 0-0 5 ♗g2 d6 6 0-0

The Fianchetto Variation is characterised by White developing his king's bishop to g2. It is a solid, restraining line where it is difficult for Black to obtain active play by the standard means we see elsewhere in this book. In fact the normal plan of attacking on the kingside is simply no longer viable, at least in the early stages of the game. Firstly, because the bishop on g2 affords extra protection to the white king and secondly because, unlike in other lines, White has no intention of blocking the centre. Attacking on the wing is a risky business when the centre is fluid. White's plan in this variation is to stifle Black's active play and gradually use his space advantage.

Gallagher Variation

Although White's play is initially quiet, the Fianchetto is not a harmless system. It is, in fact, an extremely dangerous line for the typical King's Indian player. The positions can be very difficult to handle. In my early King's Indian days I suffered horribly in this line. Things got so bad that I just felt like resigning when I saw my opponent reaching for the g-pawn. These problems continued for many years until I discovered a way to create chaos on the board. In order to create this chaos Black has to take great positional risks but these risks seemed justifiable against the sort of player who plays the Fianchetto Variation. Above all these play-

ers want to control the game and they begin to feel uncomfortable when they feel this control slipping away. Make them dance to your tune and they won't like it – even if the position is objectively in their favour. This system which I helped to develop actually ended up bearing my name. I didn't invent it but did most of the early work on it. I remember playing a never-ending tournament in Baku in 1988 where instead of spending my time preparing for the rather dangerous Soviet opposition I just immersed myself in this fascinating variation. On my return home I started to play it in tournaments (I didn't get the chance in Baku) with amazing results. In those early, heady days of the variation I won game after game, and often in crushing style, against rather confused opposition. Information travelled much slower then and it took sometime for the rest of the world to cotton on. But when they did the variation suddenly became the height of fashion! Everyone started playing it including some of the world's top players. This was of course very pleasing but it had an inevitable downside. White players began to take the variation seriously and, in the quiet of their studies, started to work out the optimum set-up for their pieces. Suddenly the ...c5 and ...b5 attack was no longer blowing White away and the variation began to look rather dubious. The crowds departed almost as suddenly as they had arrived and even I became increasingly unfaithful to the variation. But there seems to have been a mini-revival recently with the new brand of players not so willing to give up their d6 pawn. Nowadays I tend to reserve the variation in its purest form (i.e. ...c5 and ...b5 against whatever White does) for rapid play tournaments or selected opponents, and rely on a closely related but less committal system (8...a6) for more serious tournaments. That second system will form the backbone of the repertoire I am suggesting. However, it would be impossible to play that line properly without a thorough understanding of the ideas behind the Gallagher Variation (and, also, it does seem rather appropriate for me to address this topic). Therefore, the first part of this chapter details the rise and fall followed by the semi-comeback of my variation before moving on to the study of 8...a6 in Games 47-52.

Games 53 and 54 deal with early deviations from White. Let's take a look at some moves.

1 d4 ♘f6 2 c4 g6 3 ♘f3 ♗g7 4 g3 0-0 5 ♗g2 d6 6 0-0 ♘bd7

Black prepares to counter in the centre with ...e7-e5. This is known as the Classical Variation while the other main line, 6...♘c6, is known as the Panno Variation. In this book we are going to concentrate on the Classical. Not because it is a superior line but because I have played it all my life and should be able to impart its secrets better than a line I have hardly ever played.

7 ♘c3

7 ♕c2 is covered in Game 53.

7...e5 8 e4

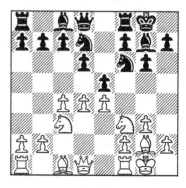

Certain players prefer 8 h3, although this often just transposes back into the main lines. A

discussion of this move order, as well as the independent lines it can lead to, follows later (Games 51-52).

8...exd4

It is anti-positional for Black to concede the centre in this fashion but he does so with a concrete method of developing counterplay in mind. The alternatives are:

a) 8...c6, the old main line which I am steering well clear of as that is where I used to suffer horribly in my youth.

b) 8...a6 will be dealt with in depth in the second half of the chapter.

9 ♘xd4 ♖e8 10 h3

In the past it was thought that 10 ♖e1 was inaccurate because of the reply 10...♘g4 but in Game 48 you can discover that this is not the case. After 10 ♖e1 Black can just play 10...a6 with a likely transposition to the main lines after White plays h3. A few White players have tried to save a tempo by omitting h3 altogether but this means they have to constantly worry about a Black piece coming to g4.

10...a6!?

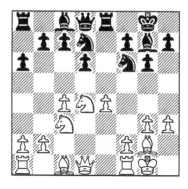

The first sign that Black has something special in mind. In the old days he would play moves such as ...c6, ...♘c5 and ...a5 and try and hold the balance, often unsuccessfully. The problem was that it was very difficult to generate active play. 10...a6 reveals Black's aggressive intentions. It is the first preparatory move in the queenside pawn storm that Black is planning. His next move will be 11...♖b8 and he will then follow up with ...c7-c5 to kick the knight from d4 and then ...b7-b5. Sometimes Black throws in ♘e5 before advancing his pawns, on other occasions he just leaves it on d7. This can be considered as the basic starting position of the Gallagher Variation. White now has various ways to deploy his pieces and these are covered in Games 43-46.

Game 43
Hohler-Gallagher
Bern 1994

---

1 d4 ♘f6 2 c4 g6 3 ♘f3 ♗g7 4 g3 0-0 5 ♗g2 d6 6 0-0 ♘bd7 7 ♘c3 e5 8 e4 exd4 9 ♘xd4 ♖e8 10 h3 a6 11 ♖e1 ♖b8

Black continues the preparation for his queenside offensive.

12 ♗e3 c5

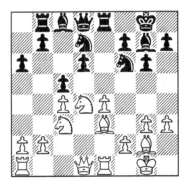

This is the move that shocks the positional men. Not only does Black give himself a backward d-pawn on an open file but he also cedes control of d5. Modern chess players are not so worried about such static details. They are more interested in the dynamics of the position. Black wants to grab the initiative and if that means making sacrificing material or making positional concessions – so be it.

13 ♘de2

Black has an interesting decision to make now. He can either play 13...b5 at once (yes, that's right, ignoring the threat to the d-pawn) or he can throw in the moves 13...♘e5 14 b3 b5 15 f4 ♘ed7 (15...♘c6? 16 e5!). In both cases Black has the same position but in the latter case he has given White the moves f4 and b3 for free! The claim is that these moves actually harm the white position. The move b3 weakens

White on the long dark diagonal while the move f4 means that the bishop on e3 is no longer protected.

White could also have retreated his knight to c2. This is what happened in Miralles-Gallagher, Bern 1991 where Black achieved a very promising position in similar fashion to the main game: 13 ♘c2 ♘e5 14 b3 b5 15 cxb5?! (there is no need for White to exchange of a c-pawn for an a-pawn – the immediate 15 f4 ♘ed7 16 ♕xd6 is the better option) 15...axb5 16 f4 ♘ed7 17 ♕xd6 b4 18 e5 ♖b6! 19 ♕d1 (19 ♕d3 ♗a6) 19...bxc3 20 exf6 ♗xf6. White is close to lost but I managed to spoil a beautiful game in time trouble and Miralles even emerged with the full point.

13...♘e5

13...b5 appears less convincing for tactical reasons. Here is a key variation. 14 ♕xd6 b4 15 ♘a4 ♘xe4 16 ♗xe4 ♖xe4 17 ♘xc5 ♖xe3 18 ♘xd7! ♖xe2 19 ♖xe2 ♖b7 (19...♗xd7 20 ♖d1 ♖b7 21 ♖e7 wins the bishop) 20 ♘f6+ ♗xf6 (or 20...♕xf6 21 ♕xf6 ♗xf6 22 ♖e8+) 21 ♕xd8 ♗xd8 22 ♖e8+ and White wins material.

14 b3 b5 15 f4 ♘ed7

Black must retreat here as 15...♘c6 is strongly met by 16 e5!

16 ♕xd6 b4

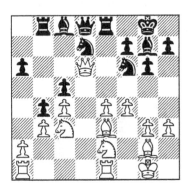

The reason that Black can get away with such opening play is that he is not really attacking on the queenside at all – White's central play would crush an attack there – but he is attacking in the centre himself. The queenside demonstration is just the means employed to destabilise White's e4-point. It can no longer be held.

---

17 e5!

White can't play as in the 13th move note as after 17 ♘a4 ♘xe4 18 ♗xe4 ♖xe4 both the rook on a1 and the bishop on e3 are hanging. The text makes better use of the moves, f4 and b3, that White has been given for free.

17...bxc3 18 exf6?

But this is a serious mistake after which White is in trouble. He should have played 18 ♘xc3! ♘h5 19 g4 ♗f8 20 ♕d2 ♘g7 when in return for the piece White has a couple of pawns and a strong grip in the centre. The position can be considered unclear.

18...♖xe3 19 fxg7 ♖b6! 20 ♕d1 ♖be6

The fine rook manoeuvre has left White stuck in an awkward pin on the e-file.

21 ♖c1 ♕f6 22 ♕c2 ♕e7 23 ♔f2 ♘f6 24 ♖cd1 ♗b7 25 ♗d5 ♗xd5

It was also possible to play 25...♘xd5!? 26 cxd5 ♖6e4 as after 27 d6 Black has a stunning combination: 27...♖f3+! 28 ♔g2 (28 ♔g1 loses to 28...♕d7 with the threat of ♕xh3) 28...♖ee3!! 29 dxe7 (White is also getting mated after 29 ♔h2 ♖f2+ 30 ♔g1 ♖g2+ 31 ♔f1 ♕d7) 29...♖xg3+ (don't forget it's double check!) 30 ♔h2 ♖g2+ 31 ♔h1 ♖xh3 mate.

26 cxd5 ♖6e4 27 ♖d3 c4!

Opening the a7-g1 diagonal so that the black queen can get at the white king.

28 ♖xe3 ♖xe3 29 d6 ♕a7 30 ♕c1?

White had to try 30 bxc4 though after 30...♘e4+ 31 ♔g2 both 31...♘xd6 and 31...♕a8 win comfortably for Black.

30...♘e4+ 31 ♔g2 ♖xg3+! 0-1

In view of 32 ♘xg3 ♕f2+ 33 ♔h1 ♘xg3 mate.

Game 44
Drasko-Gallagher
Aosta 1990

1 d4 ♘f6 2 c4 g6 3 ♘f3 ♗g7 4 g3 0-0 5 ♗g2 d6 6 0-0 ♘bd7 7 ♘c3 e5 8 e4 exd4 9 ♘xd4 ♖e8 10 h3 a6 11 ♗e3 ♖b8 12 ♕c2

At the time of this game the system was still in its infancy and I'm not even sure that Drasko understood what Black was planning? Perhaps not, as now he doesn't get to win the pawn on d6.

12...c5 13 ♘de2 b5 14 ♖ad1 ♕e7 15 ♗f4?!

White is in an ambitious mood. His plan is to lure the black knight into e5 so that he can attack it with a later f4. However, it is all going to explode in his face. A more solid continuation is 15 cxb5 axb5 16 ♘f4 with the plan of occupying d5. The game is very unclear after 16...♗b7!.

15...♘e5 16 cxb5 axb5 17 ♗g5 ♕f8

It's best to get out of the pin. Now Black doesn't have to worry about a knight landing on d5.

18 f4 ♘c4 19 ♕c1 ♗a6!

I'd seen that the tactics were going to work in my favour.

20 e5 dxe5 21 fxe5 ♘xe5! 22 ♗xf6 b4

Black regains the sacrificed piece as the knight on c3 can't move on account of ♗xe2.

23 ♗xe5 ♖xe5 24 ♘d5 ♖xd5! 25 ♖xd5 bxc3 26 ♘xc3 ♗d4+ 27 ♖f2 ♗b7

The black bishops are monstrously powerful

and the white king too exposed.
28 ♖d7 ♕e8 29 ♖c7 ♕e5! 30 ♖cxf7 ♕xg3+ 31 ♔f1 ♗a6+ 32 ♔e1 ♖e8+ 0-1

Game 45
Yin Hao-Ye Jiangchuan
Shanghai 2000

---

1 d4 ♘f6 2 c4 g6 3 ♘f3 ♗g7 4 g3 0-0 5 ♗g2 d6 6 0-0 ♘bd7 7 ♘c3 e5 8 e4 exd4 9 ♘xd4 ♖e8 10 h3 a6 11 ♖e1

For a while it became fashionable for White to withdraw his knight from d4 before it was hit with c5. The moves 11 ♘b3 and 11 ♘de2 are usually described as prophylactic but I prefer to call them cowardly. White is just trying to avoid complications at all costs. The knight was, after all, perfectly well placed in the middle of the board and could only be dislodged by Black taking positional risks. Not surprisingly, Black is able to find adequate counterplay by 'normal' means.

a) 11 ♘b3 ♘e5 12 c5 (the only way to justify his previous move as 12 ♕e2 is well met by 12...♗e6) 12...dxc5 13 ♘xc5 (13 f4 ♘d3 14 e5 ♘h5 15 ♖f3 c4 gets the White centre rolling at the cost of a pawn but the complications favoured Black in Yrjola-Cramling, Nordic zonal 1992) 13...♕e7 14 ♘b3 ♗e6 15 ♕c2 ♖ad8, Spassov-Van Wely, Munich 1992. Black's active pieces more than compensate for White's central pawn majority. The availability of the c4-square for his knight or bishop is an important factor.

b) After 11 ♘de2 Black has a choice between a complex middlegame with 11...♖b8 or a tactical trick which wins a pawn but quickly leads to a drawish endgame. Pr.Nikolic-Gelfand, Wijk aan Zee 1992 continued (after 11 ♘de2) 11...♘b6 12 b3 ♘xe4! 13 ♘xe4 ♖xe4! (13...♗xa1 14 ♗g5) 14 ♗xe4 ♗xa1 15 ♗g2 ♗f6 16 ♘f4 ♖b8 17 ♗e3 ♗d7 (Black obviously felt that keeping the extra pawn by 17...♘d7 was too risky) 18 ♗xb6 cxb6 19 ♕xd6 ♗c6 20 ♕xd8 ♖fxd8 21 ♘d5 ½-½.

11...♖b8

When I became disillusioned (see notes to Black's 14th move) with the variation I started to play 11...♘c5 here. My results were not too

bad but when grandmaster after grandmaster abandoned their normal repertoire in order to take me on in this line I felt it was time to lay it to rest.

12 ♖b1

This innocuous-looking move has caused Black quite a few problems. I think White found this move by a process of elimination. It doesn't do a lot but on the other hand it doesn't do any harm either. It doesn't interfere with the defence of the e-pawn (12 ♗e3), it doesn't expose White on the long diagonal (12 b3) and it doesn't deny White the opportunity to play ♕xd6 (12 ♕c2).

Not only did White players try and make the ...c5 and ...b5 advance less appetising (12 ♖b1) but some of them decided to prevent it altogether. The most obvious way to do this is 12 a4. At first White players were reluctant to play such an anti-positional move. The point is that if Black meets 12 a4 with 12...a5 (12...♘c5 and 12...♘e5 are also possibilities with ...a5 sometimes coming later) he obtains outposts for his pieces on c5 and b4. However, just as Black can get away with his anti-positional advance ...c5, White, too, can make a case for playing a4. The justification lies in the fact that the time spent on the moves 10...a6 and 11...♖b8 has now been lost so White obtains a sizeable lead in development

12...♘e5

Black has the usual choice between playing ...c5 and ...b5 at once or flicking in ...♘e5 first. I don't really trust 12...c5 if only because of the following variation: 13 ♘f3!? (I also have my doubts after 13 ♘c2 b5 14 ♕xd6) 14...b4 15

♘d5 ♘xd5 (15...♘xe4 16 ♕f4 is awkward for Black) 16 ♕xd5 ♗b7 17 ♕d3 ♘f6 18 ♕xd8 ♖bxd8 19 e5 ♘d7 20 ♗g5 ♖c8 21 b3 ♗xf3 22 ♗xf3 ♘e5 23 ♗d5 with an unpleasant endgame for Black. Of course this line is not forced but it's not easy to find anything significantly better for Black.

13 b3 c5 14 ♘c2

Or 14 ♘f3 ♘xf3+ 15 ♕xf3 ♗e6 16 ♗f4. What Black would like to do now his pick up his knight on f6 and place it down again on c6. That would give him maximum control in the centre and chances to occupy the tasty outpost on d4. White's last move is designed to prevent the manoeuvre ...♘d7-e5-c6 as now 16...♘d7 would be met by 17 ♗xd6. What Black must do is play 16...♘h5 and after 17 ♗d2 come straight back with 17...♘f6. He is again in a position to carry out his knight manoeuvre. White must allow the manoeuvre or agree to a repetition of moves after 18 ♗f4 ♘h5.

14...♘c6!

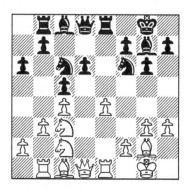

Of course Black would like to play 14...b5 but it simply doesn't work in this position. After 15 cxb5 axb5 16 f4 ♘ed7 17 ♕xd6 there is no good way for Black to continue. I became quite disillusioned with Black's chances against 12 ♖b1 as it takes the sting out of Black's counter-attack. I had assumed that if Black could not force through ...b5 then he would live to regret having played ...c5. However, it, seems that even without the hand to hand fighting of the previous games Black is able to live with his dubious pawn structure. His plan is still to play b5 but at a more convenient moment.

15 a4

This clamps down on the intended ...b5 but at the same time creates holes on the white queenside. These are well covered at the moment but as the game goes on they may become more relevant. 15 f4 is more aggressive and also prevents the immediate ...b5 on account of the reply e5. Gavrikov-Volokitin, Bad Wiessee 2000 continued 15...♗e6 16 ♕d3 b5! 17 ♗d2 (Black exploits the unprotected position of the white queen to force through ...b5; after 17 e5 dxe5 18 ♕xd8 ♘xd8 19 fxe5 ♘d7 Black has a very good position) 17...♘d7 18 cxb5 ♘d4! (more tactics from the young Ukrainian – you'll be hearing more of Volokitin in the future) 19 ♘e3 (19 bxa6 c4! 20 bxc4 ♘c5 forces White to sacrifice his queen to avoid losing the knight on c2) 19...axb5 20 ♕f1 b4 21 ♘e2 f5 with a very active game for Black, although White eventually won.

15...♗e6! 16 ♗b2 h5 17 ♕d2

17 ♘d5 was an alternative.

17...♘h7! 18 ♖ed1 ♗e5! 19 f4 ♗g7 20 ♔h1

20 ♕xd6? ♗d4+ cuts communications between the queen and rook. White is forced to give up the exchange with 21 ♖xd4 but doesn't get sufficient compensation.

20...♕a5 21 ♘d5 ♕xd2 22 ♖xd2 ♗xd5 23 cxd5

White should have played 23 exd5. Although his centre may look impressive the pawn on e4 is just a weakness which Black can attack.

23...♘a5 24 ♗xg7 ♔xg7 25 b4 cxb4 26 ♖xb4 ♘f6 27 ♘e3 ♖bc8 28 ♔g1 ♖c3 29 ♔f2 ♘b3 30 ♘d1 ♖xg3! 31 ♖c2 h4 32 ♖c3 ♘c5 33 e5?

White blunders but even 33 ♖xg3 hxg3+ 34 ♔xg3 ♘fxe4 is losing in the long run.

33...♖xc3! 0-1

White resigned because of 34 exf6+ ♔xf6 35 ♘xc3 ♘d3+.

1 d4 ♘f6 2 c4 g6 3 ♘f3 ♗g7 4 g3 0-0 5 ♗g2 d6 6 0-0 ♘bd7 7 ♘c3 e5 8 e4 exd4 9 ♘xd4 ♖e8 10 h3 a6 11 ♗e3 ♖b8 12 b3

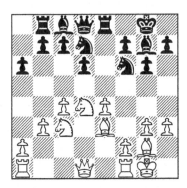

It seems that this set-up also casts doubt on the immediate ...c5 and ...b5 advance and a few players have mentioned to me that this is the refutation of the Gallagher variation.

12...c5

So it is certainly worth considering 12...♕e7!?. The idea is still to play ...c5 and ...b5 but without sacrificing the d-pawn. The game Ruck-Vajda, Hungarian Team Ch. 2003 continued 13 ♖e1 c5 14 ♘de2 b5 15 cxb5 axb5 16 ♘f4 ♕f8 17 a4 with unclear play although I would prefer 16...b4 on positional grounds. Maybe White can improve on the above, but refutation? I don't think so.

13 ♘de2 b5?!

It is better to defend the d-pawn with 13...♕c7 and after 14 a4 (to stop 14...b5) b6! 15 ♖a2 ♗b7 16 f3 ♖bd8 17 ♕d2 ♘e5 Black had a perfectly playable game in Shengelia-Mamodev, Batumi 2003. There are weaknesses in both camps.

14 ♕xd6!

I have always been amazed by how many White players unthinkingly exchange on b5 in similar positions when it is obviously in White's favour to keep the c4 and a6 pawns on the board.

14...b4 15 ♘a4 ♘xe4 16 ♗xe4

16...♖xe4

I spent ages wondering whether to take the rook or not. It seems that White is better after 16...♗xa1 17 ♖xa1 ♖xe4 18 ♘xc5 ♖e8 (I examined both 18...♖b6 and 18...♖xe3 but didn't like either) 19 ♖d1 ♕e7 20 ♕c7! ♘xc5 21 ♕xb8 as Black has insufficient compensation for the pawn.

17 ♖ad1 ♕e8 18 ♘xc5 ♖xe3 19 ♘xd7 ♖xe2

19...♗xd7 20 fxe3 ♗xh3 21 ♖f2 does not offer Black enough for the exchange

20 ♘xb8 ♗xh3 21 ♘d7?

This looks very strong but Black can maintain the balance through a queen sacrifice. The best continuation is 21 ♕b6! ♗f8 22 ♖d8 ♕e4 23 ♕c6! ♕xc6 24 ♘xc6 ♗xf1 25 ♔xf1 ♖xa2 26 ♘xb4 when the powerful white c-pawn will ensure Black has a difficult time in the ending.

21...♗xf1

Not 21...♕a8 22 ♕b8+ with advantage to White.

22 ♘f6+! ♗xf6 23 ♕xf6 ♖e1!

23...♖e6 24 ♖d8 ♗xf6 25 ♖xe8+ ♔g7 26 ♔xf1 is certainly not easier to hold.

24 ♖d8 ♗xc4+ 25 ♔h2 ♗d5?

After 25...♗b5! 26 ♖xe8+ ♖xe8 Black is in no danger as White will only be able to win the pawn on b4 at the cost of a2.

26 ♖xe8+ ♖xe8 27 ♕d6?!

27 ♕xa6 ♖e1 28 g4 should be winning for White. White is still better after the text but Williams just kept playing instantly to try and take advantage of my horrendous time trouble. **27...♗f3 28 ♕xb4 ♖e2 29 ♕c5?! h5 30 g4?! hxg4 31 ♔g3 ♖xa2 32 ♔f4 ♖e2 33 ♔g5 ♖e6 34 ♔h6 g5+ 35 ♔xg5 ♔g7 ½-½**

A tough game but this second round encounter must have put me in good stead for the rest of the tournament as I went on to become British champion that year!

That concludes my direct coverage of the Gallagher Variation.

8...a6

1 d4 ♘f6 2 ♘f3 g6 3 c4 ♗g7 4 g3 0-0 5 ♗g2 d6 6 ♘c3 ♘bd7 7 0-0 e5 8 e4 (8 h3) 8...a6

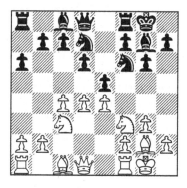

The move 8...a6 was played quite a lot in the 1970's and 80's by the East German grandmasters Vogt and Knaak but then gradually disappeared from practice. It is now back in vogue. As far as I can see White has considerable difficulty in proving any advantage against the semi-waiting move, 8...a6. The basic idea is the same as in the Gallagher Variation – to aim for active play on the queenside with ...b5. This time, though, Black delays his decision on whether to exchange on d4 or not. It all depends on what White does next. The basic rule is that if Black can play ...b5 without having to concede the centre (...exd4) then he will do so. The material is split up as follows:

Game 47: White plays 9 h3. This can be met by 9...b5 as White cannot win a pawn because

of a pin on the a6-f1 diagonal.

Game 48: White plays 9 ♖e1. Now 9...b5 is not playable but by 9...exd4 10 ♘xd4 ♘g4! Black obtains a level game.

Games 49-50: White plays 9 ♕c2 (and others). This has become quite popular and Black can revert to a sort of delayed Gallagher Variation.

Games 51-52: 8 h3 a6 (White delays e4). Quite often this will just transpose into other lines but there are alternatives for both sides.

Game 47
Renet-Gallagher
French League 2003

---

1 d4 ♘f6 2 ♘f3 g6 3 c4 ♗g7 4 g3 0-0 5 ♗g2 d6 6 ♘c3 ♘bd7 7 0-0 e5 8 e4 a6 9 h3

White is very fond of the move h3 in these Fianchetto systems and we shall see in the next game that allowing ...♘g4, and on other occasions ...♗g4, can be irritating for White. It should be said that this position is often reached via the alternative move order 8 h3 a6 9 e4.

9...b5

This may look like a sacrifice but the pawn can't be taken. After 10 cxb5 axb5 11 ♘xb5? ♗a6! Black wins material. For example, 12 a4 ♗xb5 or 12 ♕e2 c6. After 9...b5 the central situation has become very tense. White must now decide what pawn exchanges, if any, he is going to make.

There was of course still the chance to

transpose into the Gallagher Variation with 9...exd4.

10 dxe5

Or:

a) 10 cxb5 can be considered a slight positional concession as White gives up a central pawn for a wing one and at the same time opens the a-file for the black rook. Filippov-Lyrberg, Minsk 1996 continued 10...axb5 11 b4 (An attempt to blockade the position on the queenside. It is perfectly feasible for Black to just play 11...c6 and aim, in the long run, to occupy the square on c4 with a knight. In the game, though, Black prefers to challenge White at once on the queenside.) 11...c5!? 12 bxc5 (Safer was 12 dxe5 dxe5 13 bxc5 b4 14 ♘d5 ♘xc5 with an equal game.) 12...b4 13 ♘e2 (13 ♘a4 exposes the knight and is well met by 13...♕a5 while 13 ♘d5 ♘xd5 14 exd5 e4 is good for Black.) 13...♗b7! (The main point behind Black's play as now there will be no tactical problems on the long diagonal like there would have been after the immediate 13...♘xe4.) 14 cxd6 ♘xe4 15 dxe5 ♘xe5 16 ♘xe5 ♗xe5 17 ♗h6 ♖e8 18 ♖b1 (On 18 d7 Black just plays 18...♖e7 and takes the pawn next move.) 18...♕xd6 19 ♕b3 (Exchanging queens was certainly an option though Black has a slight advantage in the ending as White's pawn on a2 is weaker than Black's on b4.) 19...♘d2 20 ♗xd2 ♗xg2 21 ♔xg2? (21 ♗xb4 ♕c6 probably looked to risky for White as Black gets to keep the powerful light-squared bishop, but the game just looks like a draw after 22 ♖fc1 ♕b7 23 ♗c3 ♕xb3 24 axb3 ♗xh3.) 21...♕xd2 22 ♘c1? (White's previous error should have just cost him his a-pawn but he must have planned all along to defend it in this fashion.) 22...♖a3! (Only now did White realise that if he moves the queen 23...♖xg3+! leads to a mating attack.) 23 ♘d3 ♖xb3 24 ♖xb3 ♗c3 0-1.

b) 10 ♕c2 c6 11 ♖d1 ♕e7 12 ♗e3 exd4 13 ♘xd4 ♗b7 14 cxb5 axb5 15 a3 ♖fe8 was fine for Black in P.Nielsen-Hillarp Persson, Malmö 2003.

10...dxe5 11 ♗e3

Others:

a) 11 ♕e2 c6 (this secures a home for the queen on e7 without having to worry about ♘d5) 12 ♖d1 ♕e7 13 ♘e1!? (the knight wasn't doing a great deal on f3 so it heads off towards the queenside) 13...♘b6 14 c5!? (I must admit that I hadn't seen that one coming at all) 14...♘bd7 (14...♘xc5?? 15 ♗e3 wins a piece) 15 b4 a5 16 ♗a3 (White would be able to claim an edge if he could support his pawn chain with 16 a3 but this is of course impossible because of the pin on the a-file) 16...♘b6! (back we go! the knight wishes to install itself on c4 and 17 cxb6 axb4 is not good for White) 17 bxa5 ♘c4 18 ♗b4 ♘xa5 19 ♘c2 ♗e6 20 ♕e1 ♘c4 21 ♘e3 ♘xe3 22 ♕xe3 ♖fd8. The game is about level and Fedorowicz-Gallagher, Chicago 1999 was drawn in 48 moves.

b) 11 ♕c2 c6 (preparing ...♕e7 again and better than the greedy 11...bxc4? which wrecks Black's queenside for a pawn that he won't even be able to hold on to in the long run) 12 ♗e3 ♕e7 and now:

b1) 13 cxb5 axb5 14 ♖fd1 ♗b7 15 b3 ♖fc8 16 a4 ♘c5 17 a5 ♗f8 18 ♘e1 ♘e6 19 ♘d3 ♘d4 with a good game for Black, Vaulin-Smirnov, Tomsk 1998. The manoeuvres in this game are very typical for this type of position. The hole on d4 makes a fine home for a black knight. Here the queen's knight made it via c5 and e6 while in other games the king's knight heads for d4 via e8-c7-e6.

b2) 13 a3 ♗b7 14 ♖fd1 ♖fc8 15 ♘d2 transposes into Renet-Gallagher.

11...c6

11...b4 12 ♘d5 ♘xe4 13 ♘d2 ♘xd2 14 ♕xd2 ♖b8 15 ♘xb4 is better for White.

12 ♕c2 ♕e7 13 ♘d2 ♗b7

The bishop doesn't really belong here but the idea, in conjunction with the next move, is to be ready to meet an early b4 by White with ...c6-c5 or ...a6-a5.

A reasonable alternative could be 13...♘e8, intending ♘c7-e6. Black could, for example, meet 14 ♘b3 ♘c7 15 ♘a5 with 15...♘b8 as the white knight is not particularly well placed on a5. The move ...f7-f5 may even be on the cards one day but this desirable move is difficult for Black to arrange once he has played ...b7-b5 as there may be trouble on the long diagonal after White plays exf5. I think I will try that next time.

14 a3 ♖fc8 15 ♖fd1

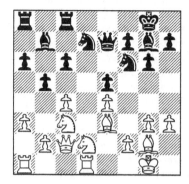

15...♘c5?

This just plays into White's hands and allows him to set up his ideal position.

15...a5 is a better move which I had actually played before. I am afraid that I was totally shocked to see that game on the database afterwards. My memory isn't what it used to be! Perhaps it was because it occurred via a different move order and was actually agreed drawn after 16 ♘e2 (Cvitan-Gallagher, Pontresina 2000). I had assumed the critical test to be 16 cxb5 cxb5 17 ♕b3 attacking the pawn on b5. The natural move is 17...b4 but this runs into 18 ♘d5. Now exchanging on d5 gives White a strong passed pawn but because of his 17th move Black is no longer in a position to play 18...♕d6 as this just runs into 19 ♘c4. After 17 ♕b3 Black does best to sacrifice a pawn with 17...♗c6 18 ♘xb5 (18 ♘d5 ♕d6) 18...♘c5 19 ♗xc5 ♕xc5 as his bishop pair and open lines on the queenside provide adequate compensation.

Interestingly enough, since I wrote that there did occur a game with 15...a5 where the strong grandmaster Predrag Nikolic ground out a win in typical fashion (he once did the same to me in this line): 16 ♖ac1 ♗a6 (16...♘c5? 17 cxb5 cxb5 18 ♘d5 ♘xd5 19 ♗xc5) 17 ♗f1 ♕e6 (17...b4 18 ♘a4 c5 19 ♘b3 ♗b7 20 ♗g2 looks a bit better for White but 17...♕f8 may be a better move) 18 cxb5 cxb5 19 ♕b3! ♕xb3 20 ♘xb3 b4 21 axb4 ♗xf1 22 ♔xf1 axb4 23 ♘d5 with an unpleasant ending for Black, Pr.Nikolic-Stevic, Istanbul 2003.

So perhaps life is not that easy after 15...a5 after all. What should Black play then? Well, it

may be best not to touch the queenside at all, waiting for White to play ♘b3 before playing ...a5. How about 15...h5!?. That was the move Renet was most concerned about and afterwards he revealed that he was not too happy with his position around here. Another idea is 15...♕f8 intending to follow up with ...♗h6. I consider the chances to be about level although the line is not as straightforward for Black as I once thought it to be (and not only me – a lot of annotators were awarding 9 h3 the '?!' symbol until recently).

16 b4 ♘e6 17 ♘b3 bxc4 18 ♘c5!

For some reason I had thought he was going to play 18 ♘a5 when 18...c5! is a good reply.

18...a5

I had just assumed, without any calculation, that I would be able to play 18...♘d4 here but on closer inspection 19 ♗xd4 exd4 20 ♖xd4 ♘d5 21 exd5 ♗xd4 22 d6 ♕f6 23 ♘xb7 ♗xc3 24 ♖d1 persuaded me against this line. Reluctantly, I decided to sit tight and try and soak up the opponent's pressure. The text at least gets rid of one of my weak pawns.

19 ♘3a4 axb4 20 axb4 ♘xc5 21 ♘xc5 ♖d8 22 ♖xd8+ ♕xd8 23 ♖a5 ♕c8 24 ♕a2 ♖b8 25 ♕xc4 ♘d7

The move I had been relying on to ease the situation.

26 ♘d3 ♕d8 27 ♗f1 ♕e7 28 ♖a7 ♕d8

Both players were extremely short of time here. We were down to 30 seconds per move until move 40. Don't ask me why we played so slowly.

29 ♔h2 h5 30 h4 ♘b6 31 ♕a2 ♘c8 32 ♖a5 ♘d6?!

A bluff which worked but 32...♛e7 was more sensible.

33 ♘c5?!

I was planning to meet 33 ♘xe5 with 33...c5 but 34 ♖xc5 ♗xe4 (34...♛e8 35 ♗f4 ♖a8 36 ♛b3) 35 ♘c6 ♗xc6 36 ♖xc6 ♘f5 (36...♖xb4 37 ♛d2) 37 ♗g5 is obviously good for White.

33...♗c8 34 ♖a8 ♛c7 35 ♖a7 ♛d8 36 ♛a5 ♗g4 37 ♛xd8+ ♖xd8 38 ♖c7 ♖c8 39 ♖a7 ♖b8 40 ♘a6 ♖d8 41 ♔g2

I was quite pleased with myself for wriggling out into this roughly level endgame and was looking forward to splitting the point when my team captain suddenly informed me that I had to try to win!

41...♘b5 42 ♖b7

42 ♗xb5 cxb5 43 ♘c7 ♗e2 44 ♖b7 ♗f8 is level.

42...♘d4 43 ♗xd4

43 ♗c4 ♗f3+ 44 ♔h2 ♘e6! was the main idea as after 45 ♗xe6 ♖d1 White gets mated while 45 ♖b8 ♖xb8 46 ♘xb8 ♗xe4 leaves him fighting for a draw.

43...♖xd4!?

The winning attempt. I certainly hadn't imagined it would go quite so smoothly. Instead 43...exd4 44 ♗d3 ♗c8 45 ♖a7 ♗xa6 46 ♖xa6 ♖b8 is a draw.

44 ♘b8 ♗e6 45 ♘xc6 ♖xe4

White has a dangerous pawn but, as we shall see, the white king is not immune from attack.

46 f3 ♖e1 47 ♔f2?!

Renet's attempt to centralise his king ends in disaster. He should have just pushed his b-pawn.

47...♖c1 48 b5 ♖c2+ 49 ♔e1?

It was only now that Renet spotted the variation 49 ♔e3 ♗h6+ 50 ♔d3 ♗f5 mate!! This brought on a fit of panic and he retreated his king. He should still have played this as 50 f4 (instead of 50 ♔d3) 50...♖c3+ (50...exf4+ 51 gxf4 ♗xf4+ 52 ♔xf4 ♖f2+ 53 ♔e5 ♖xf1 54 b6 ♖b1 looks like a draw as well) 51 ♗d3 e4 52 ♘e7+ ♔f8 53 ♔xe4 ♗g7 54 b6 ♖b3 55 ♖c7! should be a draw.

49...e4!

The rest is a massacre.

50 fxe4 ♗c3+ 51 ♔d1 ♖d2+ 52 ♔c1 ♗b3 53 ♖b8+ ♔g7 54 ♖d8 ♖c2+ 55 ♔b1 ♖a2 0-1

Perhaps this is not the greatest advert for the system with 8...a6 but note the suggested improvements in the opening for Black.

Game 48
Tregubov-Gallagher
French League 2002

---

1 d4 ♘f6 2 c4 g6 3 ♘f3 ♗g7 4 g3 0-0 5 ♗g2 d6 6 0-0 ♘bd7 7 ♘c3 e5 8 e4 a6 9 ♖e1

This move prevents 9...b5 as after 10 cxb5 axb5 11 ♘xb5 ♗a6 the knight on b5 is not pinned to the rook on f1 and so can just go back to c3. However, Black now has a simplifying manoeuvre which equalises the game.

9...exd4 10 ♘xd4 ♘g4!

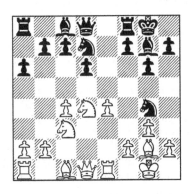

11 h3

Let's have a look at the alternatives:

a) 11 ♛xg4 ♗xd4 12 ♛e2 ♗g7 leads to a

roughly level game. If possible Black will look to continue his development with ...♘e5 and ...♗e6. Note that 12 ♗h6? would be a mistake on account of 12...♘e5! when White doesn't have a good square for his queen, e.g. 13 ♕f4 ♘d3, 13 ♕d1 ♗xf2+! 14 ♔xf2 ♘g4+ wins a pawn and 13 ♕e2 ♘g4! is good for Black.

b) 11 f3 ♘ge5 12 b3 c5!? 13 ♘de2 b5 gives Black good play. Baburin-Robovic, Liechtenstein 1993 continued 14 cxb5 axb5 15 ♗e3 b4 16 ♘a4 ♘c4! 17 bxc4 ♗xa1 18 ♘xc5 ♖xa2 19 ♘d3 ♗g7 20 ♘xb4 and with just one pawn White doesn't have enough compensation for the exchange.

c) 11 ♖f1 ♘ge5 12 b3 ♘c5 13 h3 b5 14 cxb5 axb5 15 f4 ♘ed3 16 ♗e3 b4 17 ♘d5 ♗b7 led to a promising position for Black in Chiburdanidze-Su.Polgar, World Championship match 1995. Not surprisingly White can't get away with playing 9 ♖e1 and then two moves later going back to f1.

d) 11 f4?! c6 12 h3 ♕b6 13 ♘ce2 ♘gf6 14 ♕c2 ♖e8 15 ♗e3 c5! 16 ♘b3 ♘xe4!! 17 ♗xe4 ♘f6 18 ♘c3 ♘xe4 19 ♘xe4 ♗f5 20 ♗f2 ♕c6 21 ♘bd2 ♗xh3 (Black swaps one pin for another) 22 ♖e3 ♖e6 23 ♖ae1 ♖ae8 and White is caught in a terrible bind, Wojtkiewicz-Vogt, Altensteig 1995.

11...♕f6! 12 hxg4

The alternatives:

a) 12 ♘f3 ♘ge5 13 ♘d5 ♕d8 14 ♘xe5 ♘xe5 15 ♕e2 ♖e8 is about level. 15...♗e6 is also a good move. Black's ...♘g4 trick has enabled him to exchange off a minor piece. This means that his space disadvantage is hardly a disadvantage at all as he has enough squares for all his pieces.

b) 12 ♘f5 is another important variation but Black has the strong reply 12...♘xf2! (12...gxf5 13 hxg4 is better for White) 13 ♔xf2 and now not 13...gxf5 14 ♘d5 ♕d4+ 15 ♕xd4 ♗xd4+ 16 ♔f1 which is promising for White, but 13...♘b6! to stop White from playing ♘d5. The knight on f5 is pinned and can be collected later. The game Obukhov-Pugachev, USSR 1990 continued 14 ♗f4 gxf5 15 e5 ♕d8! 16 exd6 cxd6 17 ♗xd6 ♘xc4 18 ♗xf8 ♕xf8 with excellent attacking prospects for Black in return for the exchange.

12...♕xd4 13 ♘d5 c6

Much better than 13...♕xc4 14 ♗f1 with advantage to White. In fact the insignificant-looking text (13...c6, that is) was quite instrumental in Black taking up 8...a6 again. The point is that in the similar position that can arise after 8...exd4 (instead of 8...a6) 9 ♘xd4 ♖e8 10 ♖e1 ♘g4?! 11 h3 ♘f6 12 hxg4 ♕xd4 13 ♕xd4 ♗xd4 14 ♘d5 is very annoying for Black – 14...c6 is not playable as 15 ♘c7 forks the black rooks. With the rook on f8 White cannot play ♘c7 as after ♖b8 the knight on c7 is stuck.

14 ♘e7+

14 ♘e3 ♕xd1 15 ♖xd1 ♘e5 16 ♖xd6 ♘xg4 ½-½ Grabarczyk-Wojtkiewicz, Polish Team Ch. 1997 is not very troubling for Black.

14...♔h8 15 ♕xd4 ♗xd4 16 ♗e3!

This was a novelty from Tregubov as he had played all his moves up to here instantly. Perhaps he believes White has an endgame edge. I don't think so but it is certainly the best try.

16...♗xe3 17 ♖xe3 ♘e5 18 ♘xc8 ♖axc8 19 b3

He still hadn't paused for thought.

19...c5

I decided the most important thing was to secure d4 for the knight in order to try and get a good knight via bad bishop position.

Both 19...♘xg4 20 ♖d3 ♖cd8 21 ♖ad1 and 19...f6 20 ♖d1 ♘f7 are a little uncomfortable for Black, though still tenable.

20 ♖d1 ♖cd8 21 g5

21 f4 ♘c6 22 e5 ♘d4 23 exd6 ♖xd6 24 ♔f2 b6 is fine for Black.

21...♘c6

This allows White to activate his bishop. It would have been safer to play 21...b6 before manoeuvring the knight into d4.

22 e5! ♘d4 23 ♗xb7 dxe5 24 ♔g2??

An unbelievable error. The best way to deal with the threatened ...♘e2+ was 24 ♔f1 when I was planning 24...♖fe8 25 ♗xa6 e4 with some compensation for the pawn. The main point is that after 26 ♗b7 Black wins the exchange with 26...♘c2 although this time after 27 ♖xd8 ♘xe3+ 28 ♔e2! ♖xd8 29 ♔xe3 there is no danger of White losing the game.

24...♘c2!

Black wins the exchange, as 25 ♖ed3, which would have been the response if he had played 24 ♔f1, is no longer possible. It is still not that easy for Black to win but I certainly missed a few chances. The remaining moves were:

25 ♖ee1 ♘xe1+ 26 ♖xe1 f6 27 gxf6 ♖xf6 28 ♖xe5 ♖d2 29 ♗f3 ♖f5 30 ♖e8+ ♔g7 31 g4 ♖f7 32 a4 ♖b2 33 ♖c8 h5! 34 gxh5 gxh5 35 ♖xc5 h4 36 ♖g5+ ♔f6 37 ♖h5 (37...♖xb3! 38 ♖xh4 ♖g7+ looks winning) **38 ♔f1 ♖b1+** (38...♖xb3) **39 ♔e2**

♖e7+ 40 ♔d2 ♖xb3 41 ♗d5! h3 42 ♔c2 ½-½

I could have continued a little with 42...♖a3 43 ♔b2 ♖xa4 44 ♔b3 ♖a1 45 ♖xh3 but I don't even think Black is better here, and this time I just needed a draw to secure an important victory for my team.

1 d4 ♘f6 2 c4 g6 3 g3 ♗g7 4 ♗g2 0-0 5 ♘c3 d6 6 ♘f3 ♘bd7 7 0-0 e5 8 e4 a6 9 ♕c2!?

This became the main line for a while as it more or less prevents Black from playing 9...b5 (see next note for explanation). Black must, therefore, put plan B into operation, i.e. exchange in the centre and aim for a quick ..c5 followed by ...b5. Let's take a quick look at White's other 9th move possibilities which don't merit a game of their own.

a) 9 dxe5 dxe5 10 ♕c2. This is actually played quite often but doesn't have much independent significance as play will be very similar to Game 47. For example, 10...c6 11 ♖d1 ♕e7 12 h3 b5 13 ♗e3 ♗b7 14 a3 ♖fc8 15 ♘d5 a5 16 ♘e2 ♘c5 was the actual move order of the Cvitan-Gallagher game considered in the notes to move 15.

b) 9 d5 can be met by 9...b5 although the position after 10 cxb5 axb5 11 b4 is less trustworthy than the similar one we saw in the notes to Game 47. The difference is that Black cannot play ...c6. In fact after White has blocked the centre with d5 there is no reason why Black shouldn't fall back on the trusty old King's Indian plan of playing for ...f5.

Hübner-Gallagher, Baden 1999 continued 9...♘e8 10 ♗d2 c5 (this makes it difficult for White to create active play on the queenside) 11 a4 a5 (sealing up the queenside is logical as Black is inferior on this side of the board; now the action will take place on the kingside) 12 h4 ♘df6 (it's too early to play 12...f5 as White has the reply 13 ♘g5, threatening ♘e6, so Black brings some more pieces to the kingside) 13 ♕e2 ♘h5 14 ♖e1 ♘ef6 15 ♘c2 ♘g4 (15...f5 would have led to a more complicated game) 16 ♘e3 ♘h6 17 ♘xg4 ♗xd2 18 ♕xd2 ♗xg4 19 ♘b5 ♕e7 with an equal game.

c) 9 ♖b1 b5 10 cxb5 axb5 11 b4 (11 ♘xb5 ♗a6 12 a4 c6 13 ♘xd6 ♗xf1 is unclear but Black can also consider 11...♗b7) 11...c6 (c5 is not available to Black with the white rook on b1 so she must adopt the more solid plan) 12 ♕c2 (the boring 12 dxe5 comes into consideration) 12...exd4 13 ♘xd4 ♘e5! 14 h3 (14 f4 ♘c4 15 ♘xc6? fails to 15...♕b6+) 14...♗d7 15 ♖d1 ♕c8 16 ♔h2 h5 with active play for Black, Pr.Nikolic-J.Polgar, Monte Carlo (rapid) 1995.

9...exd4

9...b5?! is not so promising as the position after 10 dxe5 dxe5 11 ♖d1! (better than 11 ♘xb5) is uncomfortable for Black. He would like to play 11...♕e7 but this is strongly met by 12 ♘d5.

10 ♘xd4 ♖e8 11 ♘de2

It's not completely clear if Black is threatening to take on e4, e.g. 11 h3 ♘xe4 12 ♘xe4 ♗xd4 13 ♗g5 gives White play for the pawn but this tactic is usually prevented by the natural move 11 ♖d1. Rogozenko prefers to beat a prophylactic retreat with his knight. He knows that Black wants to play ...c5 and ...b5 so he gets his knight out of the way of c5 and plays a4 on his next move to prevent ...b5. Tigran Petrosian, World Champion 1963-69, would have been proud of him. His approach to chess was to stop the opponent's aggressive ideas before they even thought of them!

For 11 ♖d1 see Game 50.

11...♖b8 12 a4

White continues the prophylactic approach.

In Stohl-Kindermann, Bundesliga 1999 he played 12 ♗e3 and after 12...b5 13 cxb5 axb5 14 ♘d4 ♘e5 15 f4 ♘fg4 16 ♗c1 c5 17 ♘dxb5 ♘c6 18 h3 Black should have played 18...♘d4 19 ♘xd4 ♗xd4+ 20 ♔h1 ♘f6 with good compensation for the pawn.

12...a5!

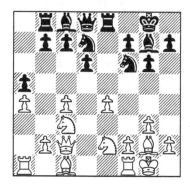

White's last move prevented Black from playing ...b5 so he had to find another idea. The first thing is to secure the c5-square for his knight.

13 b3 ♘c5 14 ♗a3 b6 15 ♖ad1 h5!?

Advancing the h-pawn to soften up the white king position is not an uncommon way for Black to treat such positions. 15...♗b7 and 15...♕e7 are more solid alternatives.

16 ♘d4 ♗d7 17 ♖fe1 h4!?

When playing this move I had obviously seen White's central breakthrough but hadn't appreciated the sort of gymnastics I would have to perform to stay in the game.

18 e5 ♘g4!

My original idea had been to play 18...♘h5 but I couldn't find a satisfactory defence to the powerful move 19 ♗d5!. The threat is 20 ♕xg6 and 19...♔f8 20 e6! didn't inspire confidence. Still, I wasn't too unhappy with the text as White can't play 19 exd6 on account of 19...♖xe1+ and 20...♗xd4.

19 f4 hxg3 20 hxg3

This game was played in the German Bundesliga and at this point I thought for so long that my captain started to give me a lot of funny looks. I eventually moved when I had less than a quarter of an hour left to reach move 40. I had assumed that I would be able to give up an exchange for an attack but now realised this wasn't possible. I was going to have to give up a lot more.

20...dxe5 21 ♘c6 exf4!!

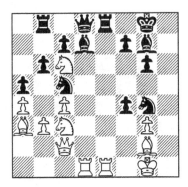

Yes, a whole queen! This move made it into grandmaster John Emms' book on the most amazing moves of all time. The alternatives are hopeless.

22 ♘xd8

What now?

22...♗d4+! 23 ♔h1

The beautiful point is that 23 ♖xd4? loses to 23...♖xe1+ 24 ♗f1 ♖xf1+! 25 ♔xf1 ♘e3+ 26 ♔g1 ♘xc2 forking the rook on d4 and the bishop on a3. After 27 ♗xc5 ♘xd4 28 ♗xd4 ♖xd8 Black wins the ending. The other nice point is that the white king is forced into the corner as 23 ♔f1 ♘h2! is checkmate.

23...♖xe1+!

Black must exchange rooks before giving the knight check. After 23...♘f2+ 24 ♕xf2! White is winning.

24 ♖xe1 ♘f2+ 25 ♕xf2?

I think my opponent was in a state of shock by what had just happened on the chessboard and he played this losing move almost instantly. He probably just saw that 25 ♔h2 ♘g4+ 26 ♔h1 ♘f2+ was a draw by perpetual check and played the text by a process of elimination. Remember I hardly had any time left so he wanted to keep the game going at all costs. In fact White can avoid the draw by 25 ♔g1

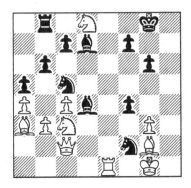

as with no black rook on the e-file 25...♘g4+ 26 ♔f1 ♘h2+ is no longer mate. True, Black still has a vicious attack after 27 ♔e2 ♗g4+ 28 ♔d2 ♖xd8 but it is hard to believe that it can succeed with only one piece for the queen. This variation was not what I had in mind when I sacrificed the queen. On 25 ♔g1 my idea was to play 25...♘e4+. Now 26 ♔f1 ♘xg3 is mate and 26 ♔h1 ♘f2+ the same draw by perpetual check we have already seen. Therefore if White wants to play for a win he must try 26 ♔h2 fxg3+ 27 ♔h1 ♘f2+ 28 ♔g1 with the difference being that after 28...♘e4+ 29 ♔f1 Black can no longer play 29...♘g3 mate as he now has a pawn on this square!. All is not lost though. Instead of 28...♘e4+ Black should play 28...♘fd3+ 29 ♔f1 ♘xe1 30 ♔xe1 ♖xd8 when he has a rook, three pawns and an ongoing attack for the queen. Rogozenko annotated this game in famous periodical *Chess Informator* and claimed that White has the advantage here (although he stopped short of saying that White was winning). I have my own ideas. Perhaps next time we play the game can start from this position!

25...♗xf2 26 ♖f1 fxg3 27 ♘c6 ♖e8

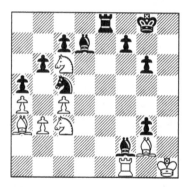

So the dust has more or less settled and Black has emerged with three pawns for a piece. Normally this would mean approximate equality but not here. Despite the fact that queens have been exchanged the white king is still in grave danger of getting checkmated. The bishop on f2 supported by the pawn on g3 is a particularly potent combination. All Black needs to do now is to get a rook to the h-file. White's next move was motivated by the fact that he wanted to stop ...♔g7 and ...♖h8 but he forgot that Black has other ways to get his rook to the h-file. The last chance, albeit a very small one, was offered by 28 ♗xc5.

28 ♗b2? ♘d3 29 ♗a1 ♖e6! 30 ♘b8 ♖e5

The cleanest route to victory was offered by 30...g5! 31 ♘xd7 ♖h6+ 32 ♗h3 ♖xh3+ 33 ♔g2 ♘f4+ 34 ♔f3 g2+ 35 ♔xf2 ♖f3+ 36 ♔xf3 gxf1♕+ but by this stage I had just over a minute for ten moves. Any win would do!

31 ♗f3 ♗h3 32 ♖d1 ♖e1+ 33 ♖xe1 ♘xe1 34 ♗e4 g2+ 35 ♗xg2 ♗xg2+ 36 ♔h2 ♘d4! 37 ♔g3 ♗b7 38 ♘d7 f5 39 ♔f4 ♔f7 40 ♘e5+ ♗xe5+

The time scramble is over. Black should have done better than an ending with two extra pawns but it is still a trivial win.

41 ♔xe5 ♘f3+ 42 ♔f4 ♘d2 43 ♘b5 ♘xb3 44 ♗e5 c6!

The last tactical trick of the game. Now after 45 ♘d6+ ♔e6 46 ♘xb7 g5+! 47 ♔xg5 ♔xe5 nothing can stop the black f-pawn.

45 ♘c3 ♘c5 46 ♗b8 ♗a6 47 ♗a7 ♘d7 0-1

White called it a day. Not only is he three pawns down but his bishop is boxed in the corner.

Game 50
Hübner-Polzin
Bundesliga 2003

1 d4 ♘f6 2 c4 g6 3 g3 ♗g7 4 ♗g2 0-0 5 ♘c3 d6 6 ♘f3 ♘bd7 7 0-0 e5 8 e4 a6 9 ♕c2 exd4 10 ♘xd4 ♖e8 11 ♖d1 ♖b8 12 a4

Hübner decides to prevent ...b5 and as a good classical player he probably thought that ...c5 would be no good if Black can't follow up with ...b5.

12 h3 has been played more often and we can see from the course of the main game how useful it is to have the g4-square protected. However, Black does not seem to have too many problems after 12 h3 c5, e.g.

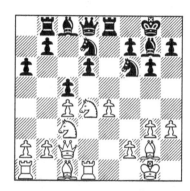

a) 13 ♘f3 b5 14 ♖xd6 (14 cxb5 axb5 15 ♖xd6 b4 is similar) 14...b4 (if the knight now moves then Black plays 15...♘xe4) 15 e5 bxc3 16 exf6 cxb2 17 ♗xb2 ♖xb2 18 ♕xb2 ♗xf6, C.Hansen-Van Wely, Groningen 1995, and now 19 ♕xf6 ♕xf6 20 ♖xf6 ♘xf6 21 ♖b1 leads to a level endgame.

b) 13 ♘de2 ♘e5 14 b3 b5 and now we have two games:

b1) 15 f4 ♘c6! 16 e5 (normally Black can't retreat to c6 after White plays f4 but Black has spotted a tactical resource which saves the piece) 16...♗f5! 17 ♕d2 (17 ♕b2 ♘d4! is also fine for Black) 17...♘d4 18 exf6 ♘xe2+ 19 ♘xe2 ♕xf6 20 ♗a3 b4! (20 ♗a3 was the only move to save the rook on a1 but now Black regains the piece with an equal game) 21 ♗xb4 ♖xb4 22 ♖ac1 ♖bb8 23 g4 ♗e4 24 ♘c3 ♗xg2

25 ♔xg2 ♕d4 26 ♖c2 ♕xd2+ ½-½ Filippov-Khalifman, Ubeda 1997.

b2) In view of the above, in a game between the Indian stars, Harikrishna-Sasikiran, Lausanne 2001 White tried 15 ♗e3. This contains a nasty trap as 15...b4? is strongly met by 16 ♗xc5! bxc3 17 ♗xd6!. Young prodigies see this sort of thing so Black preferred 15...♕c7 and after the further moves 16 cxb5 axb5 17 ♘f4 ♗e6 18 ♖ac1 b4 19 ♘xe6 ♖xe6 (19...fxe6!?) 20 ♘a4 the game was unclear.

12...c5!?

12...a5 to take control of the c5 and b4-squares is another approach but Black may not have liked this because of the reply 13 ♘db5.

13 ♘de2 ♘e5 14 b3

Hübner must have been tempted by 14 f4 but eventually settled on the solid choice. After 14...♘xc4 15 b3 (15 e5 ♗f5 16 ♕b3 ♘a5 is not an improvement for White) 15...♘a5 16 e5 ♗f5 17 ♕a2 ♘d7 18 ♖xd6 White has a positional advantage but lacks co-ordination. Unclear is my verdict.

14...♗g4! 15 ♗e3

15 f4 ♘f3+ 16 ♗xf3 ♗xf3 17 e5 ♕c8! 18 ♖xd6? ♕h3 and rather embarrassingly the knight on e2 has no square.

15...♘f3+ 16 ♔h1 ♘d4!

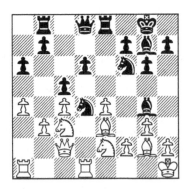

By exploiting the pin Black is able to steer the game towards a drawish position.

17 ♗xd4

17 ♘xd4!? ♗xd1 18 ♖xd1 cxd4 19 ♗xd4 is also about equal and may be a better winning chance.

17...cxd4 18 ♖xd4 ♗xe2 19 ♕xe2 ♘xe4

19...♕b6 looks like a serious alternative as after 20 ♖d3?! Black can safely take the pawn, e.g. 20...♕xb3 21 ♘b5 ♕b4 (21...♕xc4 22 ♘xd6) 22 ♘xd6 ♘xe4 23 ♘xe8 ♖xe8 24 ♗xe4 ♗xa1 with advantage to Black.

20 ♖xe4 ♖xe4 21 ♗xe4 ♗xc3 22 ♖d1 ♕e7

Black's choice has led to an endgame with a token advantage to White, but one where he shouldn't really have any difficulty holding the draw.

23 ♕f3 ♗b4 24 ♗d5 ♗c5 25 ♔g2 ♔g7 26 ♕c3+ ♕f6 27 ♕xf6+ ♔xf6 28 ♖e1 b6 29 h4 h6 30 f4 h5 31 ♔f3 a5 32 ♖e2 ♖c8 33 ♖e1 ♖b8 34 g4 hxg4+ 35 ♔xg4 ♖h8 36 ♖f1 ♔g7 37 f5 gxf5+ 38 ♖xf5 f6 39 ♖f4 ♖e8 40 ♖e4 ♖e5 41 ♖xe5 ½-½

As is often the case in these type of positions Black's initiative proved strong enough to overcome the positional defects.

Game 51
Galliamova-Renet
Koszalin 1997

---

1 d4 ♘f6 2 c4 g6 3 ♘f3 ♗g7 4 g3 0-0 5 ♗g2 d6 6 0-0 ♘bd7 7 ♘c3 e5 8 h3

This is a common move order. Most of the time White will follow up with e4 and we have transposed into lines already considered. This game deals with lines where White refrains from playing e4. Why would he (or she in this case) want to do that? Well, there are a couple of main reasons. Firstly, the bishop on g2 may now exert more influence on the game as its diagonal is not blocked by a pawn on e4. Secondly, White may be able to use the e4-square for his, or her, pieces. Usually this means a knight using the square as a stepping stone towards d6. There are also drawbacks to White not playing e4, the principal one being that it is easier for Black to advance his pawns.

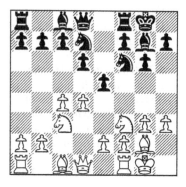

8...a6

There is no need for Black to react any differently. Remember that most of the time White is just going to play 9 e4. However, if you are concerned about the dull games that can, but not necessarily, arise after 9 dxe5 then you can play 8...exd4 9 ♘xd4 and then either 9...♖e8, when White has nothing better than 10 e4 (Games 43-46), or 9...♘b6 which is covered in Game 52.

9 dxe5

Such an exchange is usually considered wimpish and played by those who are angling for a quick draw. Here White can claim that he is trying to prove that Black's ...a6 was premature. The point is that Black will not be able to get by without playing ...c6 and this will create a hole on the b6-square. White will then play c5 to fix the queenside pawn structure thereby creating outposts for his knights (or other pieces) on b6 and d6. In my view this is not too serious. True, Black is likely to experience some discomfort on the queenside but this is compensated for by the fact that White's exchange on e5 gives the black pieces plenty of freedom. Sometimes this freedom can be translated into a kingside attack while on other occasions it just leads to mass exchanges and an early peace treaty. Let's take a look at the White alternatives:

a) 9 e4 transposes to Game 47.

b) 9 ♗e3 exd4 10 ♘xd4 ♖e8 11 ♕d2 (otherwise Black would be sorely tempted to sacrifice an exchange on e3) 11...♘c5 (another problem with not playing e4 is that Black may be able to occupy this square with his pieces; to avoid this White now gives up his bishop for a knight) 12 ♗g5 ♕d7 13 ♗xf6 ♗xf6 14 ♖ad1 ♗g7 15 e3, Gelfand-J.Polgar, Dortmund 1996. The game is about level. White has more space but could still end up regretting having parted with the bishop pair.

c) 9 b3 is a solid move. Black could just reply 9...♖e8 but Baburin-Gallagher, Mind Sports Olympiad 1999 went a different way: 9...exd4 10 ♘xd4 ♖b8 11 ♗b2 ♖e8 12 ♖e1 ♘e5 13 e4 (I was planning to meet 13 f4 with 13...c5) 13...♗d7 (the problem with 13...c5 14 ♘c2 b5 is that after 15 f4 Black can't play 15...♘c6 on account of 16 e5!; there are no miraculous resources this time) 14 f4 ♘c6 15 ♘c2 b5 16 cxb5 axb5 17 b4 (With my queenside play halted I became concerned about drifting into a passive position. What I really wanted to do was get a knight to c4 but there is no route. Then I found one.) 17...♘h5 18 ♔h2 ♘e5! (If White now takes the piece then Black will get attacking chances against his king, e.g. 19 fxe5 ♗xe5 20 ♖e3 ♘xg3! 21 ♖xg3 h5! is very good for Black. White does better to play 20 ♔g1 but after 20...♘xg3 21 ♘d4 c5 Black has plenty of play, not only against the white king but also on the long dark diagonal. Baburin didn't like the look of all this and played...) 19 ♘e3 (...as I felt certain he would) but after 19...♘c4 20 ♘xc4 bxc4 21 a3 c5! Black had an active game. The idea is to meet 22 ♕xd6 with 22...cxb4 23 axb4 ♗xh3! and this fascinating variation actually occurred in the game. Unfortunately, I eventually lost through over-excitement.

9...dxe5 10 ♗e3 ♕e7

Black tries to hold up c5 and there is no need, just yet, to worry about 11 ♘d5 as this is well met by 11...♘xd5 12 exd5 e4.

11 ♕b3

Here are a couple of other examples to show you how play can develop:

a) 11 ♕d2 c6 12 ♖ad1 ♘c5 13 ♗g5 a5 14 ♕e3 ♖e8 15 ♘d2 ♕f8 16 g4 ♘fd7 17 ♘de4 f5 18 gxf5 gxf5 19 ♘d6 ♖e6 with good play for Black, Brunner-Gabriel, Zürich 1995.

b) 11 ♕c1 c6 12 ♖d1 ♘h5!? 13 g4 ♘f4! (there is no question of retreating once ♘h5 has been played)14 ♗xf4 exf4 15 ♕xf4 ♘c5 16 e4 ♗e6 17 e5 f6 18 exf6 ♗xf6 with good compensation for the pawn, Vaganian-Gallagher, Bundesliga 1998.

11...c6

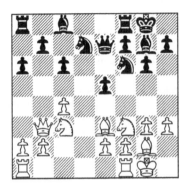

12 c5

It's funny how seldom White has played this move as if Black takes the pawn, 12...♘xc5, he gets caught in a nasty pin by 13 ♕a3 or 13 ♕b4. More often White has played 12 ♖fd1 with a couple of examples:

a) 12...♖e8 13 ♘g5 ♘c5 14 ♗xc5 ♕xc5 15 ♘ce4 ♘xe4 16 ♘xe4 ♕a5! (Black keeps e7 free for his rook as from there it defends the sensitive points b7 and f7; in a previous game Black had got into trouble after 16...♕e7 17 ♘d6) 17 ♘d6 ♖e7 18 ♖ac1 ♕c7 ½-½ Ruck-Gallagher, Charleville 2000. White has the choice between taking on c8, which kills the game, or letting the bishop out to e6 when it will in no way be an inferior piece to the white knight on d6.

b) 12...♘e8 is perhaps more logical than my choice as it frees the f-pawn and envisages a nice home for the knight on c7. From there it can go to e6, or perhaps d5 after White has played c5. Ribli-Beliavsky, Hungary 1998 continued 13 c5 ♘c7 14 ♖ac1 ♔h8 15 ♘e4 f5 16 ♗g5 (it is much too dangerous for White to play 16 ♘d6 on account of 16...f4; the bishop must get out of the way of the f-pawn) 16...♕e6 17 ♘d6 e4 18 ♘xc8 (White would prefer to not make this exchange but after 18 ♘d4 ♗xd4! 19 ♖xd4 ♕xb3 20 axb3 ♘e6 Black wins material) 18...♖axc8 19 ♘d4 ♕xb3 20 axb3 and now

Black missed a chance to win a pawn. He should have played 20...♘xc5! 21 ♖xc5 ♗xd4 22 ♖xd4 ♘e6 with a massive fork. White has nothing better than 23 ♖cc4 though after 23...♘xg5 24 ♖d7 Black can just defend his 2nd rank with 24...♖f7.

12...♔h8

Black plans to move his knight and push his f-pawn. That is how he creates counterplay in this line.

13 ♘d2 ♘g8 14 ♘de4 f5 15 ♗g5

As mentioned in the notes above White must get his bishop out of the way of f4.

15...♘gf6 16 ♗xf6 ♘xf6 17 ♘d6 e4

So the white bishop still gets locked out of the game but this time not by his own pawn on e4 but by a black one.

18 e3 ♖b8 19 ♖fd1 ♗e6 20 ♕a3 h5

Black stands well. White has one trump in this position – the knight on d6. In return Black has two good bishops, his own outpost on d5 and attacking chances against the white king. The players eventually agreed to a draw in an unclear situation, probably because of looming time trouble.

21 h4 ♘d5 22 ♘e2 b6 23 ♘d4 bxc5 24 ♕xc5 ♗d7 25 ♘b3 ♗xb2 26 ♖ab1 ♗f6 27 ♘a5 ♘c3 28 ♖xb8 ♖xb8 29 ♕a7 ♖f8 30 ♖d2 ♘d5 ½-½

Game 52
Vaganian-Volokitin
European Ch., Istanbul 2003

1 ♘f3 ♘f6 2 c4 g6 3 d4 ♗g7 4 g3 0-0 5

♗g2 d6 6 ♘c3 ♘bd7 7 0-0 e5 8 h3 exd4 9 ♘xd4 ♘b6!?

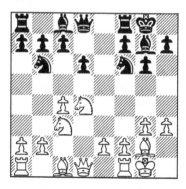

An interesting idea to try and punish White for delaying e4 by forcing through a quick ...d5.

10 b3 d5

10...c5 has been played more often although White probably retains a small edge after 11 ♘c2 ♗e6 12 ♗b2 d5 13 ♘xd5 ♘fxd5 14 ♗xg7 ♔xg7 15 cxd5 ♗xd5 16 e4. In such middlegame positions the advantage is often with the side who retains the fianchettoed bishop. His king is safer!

11 ♗a3 ♖e8 12 c5 ♘bd7 13 c6 ♘e5 14 cxb7 ♗xb7 15 ♖c1 a6 16 ♘a4 ♘e4 17 ♘c5 ♘xc5 18 ♗xc5 ♘d7

19 e3

The last moves have been all about the battle for the c5-square. In a game not long after this one White preferred to keep his bishop and played 19 ♗a3. Play continued 19...c5 20 ♘c2 ♕g5 21 h4 ♕h5 (luring the bishop to f3 so he can hit it later with ...♘e5 but it may well have

been better to just play 21...♕e5) 22 ♗f3 ♕f5 23 ♕d2 ♕e6 24 ♖fd1 ♖ad8 25 ♗xd5 ♗xd5 26 ♕xd5 ♕xe2 27 ♖e1 and now in Illescas-Moreno Ruiz, Burgos 2003 Black played 27...♘e5? and lost the ending. But 27...♕b5! is much better. Why exchange queens when you have the worse pawn structure and the opponent's king is more exposed? After 27...♕b5 the chances look about equal.

19...♘xc5 20 ♖xc5 ♗f8 21 ♖c2 c5 22 ♘e2 ♕d7 23 ♘f4 ♖ad8 24 ♖d2 d4! 25 ♗xb7 ♕xb7 26 exd4 ♕b4!

27 ♖e2

27 d5 ♗h6 28 ♖e1 ♗xf4 29 ♖xe8+ ♖xe8 30 gxf4 ♕xf4 31 d6 ♖d8 should be a draw because of the exposed position of the white king.

The position is also drawn after the text and the remaining moves were 27...♕xd4 28 ♕xd4 cxd4 29 ♖xe8 ♖xe8 30 ♖d1 g5 31 ♘h5 ♖e2 32 ♖xd4 ♖xa2 33 ♖d8 h6 34 g4 ♖b2 35 ♖b8 a5 36 ♖b5 ♗b4 ½-½,

This appears to be a good and solid way for Black to meet 8 h3.

Early Deviations

Now we shall look at two other variations for White. Game 53 deals with 7 ♕c2 and Game 54 with an early b3 from White.

Game 53

Loginov-Ryskin

Wisla 1992

1 ♘f3 d6 2 d4 ♘f6 3 c4 g6 4 g3 ♗g7 5

♗g2 0-0 6 0-0 ♘bd7 7 ♕c2

This queen move is the main alternative to 7 ♘c3. White plans a quick ♖d1 to create pressure on the d-file. This variation was initially pioneered by the Ukrainian grandmaster Oleg Romanishin.

7...e5 8 ♖d1 exd4

The main line runs 8...♕e7 9 ♘c3 c6 but that would force Black to play another type of game to the one I've been recommending throughout this chapter. There is no reason why Black should not follow the usual recipe, i.e. exchange on d4, play ...♖e8, ...a6 and ...♖b8 and then try and force through ...c5 and ...b5.

9 ♘xd4 ♖e8 10 ♘c3 a6 11 b3

After 11 h3 ♖b8 12 e4 we have transposed to the 12th move notes in Game 50.

11...♖b8 12 e4

When White plays b3 in these fianchetto lines it does not necessarily mean that he is going to follow up with ♗b2. Most White players believe that the bishop is more actively placed on e3. The move b3 is played with the primary objective of protecting the pawn on c4.

12 ♗b2 is still perfectly playable in this position. After 12...♘e5 (the plan of ...c5 and ...b5 is not so effective when White has not played e4 as this pawn is not a target back on e2) there are a couple of Van Wely games:

a) 13 ♖d2 h5 14 ♖f1 h4 (as in Rogozenko-Gallagher , Black uses his h-pawn to pound the position around the white king) 15 ♘d5 ♘fd7 (rather than exchanging on d5 Black plans to drive the white knight back by playing ...c6) 16 e4 hxg3 17 hxg3 ♘g4 18 ♖e1 c6 19 ♘e3 ♘de5 with quite a promising game for Black, Piket-Van Wely, Dutch Ch. 1991.

b) 13 c5 is the most critical test of ...♘e5. Of course Black can't play the capture 13...dxc5 on account of 14 ♘c6 but 13...d5 14 e4 c6 15 h3 ♕e7 16 exd5 cxd5 17 b4 ♘c6 18 ♕b3 ♗e6 led to an unclear game in Gross-Van Wely, Bundesliga 1997.

12...♕e7!?

In Baburin-Van Wely, Leukerbad 1992 Black played the traditional 12...c5 13 ♘de2 b5 but after 14 cxb5 axb5 15 ♗f4 ♘e5 16 ♗xe5! ♖xe5 17 f4 ♖e7 18 e5 found himself in trouble because his queen was badly placed opposite the black rook. The text, therefore, is a sensible

precaution to take before embarking on the queenside advance.

See also the suggested improvement in Game 46.

13 f3

White reinforces his e-pawn. An alternative was to play 13 ♗b2 when Black can play 13...♘e5 or the immediate 13...c5 14 ♘de2 b5 15 cxb5 axb5 16 ♘f4 ♗b7 (so as to be able to keep taking white knights that arrive on d5) 17 ♘xb5 ♗xe4 18 ♗xe4 ♕xe4 19 ♕xe4 ♘xe4 20 ♗xg7 ♖xb5! (20...♔xg7 21 ♘xd6) 21 ♗b2 c4 when White has a strong bishop on b2 but Black has pressure against the queenside pawns. A draw is the most likely outcome.

Before playing a move such as 12...♕e7 Black would also have had to take the reply 13 ♘d5 into account. In certain positions Black would avoid ♕e7 because of this move. Here, Black seems to be doing all right after 13 ♘d5 ♘xd5 14 cxd5 ♘c5 15 ♗b2 ♗d7 (so that b4 can be met by ♗a4; 15...♘xe4? 16 ♖e1 would have left Black stuck in a fatal pin). Black will seek counterplay by either ...c6 or ...f5 at an appropriate moment.

13...♘e5 14 ♗e3

The alternative 14 f4 ♘c6 did not concern Black. The white position is very loose. After the text Black is ready for the customary queenside offensive.

14...c5 15 ♘de2 b5 16 cxb5 axb5

17 ♕d2?

This allows Black to take over the initiative. Although the pawn on d6 is attacked White won't be able to find the time to take it. 17 ♘f4 was better. This would avoid the tactical problems he ran into by having too many pieces on the e-file and also threaten to play a knight to d5. 17...♗e6 or 17...♗b7 (18 ♘xb5 ♗xe4 19 fxe4 ♖xb5) are reasonable replies while a case could also be made out for 17...b4 18 ♘cd5 ♘xd5 19 ♘xd5 ♕a7.

17...b4 18 ♘a4 ♗a6?!

This is a strong move which prevents White capturing the d-pawn as the white knight on e2 would then be lost, but 18...♘xf3+! 19 ♗xf3 ♘xe4 is more powerful. I don't see how White can obtain a playable game, e.g. 20 ♗xe4 ♕xe4 21 ♔f2 ♗b7 and White can resign. 20 ♕d3 ♗f5! 21 ♗xe4 ♗xe4 22 ♕d2 ♗c6 is equally hopeless while 20 ♕c1 ♗xa1 21 ♕xa1 ♘xg3 22 ♘xg3 ♕xe3+ leaves White with a material deficit and an exposed king. Black didn't miss this idea when presented with a second chance a few moves later.

19 ♖ac1 ♗b5 20 ♖c2 ♗d3 21 ♖cc1 ♘xf3+! 22 ♗xf3 ♗xe4 23 ♗xe4 ♕xe4 24 ♗f4 ♕xe2 25 ♕xe2 ♖xe2 26 ♗xd6 ♖be8 27 ♘xc5 ♘g4

Black's little combination has led to a winning endgame. Although White has won back his pawns his king is now in serious trouble. One doesn't always need queens to conduct a mating attack.

28 h4 ♖xa2 29 ♘e4 ♗h6 30 ♖c4 ♗e3+ 31 ♔f1 ♖xe4?

This wins easily but 31...♘h2+ 32 ♔e1 ♗f2 mate was slightly more accurate!

32 ♖c8+ ♔g7 33 ♗f8+ ♔f6 34 ♖d6+ ♖e6 35 ♖xe6+ fxe6 36 ♗xb4 ♘h2+ 37 ♔e1 ♗d2+ 38 ♗xd2 ♘f3+ 39 ♔e2 ♘xd2 40 b4 ♘e4+ 41 ♔f3 ♔e5 0-1

Game 54
Villamayor-Gallagher
Calcutta 2001

1 ♘f3 d6 2 d4 ♘f6 3 g3 g6 4 ♗g2 ♗g7 5 b3

The double fianchetto can be an irritant for the King's Indian player who is hoping for an active game. In my younger years I had quite a few reversals against this line as I was striving for too much. My results improved dramatically once I decided to settle for equality.

After 5 0-0 d6 6 b3 Black can play 6...c5 with similar play to the game or he can also play 6...e5 7 dxe5 dxe5!, e.g.

a) 8 ♗b2 (not 8 ♘xe5? ♘g4) e4 and now:

a1) 9 ♘e5 ♕e7 10 ♕c1 ♗f5 (10...♘bd7 is also good) 11 ♘c4 ♕e6 12 ♘c3 ♘c6 and Black was already better in D'Amore-Gallagher, Istanbul Olympiad 2000.

a2) White can maintain the balance by exchanging queens, e.g. 9 ♕xd8 ♖xd8 10 ♘g5 ♗f5 11 g4 ♗xg4 12 ♘xe4 ♘xe4 13 ♗xg7 ♔xg7 14 ♗xe4 ♘c6 15 ♘c3 with a level game.

b) 8 ♗a3 ♖e8 9 ♘c3 ♘c6 10 ♘g5 ♗f5 11 ♘ge4 ♘xe4 12 ♘xe4 ♕xd1 13 ♖fxd1 ♘d4 14 ♖d2 ♖ad8 15 ♔f1! ♘b5?! (15...♗xe4!? 16 ♗xe4 ♘b5 17 ♖xd8 ♖xd8 18 ♗b2 c6 19 c4 ♘c7 and even though White has the bishop pair he can claim no advantage) 16 ♖xd8 ♖xd8 17 ♗b2?! (17 ♗e7! gives White a clear advantage after 17...♖d4 18 ♘f6+ ♔h8 19 ♗xb7 ♗xc2 20 ♖c1 and an edge after 17...♖e8 18 ♘f6+ ♗xf6 19 ♗xf6 ♘d6 20 c4 ♘e4 21 ♗xe4

♗xe4 22 ♖d1 ♗f5) b6 18 e3 ♖d7 19 ♔e1 ½-½
Ekström-Gallagher, Swiss League 1994.

5...c5!

Playing d5 is also quite reasonable but may not suit the style of the King's Indian player. Although many sources suggest that Black can equalise by playing a quick ...e5, my experience there is that White can easily end up with a nagging edge. The difference to the above note is that Black will no longer be able to recapture at once on e5 but will have to meet dxe5 with ...♘g4 or ...♘d7. The text quickly brings things to a head and promises Black an easier life

6 c4

After 6 ♗g2 cxd4 7 ♘xd4 d5! Black has a comfortable game. For example: 8 c4 dxc4 (8...e5!?) 9 bxc4 0-0 10 0-0 ♕b6 11 ♖c1 ♗d7 12 ♘d2 ♘c6 13 c5 ♕c7 14 ♘b5 ♕c8 15 ♘e4 ♘xe4 16 ♗xe4 ♗e5 17 ♘d4 ♖b8 18 ♖b1 ♕c7 19 ♕c2 ♖fc8 20 ♖fc1 ♕a5 21 ♕c3 ♕xc3 22 ♖xc3 ♘c6 23 ♘xc6 ♗xc6 24 ♖c4?? (24 ♖e3=) 24...b5! 0-1 Dizdarevic-Svidler, Bled Olympiad. 2002. White loses material after both 25 ♖b4 a5 and 25 cxb6 ♗xe4 26 ♖xe4 ♖xb6.

6...0-0

6...♘e4 7 ♗g2 ♕a5+ 8 ♘fd2 ♘xd2 9 ♗c3! is a nice trick which enables White to maintain an edge

7 ♗g2 d5!

7...♘c6 transposes into the Yugoslav variation but the text is better. I worked this line out over the board against Panchenko 9 years ago.

8 cxd5

8 dxc5 dxc4 is fine for Black

8...♘xd5 9 0-0

9 ♕d2 ♘c7! 10 0-0 ♘c6 was the move or-

der in Stocek-Gallagher.

9...♘c6 10 ♕d2 ♘c7!

The key move. This, as we shall see, is a very good square for the knight. Neither side can now profitably avoid the coming exchanges.

11 ♖d1 cxd4 12 ♘xd4 ♘xd4 13 ♗xd4 ♕xd4 14 ♕xd4 ♗xd4 15 ♖xd4 ♘b5!

The idea behind 10...♘c7 is revealed. The knight is heading for its ideal home on d6, closing the d-file and defending b7 so that the bishop can be developed. That the move also contains a nasty trap is merely incidental. I didn't believe for a second that my grandmaster opponent was going to fall for it.

16 ♖b4??

But he did! Instead:

a) 16 ♖d5 has been played against me the two other times I have reached this position. White has no advantage, e.g. 16...♘d6 17 ♘c3 ♗e6 18 ♖d2 (18 ♖dd1 ♖fc8 19 ♖ac1 ♖ab8= Panchenko-Gallagher, Bad Wörishofen 1994) ♖ac8 19 ♘d5 ♗xd5 20 ♗xd5 ♖c3. Normally the bishop would give White a slight edge in such a position but if anyone is better here it is Black. The knight is beautifully placed on d6 and he has control of the c-file. The remaining moves were 21 ♔g2 ♔g7 22 ♖ad1 f5 23 ♖d3 ♖fc8 24 b4 ♔f6 25 ♗b3 ♖xd3 26 ♖xd3 ♖c6 27 ♖e3 ♘c4 28 ♖d3 ♘d6 29 ♖e3 ♘c4 (perhaps Black could play on with 29...e5 but in these team matches a draw with Black is the usual aim) 30 ♖d3 ½-½ Stocek-Gallagher, European Team Ch., Plovdiv 2003.

b) 16 ♖d2 ♖b8 (it's best to wait for White to weaken his queenside before playing ♘d6) 17 a4 and only now 17...♘d6 18 ♘c3 ♖d8! is level.

16...♖d8!

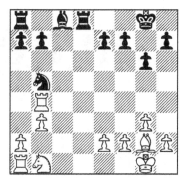

My opponent sunk dejectedly in his chair as he came to terms with the fact that 17 ♖xb5 just loses to 17...♖d1+ 18 ♗f1 ♗h3, and that with the knight on b5 dominating its opposite number on b1 he has no way to defend his back rank.

17 ♘d2

The only chance, albeit a slight one, was offered by 17 ♗e4 ♖d1+ 18 ♔g2 ♘d6 19 ♗c2 ♖c1 20 ♗d3. White will now attempt to break the pin with a4 and ♖a2. However, after 20...♗d7 21 a4 ♗c6+ 22 f3 a5! the rook on b4 is embarrassed. It is trapped after 23 ♖b6 ♘c8 while both 23 ♖d4 and 23 ♖h4 are strongly met by 23...♘f5 as if White takes the knight the pin will remain permanent.

17...♘d4! 0-1

Not 17...♖xd2 18 ♖xb5 when White should escape with a draw. Now after prolonged thought a disgusted Villamayor threw the towel in. His defensive attempts were:

a) 18 ♖e1 ♘c2

b) 18 ♖d1 ♘xe2+ 19 ♔f1 ♘c3 20 ♖c1 ♘xa2.

c) 18 ♖xd4 ♖xd4 19 ♘c4 ♖b8 and Black is just a clear exchange up.

Summary

1) The Fianchetto Variation is a solid line played by players who like to retain total control of the position. Therefore I am recommend an aggressive, risky approach as the most unpleasant for them to face. In order to arrest the initiative from White Black is willing to make positional concessions and, if need be, sacrifice material.

2) The key move in the two variations discussed is the little pawn move ...a6. This is played to prepare the advance ...b5. In the old days Black used to play with ...a5 to prevent White from advancing on the queenside. In the Fianchetto variation the move ...a6 can be considered aggressive and the move ...a5 defensive.

3) Don't play the move ...c7-c5 lightly. Make sure you have a concrete follow-up as this move can seriously compromises the long-term health of Black's position.

4) The queenside advance is not really a queenside attack at all but an attack on the white centre. Note how often Black wins the important pawn on e4 in the Gallagher Variation

5) Sometimes after Black has sacrificed the pawn on d6 the manoeuvre ...♖b6-e6 helps to increases the pressure.

6) My current assessment of the Gallagher Variation is that Black gets a playable middlegame but that against certain set-ups (see Games 45 and 46) he cannot get away with sacrificing the pawn on d6. Positions that look bad for him, and which I previously thought were bad for him, are probably not bad for him.

7) In the lines with 8...a6 when White plays the move ♕c2 (or ♕e2) Black must ensure that the move ♖d1 is not going to embarrass his queen. The best square for the black queen is usually e7, but only if the reply ♘d5 is not dangerous. In practice this often translates into meeting ♕c2 with ...c6.

8) When White exchanges on e5 the pawn structure (c4 and e4) means there is a hole on d4. It is usually a good idea for Black to manoeuvre his knights towards this square.

9) Advancing the h-pawn to soften up the position around the white king can be a good idea. This advance should be considered when Black has no chance of active play on the queenside, or conversely, after his initial queenside play has tied White down and the opening of a new front may over-stretch the opponent.

10) If White refrains from playing e4 Black can exploit this by trying to occupy the e4-square with a knight, or by advancing ...d6-d5 or ...f7-f5, depending on circumstances..

CHAPTER NINE

The Four Pawns Attack

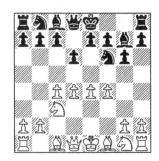

1 d4 ♘f6 2 c4 g6 3 ♘c3 ♗g7 4 e4 d6 5 f4

The Four Pawns Attack is the most overtly aggressive line available to White in the King's Indian. By move 5 he has already managed to construct a massive centre. Such a centre may look impressive but there are drawbacks to it. Firstly, pawns don't move backwards. As the game progresses White may regret his rash start to the game as key squares deep inside his camp become vulnerable to invasion by enemy pieces. The point is that they can no longer be protected by pawns and never will be. However, this ideal scenario of the black army occupying the heart of the white position is still a long way off and for now, Black must recognise that his situation is already verging on the critical. If he just develops passively then before long White will hit him with e4-e5 and he will, in all likelihood, be blown away. White is not ready to do this yet as by spending 4 of his first 5 moves moving pawns he is somewhat lagging in development. Blasting open the centre with his king still resident on e1 and with Black's nicely tucked away in the corner would be tantamount to suicide. In fact, it is Black who should be looking to open the centre as quickly as possible in order to try and take advantage of his lead in development. In the King's Indian Black usually counters in the centre by ...e5 or ...c5. In the Four Pawns Attack it is not easy for Black to arrange ...e5. There is a system based on playing ♘a6 followed by ...e5 which has become quite popular in recent years but as

White appears to be coming to terms with this plan I am suggesting that Black reacts with the more traditional ...c7-c5.

5...0-0 6 ♘f3

Sometimes White plays 6 ♗e2 first but as White nearly always develops his king's knight to f3 and his king's bishop to e2 this move order has no independent significance. Play should just transpose into one of the main lines, e.g. after 6 ♗e2 c5 7 d5 e6 8 ♘f3 exd5 9 cxd5 ♗g4 we have transposed back to the main line.

6...c5! 7 d5

This is by far the most common reaction. White blocks the centre and plans to follow-up with e5 once his king has been evacuated to safety.

There are two other strategies available to White. He can take on c5 (7 dxc5) when Black should not recapture with 7...dxc5 as after 8 ♕xd8 ♖xd8 9 e5 he is already worse, but instead should play 7...♕a5! This move reveals the tactical justification for Black's 6th move. The point is that if White now plays 8 cxd6 Black can take advantage of the pin on the knight on c3 to play 8...♘xe4! White should avoid this at all costs and instead defend his e4 pawn with 8 ♗d3. This line is examined in Game 59.

The other possibility for White is to maintain the tension in the centre and prepare castling with 7 ♗e2. Black should then capture on d4. This is also examined in Game 59.

7...e6

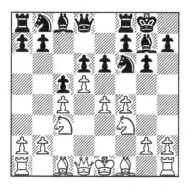

The most logical move. Black plans to exchange on d5 in order to open the e-line. His king's rook will then be able to occupy the open file or exert pressure against the White pawn on e4 (depending on how White recaptures on d5).

Certain players prefer to transpose into a type of Benko by sacrificing a pawn with ...b7-b5. This can be done immediately with 7...b5!? 8 cxb5 a6, or by starting with 7...a6 and following up with ...b7-b5. Whilst these Benko strategies are interesting I have decided to stick to the main lines for my suggested repertoire.

8 ♗e2

The alternative is to exchange with 8 dxe6. This is examined in Game 58.

8...exd5 9 cxd5

White can also recapture with the e-pawn or play the speculative 9 e5?!. These are both examined in Game 57.

9...♗g4

This is the approach I am recommending against the main line and the ideas behind the move 9...♗g4 are examined in Game 55. This position is very well known to chess theory as it arises not just from the King's Indian but also from the Benoni. The Benoni move order is 1 d4 ♘f6 2 c4 e6 3 ♘c3 c5 4 d5 exd5 5 cxd5 d6 6 e4 g6 7 f4 ♗g7 8 ♘f3 0-0 9 ♗e2 ♗g4 and we have reached the diagram position.

> *Game 55*
> **Banikas-Gallagher**
> *French League 2001*

---

1 d4 ♘f6 2 c4 g6 3 ♘c3 ♗g7 4 e4 d6 5 f4

0-0 6 ♘f3 c5 7 d5 e6 8 ♗e2 exd5 9 cxd5 ♗g4

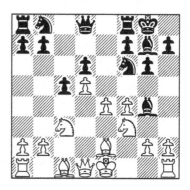

This is the most solid and reliable way to meet the main line of the Four Pawns Attack. Black is going to give up his bishop for the knight on f3 and there are two good reasons for doing this. Firstly, the knight plays an important role in supporting the advance e4-e5 and without its presence this plan becomes less dangerous. Secondly, Black has less space and will, therefore, find it difficult to accommodate a full set off minor pieces within his camp. In general, it is a good idea to aim for exchanges when you have less space (and of course avoid them when you have a space advantage).

There are two main alternatives which I do not consider here, 9...b5 and 9...♖e8. These lines have their followers but I don't like them as they allow White to play 10 e5. I prefer to frustrate my opponent's ambitions, especially when playing an aggressive player who is just lusting to play e4-e5. A good rule of thumb: against sharp guys, play solid and against solid guys, play sharp (Fianchetto Variation, for example). Anyway, solid and sharp is all relative. It is hardly possible to avoid complications in the Four Pawns Attack!

10 0-0

Black's last move did not actually prevent White from playing 10 e5 – it just rendered it harmless.

For example 10 e5 dxe5 11 fxe5 ♘fd7 12 e6 ♗xf3! 13 ♗xf3 ♘e5 and now:

a) After 14 exf7+ ♖xf7 15 0-0 ♘bd7 Black has a good central position. The mobility of White's minor pieces are somewhat restricted by the pawn on d5 and if he advances it any further it is liable to be lost – passed pawns are very strong when they are supported by another pawn but isolated in the opposing camp they are just a weakness.

b) 14 0-0 fxe6 15 ♗e3 (15 dxe6? ♘xf3+ 16 ♖xf3 ♕xd1+ 17 ♘xd1 ♖xf3 18 gxf3 ♘c6 and the pawn on e6 is doomed) 15...♘xf3+ 16 ♖xf3 ♖xf3 17 ♕xf3 exd5 18 ♘xd5 ♘c6 19 ♗xc5 ♔h8 with a roughly level game.

10...♘bd7

Although Black is going to take the knight on f3 he doesn't have to do so at once. He might as well wait for White to spend a tempo on h3. The only reason for Black to exchange at once is if he is worried about the knight running away. Practice has shown, though, that 11 ♘d2 ♗xe2 12 ♕xe2 ♖e8 13 ♕f3 ♖c8, preparing ...c4, is nothing for Black to worry about.

11 ♖e1

The main line but White can also play 11 h3 ♗xf3 12 ♗xf3. Black has tried many moves now but I am suggesting 12...♖e8, as very often White will just play 13 ♖e1 transposing into the main line. It is a good idea to link up your repertoire in this fashion as it cuts down the workload. Apart from 13 ♖e1 White has two other ideas which need to be examined:

a) 13 g4 h6 (this is the usual reaction to g4) 14 h4 h5!? and now:

a1) 15 gxh5? ♘xh5 16 ♗xh5 ♕xh4!! (theory had originally given 16...gxh5 17 ♕xh5 b5 as offering compensation for the pawn but Vaisser's analysis demonstrates than the text is much stronger) 17 ♕g4 (White can't keep the piece with 17 ♗g4 as after 17...♗xc3 18 bxc3

♕g3+ 19 ♔h1 ♔g7! he will be mated by ...♖h8; 18 ♔g2 is a better try but Vaisser points out that after 18...♘f6 19 ♗f3 ♗d4! Black is winning as 20 ♖h1 can be met by 20...♕f2+) 17...♕xh5. White should now settle for the bad ending that arises after 18 ♕xh5 gxh5 – bad because he is going to lose his e-pawn. Instead, if he plays 18 ♕xd7? he will be put to the sword: 18...♖ad8 (forcing the queen far away from his king) 19 ♕b5 ♕g4+ 20 ♔f2 (or 20 ♔h2 ♗xc3 21 bxc3 ♔g7! with the same ...♖h8 mate we have already seen) 20...♗d4+ 21 ♔e1 (21 ♗e3 ♕xf4+) ♗xc3+ 22 bxc3 ♖xe4+ with a crushing attack.

a2) 15 g5 ♘g4 16 ♗xg4 hxg4 17 ♖e1 (17 ♕xg4 ♗xc3 18 bxc3 ♖xe4 19 ♗d2 ♕e7 20 ♖ae1 ♘b6 is fine for Black) 17...c4 (Black offers his g-pawn in order to activate his knight as quickly as possible) 18 ♗e3 (18 ♕xg4 ♘c5 19 ♕f3 ♘d3 20 ♖e2 ♕a5 gives Black good compensation for the pawn) 18...♗xc3 19 bxc3 ♖xe4 20 ♕xg4 ♕e7 21 ♗f2 ♘c5 with an unclear game, Kouatly-Kindermann, Trnava 1987. It is not easy for White to get at the weak dark squares around the black king and meanwhile he has to watch out for his own weak pawns and naked king.

b) 13 a4 c4 14 ♗e3 ♕a5 (there are other plans for Black but this is similar to the one we adopt in the main line – the main idea is to play ...♘c5) 15 ♗d4 (15 ♖e1 would actually transpose to the notes to move 14) 15...♖e7!? (now 15...♘c5 is not so good because of 16 e5 so Black changes plan – he intends to double rooks on the e-file and maybe sacrifice the exchange on e4) 16 ♔h1 a6 (the immediate 16...♖ae8 17 ♘b5 is complicated but probably good for White) 17 g4 (17 ♕e1 is more solid when 17...♖ae8 18 ♕h4 ♘h5 19 ♗xg7 [19 ♗xh5 ♗xd4] ♘xg7 20 ♖ae1 is about equal) 17...♖ae8 18 g5 ♘xe4! 19 ♘xe4 (19 ♗xg7 ♘g3+) ♖xe4 20 bxe4 ♖xe4 21 ♕f3 f5! gave Black good compensation for the exchange in Peev-Velimirovic, Sofia 1972.

11...♖e8

With his rook on e1 White really was threatening to play e5. The text prevents this and forces White to play h3 in order to defend his e-pawn. There is one viable alternative to ...♖e8, namely 11...♘e8. This strange-looking retreat removes the knight out from the central firing line. It is heading for a new home on c7, from where it will help to support the advance ...b5, and it also no longer blocks the king's Indian bishop (as it did on f6). Still, this is all quite time consuming and I prefer the traditional 11...Re8.

12 h3 Bxf3 13 Bxf3

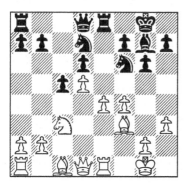

It is time to take stock and discuss what each side is trying to achieve. The most important factor in the position is the unbalanced pawn structure. White has a 2-1 majority in the centre whilst Black has 3-2 in his favour on the queenside. Pawn majorities need to be pushed so White, as we already know, will be looking to play e4-e5 while Black will be looking to expand on the queenside, usually starting with the advance ...b5. Normally it is an advantage to have an extra central pawn but here this is counter-balanced by the fact that it is easier for Black to advance his majority. Black has placed his pieces in such a way that it will be very difficult for White to play e5 and after dxe5 to recapture fxe5 without losing a pawn. Sometimes White switches to another plan – to play e5 and after dxe5 not to recapture but to play f5. Alternatively White can gain even more space on the kingside by playing g4. But exposing one's king like this is liable to backfire as we saw in the notes to move 11.

13...Wa5!

This is the most accurate way for Black to prepare ...b5. 13...a6 is also played quite often but then White can prevent b5 with 14 a4!. This is not so good after 13...Wa5 – for an explanation see the next note. After 13...a6 14 a4 Black

often plays 14...c4 in order to clear the c5-square for his knight. The main line then runs: 15 Be3 Wa5 16 Kh1 Nc5 17 Bxc5! Wxc5 18 e5 dxe5 19 fxe5 Nfd7 20 Ne4 Wb4 21 e6 fxe6 22 Bg4! Ne5 23 Bxe6+ Kh8. White is slightly better according to Vaisser.

14 Be3

So why isn't it such a good idea to play 14 a4. Well, the reason is that Black can follow a similar path to the previous note but without having to play the unnecessary ...a6. The tempo saved on this move means that White won't have the time to force through e5. Therefore 14...c4! and now:

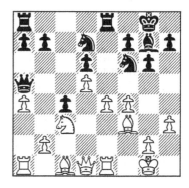

a) 15 Be3 Nc5 16 Bxc5 (White cannot be very happy to give up his strong bishop but the e-pawn is attacked and defensive moves such as 16 Bf2 are just met by 16...Nd3!) 16...Wxc5+ (the big difference to the previous variation is that this is now check) 17 Kh1 Nd7! with a pleasant game for Black. His pieces co-ordinate very well.

b) 15 Re2 (note that 15 Nb5, attacking the d6 pawn, can be met by 15...a6 as 16 Nxd6? just loses the knight to 16...Wb6+) 15...Nc5 16 e5 dxe5 17 fxe5 Nfd7 18 e6 Ne5 19 exf7+ Kxf7 20 Be4 Ned3 21 d6 Nxe4 22 Nxe4 Wf5! 23 g4 Bd4+ 24 Kh2 We5+ 25 Ng3 Wxd6 and Black had a winning position in Bosboom Lanchava-Gallagher, Cappelle la Grande 2002.

14...b5

This move is self-explanatory. Black starts the queenside attack he envisaged with his previous move.

15 a3

This little move is designed to draw the sting

from b4. White will now be able to maintain the knight on c3 as after 15...b4 16 axb4 Black must recapture with the queen.

15...♘b6

Dramatically raising the stakes. On d7 the knight was performing a good defensive duty (stopping White from playing e5) but not doing much to help the queenside offensive. Now it is heading for c4 from where it will create great confusion in the white camp. But at a price. White can now play e5. The time for generalisations is over. Tactics and the direct confrontation between the pieces will now decide who emerges with the better game.

The alternative 15...b4 is considered in the next game.

16 e5

White takes the bull by the horns.

16 ♗f2, was shelved after a couple of crushing defeats for White, but Anatoly Vaisser claims that all is not so clear. Let's take a look: 16...♘c4 17 ♕c2 (17 b3? ♕xc3 18 bxc4 ♘xe4! 19 ♖c1 ♘xf2! 20 ♖xe8+ ♖xe8 21 ♔xf2 ♕e3+ 22 ♔g3 ♗h6 0-1 was a disaster for White in Kouatly-Barencilla, Doha 1993) 17...♘d7 (threatening 18...♘xb2) 18 ♗e2 (18 a4 b4 19 ♘b5 a6!) 18...♖ab8 (18...♘xb2 19 ♘xb5) 19 a4 b4 and now:

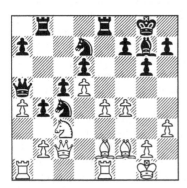

a) Kozul-Nunn, Wijk aan Zee 1991 continued 20 ♗xc4? bxc3 21 b3 a6! (keeping the bishop out of b5) 22 ♖ec1 (planning to win the pawn on c3 with ♗e1) 22...♘b6 23 ♗f1 c4! (Black gives up a pawn to open the b-file) 24 ♗xc4 ♘xc4 25 bxc4 ♖b2 26 ♕d3 ♖d2 27 ♕f3 f5! (there is no respite for White; Black is not content with having one rook in the heart of White's position so he opens the e-file to enable his comrade to join him) 28 e5 dxe5 29 fxe5 ♖xe5 (White played e5 in order to get a couple of connected passed pawns but he is under too much pressure for them to have much influence on the game) 30 ♔h1 ♖e4 31 ♗e1 ♕c7 32 ♖ab1 (32 ♗xd2 cxd2 33 ♖d1 ♖xa1 34 ♖xa1 ♖e1+ wins for Black) 32...♖de2! 33 ♗xc3 ♖2e3 34 d6 ♕xd6 35 ♗b4 ♕c6 36 ♕f1 ♖xh3+ 37 gxh3 ♖e2+0-1

b) In his notes to the above game Nunn gave the following variation: 20 ♘b5 ♘xb2 21 ♘xd6 b3 22 ♕b1 ♘xa4 23 ♘xe8 ♗xa1 24 ♕xa1 b2 25 ♕a2 ♕xe1+ 26 ♗xe1 b1♕ with a winning position for Black. It is within this minefield that Vaisser suggests an improvement for White. Instead of 23 ♘xe8 he gives 23 ♖a3! ♕b4 24 ♖xb3 ♕xb3 25 ♕xb3 ♖xb3 26 ♘xe8 as unclear.

The Croatian Grandmaster Cebalo is a great fan of Vaisser's book on the Four Pawns Attack (*Beating the King's Indian and Benoni*, Batsford 1997) and it was no surprise to see him testing this variation with White. In Cebalo-Balcerak, Biel 2000 Black preferred 23...c4!? (instead of 23...♕b4) and won an amazingly complicated game (just to give you an idea the next few moves were 24 ♘xe8 ♗f8 25 d6 ♕b4 26 ♖xa4 ♕xa4 27 ♘c7 c3). And in Cebalo-Mohr, Croatian Team Ch. 2003 Black tried 23...♖ed8 and this worked out all right for him as well.

So, to be honest, nobody really knows what's going on in this variation and it may well take weeks of computer-aided analysis to find out. I've tried a bit and still don't know what to make of it all. All that remains for me to do is wish you luck in the amazing event of any of your games actually following this much theory!

Incidentally, I once met 16 ♗f2 with 16...♘fd7 and after 17 ♕c2 b4 18 axb4 ♕xb4 we have transposed into the 17th move notes to Regez-Gallagher. Certainly an option worth considering if the above complications seem overbearing.

16...♘c4!

Such moves demonstrate the advantage of a knowing an opening well. Without prior knowledge it would take great effort and courage to play such a move, especially when there is a safer-looking alternative.

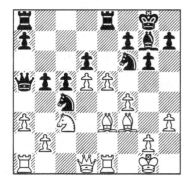

a) The fact is, though, that the safe-looking 16...dxe5 is not very good. After 17 fxe5 ♖xe5 18 ♗xc5 ♖xe1+ 19 ♕xe1 White has a considerable advantage – his passed d-pawn is actually quite strong and the position has opened more for his bishop pair.

b) There is another option, however, which has emerged relatively recently in a couple of exciting clashes involving the world's leading Four Pawns Attack experts. The move is 16...♘fd7!? and look at these fireworks: 17 e6 ♘c4 18 exd7 ♖xe3 19 ♖xe3 ♘xe3 20 ♕e2 ♕d8! 21 ♕xb5 (21 ♕xe3 ♗d4) 21...♖b8 22 ♕c6 ♖xb2 and now:

b1) 23 ♖c1 ♖b6 24 ♘b5!? (wow! 24 ♕c8 ♖b8 25 ♕c6 ♖b6 looks like a draw) 24...♖xc6 25 dxc6 (considering that Banikas later switched sides he must have an improvement on Black's play; I suspect it was here as there are certainly more useful moves than ...a6) 25...a6 (25...♗f6!?) 26 ♘xd6 ♕b6 27 ♘e8 (nothing can stop the pawns now so it's just a question of whether Black can scramble a perpetual) 27...♕b2 28 ♖d1 ♘xd1 29 d8♕ ♗d4+ 30 ♔h2 ♘e3 31 ♘d6+ ♔g7 32 ♘e8+ ♔g8 33 h4! ♕f2 34 ♔h3? (34 ♘f6+ ♔g7 35 ♘h5+! gxh5 36 ♕g5+ ♔f8 37 c7 wins) 34...♕g1 35 ♘d6+ ½-½, Banikas-Kotronias, Corinth 1998.

b2) 23 ♘e4 ♗d4 24 ♔h1 ♖b6 25 ♖e1 (here we go again) 25...♖xc6 26 dxc6 c4 27 ♘xd6 ♕h4 28 ♖b1 ♗b6 29 ♘xc4 ♘xc4 30 ♖xb6 ♘xb6 31 c7 ♘xd7 32 c8♕+ ♘f8 33 ♕b8 ½-½, Vaisser-Banikas, French League 2001.

Well that's certainly an area for further investigation for the analytically minded amongst you.

17 exf6 ♘xe3 18 ♖xe3

At first sight it may seem that White can win a piece by 18 ♕c1 as two black pieces are now attacked. The problem, though, is that after 18...♗xf6! 19 ♖xe3 ♖xe3 White can't take the rook as 20...♗d4 wins the queen.

18...♖xe3 19 fxg7 ♖ae8

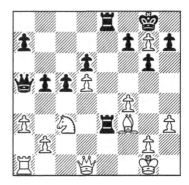

This is the position Black had in mind when he embarked on the complications with 15...♘b6. White's slight material advantage is compensated for by the fact that the black rooks are extremely active and the mobility of the white bishop restricted by the pawn on d5. The pawn on g7 is of course doomed.

20 f5 b4

Black can 'win' the queen for two rooks with 20...♖e1+ 21 ♕xe1 ♖xe1+ 22 ♖xe1 but he correctly avoids this as in the resulting position White's material advantage is more pronounced – rook and two minor pieces against a queen is usually a decisive advantage. Black certainly doesn't want to go in for such a line when it means getting rid of his main trump in this position – his active rooks.

A nightmare scenario for Black would arise if White could support his pawn on g7 with f6. The text is directed against this. Black activates his queen so that a future f6 is just likely to lose the pawn to ...♕h4 or ...♕d4. There are several other ways Black can prevent f6. The first is to play 20...♔xg7 – not a bad move but not the most accurate. Black only wants to play this when he has nothing better to do. Another possibility is to play 20...gxf5 but this would leave Black with a seriously weakened kingside.

The final possibility is perhaps the best of

all. The novelty 20...a6! was introduced in the game Segura Ariza-Moreno Carnero, Ayamonte 2002. This move also frees up the black queen as it is no longer required to defend b5, but unlike the main line, Black retains his nice positional advantage on the queenside. The game continued 21 f6? (this seems to just lose) 21...♛d8 22 ♘e4 ♖8xe4 23 ♗xe4 ♛xf6! 24 ♗c2 ♛xb2 25 a4 b4 26 ♖b1 ♛c3 27 ♖c1 ♛e5 28 ♗b3 a5 29 ♗c4 ♔xg7 and Black, who has total domination of the chessboard won in a few more moves. Look how useless White's bishop is in this type of position. It's more like a big pawn.

White can do better than 21 f6, but 20...a6 still looks like a good idea.

21 axb4 ♛xb4 22 ♛d2

Of course not 22 ♖xa7?? as then 22...♖e1+ wins the queen for just one rook.

22...♛h4!

Better than 22...♛f4 as on that square the queen can be embarrassed by a rook on f1. For example, Dearing-Moss, Hastings 1995/96 continued (after 22...♛f4) 23 ♖f1! ♛xf5? 24 ♗e4! (attacking the queen twice and cutting the lines of communication between the black rooks) 24...♛g5 (the only move to avoid immediate material loss) 25 ♖f3! and White wins the pinned rook on e3.

23 fxg6

After our game Banikas swore never to touch this line again so I was somewhat surprise to see later in the year the game Banikas-Dochev, Kavala 2001. This was the moment he chose to improve by refraining from the exchange on g6. After 23 ♖f1 a6 24 ♗g4!? ♛g3

25 ♛f2 (25 f6 looks critical but I suppose Banikas was worried that both his advanced pawns would eventually drop off; I'm not so sure) 25...♛xf2+ 26 ♖xf2 ♔xg7 27 ♗e2 I suspect the position is about equal and the game eventually ended in a draw after many adventures.

23...hxg6 24 ♖f1

It is too dangerous for White to take the a-pawn. After 24 ♖xa7 ♖xf3! 25 gxf3 ♛g3+ 26 ♔f1 (26 ♛g2? ♖e1 mate) 26...♛xf3+ 27 ♔g1 (27 ♛f2? ♛h1+ 28 ♔g1 ♖e1+ 29 ♔xe1 ♛xg1+) 27...♛g3+ 28 ♔f1 Black has at least a draw and probably more after 28...♛e5. By defending his bishop on f3 White rules out such sacrifices.

24...a6!

A nice little move. The white bishop is already restricted – now it's time to smother the knight. It can no longer go to b5 and later we see Black playing ...f5 to further reduce the knight's scope. Note how Black still hasn't bothered to capture on g7 – the pawn is not going anywhere.

25 ♘d1

This is actually the first new move of the game. Opening theory stretches far into the middlegame these days. Previously 25 ♛f2 ♛d4 26 ♔h1 ♖3e5! had been played with an unclear game according to theory. Black is certainly not worse here and I believe that White needs to defend well to maintain the balance after an exchange of queens.

25...♖3e5 26 ♘f2 f5!

As previously mentioned, this is played to limit the options of the knight – now it is denied access to the e4- and g4-squares. Still, I was a little hesitant before playing this move as now Black's king position is less secure.

27 ♗d1?!

Please don't ask me to explain this move. The only thing I can think of is that White was going to extreme lengths to lose his pawn on d5 in order to give his bishop some open diagonals. The problem is that whilst White will get diagonals Black will also get more files for his rooks.

The move White would like to play is 27 ♘d3 but this is strongly met by 27...♕d4+, creating a powerful pin on the knight. At the board I was most concerned about 27 ♖a1 – now that there are no sacrifices on f3 the rook can return to active service. It seems to me the game is about equal, for example: 27...♔g7 28 ♖xa6 ♖e1+ 29 ♔h2 ♖8e3 (Black plans ...f4 and ♕g3 mate but first prevents White from playing ♕c3+; the relevance of this is seen in the variation 29...f4?! 30 ♕c3+! ♔g8 31 ♘e4 ♖8xe4 32 ♗xe4 when the queen on c3 stops ...♕g3 mate; after 32...♖xe4 33 ♖xd6 Black has to fight for a draw) 30 ♘d3 f4! 31 ♕c3+ ♔g8 32 ♖a8+ ♔f7 33 ♖a7+ ♔e8 34 ♖a8+ ♔f7 with a draw by perpetual check. If either side tries to avoid the repetition they get mated.

27...♔xg7

A good moment to take the pawn as I was curious to see what White was going to do next. I half expected him to return to f3 with his bishop but instead he lashed out on the queenside.

28 ♕a5 ♖xd5 29 ♗f3 ♖d4

Better than going back to the e-file. I had a nasty trap in mind but wasn't really expecting my opponent to fall into it.

30 ♕xa6 ♖d2!

Now that the white queen no longer defends this square, Black penetrates to the 7th rank

31 ♗c6??

Completely overlooking Black's idea. In fact White still had good chances to defend himself with 31 ♕a3!, e.g.

a) 31...♖xf2? 32 ♖xf2? ♖e1+ 33 ♖f1 ♕d4+ 34 ♔h2 ♖xf1 wins for Black but the combination is unsound because White can flick in 32 ♕c3+!

b) 31...♕d4 looks strong as Black now threatens to take on both f2 and b2. However, again 32 ♕c3! saves the day as 32...♖xb2?! is now met by 33 ♕xd4+ cxd4 34 ♖d1. Black would do better to play 32...♖b8 here.

c) Perhaps 31...♕f6 offers Black the best chance of some advantage after 32 ♕c3 ♖b8 but the most likely outcome is a draw.

31...♖e1!

A simple but devastating tactic. The first point is that 32 ♖xe1 ♕xf2+ 33 ♔h2 ♕xe1 just loses a piece, but White's main problem is that because the rook on f1 is pinned Black is threatening ...♕xf2+ anyway. I thought the only way to stave off immediate defeat was 32 ♘h1 but my opponent said he refused to even consider this sick-looking move. The most precise way to win after 32 ♘h1 is 32...♕d4+ 33 ♔h2 ♕e5+ 34 ♔g1 (34 ♘g3 ♖xf1 35 ♕xf1 f4 wins as if the knight moves there is a devastating discovered check) 34...♖xf1+ 35 ♕xf1 ♖e2! 36 ♕f3 (the only move to save the queen) 36...♖e1+ 37 ♔f2 ♖xh1 and Black wins easily.

White chose a continuation that gave him a couple of checks but they soon run out.

32 ♕b7+ ♔h6 33 ♘g4+

What else?. Now 33 ♘h1 ♖xf1+ 34 ♔xf1 ♖d1+ is even easier.

33...fxg4 34 ♕f7

White was placing his meagre hopes on this move.

34...♖xf1+ 35 ♕xf1

35 ♔xf1 ♖d1+ 36 ♔e2 ♕e1 mate.

35...♔g7! 0-1

The black king is totally safe and White is an exchange and a pawn down for nothing.

Game 56
Regez-Gallagher
Zürich 2003

---

1 d4 ♘f6 2 c4 g6 3 ♘c3 ♗g7 4 e4 d6 5 f4 0-0 6 ♘f3 c5 7 d5 e6 8 ♗e2 exd5 9 cxd5 ♗g4 10 0-0 ♘bd7 11 ♖e1 ♖e8 12 h3 ♗xf3 13 ♗xf3 ♕a5 14 ♗e3 b5 15 a3 b4

Normally I play 15...♘b6 here but my opponent seemed to be playing so quickly and confidently that I thought it prudent to avoid the long theoretical variations. After all, when you play someone a lot lower-rated it's usually a good idea to get them out of the book as soon as possible. I had also seen the rather impressive Cebalo-Shchekachev, game that follows and thought why not give that a try.

16 axb4 ♕xb4 17 ♖a3!?

A novelty, played instantly, by my opponent, who later informed me that he had worked hard on the move with Fritz. More common had been 17 ♕c2 ♘b6 18 ♗f2 ♘fd7 19 ♖e2 and now:

a) In a couple of games Black has taken the opportunity to exchange off dark-squared bishops with 19...♗d4 and the position after 20 ♔h1 ♗xf2 21 ♖xf2 c4 22 ♖e2 a5 23 ♗g4 ♘c5! does seem fine for him, e.g. 24 e5 ♘d3 25 ♘e4 ♘xf4 26 ♘f6+ ♔g7 27 ♘xe8+ ♖xe8 28 ♖f2 dxe5, Cebalo-Krstic, Velika Gorika 2002 and White went on to win but it just looks lost for him at this point.

b) The aforementioned Cebalo-Shchekachev, Biel 2003 steered a different path: 19...a5!? 20 ♘a4 ♖eb8 21 e5?! (the standard breakthrough in the 4 pawns which White often plays even if it costs him material, as here; in my view White should have settled for something like 21 ♔h1) 21...♕xf4 22 ♖e4 ♕g5 23 exd6 ♘e5 (I suspect White may have already been regretting his decision to play e5) 24 ♖a3 ♘xa4 25 ♕xa4 (25 ♖exa4 c4! looks seriously good for Black) 25...♖xb2 26 d7 (White is relying on his d-pawn but has left his kingside vulnerable) 26...♕d2! 27 ♗e2 ♕xd5 28 ♖d3! (an excellent resource which keeps White in the game) 28...♘xd3 29 ♖e8+ ♗f8 30 ♗f3? (White had to play 30 ♗xd3! when the pawn on d7 gives him plenty of tactical opportunities to save the game) 30...♕d6 31 ♖xa8 ♖b1+ 32 ♗d1 ♘b2! 33 d8♕ ♕xd8 34 ♖xd8 ♘xa4 35 ♔h2 ♘b6! 36 ♗c2 (36 ♖xc5 ♖xd1! 37 ♖xf8+ ♔g7-+) 36...♖b2 37 ♗xc5 ♘d7! 38 ♗xf8 ♘xf8 (so the fireworks have finally died away and Black has emerged into a completely winning endgame) 39 ♗e4 ♖b5 40 ♖a8 ♗g7 41 ♖a7 ♖c5 42 ♗b1 ♘e6 43 ♗a2 ♘c7 0-1.

17...♖eb8

This move took me an hour and I can't say that I was overjoyed with it. I just didn't see a better alternative. Black's basic idea in this position is to play ...♘b6 and ...♘fd7 in order to create pressure on the queenside but I had to reject this immediately as after 17...♘b6 18 ♖b3 ♕a5 19 ♖a3 White has a forced draw. That is no good against someone nearly 400 points lower-rated.

The next thing I wondered about was whether I could get away with 17...♘xe4 (of course 17...♕xb2 loses to 18 ♖b3) but had to reject this because of 18 ♘xe4 ♖xe4 19 ♗xe4 ♕xe4 20 ♗xc5 ♕xf4 21 ♖f3! when Black does not have enough for the exchange.

So then it was time to look at the obvious move 17...c4 but it didn't appeal to me, e.g. 18 ♖a4 ♕xb2 19 ♖xc4 ♖ac8 20 ♖e2 ♕b7 21 ♖c6!? (21 ♖xc8 ♖xc8 22 ♗d4) 21...♖xc6 22 dxc6 ♕xc6 23 ♖c2 and White, despite being a pawn down is probably better.

The only idea left was to play a rook to b8 – but which one? I finally decided on the text as I wasn't sure what I was going to do after 17...♖ab8 18 ♖e2. The point is that if I can never play ...♘d7-b6 and ...♘f6-d7 (because of the draw) then, in order to get out of the way of e5 and activate the bishop on g7 I am going to have to retreat the knight on f6 to e8. Therefore it had to be ...♖eb8 even though the rook was rather well placed where it was.

18 ♖e2

I didn't look too long at 18 e5 dxe5 19 d6 exf4 as I just assumed that Black would always have sufficient compensation in such positions.

18...a5

The a8 rook needs to be brought into play.

19 ♗f2 ♘e8 20 ♔h1 ♖a7 21 ♗g3

My opponent was still playing incredibly quickly, following a typical plan for such positions. It was getting quite intimidating.

21...♗d4

Again after a long think. I finally decided that there was no good way to stop e4-e5 so I may as well at least get my bishop active. I actually came quite close to playing 21...g5?! in order to take control of the e5-square while my mind even toyed with the sick-looking 21...f6. It's bad, but not that bad.

22 e5 f5!

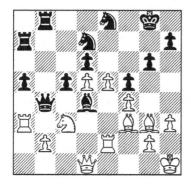

Finally it was my turn to play a move in-

stantly. Black must take control of the e4-square even at the cost of allowing White a protected passed pawn in the centre.

23 ♕e1 ♘f8?

I finally gave up on the idea of playing ...♘d7-b6 just at the moment when it was a good move. I was nervous about leaving my kingside undefended after 23...♘b6 24 exd6 ♘xd6 25 ♖e7 but 25...♖xe7 26 ♕xe7 ♘bc4 is probably just good for Black.

24 ♗h4!

By now I was getting seriously worried. My major preoccupation's were: why is this guy playing so well and where has all my time gone?

24...♖bb7

Sterling defence along the second rank as 24...♗xc3 25 ♖xc3 ♕xf4 26 exd6 ♘xd6 loses to 27 ♗g3. I was waiting for e6 so that I could grab a risky pawn and see what my opponent was like in a tactical battle. Surely he couldn't be as strong as in a strategic game!

25 e6 ♗xc3

The exchange sacrifice 25...♖e7 26 ♗xe7 ♖xe7 might be OK if it wasn't for that dreadful knight on f8 while I also thought about just playing 25...♗g7 26 e7 ♘d7 but felt that my position was too accident prone for the coming time scramble.

26 ♖xc3 ♕xf4

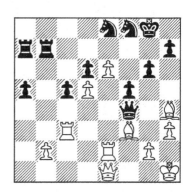

27 e7?!

Short of time it would have been more un-pleasant if White had just played 27 b3!, retaining all the advantages of his position, rather than going in for the forcing line I was ready for.

27...♘d7 28 ♗g3 ♕d4 29 ♗xd6

Whilst my opponent was thinking about this move I suddenly became terrified by 29 ♖d2 ♕f6 30 ♕e6+ when I saw that the planned 30...♔g7 fails to 31 ♗xd6! ♘xd6 32 ♕xd6! ♕xd6 33 e8♘+. I relaxed a little when I saw that I could get away with 30...♔h8.

29...♘xd6 30 e8♕+ ♘xe8 31 ♖xe8+ ♘f8 32 d6

32 ♕e6+ ♔g7 33 ♕d6 ♘d7 34 ♖e7+ ♔h6 seemed all right.

32...♖xb2 33 ♕e6+

A relief as I had seen that White can draw with 33 ♕e7! ♖xe7 34 dxe7 ♖b1+ 35 ♔h2 ♕d6+ (35...♕e5+ 36 g3 ♖b2+ 37 ♗g2 ♖xg2+ 38 ♔xg2 ♕e2+ 39 ♔g1=) 36 g3 ♖b2+ 37 ♔h1=.

33...♔g7 34 ♖e7+ ♔h6

34...♖xe7 35 ♕xe7+ ♔g8 36 ♖c1 planning ♗e2-c4 is not so easy to deal with.

35 ♕e1 ♖d7! 36 ♕c1+?

At last a serious error. I wasn't sure where my queen was going after 36 ♖d3, just somewhere that protects h4

36...♕d2 37 ♕xd2+

There is nothing better.

37...♖xd2 38 ♖xc5 ♖2xd6 39 ♖xd7 ♘xd7 40 ♖xa5 ♔g5

Finally I made it to the time control. White's next move is a mistake as the active black king gives him a winning position. Anyway, whatever White chose it was now his turn to suffer.

41 ♖d5?! ♖xd5 42 ♗xd5 ♘f6 43 ♗b7 ♔f4 44 ♔h2 ♘e4 45 ♗a6 ♔e3 46 ♔g1 f4 47 ♗b5 g5 48 ♗e8 ♘f6 49 ♗b5 h5 50 ♗c6 h4!

The key move as Black can win by playing ...f3 and then eventually collecting the pawn

that has been fixed on h3.

51 ♗b7 ♘d7

51...♔e2 52 ♗f3+ ♔e1 was perhaps the simplest.

52 ♗c8

Or 52 ♔f1 ♘b6! 53 ♗c6 ♘c4 54 ♗b7 ♘d2+ 55 ♔e1 f3 56 gxf3 ♘xf3+ 57 ♔f1 ♘d4 and Black wins.

52...♘e5 53 ♗b7 f3 54 gxf3 ♘xf3+ 55 ♔f1

Or 55 ♔g2 ♘e1+ 56 ♔g1 ♘d3 57 ♔g2 ♘f4+ 58 ♔h2 ♔f2 and wins

55...♘d4

Now White has no time for ♗c8-g4 because Black just plays ♔f3.

56 ♔g2 ♘e2 57 ♗c8 ♘f4+ 58 ♔h2 ♔f2 59 ♗b7 ♘e2 60 ♗c6 ♘d4 61 ♗d7 ♘f3+ 62 ♔h1 ♔g3 0-1

Game 57
Conquest-Mestel
Hastings 1986/87

---

1 d4 ♘f6 2 c4 d6 3 ♘c3 g6 4 e4 ♗g7 5 f4 0-0 6 ♘f3 c5 7 d5 e6 8 ♗e2 exd5 9 exd5

A much more cautious, and less popular, approach than the 9 cxd5 of the previous games. White keeps the pawn structure balanced and relies on his extra space to provide him with the advantage. However, his position would be much healthier if his pawn were back on f2. On f4 it blocks in the bishop on c1 and weakens squares on the e-file, especially the important central square e4. Black will try and control this square while at the same time making sure that White can't play f4-f5 as this would liberate his bishop and give him attacking chances against the black king.

Before examining 9 exd5, though, we have to take a look at another White option, the speculative 9 e5?!. This move enjoyed a period of popularity in the 1980's but has virtually disappeared from practice now that the strength of the reply 9...♘e4! has been established. Previously 9...dxe5 or 9...♘g4 were played with unclear complications. After 9...♘e4 there is:

a) 10 ♘xd5 dxe5 (the immediate 10...♘c6 is often recommended but taking on e5 first cuts down White's options) 11 fxe5 ♘c6 12 ♗d3 (after 12 0-0 ♘xe5 13 ♘xe5 ♗xe5 I don't see a lot of compensation for the pawn) 12...f5 (Black could also consider 12...♕a5+!? as after 13 ♘d2 ♘xd2 14 ♗xd2 ♕d8 he will win the pawn on e5, while 13 ♔f1 f5 leaves the white king badly placed) 13 exf6 (after 13 ♗f4 ♖e8 14 0-0 Black can either take the pawn on e5 or play 14...♗e6 – both look good for him) 13 exf6 ♘xf6 14 ♘xf6+ ♕xf6 15 0-0 ♗g4. Black has a slight advantage due to his lead in development.

b) 10 cxd5 ♘xc3 11 bxc3 ♘d7! and now:

b1) 12 0-0 dxe5 13 fxe5 (the original game with 9...♘e4, Calvo-Diez del Coral, Malaga 1981 went 13 ♘g5 h6 14 ♘e4 f5 15 ♘d6 e4 with a clear advantage for Black; 20 years ago information didn't travel so well and it wasn't for another five years that the strength of ♘e4 was appreciated) 13...♘xe5 14 ♗e3 (14 ♘xe5 ♗xe5 15 ♗h6?? ♕h4 0-1 has occurred more than once) 14...♘xf3+ 15 ♗xf3 ♕d6! and White is just a pawn down for nothing, Li Zunian-Gheorghiu, Dubai Olympiad 1986. Although White has a passed d-pawn it is firmly blockaded and Black has a good grip on the dark squares.

b2) After the above Gheorghiu game White tried to revive the line with 12 e6, but this has also failed to inspire: 12...fxe6 13 dxe6 ♘b6! (Black should avoid the greedy 13...♗xc3+ 14 ♗d2 when he might win more material than in the game but also allow White more attacking chances) 14 0-0 ♗xe6 15 ♘g5 ♗d5! 16 ♕c2 ♕f6. Not only is Black a pawn up but he also has active pieces.

It is no great surprise that we no longer see much of 9 e5.

9...♗f5

The most logical move, immediately taking control of e4. 9...♖e8 10 0-0 ♗f5 leads to the same position.

There is one other, more radical idea that is worth mentioning: 9...♘h5!? 10 0-0 ♗xc3 11 bxc3.

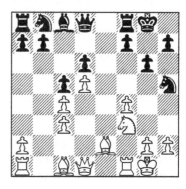

It is most unusual for Black to give up his King's Indian bishop in this fashion but here it is justified as both White's bishops are severely restricted by the pawn structure. It goes without saying that Black will now try and keep the position blocked. He has two ways to go about this:

a) 11...f5. This ensures that White can never play f5, but it also restricts Black's pieces and creates a hole on e6. In fact both sides now appear to have a bad position – lucky they are playing against each other! 12 ♘g5 (another plan would be to try and activate the dark-squared bishop by means of ♗d2-e1-h4) 12...♘g7 13 ♗f3 ♘d7 14 ♖e1 (the critical test of Black's strategy would be 14 ♘e6 ♗xe6 15 dxe6 ♘f6 16 ♗d5 ♕e7 17 ♖e1 but after 17...♘e4 Black has the advantage according to Gligoric) 14...♘f6 15 ♖b1 ♖e8 16 ♖xe8+ ♕xe8 17 ♖b2 ♗d7! 18 ♖xb7 ♖b8 19 ♖xb8 ♕xb8 (the extra pawn on the c-file is irrelevant) 20 ♕c2 h6 21 ♘h3 ♕e8 22 ♗d2 ♗a4 23 ♕c1 ♘g4 24 ♘f2 ♘xf2 25 ♔xf2 ♕e7 26 ♔g1 ♘e8 27 ♕b1 ½-½ Forintos-Gligoric, Ljubljana 1969.

b) 11...♘g7!? This time Black hopes to block f5 with pieces but it does allow White to sacrifice a pawn to open the position. 12 f5!? (the quiet 12 ♗e3 ♘d7 13 ♗f2 ♘f6 doesn't cause Black any problems – he will follow up with ...♖e8 and either bishop or knight to f5; this still may be White's best approach as the game is about level) 12...♗xf5 13 ♗f4 ♕e7 14 ♕d2 f6! (Black plugs up the holes on the dark squares and plans to block the e-file with a knight on e5) 15 ♖ae1 ♘d7 16 ♗d1 ♘e5. It is hard to believe that White has enough compensation for a pawn. After 17 ♘xe5 Black will recapture with the d-pawn in order to keep his king as safe as possible.

10 0-0 ♖e8 11 ♗d3

Black plans to meet 11 ♘h4 with 11...♘e4! not fearing the shattering of his kingside pawn structure. In return he will increase his grip in the centre, e.g. 12 ♘xf5 gxf5 13 ♘xe4 fxe4 14 ♗e3 ♗xb2 15 ♖b1 ♕f6 16 ♕b3 ♗d4 17 ♗xd4 ♕xd4+ with at least equal chances for Black, Antoshin-Boleslavsky, Leningrad 1956.

11...♕d7!

Black doesn't cede any ground in the centre. Instead 11...♘e4 12 ♘xe4 ♗xe4 13 ♗xe4 ♖xe4 14 ♘g5! allows White good attacking chances – he is not worried about losing a pawn if he can get f5 in as then both his rook and bishop can participate in an attack against the black king.

The key to this variation for Black is control of the e4-square and as the above variation demonstrates controlling a square does not necessarily mean occupying it.

12 h3

White plans to lift Black's blockade by playing g4; risky, as we shall see. On other moves Black is again not worried about the doubling of his f-pawns, e.g.

a) 12 ♘h4 ♘e4 (the usual response to ♘h4) 13 ♘xf5 gxf5 14 ♗xe4 fxe4 with about equal chances.

b) 12 ♕c2 ♘a6 13 a3 ♘c7 14 ♗xf5 gxf5 (it is better for Black to keep his queen as it defends f5) 15 ♗d2 b5 with an unclear game.

12...♘a6 13 a3

A standard reaction to prevent ...♘b4.

13...♘c7 14 g4

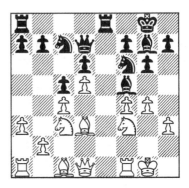

White had prepared this advance with his 12th move. It still doesn't mean that it's good. Another game, Peng Zhao Qin-J.Polgar, Novi Sad Olympiad 1990 went instead 14 ♕c2 b5! (a thematic advance – swapping the b-pawn for the d-pawn is a good deal for Black as it allows her to take more control in the centre and bring the rather passively-placed knight on c7 to life) 15 cxb5 ♘fxd5 16 ♘xd5 ♘xd5 17 ♗xf5 gxf5 18 ♖b1 ♖e4! (the black pieces dominate the centre of the board) 19 ♖d1 ♘b6 20 b4 ♕xb5! 21 ♖xd6 c4! (now the passed pawn decides the game very quickly) 22 ♕f2 c3 23 ♕g3 ♕e2 24 ♘e5 c2 0-1.

White resigned as, after 25 ♖a1 ♖xe5! 26 fxe5 ♕xe5, Black will emerge a piece to the good.

14...♗xg4!?

An interesting though not necessarily courageous decision. The point is that it is very easy for a grandmaster to calculate that the sacrifice guarantees at least a draw. The difficult decision comes later when he has to decide whether to take the perpetual check or gamble for more. In fact this position was already known to theory at the time of this game but no-one had suggested this obvious piece sacrifice. Perhaps because Black has another satisfactory continuation: 14...♗xd3 15 ♕xd3 b5! 16 cxb5 ♖eb8 17 a4 a6 with good Benko style compensation for the pawn.

15 hxg4 ♕xg4+ 16 ♔h2 ♕h5+ 17 ♔g2 ♕g4+ 18 ♔h2

White cannot avoid the draw as 18 ♔h1 ♕h3+ 19 ♘h2 ♘h5 lands him in trouble. The moment of decision has arrived for Black.

18...b5!?

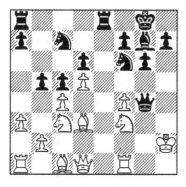

Mestel plays for the win, but with a most surprising move on the queenside. We saw a similar idea in the notes to move 14 – Black wants to weaken White's protection on d5 as if this pawn drops then more black pieces can come flooding into the attack.

19 ♖g1 ♕h5+ 20 ♔g3?!

Straightaway Black is rewarded for his bravery. Conquest chooses the wrong square for his king. He should have played 20 ♔g2 when after 20...bxc4 21 ♗xc4:

a) Look what happens if Black tries to play the same way as with the king on g3: 21...♖e7 22 ♘g5! (there is another interesting tactical shot, 22 ♘e5!?, but the text is probably stronger) and the queens are forced off as 22...♕h4 is met by 23 ♖h1. After 22...♖ae8 23 ♕xh5 ♘xh5 Black still has some compensation for the piece but the exposed position of the white king is not so crucial without queens on the board.

b) It is also to late for Black to take a draw. After 21...♕g4+ 22 ♔h1 ♕h3+ 23 ♘h2 the move 23...♘h5 is not so strong as White can defend with 24 ♕f3.

I'm not convinced that Mestel's decision to spurn the draw was objectively correct, but as the saying goes, 'Fortune favours the brave'

20...bxc4 21 ♗xc4 ♖e7!

Black prepares to double rooks on the e-file.

22 ♕d3

22 ♘g5 is not as powerful now as Black can avoid the queen exchange by 22...h6! as 23 ♕xh5 ♘xh5 is now check. After 23 ♘h3 ♕f5 24 ♗d3 ♕d7 25 ♕f3 ♖ae8 Black has excellent compensation for the piece but White has better chances of organising a successful defence than in the game.

22...♗h6 23 ♔g2

White was worried about 23...♗xf4+ 24 ♗xf4 ♕g4+ so he makes this rather sad admission of his earlier mistake.

23...♖ae8 24 ♗d2 ♗xf4!!

With the investment of a second piece the Black attack becomes irresistible.

25 ♗xf4 ♕g4+ 26 ♗g3

This is why the White king had retreated from g3 – so he would have this defence. However, it is still not enough to save him.

26...♖e3 27 ♕f1 ♘h5!

Stronger than 27...♕xc4.

28 ♔h2

There is no defence, e.g.

a) 28 ♔h1 ♘xg3+ 29 ♖xg3 ♕xg3 30 ♘h2 ♖e1 and Black wins.

b) 28 ♕f2 ♘f4+ 29 ♔h1 ♖xf3 (there are other wins as well but this is the most spectacular) 30 ♗h2 (or 30 ♕h2 ♖xc3! 31 bxc3 ♕f3+ 32 ♖g2 ♘xg2 33 ♕xg2 ♕xc3 and Black wins back his piece and emerges countless pawns to the good) 30...♕h3 31 ♕d2 ♖e2!! (a brilliant interference combination which cuts the queen's line of defence along the 2nd rank) 32 ♗xe2 (or 32 ♕xe2 ♘xe2 33 ♗xe2 ♖f2) 32...♕xh2+‼ 33 ♔xh2 ♖h3 mate.

28...♖xf3 29 ♕h3 ♕xc4 0-1

Black is three pawns up with a crushing attack.

Game 58

Christiansen-Kasparov

Moscow Interzonal 1982

---

1 d4 ♘f6 2 c4 g6 3 ♘c3 ♗g7 4 e4 d6 5 f4 0-0 6 ♘f3 c5 7 d5 e6 8 dxe6

In the previous games White played 8 ♗e2. This time he prefers to exchange in the centre himself. A very different sort of position will arise where White hopes that his active pawns on e4 and f4 will enable him to develop a kingside attack. The main drawback to 8 dxe6 is that it allows the knight on b8 easy access to White's main weakness – the hole on d4 – as there is no longer a pawn on d5 to prevent ...♘c6. First Black must decide with what to recapture on e6.

8...fxe6!

8...♗xe6 is less convincing as it encourages White to play f5, just the move he needs to play to obtain good attacking chances. For example, after 8...♗xe6 9 ♗d3 ♘c6 10 f5 ♗d7 11 0-0 White already has a healthy initiative. By playing 8...fxe6 Black keeps more control in the centre and makes it harder for White to develop an attack.

9 ♗d3

The move 9 ♗e2 also has to be examined. It is rarely played here, but the position can be reached via the alternative move order 1 d4 ♘f6 2 c4 g6 3 ♘c3 ♗g7 4 e4 d6 5 f4 0-0 6 ♗e2 c5 7 d5 e6 8 dxe6 fxe6 9 ♘f3. Black now has a good solid plan which promises him a level game, namely 9...♘c6 10 0-0 e5!?. This advance e5 has two advantages; it liberates the bishop on c8 and reinforces Black's control of d4. These two plusses outweigh the fact that the move concedes control of d5 – this square can now be occupied by a white knight. After 10...e5, the game Feletar-Jurkovic, Pula 1995 continued 11 fxe5 dxe5 12 ♕xd8 ♖xd8 13 ♗g5 ♖f8 14 ♗d3 ♗g4 with about equal chances.

9...♘c6 10 0-0 ♘d4!

There is another plan based on playing 10...a6 followed by ...b5 but it is most logical for Black to immediately occupy the important central outpost. The position after 11 ♘xd4 cxd4 12 ♘e2 e5 would be favourable for Black so White must come up with another plan.

11 ♘g5!?

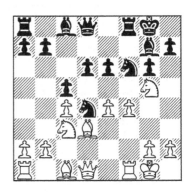

The grandmaster conducting the white pieces in this game, Larry Christiansen, is well known for his attacking instincts. His idea is to follow-up the text with f5 or e5 and then attack the black king. If Black decides to chase the knight with 11...h6 it will just return to f3. Although White will have then wasted a tempo this pales into insignificance when compared with the lasting damage created in front of the black king. The pawn on g6, in particular, would become a target for white pieces (the bishop on d3 after e5 or a knight on h4). As we shall see Black has plenty of defensive and counter-attacking resources without having to resort to the immediate ...h6. Kasparov, himself, has suggested the quieter 11 ♘e2 as an alternative while a more recent game featured a sort of deferred Christiansen plan. It is worth a look as it was quite spectacular.

Petronic-Petrovic, Yugoslavia 1995 continued 11 ♔h1 ♗d7 12 ♘g5 ♕e7 13 e5!? (White goes all in; 13 ♕e1 also comes into consideration) 13...dxe5 14 fxe5 ♘h5 15 g4 ♖xf1+ 16 ♗xf1? (16 ♕xf1 was better) 16...h6! 17 ♘ge4. White has achieved what he set out to do – trap the knight on h5 – but the price he has paid is too high. He has exposed his own king and Black now punishes him for this extravagance. 17...♗xe5! 18 gxh5 ♕h4 19 h3 ♖f8 20 ♗g2 ♗c6. Just look at the black pieces. Every single one of them (if we don't count the king and pawns) is playing a major role in the attack. White is a piece up but Black's extra firepower in the critical area of the board must have made him feel like he was a piece down. 21 ♗e3 ♖f3!! (Black takes aim at h3; he is not afraid to sacrifice more material to strip the white king bare) 22 ♕e1? (the best chance was to take the rook though extensive analysis has shown that the position after 22 ♗xf3 ♕xh3+ 23 ♔g1 ♘xf3+ 24 ♔f2 ♘d4! is very good for Black) 22...♖xh3+! 23 ♔g1 ♖h1+! 24 ♗xh1 ♕h2+ 25 ♔f1 ♕xh1+ 26 ♔f2 ♕h2+ 27 ♔f1 ♕h3+ 28 ♔f2 ♗g3+! 0-1 (29 ♘xg3 ♕g2 mate).

11...e5!

We have already seen such a reaction by Black in the notes to move 9. As well as liberating the bishop and increasing Black's control over d4 the move also prevents White from advancing e5.

12 f5

Now that e5 has been ruled out this is the only way to continue the attack. With hindsight it would probably be better to play the feeble 12 fxe5.

12...h6!

This is a good moment to attack the knight. Black has a concrete reason for playing ...h6.

13 ♘h3

White would prefer to go back to f3 but this interferes with the protection of his f-pawn. During the game Kasparov was slightly concerned about the piece sacrifice 13 fxg6 hxg5 14

♗xg5 but he finally concluded that 14...♗e6 15 ♘d5 ♗xd5 16 exd5 e4! (to open lines for the black pieces) 17 ♗xe4 ♕e7 18 ♗d3 ♖ae8 was good for him.

13...gxf5 14 exf5 b5!

By sacrificing a pawn on the queenside Black hopes to take total control of the centre. Incidentally, this is the reason he was willing to weaken his kingside with his previous two moves. Now 15 cxb5 d5 looks terrible for White and 15 b3 is strongly met by 15...b4 (according to Kasparov) so Christiansen looks for a tactical solution to his problems.

15 ♗e3?!

Kasparov thought White's best chance was 15 ♘xb5! ♗xb5 16 cxb5 d5 as the pawn centre is not quite as dangerous without the support of the knight on d4. Still, this doesn't look like much fun for White.

15...bxc4 16 ♗xc4+ ♔h8

A player of Kasparov's class is not going to fall for the trap 16...d5? 17 ♘xd5! ♘xd5 18 ♗xd4 cxd4 19 ♕b3 when White regains the pinned knight.

17 ♗xd4 cxd4 18 ♘d5 ♗a6!

An excellent move. The point is that after 19 ♗xa6 ♘xd5 the black knight will invade on e3. White prefers to give up material for some vague attacking chances rather than to play such a position.

19 ♘xf6 ♗xc4!

Now Black wins the exchange as he attacks both knight and rook

20 ♘h5 ♗xf1 21 ♕g4!

The best chance. Black must deal with the mate threat on g7 so White at least gets to activate his rook.

21...♕d7 22 ♖xf1

At first glance it appears that White has quite good compensation for the exchange. Kasparov, though, has seen deep into the position and realised that by using his d-pawn as a decoy he will be able to break White's grip on the kingside.

22...d3! 23 ♕f3 d2! 24 g4

If White drops the f-pawn he will be just losing. 24 f6 looks tempting but after 24...♗xf6 25 ♘xf6 ♕g7! Black wins back the knight (check it for yourself; don't forget the pawn on d2). This is the sort of little tactic that strong players are always using to control the game. Even when things look really quiet there is usually plenty bubbling just beneath the surface.

24...♖ac8!

Black plans 25...♖c1

25 ♕d3 ♕a4! 26 ♘f2

White must defend the pawn on g4 but now Black gets the chance to exchange queens. Don't forget that the decoy pawn is still alive and extremely dangerous. Any pawn which reaches the 7th rank should be treated with respect.

26...♕d4! 27 ♕xd4 exd4

Tripled pawns are not usually very good and it's not because they are tripled that they are good here; it's because two of them are advanced passed pawns.

28 ♘f4 ♖fe8 29 ♘e6 ♖c1 30 ♘d1 ♗f6!

The bishop plans to support the d2 pawn from g5. If White wants to remove it he has to give up his powerful knight on e6.

31 ♔f2 ♗g5 32 ♔e2 ♖c5!

A strong manoeuvre. The rook looked well placed on c1 but Kasparov understands that it can do even more damage on the e-file.

33 ♔d3 ♖e5 34 ♘xg5 hxg5 35 ♖f2

The power of the rooks is well illustrated by the following variation: 35 ♔xd2 ♖e4 36 h3 ♖f4 37 ♖g1 ♖f3. White is almost falling off the edge of the board.

35...♖e4 36 h3 ♖e3+! 37 ♔xd4

After 37 ♘xe3 dxe3 Black will soon have a new queen while 37 ♔xd2 ♖xh3 is equally hopeless for White in the long run. Rook against knight is usually a massive advantage in the endgame.

37...♖8e4+ 38 ♔d5 ♖e2 39 ♖f3 ♖e1 40 f6 ♖f4 0-1

The white pawn can be stopped by the black king; nothing will stop the pawn on d2. In fact the performance of the black d-pawn can be compared to that of a pacemaker in a long distance race who was supposed to drop out a few laps before the finish, but instead continued and won.

Game 59

Soppe-Panno

Buenos Aires 1999

---

1 d4 ♘f6 2 c4 g6 3 ♘c3 ♗g7 4 e4 d6 5 f4 0-0 6 ♘f3 c5 7 dxc5

The previous games all featured White blocking the centre with 7 d5 but this time we shall examine lines where the black c-pawn is exchanged for the white d-pawn. In the main game White exchanges on c5 while in the notes we shall look at 7 ♗e2 cxd4 8 ♘xd4. The resulting pawn structure is the same in both cases (after 7 dxc5 Black plays ...♛a5xc5) but 7 dxc5 contains more venom as White gains time attacking the black queen.

After 7 ♗e2 cxd4 8 ♘xd4

Black has two equally valid approaches. He can aim for exchanges with the idea of steering the game into a roughly level endgame (line 'a') or, if he prefers, he can direct play towards a complex middlegame where his chances are no worse than White's (line 'b').

a) 8...♘c6 9 ♗e3 and now:

a1) 9...♗g4 is played quite often but after 10 ♘xc6! (10 ♗xg4 ♘xg4 11 ♛xg4 ♘xd4 is the tactical justification of Black's 9th move; in fact, this is a very common theme in such positions) 10...♗xe2 11 ♘xd8 ♗xd1 12 ♖xd1 ♖fxd8 13 ♔e2 ♖dc8 the temporary pawn sacrifice 14 c5! ensures White of some advantage. For example, 14...dxc5 15 e5 ♘e8 16 ♖d7 ♖c7 17 ♖xc7 ♘xc7 18 ♗xc5 or 14...♖c6 15 cxd6 exd6 16 ♔f3 when in the first case White is more active and in the second he has the healthier pawn structure. The best that Black can hope for in such positions is a draw and he will have to suffer to achieve it.

This rope-a-dope strategy may be a legitimate tactic for the titans defending the black pieces in world championship matches but I certainly don't recommend this approach for the rest of us.

a2) 9...e5 is a better idea. This also leads to an endgame but one where Black has more prospects. For example, 10 ♘xc6 bxc6 11 fxe5 (11 0-0 exf4 12 ♗xf4 ♖e8 is quite good for

Black) 11...dxe5 12 ♗c5 ♖e8 13 ♛xd8 ♖xd8 14 0-0 ♖d2 15 ♖ad1 ♖xd1 16 ♖xd1 ♗e6= Uhlmann-Fischer, Varna Olympiad 1962. This variation alone is enough to explain why 7 ♗e2 is unpopular.

b) For those of you who have no desire to exchange queens so early then 8...♘a6 is a good alternative. The idea is to pressurise the white e-pawn with ...♘c5 and very often to follow up with the advance ...e5. White has:

b1) 9 ♗e3 ♘c5 10 ♗f3 ♗h6! (by pinning the pawn on f4 Black increases the power of the coming advance e5) 11 0-0 (11 ♛d2 e5 12 ♘de2 exf4 13 ♘xf4 ♖e8 is quite good for Black) 11...e5 12 ♘db5 ♘e6 13 ♛xd6 a6 14 ♗b6 ♛d7 15 ♘d5 (15 ♛e5 is interesting but the complications after 15...♛c6! are not unfavourable for Black) 15...♘xd5 16 ♛xd7 (perhaps it would be better to just play 16 exd5 axb5 17 ♛xd7 ♗xd7 18 dxe6 ♗xe6 19 cxb5 ♗xf4 with an unclear endgame) 16...♘xb6! (hardly a sacrifice as Black gets 3 pieces for the queen) 17 ♛e7 (17 ♛d6 ♘xc4 18 ♛b4 axb5) 17...axb5 18 f5 ♗g5 19 ♛b4 ♘d4 20 c5 ♘c4 21 b3?? (Black has the advantage but there is no need to lose the queen in 1 move) 21...♖d2! 0-1, Skotdad-Lesiege, Parthenay 1992.

b2) 9 ♗f3 is an alternative. Boleslavsky suggested that Black play 9...♗g4 10 ♗e3 ♛c8 while other sources offer 9...♘c5 10 ♘b3 ♘fd7. Both look OK for Black. These lines have received very little attention in tournament practice.

7...♛a5

If it wasn't for this move then 6...c5 would not be the main line against the Four Pawns Attack. Few Black players are willing to defend the passive position that arises after 7...dxc5 8 ♛xd8 ♖xd8 9 e5.

8 ♗d3

8 cxd6 ♘xe4 is not good for White, but 8 ♗d2 is OK even though it is hardly ever played. After 8...♛xc5 9 b4 ♛b6 (9...♛xb4 10 ♘d5 is dangerous for Black) 10 ♗d3 ♗g4 11 ♖b1 ♘c6 the chances are about level.

8...♛xc5 9 ♛e2

White plans ♗e3 and 0-0. Much of the play will now revolve around the battle for the d4-square. Black will play moves such as ...♘c6, ...♗g4xf3 and ...♘f6-d7, all of which increase his control of d4, while White will try and defend it with ♗e3, ♕f2 and a rook to the d-file.

9...♘c6 10 ♗e3 ♕a5

10...♕h5 is not so popular as at the end of the tricky line 11 h3 ♘g4 12 ♗d2 ♘d4 13 ♕f1 (13 ♘xd4 ♕h4+) 13...♘xf3+ 14 ♕xf3 ♗d4 White can force the exchange of queens with 15 ♔e2!. His extra space should then give him a slight plus in the ending though this line is still perfectly playable for the unambitious Black player.

11 0-0 ♗g4 12 ♖c1

Inexperienced White players sometimes prefer to immediately advance their queenside pawns. This can lead to trouble. For example, Terzic-Cvitan, Bosnia 1999 continued 12 a3 ♘d7 13 b4 ♕h5 14 ♕d2 (14 ♖c1 a5 15 b5 ♘d4 16 ♕f2 ♘c5! 17 ♗b1 ♗xf3 18 ♗xd4 ♗xd4 19 ♕xd4 ♘b3! also cost White an exchange in another game) 14...♗xf3 15 ♖xf3 ♘d4 16 ♖h3? (the only move that doesn't lose material – Black is also threatening ...♘b3 – is the unpalatable 16 ♗xd4) 16...♕xh3! 17 gxh3 ♘f3+ and Black won the exchange and the game.

12...♘d7

This move is an integral part of Black's strategy. The King's Indian bishop's diagonal is uncovered while the knight heads off towards the queenside where it may try and exchange itself in order to minimise the effects of Black's space disadvantage.

13 ♕f2

White unpins and plans to recapture on f3 with the pawn (see below for explanation). An alternative is 13 ♕d2!? when one possible reac-

tion is 13...♘c5 14 ♗b1 ♘a4 while another is 13...♗xf3 14 ♖xf3 ♗d4!?. Cifuentes-Roeder, San Sebastian 1997 now continued 15 ♔h1 ♗xe3 16 ♕xe3 ♕b6 17 ♕d2 ♕d4 18 ♘e2 ♕g7 with a roughly level game. Note how the black queen has taken over the role of the bishop on the long diagonal.

13...♘c5 14 ♗b1 ♗xf3 15 gxf3

Recapturing with the queen would allow Black to occupy the d4-square. Besides, White is happy to take with the pawn as he hopes to develop an attack along the semi-open g-file.

15...♘a4

In general it is usually a good idea for Black to swap of the white knight on c3 in the King's Indian. This is true here as without the knight Black will find it easier to develop an initiative on the queenside and neither will he have to concern himself with White playing an annoying ♘d5.

16 ♘xa4

White can avoid the exchange but only with the retreat 16 ♘d1!? This is not so stupid as the black knight on a4 is not ideally placed. Vegh-Petrov, Gausdal 2001 continued 16...♖ac8 (16...♘c5 or 16...♖fc8 are other options) 17 a3 ♕h5 18 b4 e5!? 19 ♔h1 ♘d4 20 fxe5 dxe5 21 c5 with chances for both sides.

16...♕xa4 17 h4

An extremely aggressive reaction. For White's kingside attack to work he does need to play moves such as h4-h5 and f5 in order to weaken g6 and to open more files. He usually plays a couple of preparatory moves before launching his attack. The text looks premature as White still has very few pieces ready to partake in an attack. A couple of examples where White's play was more measured:

a) 17 b3 ♕a3 18 c5 dxc5 19 ♗xc5 (19 ♖xc5!?) 19...♕xc5! 20 ♖xc5 ♗d4 21 ♖d1 ♗xf2+ 22 ♔xf2 ♖fd8 23 ♖cd5 e6 24 ♖xd8+ ♖xd8 25 ♖xd8+ ♘xd8 with a level endgame, Topalov-Kasparov, Linares 1994. The bishop is better than the knight but Black's superior pawn structure compensates.

b) 17 ♖fd1 ♖ac8 18 b3 ♕a5 19 ♖d5 ♕c7 20 ♖cd1 b6 21 a3 ♖fd8 22 h4 e6 23 ♗g5 ♕e7 24 h5 ♕f6 25 hxg6 fxg6 with a roughly level game, Topalov-Dolmatov, Elinite 1995.

17...♕b4 18 b3 ♗h6!?

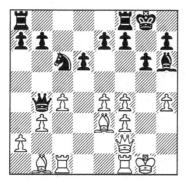

Often in such positions Black will play ...a5-a4 in order to create a weakness on the queenside and to open the a-file for his rooks. Here, though, with the white attack already underway such a policy was deemed too slow. The idea behind the text is to play ...e5 and exchange off the dark-squared bishops. If Black can then patch up the holes around his king his superior minor piece (his knight is much stronger than White's light-squared bishop) should give him the better game.

19 ♔h1 e5 20 f5 ♗xe3 21 ♕xe3 ♕b6!

Black knows that White won't exchange queens he is looking to transfer his own queen to the kingside. White's attack will only be dangerous if Black ignores it.

22 ♕h6 ♕d8 23 ♖c2 ♔h8 24 ♖g2 ♖g8 25 f4 ♕f8! 26 ♕g5 f6 27 ♕g4 ♕h6

By some accurate defensive play Black has

ensured that the white attack is over even before it got started. Note how Black hasn't rushed to occupy the outpost on d4. In fact the square he really wants for his knight is e5 as this is nearer the kingside where the action is taking place.

28 fxe5 ♘xe5 29 ♕f4 g5! 30 ♕d2 ♖ad8 31 ♖h2 ♕f8 32 h5?! g4 33 ♕f4 ♕f7 34 ♔g2 ♖g5 35 h6 ♕c7 36 ♖d1 b5!

White was hoping to save himself by blocking everything up but by means of a pawn sacrifice Black can infiltrate via the c-file.

White is now held to account for recklessly advancing the pawns in front of his own king.

37 cxb5 ♕c3 38 ♖hh1 ♕f3+!

The exchange of queens doesn't mean the end of the attack. In fact, with the open g-file and pawn on f3 it becomes even stronger.

39 ♕xf3 gxf3+ 40 ♔f2 ♖g2+ 41 ♔e3 ♖dg8 42 ♗d3 ♖8g3 43 ♗c4 f2+ 44 ♔e2 ♖g1 45 ♖h2 ♘xc4?!

45...♘g4! would have cost White a whole rook. Now Black just wins a piece but it is still good enough to win the game. The remaining moves were: 46 ♔xf2 ♖xd1 47 ♔xg3 ♖d3+ 48 ♔h4 ♘d2 49 ♖g2 ♘f3+ 50 ♔h5 ♖d2 51 ♖g3 ♖h2+ 52 ♔g4 ♘e5+ 53 ♔f4 ♖h4+ 54 ♔e3 ♖xh6 55 ♔d4 ♖h2 56 ♔c3 ♖d2+ 57 ♔e3 ♖xa2 58 ♖c8+ ♔g7 59 ♖a8 ♖a3 60 b6 ♖xb3+ 61 ♔d4 ♖d3 mate.

Summary

1) I have no magic wand to wave here. I am just suggesting that Black enter the main line with 6...c5 and follow its most reliable branch 9...♗g4.

2) 9...♗g4 is supposed to be the solid option but it still leads to incredibly sharp positions. The theory is more important here than in many other lines as a small slip can cost one the game. So if you are trying to learn the King's Indian, make this line one of your priorities.

3) Games 57-59 tackle variations that are not quite as popular at they used to be, but they have all enjoyed their moments in the sun and may well do so again. 7 dxc5 of Game 59 is the most difficult for Black to deal with.

CHAPTER TEN

White Plays an early h3

1 d4 ♘f6 2 c4 g6 3 ♘c3 ♗g7 4 e4 d6 5 h3

This is a popular way of meeting the King's Indian amongst White players looking for an uncompromising struggle. The move h3 has two main ideas. The first is to pave the way for ♗e3 without having to worry about been harassed by ...♘g4. Very often the bishop will go to g5 first but if Black attacks it with ...h6 then it drops back to e3. The second idea behind h3 is to support the advance g4. This is played both to gain space on the kingside and to dissuade Black from playing ...f5. The intentions behind h3 are similar to those behind f3 in the Sämisch Variation but the two variations usually lead to quite different types of games. In h3's favour is the fact that White can still develop his knight to f3 and that the dark squares are not further weakened (the move f3 opens the diagonal g1- a7 upon which White's king is often to be found) but, on the other hand, h3 does nothing to protect the all important e4-square.

My main recommendations are centred around Black playing the traditional ...e5 in conjunction with the modern ...♘a6 which has, in fact, been the main line for many years. The struggle can be very sharp and both players can attack on either wing (the centre is almost always blocked). White tends to win games by taking control over the crucial e4-square, whilst Black's victories usually occur when he achieves the advance ...e5-e4 or when White has neglected the safety of his king (or a combination of both).

The material is split up into two sections de-

pending on whether White plays ♘f3 or not.

White plays 6 ♘f3
1 d4 ♘f6 2 c4 g6 3 ♘c3 ♗g7 4 e4 d6 5 h3 0-0 6 ♘f3

The move order 5 ♘f3 0-0 6 h3 is at least as frequent.

6...e5

There are several move orders Black can employ to reach the desired set-up. Most of them quickly converge. For example, 6...♘a6 7 ♗g5 e5 8 d5 takes us back into Game 60.

7 d5

7 dxe5 dxe5 8 ♕xd8 ♖xd8 9 ♗g5 ♖e8 is very similar to the Exchange Variation (Chapter 6). In the line that I am recommending for Black it doesn't really make any difference that White has played h3 instead of ♗e2.

7...♘a6

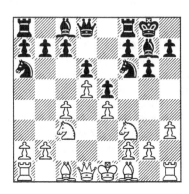

and now:

a) 8 ♗g5 is the subject of Game 60.

b) 8 ♗e3 of Game 61.

As I recommend that Black meets 8 ♗g5 with 8...h6 9 ♗e3 the positions are very similar. The difference between having the pawn on h6 and h7 will be explained later. The games below are model games for Black. Life will not always be so smooth but I have a lot of faith in the systems I'm proposing.

Game 60
Barsov-Gallagher
Calcutta 2001

---

1 d4 ♘f6 2 c4 g6 3 ♘c3 ♗g7 4 e4 d6 5 ♘f3 0-0 6 h3 e5 7 d5 ♘a6

The actual move order of this game was 7...a5 8 ♗g5 ♘a6 9 g4 ♘c5 10 ♘d2 h6 11 ♗e3. As the knight is just en route to c5 it would have been equally possible to get there via d7 (i.e. 7...♘bd7).

8 ♗g5

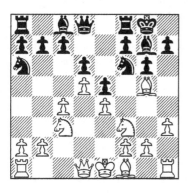

8...h6

White played ♗g5 in order to encourage this move which is often a liability for Black in the King's Indian. Here, though, I am suggesting that we fall in with White's plans as it is possible to play a system where h6 is actually quite useful.

You may well ask why not just play 8...♕e8 as we do when White delays ♘f3 (see Games 62-63) Well, that is also perfectly playable but the slight difference in the position (♘f3 instead of ♗d3) means that it is harder for Black

to achieve ...f5. For example, 8...♕e8 9 g4 ♘d7 10 ♖g1 ♔h8 11 ♕d2 ♘dc5 12 ♘h4 and f5 is not such a good idea anymore (12...c6 is still reasonable).

9 ♗e3 ♘c5

9...♘h5, which is a popular line with the pawn back on h7, is not so good here as White, at some point, will be able to gain an important tempo with ♕d2.

10 ♘d2 a5

The knight's position on c5 must be secured against b4.

11 g4

A quieter line is 11 ♗e2 ♗d7 (on the immediate 11...♘h7 White may try 12 h4!?; ...♗d7 is a useful developing move if only because the queen's rook is now more in the game) 12 0-0 (12 g4 would of course transpose into the main game) 12...♘h7!? with ...f7-f5 to soon follow. White has tried many moves now. Here are a few examples:

a) 13 ♕c2 ♘g5!? 14 h4 ♘h7 15 h5 ♘f6 (of Black's last five moves four have been with this knight and it has ended up where it started; in return for this scandalous waste of time he has lured the white h-pawn forward and White is about to take back his move ♕c2) 16 ♕d1 gxh5 17 ♗xh5 ♘d3 18 ♗f3 ♕c8 19 ♕c2 ♘f4 20 c5 dxc5 21 ♗xc5 ♖e8 22 ♘e2 ♗b5 23 ♘c4 ♘4xd5! with a good game for Black, Beliavsky-Sher, Bern 1995.

b) 13 ♖e1 f5 14 exf5 gxf5 15 f4 exf4 16 ♗xf4 ♕f6 17 ♘f3 ♘g5 18 ♖c1 ♖ae8 with an active game for Black, Jokovic-Tratar, Bled 2003

c) 13 ♔h2 ♘g5 14 f3 ♕e7 15 ♘b3 ♘xb3 16 ♕xb3 b6 17 ♕c2 f5 18 exf5 gxf5 19 f4 exf4 20 ♗xf4 ♘e4 21 ♗d3 and White was fractionally better although he over-pressed and lost in Krasenkow-Radjabov, Wijk aan Zee 2003. I don't see why Black didn't just play 14...f5.

11...c6

A useful rule of thumb in these lines is to play ...c7-c6 only in reply to White's g2-g4. Once White has played g2-g4 his king won't be very safe on the kingside so he will usually be looking to castle queenside (this game is the exception that proves the rule). It is therefore a good idea for Black to be ready to open lines in this sector of the board at a moment's notice.

Playing ...c7-c6 is quite safe but Black must be more careful about taking on d5. If he mistimes this exchange then the white pieces may become very active on the queenside (after White recaptures with cxd5 a diagonal is opened for his light-squared bishop and the knight on d2 may be able to jump into c4). A second rule of thumb for Black, therefore, is to only play ...cxd5 when you can follow up with ...b7-b5.

12 ♗e2 ♗d7

The plan is to play ...a5-a4 and ...♕a5 to develop a queenside initiative.

13 0-0!?

I was completely taken aback by this move, a novelty my opponent had prepared beforehand. Still, it was not an unpleasant surprise. I just assumed that my opponent had lost his marbles. Who in their right mind would castle kingside in such a position?

The main move is 13 h4 and after 13...a4 there is:

a) 14 h5 (It is not such a good idea for White to ignore the threat of ...♕a5) 14...♕a5 (threatening ♘xe4 as one of the white knights will be pinned) 15 f3 a3! (and this was the other threat; ideally White would like to meet this move with 16 b3 but this just loses the knight on c3) 16 ♕c2 axb2 17 ♕xb2 (exchanging his a-pawn for White's b-pawn has gained Black a positional advantage on the queenside) 17...cxd5 18 cxd5 b5! 19 ♖b1 (The pawn could not be taken. 19 ♘xb5 ♖fb8 20 a4 ♗xb5! and now 21 axb5 loses a rook and 21 ♗xb5 ♘d3+! a queen) 19...♖fc8 (It's not unusual for Black to sacrifice the pawn on h6 in this fashion in the King's Indian. In return he hopes to take control of the dark squares) 20 hxg6 fxg6 21 ♗xh6 ♘d3+! 22 ♗xd3 ♖xc3 23 ♗xg7 ♔xg7 24 ♔e2 (24 ♗e2 was better although Black has more than enough for the pawn after 24...♖ac8) 24...♘xg4! 25 ♕b4 ♖xd3! 26 fxg4 (26 ♕xa5 ♖e3+! 27 ♔f1 ♖xa5 28 fxg4 ♖xa2 is an even worse endgame) 26...♕xb4 27 ♖xb4 ♖g3 28 ♖b2 ♖f8 29 ♔d1 ♗xg4+ 30 ♔c1 ♖c8+ 31 ♔b1 ♗e2 32 ♖e1 ♗d3+ 33 ♔a1 ♖g2 34 ♘b3 ♖xb2 35 ♔xb2 ♖c4 0-1 J.Ivanov-V.Georgiev, Salou 2000. White loses a second pawn. A wonderful King's Indian game.

b) 14 ♗xc5 dxc5 15 ♘xa4 cxd5 16 ♘xc5 dxe4 is promising for Black according to Nunn.

White may pick up a pawn but his king has no home.

c) 14 g5 is probably White's best move. After 14...hxg5 15 hxg5 (better than 15 ♗xg5 ♕a5 16 ♕b1 cxd5 17 cxd5 b5 18 a3 ♖fb8 with an excellent game for Black, Chiburdanidze-Nunn, Linares 1988) 15...♘h7 we have:

c1) 16 ♘f3 cxd5 17 cxd5 ♕a5 18 ♕d2 ♖fc8 19 ♔f1 b5 Black had active play in Akesson-Gallagher, Istanbul Olympiad 2000.

c2) 16 ♖g1 ♕a5 17 ♕b1!? (ugly but it does defend against the threat of ...a4-a3 and by defending e4 allows White to recapture on d5 with the knight; previously 17 ♖c1 cxd5 18 cxd5 b5 had been played which is quite promising for Black) 17...cxd5 (I prefer to clarify things straight away) 18 ♘xd5 ♖fe8 19 f3 ♕d8?! 20 ♕c1! ♗c6 21 ♘b1! ♘e6 22 ♘bc3 ♘d4 23 ♕d2 ♖c8 24 ♔f2 ♖f8 25 ♖g3 with some advantage to White, Sadler-Gallagher, Bundesliga 2002 (1-0, 40).

It was better to play 19...♗c6! when 20 ♔f2 is met by 20...♘e6 and 20 ♕c2 by 20...b5! 21 cxb5 ♗xd5 22 exd5 e4 with a mess from which Black is more likely to emerge triumphant.

Before moving on a word about another move White has played here, 13 f3. It takes the sting out of the ...a4 and ...♕a5 idea as the e-pawn is now protected. 13...♖b8!?, intending 14...cxd5 followed by ...b5, has been played by the strong grandmasters Ehlvest and Smirin.

13...h5!

There is no longer any point in continuing with ...a4 and ...♕a5 as Black's main target, the white king, has unexpectedly disappeared to the other side of the board. My main plan now was to blast open the whole kingside as quickly as possible. True, this could backfire as Black's king is there as well but it is easier for Black to feed his pieces into a kingside attack than it is for White.

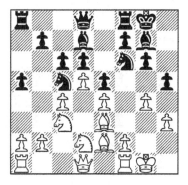

14 &g2 cxd5 15 exd5

White usually recaptures with the c-pawn in such positions but 15 cxd5 is strongly met by 15...b5! (remember the rule of thumb). By recapturing with the e-pawn he hopes to use the e4-square for his knights.

15...hxg4 16 hxg4 &h7

It should come as no surprise to you that Black plans to play ...f5. The knight is also quite handily placed on h7 as in some lines it can jump out to g5.

17 &de4

17 &xc5 dxc5 18 &de4 is nothing for Black to worry about. He just plays 18...b6 followed by ...f5

17...&xe4 18 &xe4 f5!

White had been hoping for 18...&e7 19 c5! when his central attack crashes through before Black's kingside attack is even out of the starting blocks. To be honest I didn't consider defending the d-pawn pawn for a second but it did take me a long time to find the correct follow up to the sacrifice.

As an aside, a warning if you get *ChessBase Magazine* or the *MegaBase*. They have a guy called Tsesarsky who annotates King's Indian games. The guy ruins many good games with his forthright but erroneous annotations. Here for example he awarded my fine move a '?' and said that Black could gain the advantage with 18...&c7. Not true. He didn't even consider the

possibility of White playing c5 (or even 19 g5). That's better, got that off my chest.

19 &xd6 b6!

It's always nice to sacrifice and then play a quiet move. This is the star move of the game. Initially I was trying to make the direct approach work (something with ...f4 and ...&g5) but the problem was always the c5-square – both for the bishop after ...f4, &c5 and, in other variations, for the knight after &xb7-c5. It's well worth spending a tempo to cut out these possibilities. The shaky position of the white king cannot be repaired so easily.

20 f3?!

After this White is in trouble. I was expecting him to return the pawn by 20 c5. After 20...f4 21 &d2 bxc5 22 &e4 I consider the chances to be about level. Black also has a very interesting sacrificial possibility in 21...&g5 22 f3 &xg4!

20...f4 21 &f2 &xg4 22 fxg4?

The decisive mistake. White should have tried 22 &e4 even if 22...&f5 with the idea of capturing on e4 and attacking the black king gives Black a good game.

22...&xd6 23 &f3 &g5 24 &h4 &xf3 25 &xf3

Barsov said after the game that he was totally oblivious to the coming danger. He had assumed that he would be able to blockade the passed pawns but Black's idea is just to get rid off them to open up lines around the white king.

25...e4! 26 &xe4 &ae8 27 &f3?!

This is just hopeless and Barsov played it in a panic when he suddenly realised that 27 &c2

f3+ 28 ♖xf3 ♖xf3 29 ♔xf3 ♕f8+ 30 ♔g2 ♕f4 gives Black a decisive attack.

27...♖e3 28 ♕d1

28 ♕f2 ♕d7 is crushing.

28...f3+ 29 ♔h3

29 ♔h1 g5 30 ♗xg5 (30 ♗f2 ♕h6+ 31 ♔g1 ♕h3) 30...♖e2 wins.

29...♖e2 30 ♗g3 ♗e5

It's a real shame that I didn't find 30...♕xg3+ 31 ♔xg3 ♗e5+ 32 ♔h4 ♖h2+ 33 ♔g5 ♗f4+ 34 ♔xg6 ♖h6 mate

31 c5 ♕f6 32 ♗xe5 ♕xe5 33 ♖h1 0-1

White lost on time but it's mate in two anyway.

Game 61

Nikcevic-Tkachiev

Cannes 1996

---

1 d4 ♘f6 2 c4 g6 3 ♘c3 ♗g7 4 e4 d6 5 ♘f3 0-0 6 h3 e5 7 d5 ♘a6 8 ♗e3

This time White doesn't bother trying to squeeze ...h7-h6 out of Black but develops his bishop directly to e3.

8...♘c5

8...♘h5 is an important alternative that can even be considered as the main line. However, I see no reason to complicate life. The plan we used against ♗g5 works perfectly well here as well (I did cover 8...♘h5 in SOKID for those of you who prefer that move).

9 ♘d2

9 ♗xc5 dxc5 10 ♘xe5 ♘xe4 is not a very good idea for White.

9...a5 10 g4 c6 11 ♗e2

The position is the same as in the previous games apart from the fact that the black pawn is on h7 instead of h6. This seemingly insignificant difference is enough to make the way Black played in the previous game unattractive, but at the same time introduces a new possibility that wasn't really available to Black in the last game.

11...a4!

11...♗d7 is less promising because of the reply 12 g5. It is better for Black to get on with his queenside play at once, even if it means sacrificing a pawn. The Russian grandmaster Dolmatov pioneered the text in this particular position, but it is a well-known idea from other King's Indian variations. The point is that if White wants to take the pawn he will have to give up his important bishop for a knight. In the resulting position Black's control of the dark squares guarantee him long-term positional pressure. The reason that such an approach was not recommended in the previous game is that Black needs to activate his bishop via the h6-square – which was not available to him there.

12 b4

I have my doubts about this move as White opens the queenside before he is ready to take over the initiative there. Let's have a look at the alternatives.

a) Few strong players are willing to accept the pawn sacrifice. The one example I have, Bagirov-Dolmatov, Lucerne 1993 wasn't very informative: 12 ♗xc5 dxc5 13 ♘xa4 ♕a5 14 ♘c3 ♗h6 15 ♕c2 ♗d7 16 ♖g1 ½-½. Black's next move would have been 16...♗f4 with good play for the pawn.

b) 12 h4 ♕a5!, with the double threat of ...♘xe4 and ...a3, should be compared to the previous game.

c) 12 ♕c2 ♕a5 13 0-0-0 ♗d7 14 ♔b1 cxd5 15 cxd5 b5 16 ♗xc5 dxc5 17 ♖c1 ♖ac8 18 g5 ♘e8 19 ♗g4 f5 20 gxf6 ♘xf6 21 f3 c4 was good for Black in Kalantarian-Dolmatov, Linares 2000.

d) I mentioned that Black didn't play 11...♗d7 because of the reply 12 g5. What about 12 g5 here? Well, nobody has played it but the main difference is that Black can retreat his knight to d7 instead of e8, which is important as he retains control over c5.

12...axb3 13 axb3 ♖xa1 14 ♕xa1 ♘a6!

Black prevents White from playing b4 and plans to play c5 in order to secure the useful outpost on b4 for his knight. White's next move re-introduces the threat of b4 but it forces Black to play what he was going to do anyway.

15 ♕a3 c5 16 ♘f1

White should probably play 16 ♘a2 to prevent Black's next move and to force through b4. This is the only way for White to generate some play in this position and is certainly preferable to doing nothing as he did in the game. Black would reply with either 16...♘e8 or 16...♘d7 and then ...f5.

16...♘b4

Threatening 17...♘c2+ .

17 ♕c1 h5!

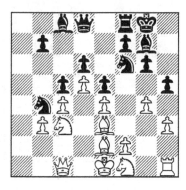

With the queenside more than secure it is time for Black to turn his attention to the kingside. As usual in this variation the white king

does not have much cover.

18 f3

Of course 18 gxh5 ♘xh5 19 ♗xh5?? fails to 19...♘d3+.

18...♗d7 19 ♔f2 ♘h7 20 ♔g2 h4 21 ♘d2 ♕e7 22 ♘db1 ♗f6!

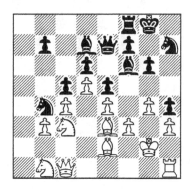

Note how Tkachiev, a very strong grandmaster, calmly manoeuvres his pieces to their best squares before launching his attack. He can do this because White has no counterplay and is reduced to fiddling about with his knight on the back couple of ranks (he's trying to get it to c2 to exchange of Black's knight on b4 – he doesn't quite make it).

23 ♗f2?!

White is trying to avoid the exchange of bishops that Black had planned with ♗f6. This is because his bishop is, theoretically speaking, the better piece (his pawns are on light squares while Black's are on dark squares) But which bishop would you prefer in the middlegame? White's passive one on f2 or Black's active one on g5. The lesser evil was to acquiesce to the bishop exchange.

23...♗g5 24 ♕b2 f5

At last.

25 ♘a3 fxg4! 26 hxg4

On 26 fxg4, 26...♖xf2+!? 27 ♔xf2 ♕f6+ 28 ♔e1 ♕f4 would be very strong but there is an even more decisive line for Black: 26...♕f6! 27 ♖f1 (27 ♔e1 ♘d3!) 27...♘d3! (we'll see this combination again in a minute) 28 ♗xd3 ♕f3+ 29 ♔g1 ♕xd3 with a completely winning position.

26...♕f6 27 ♘d1

White defends his bishop on f2 to stop

Black from playing ♗xg4. But...

27...♗xg4!

...Black plays it anyway.

28 ♕c3

And White can't take as after 28 fxg4 he is blown away by 28...♘d3!. The text, however is no better.

28...♘a2! 0-1

White resigned as his only move to stay defending f3 is 29 ♕d3 but then 29...♘c1! is a killer.

White delays, or omits, ♘f3

1 d4 ♘f6 2 c4 g6 3 ♘c3 ♗g7 4 e4 d6 5 h3 0-0 6 ♗g5

In this section White delays the development of his king's knight as he usually prefers a setup with ♗d3 and ♘ge2 although he has been known to change his mind and develop his knight to f3 later. I am recommending that Black plays the very modern system 6...♘a6 7 ♗d3 e5 8 d5 ♕e8!?

If you can learn how to handle such positions then you will be well on your way to King's Indian mastery.

> *Game 62*
> ## Zotnikov-Gallagher
> *Arosa 1996*

1 d4 ♘f6 2 c4 g6 3 ♘c3 ♗g7 4 e4 d6 5 h3 0-0 6 ♗g5 ♘a6 7 ♗d3

The main line. For early deviations, see Game 63.

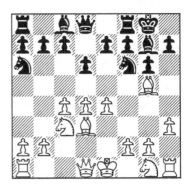

7...e5 8 d5 ♕e8

This is the modern, dynamic approach to the King's Indian. The alternative, 8...c6, can be considered the traditional approach. The idea behind 8...♕e8 is, I hope, obvious to you. Black unpins the knight on f6 so that he can move it and play ...f7-f5. Black could also have unpinned with 8...h6 when the bishop normally drops back to e3. Although that is how I recommended Black play against 6 ♘f3 I am not so keen on that against the ♗d3, ♘ge2 set-up. After 8...♕e8 one of Black's hopes is that the bishop on g5 may actually turn out to be misplaced. It could end up just pointing into thin air, or it may block the g-file for the white rooks while it will also have to watch that it doesn't get stranded by Black playing f4.

9 g4

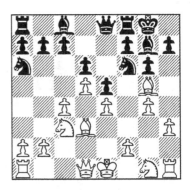

This double-edged move is the consistent follow-up to an early h3. The idea is not to start a kingside pawn storm but to make Black think twice about playing ...f5. If Black goes ahead with the ...f7-f5 idea, the g-file, where the black king is currently in residence, will open. However, the piece which has the least reason to be satisfied with g2-g4 is the white king. His preferred home on g1 is now out of bounds (unless your name is Barsov) so he will have to stay in the centre or risk the queenside. Playing Black in the King's Indian I am always happy to see White playing g4 as even if things go wrong there should still be swindling chances.

A couple of other tries for White:

a) 9 ♘ge2 is a more solid alternative, when after 9...♗d7 we have a couple of examples:

a1) 10 a3 is interesting. The idea is to follow up with b4 in order to make the knight on a6 look silly. I suppose 10...♘ac5 11 ♗c2 a5 is possible but Black can also just play 10...f5 11 b4 when 11...h6 12 ♗d2 c5! 13 dxc6 bxc6 14 0-0 ♘c7 led to a tense game in Atalik-Ivanesevic, Halkidiki 1998. Also possible is 11...f4 12 f3 ♗f6 13 ♗xf6 ♘xf6 14 ♕d2 ♕e7 with reasonable prospects for Black. Such a position is only playable because he has exchanged off his passive bishop. If White now plays 15 0-0-0 then 15...c5 looks like a decent reply.

a2) 10 0-0 f5 11 exf5 gxf4 12 f4 e4 13 ♗c2 ♕h5! (threatening h6) 14 ♘d4 ♕xd1 15 ♖axd1 ♘b4 16 ♗b1 ♘c5 with an active game for Black, Cramling-Gallagher, Bern 1992.

b) 9 a3 ♘c5 10 ♗c2 a5 11 ♕f3?! ♘fd7 12 ♘b5 ♘a6 13 g4 ♘dc5 14 ♘e2 (14 b4 axb4 15 axb4 ♘xb4! is good for Black) f5 15 ♕g2?! fxe4 16 ♗xe4 ♘xe4 17 ♕xe4 ♗d7! 18 a4 ♘c5 19 ♕e3 ♗xb5 20 axb5 e4! and the rest was carnage, Chernin-Gallagher, Basle (rapid) 1995. What I like about these h3 systems is that when things go wrong for White they go really wrong.

9...♗d7

Black is not bluffed out by White's g4. He is still going to play ...f5 even if it means exposing his own king. Better that than a passive position with nothing to do.

10 ♘ge2

Or:

a) 10 ♘f3 f5 11 gxf5 gxf5 12 ♖g1 (12 exf5 is very strongly met by 12...e4!) 12...♔h8 13 ♘h4 ♘dc5 14 ♗c2 fxe4 15 ♘xe4 ♘xe4 16 ♗xe4 ♘c5 17 ♕c2 (the bishop must be protected as retreating it would allow 17...e4!) 17...♘xe4 18

♕xe4 ♕h5!? (18...♕f7) 19 ♖c1 (with the intention of swinging his queen's rook to the kingside) 19...♗d7 (an attacking player like Kupreichik would be considering ...♖f4 at each turn – here it was rejected because of 20 ♗xf4 ♕xh4 21 ♕g2 – but it is clear that it, and other attacking ideas, will be more effective once the queenside is developed) 20 ♖c3 ♖ae8 21 ♖cg3 b5! (21...♖f4 22 ♕g2! is less good as Black can't play ...e4) 22 ♕g2 e4! 23 ♗e7 (after something like 23 ♗e3 ♗xb2 White has no killer blow) 23...e3! 24 f3 (completely hopeless, but so is everything else) 24...♖xe7 0-1 Paunovic-Kupreichik, Yugoslavia 1992. After 25 ♖xg7 ♕xh4+ there is no good square for his king.

If a game is lost so quickly without any clear error then it must mean that the whole strategy is wrong. I have serious doubts about White's combination of g4 and ♘f3 in this game.

b) 10 a3 (danger!) and now:

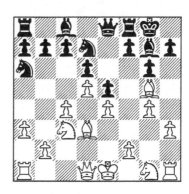

b1) 10...♘ac5 11 ♗c2 a5 and now Agrest-Milov, European Ch., Ohrid 2001 continued 12 ♘ge2 ♘b6! (a rare exception to the good King's Indian rule of not putting one's knights on b6) 13 b3 f5 14 ♖g1 fxe4 15 ♘xe4 ♘xe4 16 ♗xe4 a4! (White's queenside structure will now be spoiled as he can't play 17 b4) 17 ♘c3 axb3 18 ♕xb3 ♘d7 19 ♗e3 b6 20 ♖a2 ♕e7 21 ♖g3 ♘c5 (this is such a good square for the knight that now White feels obliged to give up his strong bishop for it) 22 ♗xc5 bxc5 23 a4 ♗h6 24 ♘e2 ♗d7 25 ♕c2 ♗f4 26 ♖f3 ♖a5 27 ♘c3 ♖fa8 ½-½. Black could certainly have continued the game.

b2) Black can also play the other knight to

c5, e.g. 10...♘dc5 11 ♗c2 f5 but after 12 b4 ♘xe4 13 ♘xe4 fxe4 14 ♗xe4 he must immediately bring the knight on a6 back into play with 14...♘b8.

10...♘dc5

10...f5 at once has also been played but the text is more accurate. Black wants to be in a position to recapture with the bishop if White takes twice on f5.

11 ♗c2

11 ♘g3!? has been suggested as an improvement but it seems to me like an admission of defeat to give up the bishop so easily when Black is about to open the position with ...f5.

11...f5 12 a3

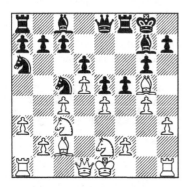

It may look like a quiet little move but a3 spells danger for Black in this system. White is threatening to lock the knight on a6 out of the game. Black is forced to take action immediately and that means exchanging in the centre. Alternatively:

a) In Eliet-Gallagher, Charleville 2000, White tried the over-ambitious 12 exf5 gxf5 13 a3 but overlooked that after 13...e4 14 ♗e3 ♘d3+ 15 ♗xd3 exd3 that he cannot play 16 ♕xd3 as 16...f4! wins a piece. If the bishop moves there follows 17...f3. Instead he was reduced to 16 ♘f4 but after 16...fxg4 17 ♘xd3 g3 Black had a strong attack. In passing, I should just mention that 12 gxf5 gxf5 13 ♘g3 should be met by 13...f4.

b) Hazai awards the move 12 f3 an '!' but after 12...♘b4 13 ♗b1 fxg4 14 fxg4 he fails to consider Black's best move, 14...♕f7!

12...fxe4 13 ♘xe4?

This natural recapture allows Black to take over the initiative. White should have played 13 b4 ♘d3+ 14 ♗xd3 exd3 15 ♕xd3 in order to try and keep the knight on a6 out of the game. I had envisaged a neat way to get the beast back into play: 15...e4 16 ♕d2 c5! 17 b5 ♘b4! although the position after 18 axb4 cxb4 19 ♘d4 bxc3 20 ♕xc3 is just unclear.

13...♘xe4 14 ♗xe4 ♘c5 15 ♘c3

It is essential for White to keep a piece on e4 to prevent Black from playing ...e4. Black must take quick action as if White has the time to consolidate then his blockade of e4 will give him a positional advantage. The first move King's Indian players look at in such positions is the exchange sacrifice ...♖f4. Here there is an even more dynamic solution.

15...b5!

Not deep, but a visually surprising move. Of course 16 ♘xb5 is impossible but Black's main point is that after 16 cxb5 ♘xe4 17 ♘xe4 ♕xb5 the position has opened and White's king is very exposed. Rather than go for this White prefers to give up a pawn to retain his blockade.

16 ♗e3 ♘xe4 17 ♘xe4 bxc4 18 ♕c2 ♕b5 19 0-0-0

White was well aware that his king was not going to lead a quiet life on the queenside but castling kingside is at least as risky and staying in the centre is out of the question.

19...♗d7 20 ♖he1

White plans to use his rooks on the 2nd rank to defend b2.

20...♕a6

Threatening 21...♗a4

21 ♘c3 ♖ae8?! 22 ♖d2 ♖b8

Correcting my previous error which had

been prompted by some imaginary concerns about White playing f4. Of course the rooks belong on the open b-file.

23 ♕e4 ♖b3 24 ♖c2 ♖fb8 25 ♖ee2

White has successfully defended his main weakness on b2. It is hard to see how Black can make further progress on the queenside. How can he increase the pressure then? Well, ever since White played ♕e4 the old adage that a queen is a bad blockader (the black e-pawn must be blockaded and the queen is too strong a piece to be reduced to the role of blockader) would not leave my head. If only the queen could be attacked then the white position is sure to fall apart.

25...g5!!

Oh, what pleasure I got from that move! I particularly enjoyed the fact that the two key moves in the game were sacrifices of the knight's pawn (15...b5!). Black's plan is simple – to transfer his bishop to g6. The move g5 had to be played at once as otherwise White could prevent the manoeuvre with h4-h5.

26 ♗xg5 ♗e8 27 f4

White allows the opening of the long diagonal in order to get some vague attacking chances of his own against the black king. A couple of other moves are also worth examining:

a) 27 ♕g2 ♗g6 28 ♘e4 is a fragile attempt to keep e4 blockaded and the black bishops out of the game. However, 28...c3! 29 ♘xc3 ♖xc3! 30 bxc3 ♖b1+ 31 ♔xb1 (31 ♔d2 ♕d3 mate) 31...♕xe2! and Black wins the other rook as well. A nice combination but there are also other ways to win. It is simply inevitable in such

a position.

b) The best chance was offered by 27 ♕f5 ♗g6 28 ♕e6+ as after 28...♔h8 29 ♗f6 ♗xc2 30 ♗xg7+ ♔xg7 31 ♕e7+ White scrambles a draw by perpetual check. Black shouldn't be so greedy. Instead, he can play 28...♗f7 29 ♕f5 c6! when his big centre gives him a clear advantage in a still complex position.

27...exf4 28 ♕xf4 ♗xc3!

This is not the sort of move one should play lightly and I didn't. I used up most of my remaining time making sure there would be no nasty surprises on the weakened dark squares around my king. 28...♗g6 looks good but I didn't want to give him the chance to play 29 ♗f6.

29 bxc3 ♕xa3+ 30 ♔d2 ♖xc3!?

This is actually the safest move in the position as with best play it leads to a very favourable endgame.

31 ♖xe8+?

The main line was 31 ♖xc3 ♖b2+ 32 ♖c2 (32 ♔d1 ♗a4+ 33 ♖cc2 ♖b1+) 32...♖xc2+ 33 ♔xc2 ♕d3+ 34 ♔c1 ♕xe2 35 ♗h6 ♕e7 which should be winning for Black.

31...♖xe8 32 ♖xc3 ♕a2+!

Not 32...♕b2+ 33 ♖c2 ♕b4+ 34 ♖c3 which is just a draw.

33 ♖c2

33 ♔d1 ♕e2+ 34 ♔c1 ♕e1+ 35 ♔c2 ♖e2+ and Black wins.

33...♕a5+! 34 ♖c3 ♕xd5+

Now the king is forced to the open files on the queenside.

35 ♔c1 ♖e1+ 36 ♔b2 ♕b5+ 37 ♔a2 ♖e2+ 0-1

Game 63

Partos-Gallagher

Swiss League 1997

1 d4 ♘f6 2 c4 g6 3 ♘c3 ♗g7 4 e4 d6 5 h3 0-0 6 ♗g5

Incidentally, 6 ♗e3 is played from time to time when 6...♘a6 followed by e5 is again the right plan. For example,

After 6 ♗e3 ♘a6 there is

a) 7 ♘f3 e5 8 d5 transposing to Game 61.

b) 7 g4 e5 8 d5 ♘c5 (8...c6 is an alternative) 9 f3 a5 10 ♕d2 c6 11 dxc6!? bxc6 12 0-0-0 ♘b7 13 c5 d5 14 exd5 (14 g5 d4) ♘xd5 15 ♗c4 (15 ♘xd5 cxd5 16 ♕xd5 ♕xd5 17 ♖xd5 ♗e6) ♘xe3 16 ♕xe3 ♕e7 with a roughly level game, Gomez-Topalov, Seville 1992.

c) 7 ♗d3 (more common) 7...e5 8 d5 ♘d7 (8...♘h5 is also interesting) and now White has several possibilities:

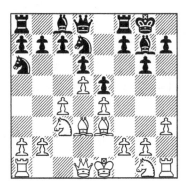

c1) 9 ♘ge2 ♘dc5 10 ♗c2 f5 11 exf5 (11 f3 ♗h6) gxf5 12 0-0 f4 13 ♗xc5 ♘xc5 14 f3 is unclear according to Kuzmin.

c2) 9 g4 ♘dc5 10 ♗b1?! (10 ♗c2) f5 11 exf5 gxf5 12 ♘ge2 ♕h4 13 a3 e4 14 gxf5 ♗xf5 15 ♘d4 ♗g6 16 ♗c2 ♘d3+ 17 ♗xd3 ♗xd4! was excellent for Black in Avshalumov-Kupreichik, Blagoveshchensk 1988.

c3) 9 a3 ♘ac5 10 ♗c2 f5 11 b4 (11 f3 ♗h6) ♘xe4 12 ♗xe4 fxe4 13 ♘xe4 ♕h4 14 g4!, Barlov-Kir.Georgiev, Yugoslavia 1991 is given as better for White by several commentators, but the simple 13...♘f6! promises Black a good game. White is far too underdeveloped to main-

tain his grip on e4. 14 ♗g5 should be met by 14...♗f5.

To sum up, Black has a slightly easier time after 6 ♗e3 than 6 ♗g5. He can follow the same plan but doesn't need to spend a tempo unpinning on ...♕e8.

6...♘a6

Black prepares the traditional King's Indian central strike, ...e7-e5.

If he plays this at once then 6...e5 7 dxe5 dxe5 8 ♕xd8 ♖xd8 9 ♘d5 wins a pawn although Black may have some slight compensation after 9...♘bd7 10 ♘xc7 ♖b8. Still, I certainly don't recommend that you follow this path. I can't work out whether the few grandmasters who have played like this did so on purpose or because they were drunk or something like that.

Another way to prepare ...e5 is the immediate 6...♕e8 which has been gaining in popularity recently. It is fine for Black to use this move order if he is planning to transpose into our main line, but some of the independent lines there do not look so trustworthy to me.

6...c5 is also quite popular, but after 7 d5 e6 8 ♗d3 exd5 9 cxd5! we are in the Modern Benoni which is outside the scope of this book.

7 ♘f3

a) 7 ♗d3 was covered in the previous game.

b) 7 g4 is not so common although I have had to face it a couple of times.

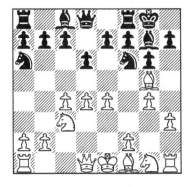

Black can either continue with his ...e5 plan or switch to a Benoni now that White has played the weakening g4 move. Here is an example of each strategy:

b1) 7...e5 8 d5 ♕e8 (8...c6 is an alternative) 9

♘ge2 ♔h8 (I wanted to be ready to play ...♘g8 and ...f5 at a moment's notice) 10 ♕d2 c6 11 ♘g3 cxd5 12 cxd5 ♗d7 13 ♗e2 ♘c5 14 f3 ♘g8! 15 h4 f5 16 gxf5 gxf5 17 exf5 ♗xf5 18 ♘ce4 (18 ♘xf5) ♗xe4 19 ♘xe4 ♘xe4 20 fxe4 ♕a4! 21 ♗d3 ♘f6 22 ♕e2 ♘d7 with an unclear position, Suba-Gallagher, Kuala Lumpur 1992. White has the bishop pair but his king is exposed.

b2) 7...c5 8 d5 e6 9 ♗d3 exd5 (9...♕e8!?) 10 exd5 (the white position would be too loose after 10 cxd5) 10...♕e8+! (unpinning) 11 ♕e2 (11 ♘ge2 ♘d7 looks all wrong for White) 11...♘c7 (Black is going to play ...b7-b5) 12 0-0-0 b5 13 cxb5, Gyimesi-I.Botvinnik, Tel Aviv 2001, and as Hazai points out Black should just play 13...♘fxd5! as 14 ♘xd5 ♘xd5 15 ♗e4 is refuted by 15...♗xb2+ 16 ♕xb2 (16 ♔xb2 ♕e5+ 17 ♔c2 ♘c3 is very good for Black) 16...♕xe4 17 ♗h6 ♕c4+ 18 ♔d2 f6 with a decisive advantage for Black.

Obviously White can do better than this but this shows you the sort of thing to aim for.

7...♕e8!?

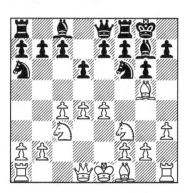

Of course Black could just play 7...e5 as after 8 d5 we have transposed into Game 60 and 8 dxe5 dxe5 9 ♕xd8 ♖xd8 10 ♘d5 ♖d6 is fine for Black, but the text is an interesting alternative. The idea is to play ...e7-e5 next move, but since Black will already be unpinned he can then meet d4-d5 with ...♘f6-h5.

8 ♗e2

Let's take a look at a few other moves:

a) 8 ♗d3 e5 and now:

a1) 9 d5 ♘h5 falls in with Black's plans, e.g.

a11) 10 g4 ♘f4 11 ♗xf4 exf4 12 ♕d2 ♘c5

13 0-0-0 a6 14 ♗c2 b5 15 ♘d4 bxc4 16 ♕xf4 ♗d7 17 ♕e3 ♕b8 18 f4 ♕b6 19 ♖d2 ♘d3+ 0-1 Kunte-Zhang Zhong, Shenyang 1999.

a12) 10 g3 f5 11 ♗d2 ♘c5 12 ♗c2 fxe4 13 ♘xe4 ♘xe4 14 ♗xe4 ♘f6 15 ♗c2 e4 with a decisive advantage for Black, Bronstein-Nijboer, Wijk aan Zee 1992.

a2) Therefore a number of White players have tried 9 0-0 when 9...exd4 10 ♘xd4 ♘c5 seems fine for Black as White has no time for 11 ♗c2 ♘fxe4! and must play something like 11 ♖e1. But more Black players have continued with 9...♘h5, e.g.:

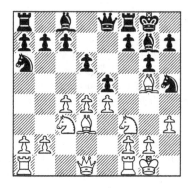

a21) 10 ♖e1 exd4 11 ♘d5 f6 12 ♗c1 c6 13 ♘f4 ♘xf4 14 ♗xf4 ♕d8 15 ♘xd4 f5 with advantage to Black, Shabalov-Edelman, New York 1993.

a22) 10 ♕d2 was played in Akesson-Shulman, Stockholm 1999. Black played 10...f5 and got in some trouble after 11 exf5 gxf5 12 dxe5 dxe5 13 ♖fe1 e4 14 ♘xe4! but 10...f6 11 ♗h6 ♗xh6 12 ♕xh6 ♘f4 13 ♖ad1 ♕f7 14 b3 ♕g7 seems like a relatively easy way to equalise.

a23) 10 dxe5 dxe5 11 ♖e1 led to victory for White in Barsov-Sutovsky, York 1999, but only because Black went in for a speculative exchange sacrifice. Such a continuation cannot be dangerous for Black. 11...c6 is a good solid choice while even after 11...♘c5 12 ♘d5 ♕d7 (Sutovsky played 12...c6?! 13 ♘c7 ♕d7 14 ♘xa8 ♘xd3 15 ♖e3 but it didn't work out) 13 ♘e7+ ♔h8 14 ♗c2 ♘e6! Black has no problems.

b) 8 e5 may look quite dangerous but is actually quite harmless. After 8...dxe5 9 dxe5 ♘d7 we have a couple of quick draws:

b1) 10 ♕e2 f6 11 exf6 exf6 12 ♗e3 ½-½, Bykhovsky-Istratescu, Tel Aviv 1994.

b2) 10 ♗f4 b6 (10...♘dc5 certainly deserves consideration) 11 ♗d3 ♗b7 12 be4 ♗xe4 13 ♘xe4 ♘dc5 14 ♘xc5 ♘xc5 15 0-0 ♖d8 16 ♕c2 ♕c6 17 ♖ad1 ♘e6 ½-½, San Segundo-Spassov, Moscow Olympiad 1994.

c) 8 g4 can be met by 8...e5 9 d5 ♘d7 transposing to Zotnikov-Gallagher, or by 8...c5 9 d5 e6 10 dxe6 ♕xe6 (10...♗xe6 11 ♕xd6 h6! is a playable pawn sacrifice) 11 ♕e2 ♖e8 12 0-0-0 ♘xe4 13 ♘xe4 ♕xe4 14 ♕xe4 ♖xe4 15 ♖xd6 ♖e8 was comfortable for Black in Flear-Wood, London 1993.

Recently White has played 9 ♗g2 here a few times and I think Black should just head for the strange Maróczy with 9...cxd4 rather than getting involved with 9...h5 10 ♗xf6 exf6 11 gxh5 f5 12 hxg6 fxe4 13 ♘g5 fxg6 14 ♘cxe4 ♗xd4 15 0-0, as he did unsuccessfully in the game Nielsen-Michelakis, Copenhagen 2003. I believe this messy position to be somewhat in White's favour.

8...e5 9 d5

9 dxe5 dxe5 10 ♘d5 ♘xe4! 11 ♗e7 c6 12 ♗xf8 ♕xf8 is the sort of exchange sacrifice King's Indian players dream about.

9...♘h5 10 g3

Not a desirable move, but otherwise Black will play ...♘h5-f4 with an easy game.

10...f5

Shirov has played 10...f6 here but considering the move my opponent played after 10...f5 I am reluctant to recommend this.

11 ♗c1

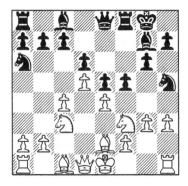

The move of a man who is not happy with his position. White wants to support his e4-square with ♘f3-d2 but is worried about his bishop stuck out on g5. A retreat to e3 will only encourage Black to play ...f4, d2 is required for the knight so the bishop went all the way home. A more testing continuation would be 11 exf5 gxf5 12 ♘h4 (and not 12 ♘xe5? ♕xe5 when the bishop on e2 is pinned) 12...♘f6 with a double-edged game.

11...♘c5 12 ♘d2 ♘f6

I was quite tempted by the continuation 12...a5 13 exf5 e4! but in the end opted for the solid text. White is virtually forced to give up a pawn now as if Black can play ...a5 next move he will have achieved a perfect King's Indian position.

13 b4 ♘cxe4 14 ♘dxe4 ♘xe4 15 ♘xe4 fxe4 16 ♗e3 ♗d7 17 a4 ♕e7 18 ♕b3 ♖f7 19 c5 ♕f8!

My original plan had been to double rooks on the f-file but now that White can't stop the threatened ...♗g7-h6 with ♕d2 the text is a good choice which forces White to weaken his kingside. He doesn't want to allow ...♗g7-h6 as the bishop on e3 is holding his position together.

20 g4 ♕e7!? 21 ♖c1 ♖af8 22 b5?!

22 cxd6 cxd6 23 ♗xa7 ♖h6 is very good for Black but 22 g5, trying to keep the black queen out of h4 makes more sense. I was planning the typical rejoinder 22...♖f4 23 h4 h6 but 23...♗g4 is interesting.

22...♕h4 23 ♖h2 ♗h6 24 ♗xh6 ♖xf2!?

A rather speculative continuation. I considered 24...♕xh6 25 ♕e3 ♕f4 to be a bit better for Black but couldn't resist the text.

25 ♖xf2 ♖xf2 26 ♗e3 ♖h2+?

26...♖g2+ 27 ♔d2 ♕xh3 was more accurate, preventing the defence with ♖g1 given in the next note.

27 ♔d2 ♕xh3

28 ♖e1?

Missing his last chance. After 28 ♖g1! ♗xg4 29 ♖xg4 ♕xg4 30 ♕c4 h5 31 cxd6 cxd6 32 ♔d1! Black has a draw with 32...♖h1+ 33 ♔d2 ♖h2. He could play on with something like 32...♕h3 but not without risk. After the text White gets caught in a pin and has no good way to prevent the advance of the black kingside pawns.

28...♗xg4 29 cxd6 cxd6 30 ♕c4 ♕f3! 31 a5 h5 32 a6

White was reluctant to play 32 ♗xa7 as this allows the black queen to penetrate to the queenside. For example, after 32 ♗xa7 ♕a3! 33 a6 bxa6 34 bxa6 (34 b6 e3+) 34...♖h3! Black has a decisive attack. Note how in many variations the bishop on g4 plays an important defensive role by preventing ♕c8+

32...b6 33 ♗g5

White has no move, e.g. 33 ♗xb6 axb6 34 a7 ♕a3.

33...h4 34 ♕c7

Or 34 ♗xh4 ♕f4+ 35 ♔d1 ♖xh4.

34...♖xe2+ 35 ♖xe2 ♕xe2+ 36 ♔c1 ♕f1+ 37 ♔d2?!

37 ♔c2 poses slightly more problems but Black is still winning easily after 37...h3!

37...e3+! 38 ♔c2 ♕f5+ 39 ♔c3 ♕xg5 40 ♕b8+ ♔g7 41 ♕xa7+ ♔h6 42 ♕xb6 e2 43 ♕g1 ♕f4 44 a7 ♕f1 0-1

Summary

1) The systems with an early h2-h3 by White usually lead to a tense struggle where Black must play actively to avoid getting squashed.

2) White usually plays an early g2-g4, gaining space on the kingside and making it more difficult for Black to play ...f7-f5. Black must either go ahead and play ...f7-f5 anyway or open lines on the queenside (...c7-c6) so that the white king won't be safe on this side of the board.

3) Black must take care that the knight he often has on a6 doesn't get shut out of the game by White playing a2-a3 and b2-b4.

4) The e4-square can be of paramount importance in the lines where Black plays ...f7-f5. If White can maintain a blockade of this square, preferably with a knight, then he usually has a pleasant game whilst if Black can advance ...e5-e4 then everything changes and it is White who is usually struggling.

CHAPTER ELEVEN

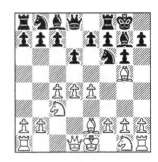

The Averbakh Variation

1 d4 ♘f6 2 c4 g6 3 ♘c3 ♗g7 4 e4 d6 5 ♗e2 0-0 6 ♗g5

This line bears the name of the famous Russian grandmaster Yuri Averbakh. It is a solid restraining system which by preventing the immediate ...e7-e5 makes it more difficult for Black to obtain his traditional kingside counterplay. It is quite reasonable for Black to switch plans and play for a quick ...c7-c5 but there is no need for him to abandon the idea of playing for ...e5. It just needs further preparation. There are several ways this can be done. The most obvious is to attack the bishop with 6...h6 and after it retreats (7 ♗e3) to play 7...e5. The problem here is that is not always a good idea for Black to play ...h6 so early in the King's Indian as White may be able to gain a tempo with ♕d2. Another way to prepare ...e5 is with 6...♘bd7. This is quite playable but I'm recommending a third, more flexible way, 6...♘a6. This prepares ...e7-e5 by defending the c7-pawn and is more flexible than 6...♘bd7 because it doesn't hem in the bishop on c8. Although Black's main idea is to play ...e7-e5 sometimes White prevents this (7 f4 for example) but, as we shall see, Black has other ways of developing counterplay.

White has a wide variety of replies to 6...♘a6 and each of these is examined in their own game. The most popular response is 7 ♕d2 and this is examined in the first game below. The sharpest moves are 7 f4 and 7 h4. These are examined in Games 65 and 66. 7 f4 makes it

difficult for Black to play ...e5 but playing a quick ...c6 and ...♘c7 introduces many interesting ideas into the position. Such a plan would be too slow in the real Four Pawns Attack (see Chapter 9) but is quite acceptable here as White's bishop is offside on g5. Against 7 h4 Black can react in traditional fashion with 7...e5. The system recommended involves a very thematic pawn sacrifice. In the 67 game we look at the solid 7 ♘f3 whilst in the Game 68 we take a look at Uhlmann's speciality 7 ♕c2.

Game 64
Korniushin-Ozolin
Tomsk 1997

---

1 d4 ♘f6 2 c4 g6 3 ♘c3 ♗g7 4 e4 d6 5 ♗e2 0-0 6 ♗g5 ♘a6 7 ♕d2 e5 8 d5

After 8 dxe5 dxe5 9 ♕xd8 ♖xd8 neither 10 ♘d5 ♖d6 nor 10 ♘xe5 ♘xe4 cause Black any problems.

8...♘c5

8...c6 and 8...♕e8 are commonly played alternatives. I covered the former in SOKID and it can easily lead to similar positions to the text where Black is merely delaying ...c7-c6 until his knight has been established on c5.

9 f3

An important point is that Black can meet 9 b4 with 9...♘cxe4! 10 ♘xe4 ♘xe4 11 ♗xd8 ♘xd2. The position is very complicated but practice has shown that after 12 ♗xc7 both

12...♘e4 and 12...e4 give Black good play. An example of the latter: 13 ♖c1 e3! 14 fxe3 (14 ♗d3 exf2+ 15 ♔xf2 ♗f5 and 14 ♗xd6 ♘e4!) 14...♘e4 15 ♗d3 ♖e8 and Black has excellent compensation for his pawn.

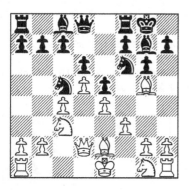

9...a5

Now that White's e-pawn is protected b2-b4 must be prevented.

10 g4

White's standard plan in this position is to advance his kingside pawns. There is not much chance of Black getting mated but White hopes that the space he will gain will further restrict Black's active options. Sometimes White starts with 10 h4 but it usually just comes to the same thing.

10...c6

Black needs to seek counterplay on the queenside as ...f5 is not really on the cards. At least not yet!

11 h4 cxd5

Black takes immediately on d5 as delaying

may mean him having to worry about White recapturing with the knight. 12 ♘xd5 is well met by 12...♘e6.

12 cxd5 ♗d7 13 ♘h3 ♕e8

A slightly awkward move but it does unpin the knight and prepare the desirable queenside advance ...b5. How brave are you? If you are willing to sacrifice a piece to create chaos on the board then the immediate 13...b5!? (patented by the Cuban master A.Perez) is the move for you. The quiet manoeuvring game that one is likely to get after 13...♕e8 is now likely to be replaced by a roller-coaster ride. Take a look at the following variations before you make your mind up. After 13...b5:

a) Firstly, White can politely decline the offer with 14 ♘f2 but then Black can develop his queen actively with 14...♕b6. A logical follow up for Black would then be to double rooks on the c-file.

b) 14 ♗xb5? is a mistake. The point is that after 14...♗xb5 15 ♘xb5 ♖b8 White cannot retreat with 16 ♘c3 on account of 16...♖xb2! when 17 ♕xb2? loses to 17...♘d3+. 16 ♕e2 ♕d7 17 a4 is better but Black still has a good game after 17...♘xa4!

c) 14 ♘xb5 is the critical test. The amazing response is 14...♘fxe4!!

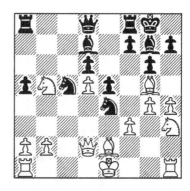

and White has two moves:

c1) 15 ♗xd8 ♘xd2 16 ♗e7 (16 ♔xd2 ♖fxd8 17 ♘xd6 ♗xg4 is good for Black) 16...♘xf3+ 17 ♗xf3 ♗xb5 18 ♗xf8 ♖xf8, Keipo-Perez, Cuba 1996. The dust has settled and in return for the exchange Black has a pawn, active pieces and two potential passed pawns in the centre. Quite adequate compensation c2) 15 fxe4 f6 when White has a couple of possible bishop moves (returning the piece offers no advantage):

c21) 16 ♗h6 ♘xe4 17 ♕e3 ♗xh6 and whichever recapture White makes Black will have compensation for the piece. I'll just mention that 18 ♕xe4 can be met by 18...f5 19 gxf5 ♗xf5 and 18 ♕xh6 by either 18...♘g3 or 18...♕b6. Of course the reason Black has compensation is the terribly exposed position of the white king.

c22) 16 ♗e3 ♘xe4 17 ♕c2 f5. At first sight it seems that Black doesn't have much but on closer inspection we can see that White is facing serious problems. For example, 18 gxf5 ♘g3! 19 0-0-0 (19 ♖g1 ♕xh4 is good for Black after both 20 ♘f2 ♘xf5 21 ♗g5 ♕xf2+! 22 ♔xf2 ♘d4+ and 20 ♗g5 ♕xh3 21 ♕c3 ♘xe2! 22 ♕xh3 ♘xg1) ♖c8 20 ♘c3 ♗xf5 21 ♗d3 ♗xd3 22 ♕xd3 e4! 23 ♕d2 ♗xc3 24 bxc3 ♖xc3+! (this is why Black was in no rush to take the rook in the corner; after 25 ♕xc3 ♘e2+ 26 ♔b2 ♘xc3 27 ♔xc3 ♕c7+ 28 ♔d2 ♕c4 he has a winning position) 25 ♔b2 ♖d3 and Black is winning. Instead of taking on f5 White can try 18 ♘g5 but here too Black has good play after 18...♘g3, e.g. 19 ♖g1 ♘xe2 20 ♕xe2 f4 21 ♗f2 e4! or 19 0-0-0 ♘xh1 20 ♖xh1 ♖c8.

To conclude, 13...b5 looks worth a try if you have a gambling nature. The above variations are only the tip of the iceberg, given to demonstrate the sort of possibilities open to Black. There are no guarantees that it won't end in tears against a strong defensive player but I, myself, would be inclined to take the risk.

14 ♘f2 b5 15 h5 b4 16 ♘cd1 ♗b5

It is a good idea for Black to exchange some pieces as he has less space. Without the bishop on d7 this square will become available to either the queen or king's knight.

17 ♘e3

Black is not worried about 17 h6 as if White closes the h-file he will no longer have any attacking chances on the kingside. Although the bishop on h8 will be locked out of the game this is not irreversible.

17...♗xe2 18 ♕xe2 b3 19 a3 ♖c8 20 0-0 a4 21 ♖ac1 ♕d7

White's position has one main drawback – the exposed position of his king. For the moment the black pieces cannot get anywhere near it but this may change as the game progresses. For the time being both sides concentrate on doubling their rooks on the only open file.

22 ♖c4 ♖c7 23 ♖fc1 ♖fc8 24 ♖1c3 ♕e8 25 ♖b4 ♘fd7 26 ♘c4 ♕f8 27 ♗e3 ♕e7 28 ♘a5?!

It would have been better for White to exchange on g6 at some point as now Black will be able to open lines advantageously on the kingside.

28...♕h4 29 ♔g2 gxh5 30 g5 ♘f8

The knight is heading for f4.

31 ♘h3?

Now that the black queen can't defend d6 White should have brought his knight back with 31 ♘c4! That would have left the situation far from clear whereas after the text Black should be winning.

31...♘g6 32 ♕f2 ♘f4+ 33 ♘xf4 ♕xf2+?

33...♕xg5+! 34 ♔h1 exf4 would have been even stronger.

34 ♔xf2 exf4 35 ♗d4 ♘a6 36 ♗xg7?

White could have offered more resistance with 36 ♖xc7 ♖xc7 37 ♖xa4.

36...♘xb4 37 ♗d4 ♖xc3 38 ♗xc3 ♖xc3 0-1

Game 65
S.Mohr-Uhlmann
Bundesliga 1994

---

1 d4 ♘f6 2 c4 g6 3 ♘c3 ♗g7 4 e4 d6 5 ♗e2 0-0 6 ♗g5 ♘a6 7 f4!?

An aggressive move which leads to a strange version of the Four Pawns Attack. One of the main points behind 7 f4 is to prevent Black from playing ...e5. In this way White hopes to show that the knight on a6 is misplaced. Don't forget that the main point of 6...♘a6 was to prepare the advance ...e5. This approach will not suit all White players, though, as with the bishop on g5 stuck outside the pawn centre there is an element of risk involved in White's strategy. Black should not react with the traditional response to the 4 Pawns Attack, 7...c5, as after 8 d5 the knight on a6 would indeed be condemned to passivity. Instead, he should prefer the modest-looking 7...c6 followed by 8...♘c7 and then decide between establishing a foothold in the centre with ...d5 or seeking active play on the queenside with ...b5. The potentially problem piece on a6 often settles down on the healthy central square e6.

7...c6 8 ♘f3 ♘c7

9...♘e6 can now be considered a threat. For example, after 9 0-0 ♘e6 White can't play 10

♗h4 on account of 10...♘xf4 so he would have to part with his important dark-squared bishop. White has three ways to deal with the threat of 9...♘e6. He can prevent it with d5, retreat the bishop from g5, or defend his f-pawn.

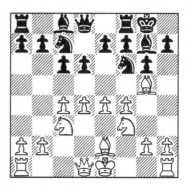

9 ♕d2

Defending the f-pawn, so that 9...♘e6 can be met by 10 ♗h4, is considered the main line. The alternatives:

a) 9 ♗h4. This prophylactic retreat is becoming increasing popular as White has failed to prove any advantage in the main line. The bishop is less vulnerable to attack on h4 than g5, from where it could be hit by a knight on e6 or e4 or a pawn on f6. By retreating the bishop now White reasons that he won't have to waste a tempo at a more important moment. As in the main game Black has a choice between 9...b5 or 9...d5. We are going to concentrate on the latter. After 9...d5 10 e5 ♘e4

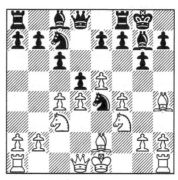

we can already see the benefit of 9 ♗h4 – the bishop is not attacked. A number of games have gone 11 ♘xe4 dxe4 12 ♘g5 f6 13 exf6 exf6 14 ♘xe4 but 14...♘e6 gives Black good play. In Korchnoi-Xie Jun, Schuhplattler Veterans-Ladies 2000 White introduced 11 0-0! and quickly built up strong pressure after 11...♘e6 12 g3 f6 13 cxd5 cxd5 14 ♕b3. Black needs to improve on this. Annotations to the game suggest that White is doing very well after 11...♗f5 12 ♘xe4 ♗xe4 13 ♘g5 ♗f5 14 g4 ♗c8 15 f5 as Black has wasted so much time moving his bishop. But what has White done with this time? Pushed all the pawns in front of his king which may give him attacking chances but also leaves his own monarch quite exposed. I believe 15...f6 leads to an unclear game. This is just an untested suggestion while the latest development in the variation is the 11...f6 that was introduced in Illescas-Comas, Spanish Ch. 2002. After 12 ♘xe4 dxe4 13 ♘e1 ♘e6 14 ♘c2 g5 15 fxg5 fxe5 16 ♖xf8 ♕xf8 White could have obtained an edge with 17 d5! ♘f4 18 ♘e3. A possible improvement for Black is to play 16...♗xf8 with the idea of meeting 17 dxe5 with a spot of pawn grabbing – 17...♕b6+ followed by ...♕xb2.

b) 9 d5 is a radical way to prevent ...♘e6. It is not very popular although it is probably no worse or better than any of the other lines. The recommended antidote is 9...cxd5 10 cxd5 ♘h5! (threatening ...f6).

b1) Now 11 f5 ♘f6 12 fxg6 hxg6 13 ♕d2 (13 0-0) 13...♘a6! is good for Black according to Seirawan. This is all deep stuff where you may be forgiven for thinking that the black knights are aimlessly wandering backwards and forwards. In fact the purpose of their meanderings was to clarify the central situation and to carve out some reasonably safe squares for themselves. The f6-square is now secure for the king's knight (there is no longer e5 to worry about) while the queen's knight can go to c5.

b2) 11 ♕d2 looks better when 11...f6 12 ♗h4 ♗h6 13 g3 e5!? 14 dxe6 ♗xe6 leads to a very double-edged position where Black has weaknesses but the white bishop on h4 is in trouble.

9...d5

Finally Black reacts in the centre. As previously mentioned there is an alternative plan which involves not striking in the centre but on the queenside. Yakovich-Atalik, Beijing 1997 continued 9...♕e8 (if Black is willing to sacrifice a pawn he can also play the immediate 9...b5!?) 10 ♕d2 b5 11 e5 b4! (an important counterattack) 12 exf6 exf6 13 ♗h4 bxc3 14 ♕xc3?! (14 bxc3 is better when the game is about level after 14...♗f5) 14...♕xe2! 15 ♖fe1 (it looks as though Black has fallen into a childish trap – how does the queen escape?) 15...♘b5!! Brilliant. The point is that after 16 cxb5 Black has 16...♕xb5 while 16 ♕b3 ♘xd4! 17 ♘xd4 ♕g4 is also good for Black. White decided to settle for the slightly worse endgame that arises after 16 ♖xe2 16...♘xc3 17 bxc3 ♗a6 and managed to hold the game with some careful defence.

10 ♗xf6

10 e5 is of course met by 10...♘e4.

10...exf6!

Rules are made to be broken, though you have to know when to break them! The natural recapture, 10...♗xf6, leaves Black with a difficult game after 11 cxd5 cxd5 12 e5 ♗g7 13 h4!. White has a space advantage and attacking chances and Black has no counterplay. Black's choice of recapture obviously compromises his pawn structure but there are certain compensations. For example, it is not so bad to have doubled f-pawns in front of the castled king. The back one can stay at home on defensive duty while the front one can happily advance. With just one f-pawn you can't do both. Recapturing with the pawn should also give Black first use of the open e-file.

11 exd5

11 0-0 is well met by 11...dxe4 12 ♘xe4 ♗g4! Black's strategy is based on pressurising

the d4 pawn. By eliminating the knight on f3, playing ...f5 and a rook to the d-file Black should be able to force the pawn to advance to d5. He will then look to blockade the pawn with a knight on d6, which in conjunction with his better bishop and safer king should, at the very least, compensate for White's central passed pawn. All this was demonstrated in the first important game in this line, Yakovich-Smirin, Munich 1993. Play continued: 13 ♖ad1 ♕e7 14 ♘f2 ♗xf3 15 ♗xf3 f5 (this must be played before White can play f5) 16 d5 cxd5 17 cxd5 ♕d6 18 g3 ♘b5 19 ♗g2 and now 19...♕b6!, followed by ...♘d6 would have given Black a good game (20 d6 would just push the pawn to its doom). Many years ago Nimzowitsch taught us that the knight is an ideal blockader, especially of an advanced central pawn. Here Black originally blockaded the pawn with his queen but this was never intended to be a permanent state of affairs. After the Yakovich-Smirin game White searched for other ways of injecting life into this system and came up with the plan in the main game. Initially, Black struggled but his recent results have improved.

11...cxd5 12 c5 ♗f5!

White has a potentially dangerous queenside pawn majority but also weaknesses in the centre created by the move f2-f4. If this pawn were back on f2 White would have a clear positional advantage but now Black is able to park his bishop on the dominant e4-square. White will be extremely reluctant to take the bishop as it will then be replaced by a strong passed pawn.

13 0-0 ♗e4 14 b4 ♘e6 15 ♖ac1

In other games White has preferred 15 ♖ad1 f5 16 ♘e5 to tempt Black into playing ...f6, the reasoning being that the time is well spent as the long diagonal of the bishop on g7 will now be closed. Black is advised to fall in with White's plans as he has another way to activate his bishop. After 16...f6 17 ♘f3 ♗h6 18 g3 g5 Black has good play. This is the same strategy Black uses in the main game.

15...f5 16 ♘b5?!

Rather optimistically sending his knight on a journey to d6. True, this is a nice outpost but Black now has the time to develop a kingside attack. Note that White no longer has the possibility to remove the masterful bishop on e4.

16...♗h6! 17 g3 g5!

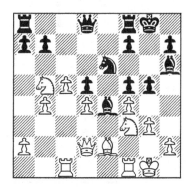

There has been a wonderful economy about Black's play in this game. No useless moves, everything done with a clear purpose. Uhlmann used to be one of the world's best players and even now, well into his eighth decade, he still knows how to pack a punch. I can testify from personal experience.

18 ♘e5?

White's best chance was to sacrifice the exchange with 18 fxg5 ♘xg5 19 ♘xg5 ♗xg5 20 ♕c3 ♗xc1 21 ♕xc1 when he has some compensation though Black's game is still to be preferred after 21...a5! (opening lines for the rooks). The text leads to complications that are only ever going to end in Black's favour.

18...gxf4 19 c6 bxc6 20 ♖xc6 ♕g5

Black was unable to play ...fxg3 on the previous move as the f4 pawn was pinned to his bishop on h6. Now with Black threatening this capture White can find nothing better than a desperate piece sacrifice.

21 ♘xf7 ♔xf7

Of course Black takes this way to defend the knight on e6.

22 ♘d6+ ♔e7 23 ♘xe4

Now White has no pieces left to attack with but the reality was that if he didn't make this exchange it was Black who had the stronger attack. In fact, he still does. White may as well have resigned here.

23...fxe4 24 b5 f3 25 ♕b4+ ♔f7 26 ♕d6 ♖ae8 27 ♗xf3 ♔g8! 28 ♗g2 ♕e3+ 29 ♔h1 ♖xf1+ 30 ♗xf1 ♕f3+ 0-1

It's mate in two.

Game 66

Yakovich-Smirin

European Ch., Saint Vincent 2000

---

1 d4 ♘f6 2 c4 g6 3 ♘c3 ♗g7 4 e4 d6 5 ♗e2 0-0 6 ♗g5 ♘a6 7 h4

Another aggressive move. When playing Black in the King's Indian and your opponent starts an attack on the h-file, don't panic. It's never mate. The text was quite popular in the early 1990's when the world class Russian Grandmaster Bareev lost a lot of games with it. Nowadays it is not seen so much but the way Black deals with it is very instructive and shows how the King's Indian should be played – with great energy!

7...e5 8 d5 h6 9 ♗e3 ♘c5 10 ♕c2

10 f3 doesn't fit with an early h4 on account of 10...♘h5 but 10 ♗f3 is played sometimes. A recent example is Kogan-V.Georgiev, Salou 2000. Play continued 10...a5 11 g4 ♕d7! 12 g5 ♘g4 13 ♗xg4 ♕xg4 14 gxh6 ♗f6 15 ♕xg4 ♗xg4 16 f3 ♗h5. White has won a pawn but he will be unable to hold onto it for long. He now felt obliged to part with his strong bishop as he was quite fearful of the damage that Black's knight might inflict. After 17 ♗xc5 dxc5 18 ♘ce2 ♔h7 19 ♘g3 ♔xh6 20 ♘xh5 ♔xh5 21 ♘e2 ♗xh4+ 22 ♔e2 ♖h8 23 f4 exf4 24 ♘xf4+ ♔g4 25 ♘d3 ♗g3 26 ♘xc5 f5 Black had the better ending (active king, superior minor piece, dangerous kingside pawns) and went on to win.

10...c6

As we also saw in Chapter 10 when White starts advancing on the kingside Black should open lines on the queenside so that the white king won't be safe there. With the white queen on c2 this becomes even more desirable.

11 h5

There was already a trap for White to fall into: 11 b4? ♘cxe4! 12 ♘xe4 ♘xe4 13 ♕xe4 ♗f5 14 ♕f3 e4 and Black wins the rook on a1.

If it weren't for this tactic then Black would have played 11...a5 in order to prevent b4.

11...cxd5

11...g5!? has been played by Kasparov. It is not a bad move in this particular position but in general Black should be very wary about blocking the kingside in this fashion. I prefer the more dynamic approach used by Smirin (and others).

12 cxd5 ♕a5

Black threatens to take on e4 so White has no time to take on g6. 13 fxg6 ♘cxe4 is good for Black.

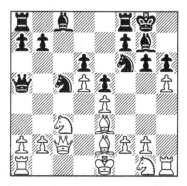

13 ♗d2 ♗d7

Discovered attacks can be devastating but Black doesn't have to worry here (at least not yet) as there is no good square for the knight on c3 to move to.

14 hxg6 fxg6 15 f3

By solidly defending the e-pawn White finally 'threatens' to take on h6. The move f3, though, can be considered a positional concession from White as it allows Black to play ...♘h5 and take over the initiative on the kingside. In Hauchard-Hebden, Cappelle la Grande 1998 White tried to live for a while without playing f3 but soon had to admit defeat. Play continued 15 ♖b1 (threatening b4) 15...♕b6 16 ♗e3 a5 17 ♘h3 ♖ac8 18 ♕d2 a4 19 f3 ♘h5! 20 ♘f2 (20 ♗xh6 ♘g3! 21 ♗xg7 ♔xg7 22 ♖h2 ♖h8 is good for Black) 20...♘f4 21 ♗f1 ♕b4 22 ♘cd1 ♘a6 23 ♘d3 ♕xd2+ 24 ♔xd2 b5 and Black's energetic play has given him a good game. In fact he continued to play with great energy. The rest of the game is worth giving: 25 ♖c1 ♖xc1 26 ♔xc1 ♘c5 27 ♘1f2 ♖c8 28 ♔b1

a3 29 b3 ♘cxd3 30 ♘xd3 ♖c3 31 ♘xf4 ♖xe3 32 ♘d3 b4 33 ♔c2 h5 34 ♔d1 ♗a4 35 bxa4 b3 36 ♔d2 ♗h6 37 f4 bxa2 38 ♗e2 exf4 39 ♗f3 ♗g7 40 e5 dxe5 41 d6 e4 42 ♘xf4 a1♕ 43 ♖xa1 ♗xa1 44 ♔xe3 exf3 45 ♘d5 fxg2 46 ♔f2 ♗e5 47 d7 ♗g3+ 48 ♔xg2 ♗h4 49 ♘b4 ♗d8 0-1.

15...♖ac8!

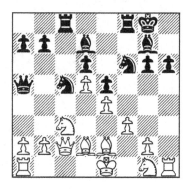

An excellent move with a cunning idea behind it. Smirin's preparation had no doubt revealed the game Yakovich-Bekker Jensen, Excelsior Cup 2000 where Black played the thematic 15...♘h5?! but landed in trouble for tactical reasons after 16 b4! ♕xb4 17 ♘b5 ♕a4 18 ♕xa4 ♘xa4 19 ♘xd6. The next note shows how Smirin planned to deal with this continuation against his move. But can't White just take on h6 now? Yes, but after 16 ♗xh6 ♗xh6 17 ♖xh6 ♔g7 Black has good compensation for the pawn. This is similar to the game continuation.

16 ♖b1

16 b4 ♕xb4 17 ♘b5 is now met by the powerful queen sacrifice 17...♕xb5!! 18 ♗xb5 ♗xb5. Although Black has just two pieces and a pawn for the queen, his threats against the white king and queen (now we see why 15...♖ac8 was better than 15...♘h5) give him a decisive attack. For example after 19 ♕b1 ♗d3 20 ♕d1 ♘fxe4! 21 ♗xh6 (what else? 21 fxe4? allows mate in one) 21...♗a6! 22 ♘e2 ♘d3+ 23 ♔f1 ♘df2 24 ♕a4 ♘xh1 Black even has a material advantage to go with his attack (25 ♕xe4 ♘g3+).

16...♕d8

16...♕b6 may look more active but White

replies 17 ♗e3.

17 ♗xh6

As White is going to suffer anyway – Black would play ...♘h5 against neutral continuations – he may as well have a pawn for his troubles.

17...♗xh6 18 ♖xh6 ♔g7 19 ♖h1 ♘h5

This is not an original pawn sacrifice – the idea is known from other variations of the King's Indian. So what does Black have for the pawn? Well, firstly in order to win it White had to exchange off his active dark-squared bishop for Black's passive one. Because of the pawn structure this means his bishop's protection of the dark squares will be sorely missed – the subsequent course of the game should drive this point home. Secondly, White's king doesn't have a safe home and thirdly his minor pieces are awkwardly developed – just look at his 21st move, influenced by the fact that he wants a knight on e2, not a bishop. I don't know if Black can claim a theoretical advantage here but all King's Indian players should delight in such positions.

20 ♕d2 ♖h8 21 ♗f1 ♕b6 22 ♘ge2

22 ♕g5 is not dangerous as Black just replies 22...♘f6.

22...♘f4 23 ♖xh8 ♘cd3+!

Games between strong players contain many more intermediate moves than games between average players. There are a few more to come!

24 ♔d1 ♖xh8 25 ♘xf4 ♘xf4 26 ♔c2 ♖h2

While White is trying to improve his king position Black piles the pressure on his Achilles heel – g2.

27 ♖c1 ♗h3 28 ♘a4 ♕d4!

Black is happy to exchange queens if it takes

place on the d4-square. He will then obtain an annoying passed pawn which also prevents the knight on a4 from returning to play.

29 ♕xd4 exd4 30 ♔b3 ♗xg2 31 ♗xg2 b5!

The previous intermediate move was quite simple – this is pure class. Black forces an ending with good knight against bad bishop. Even with all Black's pawns isolated the chances to hold such an ending are slim. If nothing else being under permanent pressure is likely to lead to an eventual collapse.

32 ♘b6 axb6 33 ♗f1 d3 34 ♔c3 ♖h1 35 ♖d1 ♔f6 36 ♔d4 b4 37 ♖b1 ♘e2+ 38 ♔e3 g5

Maybe 38...♔e5 is more accurate. For example 39 ♗xe2 ♖xb1 40 f4+ ♔f6 41 ♗xd3 ♖xb2 42 ♗c4 g5! is hopeless for White.

39 ♔f2 ♘f4 40 ♔e3 ♘e2 41 ♖d1 ♘f4 42 ♖b1 d2 43 ♔xd2 ♖h2+ 44 ♔e3 ♔e5 45 ♗a6 ♘g2+ 46 ♔d3 ♘f4+ 47 ♔e3 ♖h3 48 ♖f1?

I'm not sure that Black has made the most of his position but until here White had defended very well. He should have played 48 ♖g1 to prevent g4. Black now gets a passed pawn that quickly decides the game.

48...g4! 49 ♗e2 ♘g2+ 50 ♔d2 g3 51 ♖g1 ♖h2 52 ♗a6 ♔f4 53 e5 ♔xe5 0-1

Game 67

Burnier-Gallagher

Neuchâtel 2002

---

1 d4 ♘f6 2 c4 g6 3 ♘c3 ♗g7 4 e4 d6 5 ♗e2 0-0 6 ♗g5 ♘a6 7 ♘f3

A modest move. White has no attacking ambitions. He just wants to castle kingside and steer the game towards a Classical King's Indian where Black has committed himself to an early ...♘a6. Of course there is nothing wrong with an early ...♘a6 there; it is just that White avoids all the complex lines with ...♘c6.

7...h6 8 ♗e3

This is Milov's favourite move with which he has won a number of games including one against your author. However, I didn't play the opening so well in that game. There are two other bishop moves:

a) 8 ♗f4 e5! 9 dxe5 ♘h5 10 ♗e3 dxe5 gives Black an easy game. White has been wasting time with his bishop whilst Black has been making useful move. Neither 11 0-0 c6 12 ♕xd8 ♖xd8 13 ♖fd1 ♖e8 14 g3 ♘f6 15 ♘d2 ♘g4 16 ♗xg4 ♗xg4 17 f3 ♗e6, Milov-Smirin, Haifa 1995, nor 11 ♕c1 ♔h7 12 0-0 c6 13 ♖d1 ♕e7 14 c5 ♘c7 15 ♖d6 ♘e8 16 ♖d2 f5, Serigenko-Navrotescu, Decin 1996, gave Black cause for complaint.

b) 8 ♗h4 (the most common choice) 8...c6 (a useful waiting move: 8...e5 transposes directly into a line of the ♘a6 Classical) and now:

b1) 9 e5 can be met by 9...♘e8 but also 9...dxe5 10 dxe5 ♘g4 11 ♕xd8 (on 11 ♗g3 Black can hit e5 again with 11...♘a5) 11...♖xd8 12 ♗g3 and now Black should play 12...h5 in order to give his knight on g4 a retreat square. The game looks about equal.

b2) 9 ♕d2 e5 10 0-0-0 exd4! 11 ♕xd4 (White would prefer to recapture with the knight but this runs into a little tactical trick: 11 ♘xd4 ♘xe4! 12 ♗xd8 ♘xd2 gives Black the

advantage. If White had played 10 0-0 then Black would have continued in the same fashion, though meeting 11 ♕xd4 with 11...♖e8) 11...g5 12 ♗g3 ♘xe4! 13 ♕xe4 f5 14 ♕d3 f4 15 ♕xd6 ♕xd6 16 ♖xd6 fxg3 17 hxg3 ♘c5. Although White is a pawn up Black's powerful bishops give him good compensation. In Alexandrov-Bologan, Kstovo 1998 Black emerged victorious on the 37th move.

b3) 9 0-0 can be met by the interesting 9...g5!?. Black forces the exchange of White's bishop for a knight but in doing so weakens his kingside. As a rule such play is risky if White hasn't castled but quite acceptable once he has committed his king to the kingside. It will then be difficult for him to attack on this side of the board. The game Zakharevich-Kokorev, Moscow 1999 now continued 10 ♗g3 ♘h5 11 ♕d2 ♘c7 (or 11...e6 12 ♖e1 ♘xg3 13 hxg3 c5 ½-½ Kallai-Gallagher, French League 2002 – Black has easy equality) 12 d5 ♘xg3 13 hxg3 e6 14 ♖ad1 (after 14 dxc6 bxc6 15 ♖ad1 d5 16 cxd5 cxd5 17 exd5 ♘xd5 18 ♘xd5 ♕xd5 19 ♕xd5 exd5 20 ♖xd5 ♗e6 Black regains the lost pawn with the better game) 14...exd5 15 exd5 c5 (the game has taken on the character of a Benoni where the bishop on g7 is a particularly strong piece now that its opposite number has been eliminated) 16 ♘h2 a6 17 g4 b5 18 b3 bxc4 19 bxc4 ♖b8 20 ♗d3 ♘e8 21 ♖b1 ♖xb1 22 ♖xb1 ♘f6 23 ♗f5 ½-½.

Black could have continued the struggle.

8...♘g4 9 ♗c1

Don't worry, I also struggle to get my head around this variation. One way to look at it is that White after playing his sixth move in the

Classical offers his opponent a pact. You can have the pretty useful move ...♘a6 for free and you can even move again. But in return you must also play the possibly harmful and the positively ugly moves ...h7-h6 and ♘f6-g4. I think I would take him up on his offer.

9...e5 10 0-0 c6

In the game I lost to Milov I played 10...♕e8 here and ended up worse after 11 dxe5 dxe5 12 b3 ♕e6?! 13 ♗a3 c5 14 ♘d5 ♘f6 15 ♕c2, Milov-Gallagher, Pula 2000.

11 h3

Probably a slight inaccuracy. 11 d5 is also doubtful as Black just plays ...f7-f5. The knight sortie to g4 will then have been given real meaning. That leaves 11 dxe5 and now:

a) 11...dxe5 12 h3 ♘f6 13 ♕xd8 ♖xd8 14 ♗e3 ♘e8 (14...♗e6!?) 15 ♖fd1 ♖xd1+ 16 ♖xd1 ♗e6 17 a3 and Black had to suffer a little in Milov-Ponomariov, Biel 2000 before obtaining a draw.

b) 11...♘xe5 seems like the better recapture, e.g. 12 ♘d4 ♘c5 13 ♗e3 a5 14 f4 ♘ed7 15 ♗f3 a4 (a5 is a good square for the black queen in such positions) 16 ♖b1 ♖e8 17 ♗f2 ♕a5 18 ♕c2 ♕b4 (Black has taken over the initiative) 19 ♘ce2 ♘f6 20 ♘g3 h5 21 h4 ♘g4 22 ♗xg4 ♗xg4 23 f5 ♘d7 24 a3 ½-½ Milov-Motylev, Linares 2001. Knowing Milov rather well, I can assure you that he must have hated his position to offer a draw here.

11...exd4! 12 ♘xd4 ♘f6 13 ♖e1 ♖e8 14 ♗f3

14 f3 seriously weakens the dark squares while 14 ♗f1 is met by 14...♘c5.

14...♘h7!

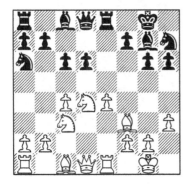

Up until here my opponent had been playing very quickly as he had been following some opening theory which said White was better here. But they didn't take the text into account. This is a standard ploy in such positions (see Game 21) and makes the set-up with the bishop on f3 look rather suspicious. It's not obvious how White can deal with ...♘g5 and in my opinion he is already fighting for equality

15 ♗f4 ♘g5 16 ♘b3?!

Simply overlooking the reply. Probably White should settle for 16 h4 ♘xf3+ 17 ♘xf3 ♗e6 with an edge for Black.

16...♗xh3! 17 ♕xd6?!

Obviously 17 gxh3 loses to 17...♘xh3+ but I assumed he was going to try 17 ♗xg5 ♕xg5 18 e5 with the idea of ♘e4 if Black captures on e5. I had planned to play 18...♗f5 as even after 19 exd6 Black has the advantage.

17...♘xf3+ 18 gxf3 ♕h4

Of course Black keeps the queens on.

19 ♗h2

White is keeping g3 free for his queen.

19...♕h5 20 ♖e3

20 ♕g3 ♗e6 is excellent for Black.

20...♖ad8 21 ♕g3 ♘b4!

21...♗e5 is also strong but after the text all Black's pieces get to join in the attack.

22 f4 ♘c2! 23 ♕xh3 ♕xh3 24 ♖xh3 ♘xa1 25 ♘a5

The point was of course that 25 ♘xa1 is met by 25...♗xc3 and ...♖d1+. Black has a decisive material advantage. The remaining moves were...

25...♖d2 26 ♘xb7 ♖b8 27 ♘a5 ♖bxb2 28 e5 ♖xf2 29 ♘xc6 ♗f8 30 ♘e4 ♖fe2 31

♘f6+ ♔g7 32 ♘e8+ ♔h8 33 ♔h1 ♖e1+ 34 ♗g1 ♖bb1 35 ♘d8 ♖xg1+ 36 ♔h2 ♖h1+ 0-1

Game 68
Bönsch-Gallagher
Bundesliga 2003

---

1 d4 ♘f6 2 c4 g6 3 ♘c3 ♗g7 4 e4 d6 5 ♗e2 0-0 6 ♗g5 ♘a6 7 ♕c2

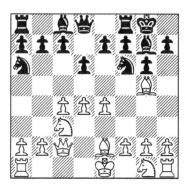

A speciality of Uhlmann so it is no great surprise to see Uwe Bönsch, a former colleague in the East German team, trying out one of the ideas of his old mentor.

7...h6

One of the main points behind 7 ♕c2 is to render the immediate 7...e5 unattractive, e.g. 7...e5 8 dxe5! dxe5 9 ♖d1 ♕e8 (9...♗d7 10 ♘d5±) 10 ♘d5 ♕e6 11 ♗xf6 ♗xf6 12 ♗g4 ♕c6 13 ♗xc8 ♖axc8 14 b4!? with an edge for White, Uhlmann-Reschke, Dresden 1995.

So before playing ...e7-e5 Black forces the bishop back to avoid this line. The main reason he is usually reluctant to play ...h7-h6 in such positions is that White sometimes gains a tempo with ♕d1-d2, but this is no longer so relevant here as White has already played ♕d1-c2.

7...c6, however, is a perfectly reasonable alternative to the game continuation. The idea, as we saw in Game 65 is to play ...♘c7-e6

8 ♗f4!?

Now 8 ♗e3 e5 is fine for Black so White decides to prevent ...e7-e5, probably assuming that this would be the most unpleasant for the

King's Indian player to face. I can't say it bothered me. It's just time to take the game into Benoni territory.

8...c5 9 d5 e5 10 dxe6 ♗xe6 11 ♖d1

Both players were probably quite content with their position. I was happy because I had a lead in development and was expecting to solve the position tactically. Better than suffering with no counterplay! Bönsch was probably quite happy as well because he is a positional player and Black has a lot of weaknesses.

This position had been reached once before and there too White immediately attacked the d-pawn but with 11 0-0-0. Then, after 11...♕a5 White decided that he had to prevent ...♘b4 so he played 12 a3 but Black played it anyway! 12...♘b4! 13 axb4 cxb4 14 ♕a4 (there is nothing better) 14...♕xa4 15 ♘xa4 ♘xe4 16 ♗e3 b5 and Black has the better game despite the exchange of queens, Bagirov-Smirin, Batumi 1999.

11...♘b4

The only thing that perturbed me about the black position was the knight on a6. It makes sense, therefore, to throw this move in and find out where the white queen is going.

12 ♕b1!?

A surprise. I had assumed he would play 12 ♕d2 when I was seriously toying with the idea of playing the speculative piece sacrifice 12...♘xa2!? 13 ♘xa2 ♘xe4 when Black has decent compensation for the piece. The more sensible continuation, however, is 12...♕a5 when 13 a3 ♘c6 14 ♗xh6 is nothing to worry about on account of 14...♘xe4! 15 ♘xe4 ♗xh6.

12...♖e8

12...♕a5 is considered a more accurate move order by Hazai (he doesn't like Black's position after 12...♖e8 13 ♘f3) meeting 13 ♗xd6 with 13...♖fd8 and 13 ♘f3 with 13...♘g4 14 0-0 ♘ge5.

13 ♗xd6?!

Another surprise. This time I thought he was finally going to start developing his kingside but Bönsch was probably scared off by variations such as 13 ♘f3 ♘xe4!? 14 ♘xe4 ♗f5. I really wanted to play this but I'm not sure Black has sufficient compensation here after 15 ♘fd2. There are plenty of other 13th move options for Black such as 13...♕a5,

13...♘d7 or 13...g5 and I don't share Hazai's opinion that Black is worse here.

13...♕a5 14 a3?!

It is a mistake to drive the knight back to the centre. He had to play 14 ♘f3 when I would still have sacrificed a piece with 14...♘xe4!?. The key line is 15 ♕xe4 ♘xa2 16 0-0 ♗xc3 17 bxc3 ♘xc3 which looks at least equal for Black.

14...♘c6 15 ♘f3 ♘xe4!

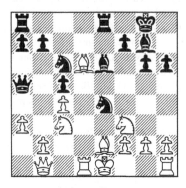

Finally I get to play the sacrifice I had been dreaming of.

16 ♕xe4 ♗h3!

A great follow-up.

17 ♕d3

After 17 ♕xe8+ ♖xe8 18 gxh3 White has enough material for the queen but a dreadful position. I believe Black is winning, e.g. 18...♗xc3+ (18...♘d4 is also not bad) 19 bxc3 ♕xc3+ 20 ♔f1 ♖xe2 21 ♔xe2 ♕xc4+ 22 ♖d3 (or 22 ♔d2 ♕d5+ 23 ♔e3 ♘d4) 22...♕e4+ 23 ♖e3 (23 ♔d2 c4) 23...♕c2+ 24 ♔f1 ♕d1+ 25 ♔g2 ♕xd6 with a decisive advantage.

17...♗xg2 18 ♖g1 ♗xf3 19 ♕xf3 ♘d4 20 ♖xd4

The point of the combination is that this move is forced because the knight on c3 is pinned and therefore not defending the bishop on e2.

20...cxd4 21 ♗b4 ♕c7 22 ♘e4??

22 ♘d1! was the only way to resist. I was unsure how to continue as I can pick up a second pawn on c4 or h2, or play for an attack by sacrificing the d-pawn. Black is clearly better

but the game is far from over. The text just drops a whole piece.

22...♕c6! 23 ♔f1

23 ♘d2 ♕xf3 24 ♘xf3 d3, 23 ♖g4 f5 and 23 ♗d3 f5 are the reasons White can't save his knight. The remaining moves were...

23...♖xe4 24 ♕d3 ♕e6 25 ♖g3 ♖e8 26 ♗f3 f5! 27 ♗d2 ♔h7 28 c5 h5 29 b4 h4 30 ♖h3 ♗f6 31 ♗d1 ♕d5 32 ♗f3 32...♕a2 33 ♔g2 ♖g4+! 34 ♗xg4 fxg4 0-1

Summary

1) Don't play 6...e5?? It loses.

2) Be careful about the knight on a6 ending up out of play. In many lines where Black plays e5 it quickly comes to c5. In others it remains on a6. That may be all right if the piece is performing an important defensive task but not if it is redundant and locked out of the game. Note how in Game 65 Black quickly brings the piece into play via c7. Remember the old adage: one badly placed piece makes the whole position bad.

3) Don't panic when White flings his kingside pawns down the board. There may be a variety of reasons for this but he is unlikely to be making a whole-hearted attempt to mate you. Black doesn't get mated very often in the King's Indian. Possible motives behind White's advance on the kingside include gaining space in this sector of the board, scaring you into exchanging queens or simply by advancing his own pawns White hopes to prevent Black from advancing his own – a sort of prophylactic measure against being attacked himself.

4) As in most variations of the King's Indian Black must play with great energy. If you just want to get your pieces out then the King's Indian is not the opening for you. Black must play with purpose or risk ending up in an inferior position.

5) Don't be afraid to sacrifice material to obtain the initiative. In the notes to Game 64 there is a very interesting piece sacrifice while Game 66 features a very thematic sacrifice of the pawn on h6 in order to take over control of the dark squares.

CHAPTER TWELVE

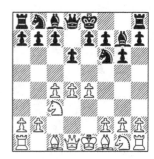

Other Systems

1 d4 ♘f6 2 c4 g6 3 ♘c3 ♗g7 4 e4 d6

The final chapter features the remaining 'important' variations in the King's Indian. These lines don't quite merit a chapter of their own but are still relatively mainstream.

5 ♗d3

1 d4 ♘f6 2 c4 g6 3 ♘c3 ♗g7 4 e4 d6 5 ♗d3

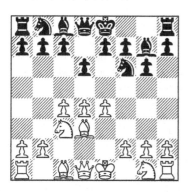

Some strong grandmasters play this system quite regularly. Its main supporter has been the American grandmaster Yasser Seirawan whilst in the last couple of years Ivan Sokolov has used it as his main weapon against the King's Indian.

White has a simple plan. He will develop his kingside quickly with ♗d3, ♘ge2 and 0-0 and be ready to meet any subsequent ...f5 by Black

with exf5 and f4 (or occasionally ♘e2-g3). This is a solid line in which Black's chances of a successful kingside attack are slim. The main drawback to an early ♗d3 is that it slackens White's already rather shaky grip on d4. Therefore, it is no great surprise that Black's most popular defences are based on a quick assault against this point.

5...0-0 6 ♘ge2 ♘c6

After 6...c5 7 d5 Black has to be ready to play a well known line in the Modern Benoni whilst 6...e5 is played surprisingly rarely.

7 0-0

Now:

1) In SOKID I concentrated mainly on 7...♘h5, the variation I have played myself for a number of years. It has also become the main line of 5 ♗d3 and Game 70 reveals the latest state of affairs there.

2) There have also been some interesting developments after 7...e5 so that is covered in Game 69.

Game 69
Bareev-Tkachiev
Cap d'Agde 2002

---

1 d4 ♘f6 2 c4 g6 3 ♘c3 ♗g7 4 e4 d6 5 ♗d3 0-0 6 ♘ge2 ♘c6 7 0-0 e5 8 d5 ♘d4 9 ♘xd4

9 ♗g5!? is a favourite of Yasser Seirawan but what works well for him does not always work

for other players. Yasser tends to operate on his own, admittedly fairly advanced, positional planet and trying to emulate his style is not advisable. After 9...h6 10 ♗h4 c5 we have:

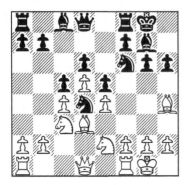

a) 11 ♘xd4 exd4 12 ♘e2 ♕e8 13 ♗xf6 .♗xf6 14 ♕d2 ♗g7 15 b4 b6 16 bxc5 bxc5 17 ♖ab1 ♕d8 18 ♖b3 h5 19 ♔h1 ♔h7 20 ♘g1= Seirawan-Nunn, Cannes 1992.

b) 11 dxc6 bxc6 12 b4 ♖e8 13 b5 cxb5 14 cxb5 g5 15 ♗g3 ♗b7 and Black had an active game in Dzhindzihasvili-Benjamin, Los Angeles 1991. However, White's plan should not be dismissed out of hand as he got into trouble in this game by playing b4-b5 prematurely.

c) 11 ♖b1, preparing b2-b4, is the most popular choice. Now we have:

c1) 11...g5 12 ♗g3 h5 13 f3 h4 14 ♗e1 ♘h5 has occurred a couple of times and is worthy of attention..

c2) 11...♗d7 12 f3 (12 b4 ♘xe2+ cxb4 14 ♖xb4 ♕c7 looks all right for Black) 12...g5 13 ♗f2 ♘h5 14 b4 b6 15 bxc5 dxc5, Graf-Kotronias, Aeroflot Open Moscow 2004.

I see no reason to be unhappy with Black's position in lines 'c1' or 'c2'.

c3) 11...♕d7!? (Black unpins – he wants to play ...f7-f5) 12 b4 b6 13 ♘xd4 exd4 14 ♘e2 ♘g4 15 bxc5 bxc5 16 ♗c2? ♘e5 17 ♗a4 ♕c7 18 ♕b3 ♗g4 19 f3 ♖fb8 20 ♕d1 ♗c8 21 ♗b3 ♗a6 22 f4 ♘xc4 23 ♕d3 ♘a3 0-1, Gonzalez de la Torre-Arizmendi, Mislata 2003. White's performance in this game was very poor and I'm sure his play can be improved upon. Even his resignation was a bit premature as after 24 ♕xa6 c4? he has 25 ♖c1. Black should still win however with 24...d3! 25 ♕xd3 c4.

9...exd4 10 ♘b5

The alternative is 10 ♘e2 ♖e8 11 f3 c5 with an unclear game. White will try and use his central majority whilst Black will try and open lines so that his passed d-pawn can be come a force. After 12 ♗g5 ♕c7 13 ♕d2 ♘d7 we have:

a) 14 ♖ac1 b5 15 cxb5 a6 16 b6 ♕xb6 17 f4 h6 18 ♗h4 a5 19 ♗f2 ♗a6 with good play for Black, Gonzalez Velez-Arizmendi, Spanish Ch., Palencia 1999. Another example of a 'Gonzalez' playing poorly against Arizmendi..

b) 14 f4 b5 15 b3 bxc4 16 bxc4 ♘f6 17 ♗xf6 ♗xf6 18 ♘g3 with chances for both sides.

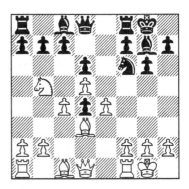

10...♘e8!?

An interesting move. It had already occurred a few times before but theory had dismissed it, rather unfairly, as just good for White. The standard line has been 10...♖e8 11 ♖e1 and now:

a) 11...♘g4 12 h3 a6 13 hxg4 axb5 14 cxb5 ♕h4 15 g3 ♕h3 16 ♗f1 ♕xg4 17 ♕xg4 ♗xg4 18 ♔g2 is well known to give White an endgame plus whilst Milov's 15 ♗f4!? may be even stronger.

b) 11...♗d7! is a much better move and, to be honest, I hadn't realised that Black could get such an easy game in this fashion. I think I may have been fooled by assessments of += in various places which are not really += at all but more like =. Now:

b1) 12 ♘xd4 ♘xd5 13 cxd5 (moves such as 13 ♘c2 or 13 ♗f1 offer White no advantage after 13...♘b6; these are easy Maróczy positions for Black as he has exchanged a minor piece and has good development) 13...♗xd4 14 ♕c2 (or 14 ♕b3 c6=) 14...c5 15 dxc6 ♗xc6 16 ♗e3 ♗xe3 17 ♖xe3 d5 with equality, Mastrovasilis-Kotronias, Athens 2003.

b2) 12 ♗g5 h6 13 ♗h4 g5 14 ♗g3 ♘g4 15 h3 ♘e5 16 ♗f1 d3 17 ♗xe5 ♗xe5 18 ♘c3 ♕f6 19 ♕xd3 h5 and Black had good dark square control in return for his pawn, Arduman-Kotronias, Zouberi 1993.

11 b4

This doesn't work out so well. Perhaps Bareev was unaware of the theoretical recommendation, 11 ♗c2 ♕f6 12 f4 with advantage to White. Or perhaps, like me, and presumably Tkachiev, he just didn't believe it. This theoretical assessment is based upon Sagalchik-Yuneev, Miedzybrodzie 1991 and the continuation 12...c6 13 ♘a3 ♕e7 14 f5 ♘f6 15 ♗g5 h6 16 ♗h4 g5 17 ♗g3 ♘d7 18 c5 which is supposed to be good for White. Well, maybe, maybe not, but Black can just play 14...♗e5. This is surely fine for him. The knight on a3 is a rather forlorn-looking creature while Black may even be able to consider taking on f5 and playing ...♔h8 and ♖g8 in some lines.

11...a5!

Carving out a potential outpost on c5 which plays an important role in the game.

12 bxa5 c6 13 ♘a3 ♖xa5 14 ♕b3

I'm not sure that Black should have been offered any encouragement to attempt to manoeuvre his knight to c5. The immediate 14 ♘c2 is probably better.

14...♘c7!

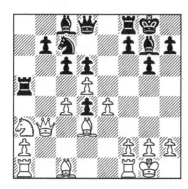

15 ♗d2?!

Now he really had to play the move 15 ♘c2

when Hazai gives 15...♖a8 16 ♗b2 c5 17 ♗c1 as best play for White. Black has an easy game after 17...f5. The reason Black didn't play 15...♘a6 is because of the awkward reply 16 ♗d2 when after 16...♘c5 17 ♗xa5 ♕xa5 18 ♕b4! ♕d8 19 ♖ad1 f5 he may have quite reasonable compensation for the exchange but it's not the sort of thing you really want to play.

15...♖a8 16 ♘c2 ♘a6! 17 ♕a3?! ♗g4!

Now White is in serious trouble as his solid blockade of d3, the bedrock of his game, is now crumbling.

18 ♗b4

So he decides his best chance is to give up his queen to try and hold the square. But it's pretty hopeless. 18 ♕b2 looks forced when after 18...♘c5 19 ♘e1 Black can choose between 19...f5 and the more spectacular 19...♗e2!? 20 ♗g5 (20 ♗xe2 d3) 20...♕xg5 21 ♕xe2 ♖a3 with a large positional advantage.

18...♘c5 19 ♗xc5 ♖xa3 20 ♗xa3 c5

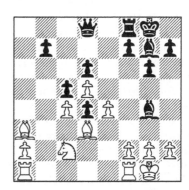

Black is just winning. The remaining moves were...

21 ♖ab1 ♕a5 22 ♗c1 f5! 23 exf5 ♗xf5 24 ♗xf5 ♖xf5 25 ♖xb7 ♕xa2 26 ♘a3 d3 27 ♘b5 d2 28 ♗xd2 ♕xd2 29 ♘xd6 ♖f8 30 ♘b5 ♕d3 31 ♖e7 ♕xc4 32 ♘c7 ♗d4 33 g3 ♕c2 34 ♔h1 ♕d3 0-1

Game 70

I.Sokolov-Golubev

Bundesliga 2003

---

1 d4 ♘f6 2 c4 g6 3 ♘c3 ♗g7 4 e4 d6 5 ♗d3 0-0 6 ♘ge2 ♘c6 7 0-0 ♘h5!?

Forcing White to deal with the threat to d4. It is most uncommon for Black to move this knight before playing ...e7-e5 in the King's Indian.

8 ♗c2

This has become the main line. I suppose the original idea was to prevent a black knight coming into d4 (now after 8...e5 9 d5 ♘d4? 10 ♘xd4 exd4 11 ♘b5 White just wins a pawn) but as we see in variation 'b' below it's not even clear that it wants to go into d4. The real reason for the text then is that the bishops are simply better placed on c2 and c1 than they are on d3 and e3 (bishops work well from a distance), There are two alternatives:

a) 8 d5!? ♘e5 9 f4 ♘xd3 10 ♕xd3 f5!? (I wasn't sure if I liked this move or not but I didn't want to let White play f4-f5) 11 ♘d4 c5 12 dxc6 bxc6 13 ♗e3 ♗d7 14 exf5 gxf5 15 c5 e5 16 ♘de2 d5 17 fxe5 ♗xe5 18 ♗d4 ♗xd4+ 19 ♘xd4 ♕g5 20. ♖ae1 (the Hungarian master Hazai, commenting in *ChessBase Magazine*, stopped his analysis here and said that White is better because he has a strong blockading knight on d4 against a passive bishop on d7; I disagree) 20...♖ae8! 21 ♖xe8 ♖xe8 22 ♘xf5 ♖f8! 23 ♘g3 ♖xf1+ 24 ♘xf1? (overlooking a little tactic; 24 ♕xf1! ♘xg3 25 hxg3 ♕xg3 26 ♕f2 ♕e5 27 ♕e2 should be a draw) 24...♕xg2+! 25 ♔xg2 ♘f4+ 26 ♔f3 ♘xd3 27 ♘a4 ♔f7 and Black has a clear advantage as the white knights are all over the place, he has a passed pawn and the so called passive bishop is not looking so passive anymore (0-1, 42), Van der Werf-Gallagher, Cannes 1997.

b) 8 ♗e3 e5 9 d5 ♘e7!? (9...♘d4 looks more

natural but 10 ♗c2!? forces Black to exchange his knight and after 10...♘xc2 11 ♕xc2 f5 12 exf5 gxf5 13 f4 ♘f6 14 h3 White probably has a slight advantage) 10 ♕d2 f5 11 exf5 gxf5 12 f4 (12 ♗g5 f4! led to a most complicated game in Christiansen-Gallagher, Bern 1996) 12...♘g6! 13 g3 ♗d7 14 ♖ae1 a6 15 b3 with equal chances.

8...e5 9 d5 ♘e7

10 a4

White's whole set-up is based on neutralising the advance ...f7-f5. The only problem is that Black hasn't even played the move yet and so White needs to find some good waiting moves until Black does play it. The text is the most popular as not only does it gain space on the queenside but it also prepares to deploy the queen's rook actively on the third rank. The other waiting moves include:

a) 10 ♔h1 f5 11 exf5 ♘xf5 (White's idea is to meet 11...gxf5 with 12 ♘g1! followed by 13 f4 which Atalik claims is good for White) 12 ♘e4 (12 g4 ♘d4 13 gxh5 ♘f3) 12...♘f6 13 ♗g5 ♕e8 14 ♕d2 ♘xe4 15 ♗xe4 ♗d7 16 ♖ae1 ♕f7 and Black is close to equality, Sokolov-Spassov, Istanbul 2003.

b) 10 ♖b1 f5 11 exf5 gxf5 (11...♘xf5 is the solid option but the text is also fine as Black doesn't have to worry about 12 ♘g1 here) 12 f4 ♘g6 13 fxe5 dxe5 (I've seen this assessed as better for White but why are we playing the King's Indian – for positions like this as far as I am concerned) 14 c5 ♔h8 15 b4 f4! (Black concedes e4 in order to bring his light-squared bishop into play; he also gains the useful f5-square) 16 ♘e4 ♗g4 17 ♖b3 ♘h4 18 ♖f2?

(White seems oblivious of the danger; he had to play 18 h3, or perhaps 17 h3 with unclear play) 18...f3! 19 gxf3 ♘xf3+ 20 ♖bxf3 ♖xf3 21 ♖g2 ♗h3 22 ♘g5 ♗xg2 23 ♔xg2 ♘f4+! 24 ♗xf4 ♖xf4 25 h4 ♖g4+ 26 ♘g3 ♖xg5 27 hxg5 ♕xg5 and Black soon won, Feletar-Gallagher, Pula 2000.

10...f5

If Black is going to play ...f7-f5 then he may as well do so at once. Many players delay for a move or so with 10...a5 or 10...♔h8 and then after 11 ♖a3 play 11...f5. This doesn't really make sense as White gains more from ♖a3 than from whatever move Black plays. However, it is perfectly feasible to play 10...a5, to block White's queenside play, and to then stubbornly refuse to play ...f7-f5 at all. For example, Dorfman-Nataf, Marseille 2001 continued (after 10...a5) 11 ♖a3 ♗g4 (to provoke f2-f3 which closes the third rank for the rook and the d1-h5 diagonal for the queen) 12 f3 ♗d7 13 ♘b5 ♔h8 14 ♔h1 ♘g8 15 ♕e1 ♗c8 16 g4 ♘hf6 17 ♕h4 c6 with a roughly level game.

11 exf5 gxf5 12 ♘g3!?

White is hoping for 12...♘xg3 13 fxg3! with pressure against f5. Black does best to avoid this.

12...♘f4

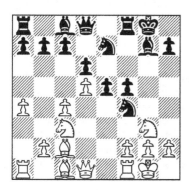

13 ♖a3

In Korchnoi-Radjabov, Buenos Aires 2001 White preferred 13 ♘h5 and after 13...♘xh5 14 ♕xh5 ♘g6 15 f4 exf4 16 ♗xf4 (16 ♘e2 has also been played) 16...♕f6 17 ♖ad1 ♘xf4 18 ♖xf4 ♕h6 19 ♖h4 ♕xh5 20 ♖xh5 ♗xc3 21 bxc3 ♗d7 Black comfortably held the draw.

13...♘eg6 14 ♔h1

Or 14 ♘ce2 c5!? 15 ♘xf4 exf4 16 ♘h5 ♗e5 17 ♖f3 ♕h4 18 ♖h3 ♕g5 19 ♔h1 ♖e8 20 ♖g1 ♖e7 21 ♖g3 ♕h4 22 ♖h3 ♕g5 23 ♖g3 ♕h4 24 ♖h3 ½–½ Pinter-Nataf, Batumi 1999.

14...♕h4 15 ♖g1

White was, presumably, worried about Black sacrificing on g2. I suspect something has already gone wrong with his preparation and I will be most surprised if we see Sokolov repeating the super prophylactic plan of ♔h1 and ♖g1.

15...e4 16 f3

White must play this before Black can play ♘e5.

16...♗d7 17 ♘f1

17 fxe4 ♘e5! 18 ♗xf4 ♘g4! is the point!

17...♘d3! 18 ♗xd3 exd3 19 ♕xd3 ♘e5 20 ♕d1 ♘xc4 21 ♖b3

After 21 ♖a1 ♗d4 22 g3 ♕f6 23 ♖g2 White saves the exchange but is left in a miserable position.

21...♘a5 22 ♖a3 ♖ae8!?

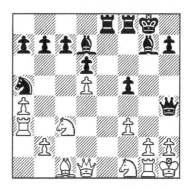

It may have been more prudent to repeat moves against a man of Sokolov's calibre but Golubev is not someone who shirks his responsibilities when he has the better of it.

23 ♘g3 ♖f6!

Black is going to try and prove that White's 14th and 15th moves were part of a helpmate combination

24 ♘ce2 ♘c4!?

How was Sokolov planning to respond to 24...f4? Obviously not with 25 ♘e4 (25 ♘f1 ♕f2! is also a killer as if the knight on e2 moves Black plays ♖e1) 25...♕xh2+ 26 ♔xh2 ♖h6 mate. Therefore, I imagine 25 ♘xf4 ♖xf4 26

♗xf4 ♕xf4 27 ♘h5 ♕e5 28 ♘xg7 ♔xg7 with some chances of survival.

25 ♖c3

25 ♖b3 loses to 25...♗xa4 and after 25 ♖a1 f4 White is forced to take on f4 again.

25...♖g6! 26 ♕c2

White gives up the exchange as variations such as 26 ♖d3 f4 27 ♘xf4 (27 ♗xf4 ♘xb2) 27...♖xg3 are extremely unpleasant.

26...♗xc3 27 ♕xc3

Black is just winning here but Golubev now played like a man who had about a minute left to reach move 40. Which he probably did! He should have just returned his knight to the centre with 27...♘e5 as he is winning comfortably after 28 ♕xc7 ♕xa4. Instead he played 27...♘b6?! and the rest was a disaster. The remaining moves were: 28 ♕xc7 ♖c8? 29 ♕xb7 ♖g7 30 ♕xa7 ♘xd5 31 ♕a5 ♕c4 32 b3? ♕xb3 33 ♘d4 ♕a2 34 ♗h6 ♖f7 35 ♕e1 ♖e8 36 ♕c1 f4 37 ♘e4 ♕xa4 38 ♕d2 ♖xe4? 39 fxe4 ♘e3 (39...♘f6!) 40 ♗xf4! ♘g4 41 h3 ♘f6 42 ♖e1 ♕a8 43 ♘f5 ♗xf5 44 exf5 ♘e4 45 ♕d4 d5 46 ♖b1 ♖f8 47 ♗h6 ♖f6 48 ♕e5 1-0

5 ♘ge2

Game 71

Liardet-Gallagher

Lenk 1998

---

1 d4 ♘f6 2 c4 g6 3 ♘c3 ♗g7 4 e4 d6 5 ♘ge2

This system was devised by Hungarian players in the 1960's and whilst it remains a fairly peripheral variation of the King's Indian it can be quite a tricky system to face for the unprepared. To spend a couple of tempi manoeuvring the knight to g3 (that's where it is going) may seem like rather strange behaviour but from there it exerts influence over the e4 and f5-squares so it is not easy for Black to play on the kingside. That is, perhaps the sophisticated part of White's strategy. The crude part is actually what most White players are interested in. They are going to play h4, h5 and try and attack on the kingside. If Black blocks the h-pawn with h5, they play ♗g5 and try and make ♗xh5 work.

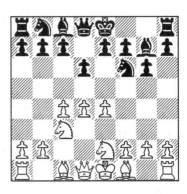

Here is an example of what I mean. This is the game Liardet-Peng Xiaomin, Geneva 1997.

1 d4 ♘f6 2 c4 g6 3 ♘c3 ♗g7 4 e4 d6 5 ♘ge2 0-0 6 ♘g3 e5 7 d5 a5 8 h4 h5 9 ♗g5 c6?! (9...♕e8! is a better move) 10 ♗e2 cxd5 11 ♘xd5! ♗e6 12 ♗xh5! ♗xd5 13 cxd5 gxh5 14 ♘xh5 ♘bd7 15 ♕f3 (White now has an unbreakable pin and it just remains for him to bring up the reinforcements and deliver mate) 15...♖c8 16 0-0 ♖c2?! 17 ♖fc1 ♖xb2 18 ♖c3! a4 19 ♖ac1 (the queenside is irrelevant) 19...♖xa2 20 ♕f5! (now the rook on c3 will swing to the kingside) 20...a3 21 ♘xg7 ♔xg7 22 ♖g3 ♔h8 23 ♗xf6+ ♘xf6 (23...♕xf6 24 ♕h5+ and mate next move) 24 ♖c8! 1-0

Quite frightening. Because of the potential dangers on the kingside quite a few players, myself included, prefer to delay castling and immediately start operations on the queenside with a6, c6 and b5. If Black also refrains from playing ...e5, which he usually does, he must be careful that White can't breakthrough in the centre with e4-e5 himself.

To be honest, it is not bad to play the normal King's Indian moves (...0-0, ...e5), it just requires accurate play. However, if you have a choice between two roughly equivalent lines, one of which thwarts the opponent's plans and the other which doesn't then one should obviously choose the former.

5...a6

Forewarned is forearmed as the saying goes. During my preparation for this game I had noticed what Liardet did to his illustrious opponent in the above game so I was more convinced than ever that it would be prudent to delay castling.

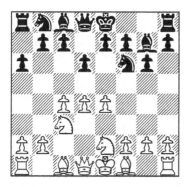

6 ♘g3

And what about if they play 6 f3, you may ask, transposing into the Sämisch? Didn't you recommend that we play 6...c5? How are we going to get back into that?

Well, I'm afraid you are not going to get back directly into that. But don't lose any sleep over it, and no, I'm not going to write a whole new chapter because of it. No-one has ever played the Sämisch via this move order against me. Just play percentage chess and forget about it. And if it does happen, then don't panic. I suggest you play 6...0-0 when you can meet 7 ♗e3 with 7...♘bd7 followed by 8...c5, and 7 ♘g3 or 7 ♗g5 with 7...c5 (8 dxc5 ♕a5!? 9 ♗xf6 exf6! 10 cxd6 f5 was the fascinating continuation in a game I had with Dorfman – very unclear). Play shouldn't be too different from what you are used to.

But whilst no-one has ever played 6 f3 against me, strangely enough, a couple of play-ers, including Korchnoi, have played 6 g3 against me. Here, though we can just play 6...0-0 7 ♗g2 ♘bd7 8 0-0 e5 and the only difference to the proposed repertoire in the Fianchetto Variation is that the white knight is on e2 instead of f3. Its unclear who this favours but if Black captures on d4 in the near future we will transpose directly to that chapter.

6...c6

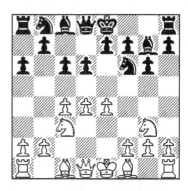

7 ♗e2

Alternatively:

a) White can also play 7 a4 to prevent ...b5 but then Black replies 7...a5!. Playing ...a6 and ...a5 may seem like a criminal waste of time but the point is that Black has secured a couple of useful outposts for himself on the queenside. b4 is obvious but after he plays ...e5 the c5-square will also fall into his hands. A possible continuation is 8 ♗e2 0-0 and then:

a1) 9 h4 e5 10 d5 ♘a6 11 ♗g5 ♘c5 12 ♕c2 ♕b6 13 ♖a3 (to prevent ♘b3-d4) 13...♗d7 with a comfortable game for Black.

a2) 9 f4 e5! 10 dxe5 (10 fxe5 dxe5 11 d5 ♕b6! looks a little awkward for White) 10...dxe5 11 ♕xd8 ♖xd8 12 f5 (White tries to make it difficult for Black to develop his queenside and doesn't allow him use of the e5-square but he is, nevertheless, still balancing on the edge of a positional precipice) 12...♘a6 13 0-0 ♘d7 14 ♗e3 ♘dc5 15 ♖ad1 ♗d7 and White is fighting for equality, Flear-Gallagher, San Bernardino 1991

b) This was not the first game I had against Liardet in this line. Some years previously he played 7 h4 against me and after 7...h5 8 ♗e2 b5 9 cxb5 axb5 10 b4 0-0 (often when Black has played ...h5 in response to h4 he has to worry about piece sacrifices on h5, but delaying castling until White has played a move such as b4 renders it extremely unlikely that White can conduct a kingside attack without allowing serious counterplay on the queenside) 11 ♗g5 ♘bd7 12 ♕d2 ♘b6 13 0-0 (13 ♖c1) ♘h7! 14 ♗e3 e6 (it turns out that it's White who has problems on the kingside) 15 d5 cxd5 16 ♗xb5 (16 exd5 bxc3 17 ♕xc3 ♘xd5 is good for Black) dxe4 17 ♘gxe4? (17 a4 d5 is less clear) 18 ♘g5? d4 19 ♖fd1 e5 and Black won material, Liardet-Gallagher, Geneva 1993.

7...b5 8 cxb5

Or:

a) 8 e5!? is not considered very dangerous, e.g. 8...dxe5 (8...♘fd7? 9 exd6 exd6 10 ♗f4 ♘f6 11 ♘ge4) 9 dxe5 ♕xd1+ 10 ♘xd1 (10 ♗xd1 ♘g4 11 f4 bxc4 12 ♗e2 ♗e6) 10...♘fd7 11 f4 with a couple of examples:

a1) In Tyrtania-Gallagher, Bad Wörishofen 1993 Black attacked the centre at once with 11...f6. After 12 exf6 exf6 13 ♘e4 f5 (on 13...♔e7 I was afraid of 14 ♗d2!) 14 ♘d6+ ♔e7 15 ♘xc8+ ♖xc8 16 ♗d2 (16 ♗e3!? ♘f6) ♘c5! 17 ♗b4 ♘bd7 18 ♘c3 (18 ♖c1 is well met by 18...a5! as although 19 ♗xc5 ♘xc5 20 cxb5 cxb5 21 ♗xb5 may appear to win a pawn it loses the game after 21...♘d3+!) 18...♔f7 19 ♖d1 ♗f8 the game was about level.

a2) Perhaps 11...♘b6 offers more chances of a complicated middlegame. Goormachtigh-W.Watson, Brussels 1986 continued 12 ♘e3 ♗e6 13 ♗d2 ♘8d7 14 ♖c1 ♗h6 15 ♖f1 (15 0-0 looks more natural, although White may have been worried about some combination of

...bxc4 and ...♘xe5, exploiting the undefended state of the bishop on d2) 0-0 16 b3 ♖ad8 17 ♘e4 bxc4 18 ♘xc4 ♘xc4 19 ♗xc4 ♗f5! 20 ♘g3 ♘xe5 21 ♘xf5 gxf5 22 ♗xa6 ♖d4! (White is allowed no peace) 23 ♖c2 ♘g4 24 h3 ♘f6 25 ♗c3 ♖e4+ 26 ♖e2 ♖a8 27 ♗xf6 ♖xa6 28 ♗xe7 ♖xa2! 29 ♖xe4 fxe4 with a favourable endgame for Black.

b) 8 0-0 0-0 9 e5! is probably better for White. Black should therefore play either 8...♘bd7, preparing ...e7-e5, or 8...bxc4 9 ♗xc4 d5 10 ♗b3 dxe4 11 ♘gxe4 when 11...♘d5 12 ♕f3 is better for White and 11...♘xe4 12 ♘xe4 ♕xd4 too risky, or so I wrote back in the mid-1990's. All I can say is that it doesn't feel quite so risky these days with Fritz 8 assisting the defence.

8...axb5 9 b4

I'm not too convinced by White's plan. It seems to me he plays half-heartedly on both wings.

The move b2-b4 can be an effective counter to an early ...b5 by Black in the King's Indian – first blockade and later seize the initiative with a4 – but here White has a slightly inferior version as he has already committed his knight to g3. In similar positions arising from the Sämisch (not part of our repertoire) the knight usually settles on the more relevant b3-square.

9...0-0 10 ♖b1 ♘bd7 11 0-0 ♗b7 12 ♗g5 h6 13 ♗e3 e5 14 ♕c2 ♕e7 15 ♖fd1 exd4 16 ♗xd4 h5 17 f3 ♘e5

I prefer Black. White is kept occupied by the hole on c4 as the last thing he would want is a black knight establishing itself there. The move f3, which was required to protect e4, has also weakened the White kingside.

18 ♘f1 h4 19 ♕d2!? ♖fe8 20 ♗f2 ♘h5! 21 g4

21 ♕xd6 ♕g5 with ...♘f4 to follow is much too dangerous for White. I wasn't too unhappy to see the text either as the white king position is beginning to open up.

21...hxg3 22 hxg3 ♖ad8 23 g4 ♘f6 24 ♘g3 ♕e6 25 ♔g2?

White should have played 25 g5. Now he is losing.

25...d5! 26 g5 ♘xf3!

White had seen that 26...dxe4 27 ♕xd8 wasn't so clear but completely overlooked this shot. Of course 27 bxf3 just loses to 27...dxe4.

27 ♕f4 ♘xe4!

If White takes on f3 Black takes on c3 and if White takes on e4 Black recaptures defending his knight on f3.

28 ♘cxe4 dxe4 29 ♘xe4 ♘d4 30 ♗xd4 ♖xd4 31 ♗f3 ♕xa2+ 32 ♔g1 c5 33 ♘f6+ ♗xf6 34 ♕xf6 ♖g4+! 35 ♔f1

35 ♗xg4 ♕g2 mate and 35 ♔h1 ♕f2! were alternative ways for the game to end.

35...♕c4+ 36 ♔f2 ♖e2+! 0-1

White resigned because of 37 ♗xe2 ♖g2+ 38 ♔e3 ♖xe2.

Systems with an early ♗g5

We shall now look at a couple of lines where White plays an early ♗g5.

1) Games 72 and 73 feature the Smyslov System, a quiet restraining line named after the ex World Champion Vassily Smyslov. It is characterised by the moves 1 d4 ♘f6 2 c4 g6 3 ♘c3 ♗g7 4 ♘f3 d6 (0-0) 5 ♗g5 and White

follows up with e2-e3. This can be quite a difficult line for the unprepared Black player. In my early days with the King's Indian I struggled a bit playing with ...e7-e5. The turning point for me came when I suddenly noticed a game where Smyslov was playing Black against his own system. He played with ...c7-c5 and won really easily. I copied him and my results improved dramatically.

2) In Game 74 White plays ♗g5 with his pawn on e4. This arises after the initial moves 1 d4 ♘f6 2 c4 g6 3 ♘c3 ♗g7 4 e4 d6 5 ♗g5. This line is not entirely respectable and if Black knows what he is doing he should be able to emerge from the opening with a good position.

Game 72
C.Horvath-Rajlich
Budapest 2002

---

1 d4 ♘f6 2 c4 g6 3 ♘c3 ♗g7 4 ♘f3 0-0 5 ♗g5 d6 6 e3 c5

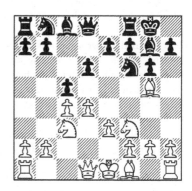

7 ♗e2

Alternatively:

a) 7 d5 is gaining in popularity as White players are beginning to accept that the main line is just a dead end. It is covered in the next game.

b) 7 h3 provides a haven for the bishop on h2, thereby preventing lines with ...h7-h6, ...g6-g5 and ♘f6-h5. Black has:

b1) 7...♗f5!? 8 g4 ♗e4 9 ♗g2 cxd4 10 exd4 ♘c6 11 ♗e3 ♗xf3 12 ♗xf3 ♘d7 13 0-0 e5 14 dxe5 ♘dxe5 15 ♗d5 ♘e7 16 ♗g5 ½-½, Hort-Kindermann, Munich 1991.

b2) 7...♘c6 8 d5 ♘a5 9 ♘d2 a6 10 a3 b5 11 cxb5 axb5 12 ♗xb5 ♗d7 13 ♗e2 h6 14 ♗f4 ♖b8 15 ♖b1 ♕c7 16 0-0 c4 (Kuligowski-Hawelko, Polanica Zdroj 1984), with compensation according to *ECO*.

c) 7 dxc5 is anti-positional. After 7...dxc5 8 ♕xd8 ♖xd8 9 ♗xf6 ♗xf6 10 ♘d5, 10...♘c6 is very comfortable for Black whilst 10...♗xb2!? 11 ♖b1 ♗f6 12 ♘c7 ♗c3+ 13 ♔e2 ♗f5 14 ♖d1 ♘c6 15 ♘xa8 ♖xa8 looks like good value for an exchange.

7...h6 8 ♗h4 ♗f5!

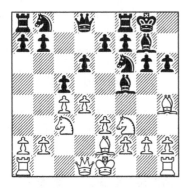

Black has tried numerous moves in this position but my attention was originally drawn to the modest-looking text when I spotted that it was the choice of Smyslov when somebody had the temerity to play his own system against him. There are at least a couple of good reasons for putting the bishop on f5. The first is to introduce the possibility of ...♘e4. Exchanging his knight on f6 for White's on c3 is almost always a good deal for Black as with all the excess baggage removed from the long diagonal the full force of the King's Indian bishop is likely to be felt. The second reason for putting the bishop on f5 is that it covers b1 and in a surprising number of variations this allows Black to mount a decisive assault against the b2 pawn, which in this variation is more likely to have a coating of sugar than the usual arsenic.

9 0-0

Or:

a) 9 h3 has been played but after 9...♘e4 White is simply a tempo down on the game.

b) I haven't seen any examples of 9 ♗d3 but perhaps White should already be looking to

equalise with a move such as this.

9...♘e4

9...♘bd7 is an important alternative which I have recommended in previous works (and still recommend it). The idea is to prepare ...♕d8-b6, which is not playable at once in view of 10 ♗xf6 followed by 11 ♘d5. After 9...♘bd7 we have:

a) 10 d5 ♕b6 11 ♘a4 (ugly, but 11 ♕d2 g5 12 ♗g3 ♘e4 13 ♘xe4 ♗xe4 and 11 ♕b3 g5 12 ♗g3 ♘e4 13 ♘xe4 ♗xe4 14 ♘d2 ♗g6 both seem to lose a pawn, whilst 11 b3 g5 12 ♗g3 ♘e4 13 ♘xe4 ♗xe4 14 ♖c1 ♗b2 costs White an exchange for uncertain compensation) 11...♕a5 12 ♘d2 ♘b6 13 ♘c3 (13 ♘xb6 ♕xb6 again leaves the b-pawn in difficulties) 13...♕b4! 14 ♕b3 (14 e4 ♕xb2! 15 ♖c1 ♗d7 looks like a relatively safe pawn) 14...♘bxd5! (the exposed position of the bishop on h4 is the key point in this simple, but pleasing combination) 15 cxd5 (or 15 ♘xd5 ♘xd5 16 ♕xb4 ♘xb4 17 ♗xe7 ♖fe8 18 ♗xd6 ♖ad8) 15...♕xh4 16 ♕xb7 ♕b4! 17 ♕xb4 (there is no choice for White as 17 ♕xe7 ♕xb2 loses material) 17...cxb4 18 ♘b5 ♘xd5! 19 ♗f3 ♗d3! 20 ♗xd5 ♗xb5 21 ♗xa8 ♗xf1 22 ♗e4 ♗a6 0-1, Pachmann-Smyslov, Amsterdam 1994.

The moral of the story: don't play the Smyslov System against Smyslov

b) 10 ♖c1 ♕b6 (10...♘e4 11 ♘xe4 ♗xe4 12 ♘d2 g5! has also been suggested as roughly level) 11 b3 ♖fe8 12 h3 g5 13 ♗g3 ♘e4 14 ♘xe4 ♗xe4 15 dxc5 ♘xc5 16 ♘d4 ♖ad8! with good play for Black, Law-Gallagher, British Ch., Hove 1997.

c) 10 ♕d2 ♘e4 is level while 10...♕b6!? 11

♘d5?! ♘xd5 12 exd5 ♖fe8, with ideas of ...♗e4 also deserves consideration.

10 ♘xe4

10 ♗d3 ♘xc3 11 bxc3 ♗xd3 12 ♕xd3 ♘c6, Poluliakhov-Kengis, Podolsk 1990, just leaves Black with the better pawn structure.

10...♘xe4 11 ♘d2

I like this line because one small slip can suddenly leave White in a lost position. For example, 11 ♕d2 g5 12 ♗g3 ♕b6 13 ♖fd1? (13 ♖ad1 is better) 13...♘c6 14 ♖ac1 (or 14 d5 ♘d8 and White can kiss goodbye to his b-pawn) 14...♖ad8?! (perhaps a touch too sadistic; Black could have cashed in at once with the same mini-combination that he played on his next move) 15 b3 (15 d5 would have saved the pawn although Black would still be better) 15...♗xf3 16 ♗xf3 cxd4 17 ♗xc6 dxe3! and Black soon won, Skare-Westerinen, Gausdal 1992.

11...♗f5 12 e4!?

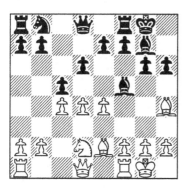

White decides to give up a pawn for a space advantage and some vague attacking chances sacrifices. I suspect this is the best practical try as the alternatives are far from awe-inspiring, e.g.

a) 12 ♘b3 ♘c6 13 d5 ♘b4 14 a3 ♘a6 15 ♕c1 ♕b6 with good play for Black, Del Rey-Gofshtein, Lisbon 1999.

b) 12 ♗f3 ♘c6 13 ♗xc6 (13 ♘b3 cxd4 14 exd4 g5 15 ♗g3 ♕b6 is very good for Black) bxc6 14 e4 ♗e6 (14...♗c8!? 15 dxc5 ♗xb2 16 ♖b1 ♗g7 is at least an edge for Black) 15 d5 ♗d7 16 ♕c2 ♖b8 17 ♖ab1 cxd5 18 cxd5 f5 with some advantage to Black, Lebel-Sharif, French League 1992.

12...♗c8! 13 d5! ♗xb2 14 ♖b1 ♗g7

14...♗f6 15 ♗g3 e5 has been played which turned out to be quite promising for White after 16 dxe6. However, Black could play 14...♗f6 just as a means of driving the bishop back to the less active g3-square and continue with, well I don't know; 15...a6, 15...♕a5 or even 15...♗g7 come to mind. The moves ...e7-e6 or ...e7-e5 remain an option for later.

15 f4 a6

Black prepares to open lines on the queen-side with ...b7-b5.

16 ♖b3 b5 17 ♖g3

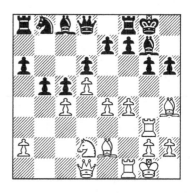

White doesn't have anything concrete for the pawn, just space and vague attacking chances. But it will also be a long time before the extra pawn can have any real effect. I consider the chances to be about equal.

17...♘d7 18 ♔h1 ♘b6

Maybe Black should keep this knight nearer to the kingside. 18...b4 is an idea followed by pushing the a-pawn at every available opportunity.

19 ♗d3 bxc4 20 ♗c2 c3 21 ♘b1 a5 22 ♘xc3 ♗a6 23 ♖e1 ♘c4 24 e5! dxe5! 25 f5

This attacking ploy has occurred hundreds of times in similar positions but that doesn't make it any less dangerous!

25...g5?

25...♘d6! 26 fxg6 f5 is winning for Black according to Hazai but I would still be pretty scared after 27 ♕h5!. It is certainly better than the text however, which just loses out of hand.

26 ♗xg5! hxg5 27 ♖xg5

Surprisingly, there is absolutely no defence here.

27...e6

Or 27...♕d6 28 ♖xg7+! ♔xg7 29 ♕g4+ ♔h8 30 f6! and Black gets mated.

28 ♖xg7+! ♔xg7 29 ♕g4+ ♔h6 30 f6 1-0

Game 73
Yusupov-Gallagher
Dresden 1998

---

1 d4 ♘f6 2 c4 g6 3 ♘c3 ♗g7 4 ♘f3 d6 5 ♗g5 0-0 6 e3 c5 7 d5

In the past I was quite puzzled as to why nobody ever played this move. In my opinion it is the only test of Black's opening strategy.

7...h6 8 ♗h4

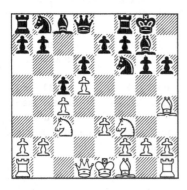

8...a6

I'm not at all sure what the best move is but I'm presenting my game with Yusupov as the main line as it contained some interesting opening play. The numerous alternatives include:

a) 8...e5, the typical King's Indian response, and the jury is still out on the position after 9 ♘d2! Most sources say White is better but I have my doubts. Black should probably start with 9...♕e8 or even 9...♕d7 as Golubev did recently in a blitz game.

b) 8...e6 9 ♘d2 exd5 10 cxd5 leads to a Modern Benoni which seems quite difficult for Black, e.g. 10...♕e7 11 ♗e2 ♘a6 12 0-0 ♘c7 13 e4 g5 14 ♗g3 ♘d7 15 ♘c4 ♘e5 16 ♘e3 ♗d7 17 a4 and White's position was preferable in Yusupov-Markowski, Netherlands 1998.

c) 8...b5 is the Benko option. It is probably slightly dubious. For example, after 9 cxb5 a6 10 ♘d2 there is:

c1) 10...axb5 11 ♗xb5 ♗a6 12 ♗xa6 ♖xa6 13 ♕e2 ♕b6 14 ♘c4 ♕b7 15 e4 ♘bd7 16 0-0 with advantage to White.

c2) 10...e6 11 dxe6 ♗xe6 12 ♗e2 axb5 13 ♗xb5 d5 14 0-0 ♕b6 15 a4 ♖d8 16 ♗xf6 ♗xf6 17 ♕f3 ♗g7 18 ♖ad1, Agrest-Cicak, Swedish Team Ch. 2003, which doesn't look like quite enough for the pawn.

d) I have suggested in the past that Black can try 8...♕b6 to try and reach similar positions to those discussed in Game 72, but even I forgot to play it when given the chance.

e) 8...g5 9 ♗g3 ♘h5 is the most principled reaction to White closing the centre and probably the reason most White players avoided 7 d5 in the past. Black does get a powerful King's Indian bishop to compensate for his kingside weaknesses. Here are a couple of examples:

e1) 10 ♗d3 f5 11 ♘d2 (11 e4? f4 12 ♘xg5 fails to 12...♕e8! whilst 11 ♘xg5 leads to a draw after 11...♘xg3 12 hxg3 hxg5 13 ♕h5 ♖f6 14 ♕h7+ ♔f7! 15 ♕h5+ ♔g8 16 ♕h7+ ♔f7 17 ♕h5+ ♔g8 18 ♕h7+ ½-½, Pert-Smirnov, Aviles 2000) 11...♘xg3 12 hxg3 and now 12...e5? 13 g4! allowed White to take control of the light squares in I.Sokolov-Radjabov, Sarajevo 2002, but 12...♘d7 13 ♘f3 ♘f6 14 ♕c2 ♘g4 seemed perfectly satisfactory for Black in Fiorito-Llanos, Rosario 2000.

e2) 10 ♕c2 ♖e8 (10...f5 is an alternative as long as Black doesn't meet 11 ♗e2 with 11...♘d7?? 12 ♘xg5! ♘xg3 13 ♘e6 when White was winning in Speelman-Polzin, Bundesliga 2002) 11 ♗e2 ♘xg3 12 hxg3 e6 13 ♘d2 exd5 14 ♘xd5 ♘c6 15 ♖d1 ♖b8 16 ♘e4 a6 17 a6 17 a3 ♗e6 18 ♘xd6 ♘d4 19 ♖xd4 cxd4 20 ♘xe8 ♕xe8 21 ♘c7 ♕c6 22 ♘xe6 ♕xe6 23 e4 (23 exd4 ♖e8) 23...♖e8 24 0-0 ♕xe4 25 ♕xe4 ½-½ Agrest-Kozul, Plovdiv 2003.

9 ♘d2

Ruling out any ...g6-g5 followed by ...♘f6-h5 ideas that Black may have still entertained.

9...♘bd7

9...b5 10 cxb5 transposes to line 'c' above. I didn't want to play this sacrifice just yet but it is certainly a useful option to have available.

10 ♗e2 ♘h7 11 e4 ♘e5!

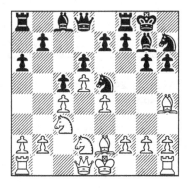

12 ♗g3

12 f4 would have been met by 12...g5! with good play for Black.

12...f5 13 f4 ♘g4 14 ♗xg4 fxg4 15 0-0 ♘f6 16 e5 ♘h5 17 ♕e2

White would like to play 17 e6 but he can't as it loses to 17...♘xg3 18 hxg3 ♗d4+ 19 ♔h2 ♖f5 and ♖h5 mate.

17...♘xg3 18 hxg3 b5!

Now is a good moment to play ...b7-b5. I believe Black has the better game here.

19 ♖ae1 ♗f5 20 ♘d1 bxc4 21 ♘xc4 dxe5 22 ♘xe5 ♕xd5 23 ♘e3 ♕e6

The game came to a sad conclusion now. I was extremely short of time but 23...♕xa2! looks like a serious advantage for Black.

24 ♘3xg4 ♖ad8 ½-½

Game 74

Spassky-Fischer

Sveti Stefan/Belgrade (m16) 1992

---

1 d4 ♘f6 2 c4 g6 3 ♘c3 ♗g7 4 e4 d6 5

♗g5 h6

It makes sense to put the question to the bishop before committing oneself in the centre.

6 ♗h4

6 ♗e3 invites Black to play 6...♘g4. Several games have continued 7 ♗c1 e5 8 d5 f5 9 ♗e2 ♘f6 10 gxf5 gxf5 11 ♗h5+ ♘xh5 12 ♕xh5+ ♔f8 with about equal chances. Black has lost the right to castle, but he has gained the bishop pair and has a strong central position.

6...g5

This is more accurate than 6...c5 as that gives White the extra possibility of 7 e5!?.

7 ♗g3 c5 8 d5

Colin Crouch, who for some reason kept repeating this line, has also tried 8 dxc5. After 8...♕a5 9 ♕d2 dxc5 10 h4 ♘h5 he suffered one painful defeat when he allowed Black to play ...♘xg3 so in the next game he played 11 ♗xb8! and managed to draw. Black could also have played 9...♕xc5.

8...♕a5 9 ♗d3?!

9 ♕d2 is the lesser evil, but White players were reluctant to play this as Black can take the bishop pair with 9...♘h5.

9...♘xe4!

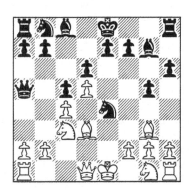

This combination is the justification of Black's play.

10 ♗xe4 ♗xc3+ 11 bxc3 ♕xc3+ 12 ♔f1 f5!

Black now wins back one of the white bishops and should remain a pawn up. In such sharp positions, though, material is not of paramount importance.

13 ♖c1

A supposed improvement over Stein-Geller,

Moscow 1966 which went 13 ♘e2 ♕f6 14 ♗c2 f4 15 h4 ♖f8! with an excellent game for Black.

13...♕f6 14 h4

After 14 ♕h5+ Black happily plays 14...♔d8 as his king has better prospects on the queenside than White's on the kingside.

14...g4!

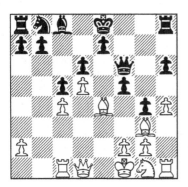

Geller only considered 14...fxe4, when 15 ♕h5+ is good for White. Many people criticised Fischer for his antiquated openings in this match, but if you had a whole stack of novelties gathering dust on the shelf after a twenty year lay-off, I'm sure you would also be trying to get them in when you made your comeback.

15 ♗d3

In Milov-Gallagher, Las Vegas 2002 I was rather surprised to see my strong opponent stumbling into this position by accident. Here he played 15 ♘e2 and after 15...fxe4 16 ♔g1 ♗f5 17 ♘c3 ♘d7 18 ♕e2 I would accept that White has one pawn's worth of compensation, but not two. I finally won in 67 moves.

15...f4 16 ♘e2

16 ♗h2 doesn't help as after 16...g3 17 fxg3 fxg3 it is check. 16 ♗xf4 was probably a slight improvement on the text.

16...fxg3 17 ♘xg3 ♖f8 18 ♖c2 ♘d7!

Black is more than happy to give back his extra pawn if it involves the rapid development of his queenside and increased attacking chances on the kingside via the open g-file.

19 ♕xg4 ♘e5 20 ♕e4 ♗d7 21 ♔g1 0-0-0 22 ♗f1 ♖g8

Black has completed his development and his forces co-ordinate beautifully. White... well, let's just mention his rook on h1 and leave it at that.

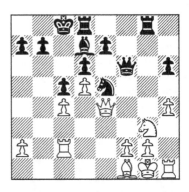

23 f4 ♘xc4! 24 ♘h5 ♕f7 25 ♕xc4 ♕xh5 26 ♖b2 ♖g3!

Black prepares the fatal doubling of his rooks on the g-file, having calculated 27 ♕a6 ♕xd5! 28 ♕xa7 ♗c6.

27 ♗e2 ♕f7

Matanovic has pointed out that 27...♕g6! was possible as after 28 ♕a6 ♖xg2+ 29 ♔f1 ♖g8 White has no mate.

28 ♗f3 ♖dg8 29 ♕b3 b6 30 ♕e3 ♕f6 31 ♖e2 ♗b5!

Not falling for 31...e5? 32 dxe6 ♗c6 33 ♗xc6! ♖xe3 34 ♖xe3 when White would be very much back in the game.

32 ♖d2 e5! 33 dxe6 ♗c6 34 ♔f1 ♗xf3 0-1

Summary

1) 5 ♗d3 tends to lead to a tough struggle where Black's chances do not seem inferior.

2) 5 ♘ge2 and 6 ♘g3 is surely not the answer to the King's Indian. I am recommending the same system I have for years, based on delaying ...0-0 and instigating immediate queenside play.

3) Lines with an early ♗g5 are best met by a quick ...c7-c5 as White can experience trouble on his queenside dark squares which are not so secure, especially after the moves ...h7-h6 and ♗g5-h4 have been included.

INDEX OF VARIATIONS

10...f5 11 f3 f4 12 &f2 g5 13 &c1
      13 a4 *Game 1*; 13 b4 *Game 2*; 13 ♘d3 *Game 5*
13...&f6 14 b4 *Game 3*; 14 c5 *Game 4*

The Sämisch
1 d4 ♘f6 2 c4 g6 3 ♘c3 &g7 4 e4 d6 5 f3 0-0 6 &e3
      6 ♘ge2 c5 7 d5 e6 8 ♘g3 exd5 9 cxd5
            9...♘h5 *Game 40*
            9...h5
                  10 &g5 *Game 38*; 10 &e2 *Game 39*
      6 &g5 c5 7 d5 e6 8 ♕d2 exd5
            9 ♘xd5 *Game 41*; 9 cxd5 *Game 42*
6...c5 7 dxc5
      7 d5 *Game 37*
      7 ♘ge2 ♕a5
            8 d5 *Game 35*; 8 ♕d2 *Game 36*
7...dxc5 8 ♕xd8 &xd8 9 &xc5 ♘c6 10 &a3 *Game 33*; 10 ♘d5 *Game 34*

The Fianchetto Variation
1 d4 ♘f6 2 c4
      2 ♘f3 g6 3 g3 &g7 4 &g2 d6 5 b3 c5 *Game 54*
2...g6 3 ♘f3 &g7 4 g3 0-0 5 &g2 d6 6 0-0 ♘bd7 7 ♘c3
      7 ♕c2 *Game 53*
7...e5 8 e4
      8 h3
            8...a6 *Game 51*; 8...exd4 *Game 52*
8...exd4
      8...a6
            9 &e1 *Game 48*
            9 h3 *Game 47*
            9 ♕c2 exd4 10 ♘xd4 &e8
                 11 ♘de2 *Game 49*; 11 &d1 *Game 50*
9 ♘xd4 &e8 10 h3 a6 11 &e1
      11 &e3 *Game 46*
11...&b8 12 &b1 *Game 45*; 12 ♕c2 *Game 44*; 12 &e3 *Game 43*

The Four Pawns Attack
1 d4 ♘f6 2 c4 g6 3 ♘c3 &g7 4 e4 d6 5 f4 0-0 6 ♘f3 c5 7 d5
      7 dxc5 *Game 59*
7...e6 8 &e2
      8 dxe6 *Game 58*
8...exd5 9 cxd5
      9 exd5 *Game 57*
9...&g4 10 0-0 ♘bd7 11 &e1 &e8 12 h3 &xf3 13 &xf3 ♕a5 14 &e3 b5 15 a3
      15...♘b6 *Game 55*; 15...b4 *Game 56*

Other Variations
1 d4 ♘f6 2 c4 g6 3 ♘c3 &g7 4 e4
      4 ♘f3 0-0 5 &g5 d6 6 e3 c5
            7 &e2 *Game 72*; 7 d5 *Game 73*
4...d6 5 &e2
      5 &g5 *Game 74*; 5 ♘ge2 *Game 71*;
      5 &d3 0-0 6 ♘ge2 ♘c6 7 0-0
            7...e5 *Game 69*; 7...♘h5 *Game 70*
      5 h3 0-0
            6 &g5 ♘a6
                7 &d3 *Game 62*; 7 ♘f3 *Game 63*
            6 ♘f3 e5 7 d5 ♘a6
                8 &g5 *Game 60*; 8 &e3 *Game 61*
5...0-0 6 &g5 ♘a6 7 ♕d2 *Game 64*
      7 f4 *Game 65*; 7 h4 *Game 66*; 7 ♘f3 *Game 67*; 7 ♕c2 *Game 68*

INDEX OF COMPLETE GAMES